Affairs to remember

The Hollywood

Affairs to remember

comedy of the sexes

Bruce Babington
& Peter William Evans

MANCHESTER UNIVERSITY PRESS
Manchester and New York

distributed exclusively in the USA and Canada by St. Martin's Press

Copyright © Bruce Babington and Peter William Evans 1989

Published by Manchester University Press
Oxford Road, Manchester M13 9PL, UK
and Room 400, 175 Fifth Avenue, New York, NY 10010, USA

Distributed exclusively in the USA and Canada
by St. Martin's Press, Inc., 175 Fifth Avenue, New York, NY 10010, USA

British Library cataloguing in publication data
Babington, Bruce
    Affairs to remember : the Hollywood comedy of the sexes.
    1. American cinema films
    I. Title II. Evans, Peter William, *1933–*
    791.43'09'0917

Library of Congress cataloging in publication data
Babington, Bruce
    Affairs to remember : the Hollywood comedy of the sexes / Bruce Babington and Peter
    William Evans
        p. cm.
        Bibliography: p.
        Includes index.
        ISBN 0-7190-2290-8 : $35.00 (est.)
        1. Comedy films — United States — History and criticism. 2. Women in motion pictures.
    3. Sex in motion pictures. 4. Love in motion pictures. 5. Sex role. I. Evans, Peter William.
    II. Title.
    PN1995.9.C55B34 1989
    791.43'09'0917—dc 19

ISBN 0 7190 2290 8 *hardback*

Typeset in Plantin Light with Present display
by Koinonia Limited, Manchester

Printed in Great Britain
by Bell & Bain, Glasgow

Contents

Preface — *page vi*
Acknowledgements — *x*

1 'EDUCATION SENTIMENTALE' — *1*
Bringing up Baby
and the golden age of Hollywood comedy

2 'THE LOVE PARADE' — *45*
Lubitsch and romantic comedy

3 'JOKING APART' — *95*
Three comedians
Bob Hope, Mae West and Woody Allen

4 THE FIFTIES — *179*
A meditation on comedy in the age of conformity, via
Pat and Mike
Rock and Doris
Wilder and Marilyn
and Douglas Sirk

5 'STARTING OVER' — *267*
Romantic comedy today

Sources — *299*
Index — *306*

Preface

Anyone who in the late 1980s attempts to write about the representation of the sexes in art charts their way through a minefield. The attempt to steer between the claims of nature and nurture, the pre-social and the social, however scrupulous, is fated to end in accusations of 'biologism' from those who wish to believe that there is no given except culture, and 'culturism' from those who will not see the malleability of what is given. But no serious analyst today can approach our subject – the great comedies of the Hollywood tradition, from the films of Lubitsch and Hawks to those of Woody Allen – innocently, without reference to the troubled terrain of sexual theory that has been the legacy, both complicatedly liberating and confusing, first of the psychoanalytic movement, then of scientific sexology, and then of feminism, the gay liberation movement and consequent revisionist views of the 'heterosexual norm'. Yet in stressing this, we feel the need to warn the reader that our approach is unapologetically first and foremost film-centred. Our concern is the peculiarity and uniqueness of cinematic art as it deals through comedy with the material of sexuality and its cultural organisation. Central to our aim is the detailed analysis of particular texts, whether they already bring with them a tradition of commentary (e.g. *Bringing up Baby* and the films of Woody Allen) or whether they have been all but untouched by it (e.g. *Pillow Talk*, *Bluebeard's Eighth Wife*, Sirk's Family comedies). Though our analyses are always acutely conscious of the place of the filmic institution within the larger social world, we insist – in opposition to critics who ignore the specificity of film in their haste to collapse works of art into the simplest negative ideological categories – upon the meanings of cinematic modes and conventions (themselves of course historically and ideologically conditioned), resisting the reduction of the cinematic into unmediated meanings. It will be clear also that our view of Hollywood cinema is not one of a simply monolithic, oppressive and conservative force, but of a multi-levelled and contradictory phenomenon capable of producing from within its contradictions works of art that are worth our constructive as well as deconstructive meditation.

In two ways we separate ourselves from some major tendencies in contemporary film theory. Firstly, we assert the centrality and importance of comedy. Here, of course, *pace* Stanley Cavell, Andrew Britton and others, let alone Freud, we are not alone. Yet there has been a general trend that has marginalised comedy, a point illustrated by the recent authoritative British Film Institute publication, *The Cinema Book* (ed. Pam Cook, 1985), very much a radical state of criticism dossier, which privileges melodrama among the genres, but ignores its more optimistic sister. Further, as regards the depiction of the relations of the sexes, and the representation of women in particular, we again (in the tradition of Meredith's *An Essay on Comedy*, 1877) assert comedy's centrality, disagreeing with the prevalent kind of generalisation illustrated in the following quotations from a highly respected book by E. Ann Kaplan, *Women and Film: Both Sides of the Camera* (1983):

It is important that women are excluded from the central role in the main, highly respected Hollywood genres; women, and female issues, are only central in the family melodrama . . . The idealized male screen heroes give back to the male spectator his more perfect mirror self, together with a sense of mastery and control. In contrast, the female is given only powerless victimized figures who, far from perfect, reinforce the basic sense of worthlessness that already exists.

Whatever validity the statements have as a critique of the tendencies of Hollywood production (and clearly they articulate fundamental issues), they are enormously simplifying as regards many romantic comedies where women and female issues are far from denied centrality, and where it is untrue to say of the complex characters played by, let us say, Katharine Hepburn, Claudette Colbert, Miriam Hopkins, Rosalind Russell or Irene Dunne, that they are simply 'powerless victimized figures' who simply reinforce a 'sense of worthlessness'. Such a caveat should not be interpreted as in any way belittling the major achievements of the feminist re-reading of the Hollywood cinema, but rather, we hope, as, among other things, a contribution to that process of re-reading, at least as conducted by that branch of feminist criticism which regards 'patriarchal' texts as the part-creation of women and the property of female as well as male viewers and analysts, and takes the line that the texts themselves may be less reactionary than the often chauvinist criticism that has until recently owned them.

Secondly, we find ourselves sceptical of the theories (practically dogma in advanced film theory) of writers such as Robin Wood and Andrew Britton concerning (i) the supposed universality of bisexual needs in the adult and the malign consequences of their repression and (ii) the assertion of the moral superiority over heterosexuality of male and female homosexuality. Major critics though they are, it seems to us that here their approach is basically flawed, and that the closed nature of their audience (more concerned in a still repressive political–sexual situation to argue what it may be self-enhancing for sexual minorities to believe than to respect the claims of reality) perpetuates dogma over analysis or, rather (to do justice to their abilities), analysis in the service of dogma. In their recent work on film the homosexual's intolerable position as the outcast in Western culture is totally reversed, so that he or she becomes not just a sexual difference demanding equality and representation, but a moral and evolutionary superior whom all heterosexuals should imitate, the sexual proletariat whose revolution will institute the new society. In Britton and Wood the most relentless analysis of the ills of bourgeois patriarchy ends, we believe, in a sentimental Utopianism which defies reason and experience in its claims for innate superiority. What is more, their arguments contain an area of bad faith, since the 'bisexuality' they advocate turns out on inspection to mean exclusive homosexuality, reducing the heterosexual male and female to the despised marginality at which the homosexual critic originally protested. Also, given that their work is so much grounded in psychoanalysis, they seem curiously unaware of the dangers in their own procedures of a splitting and projection whereby homosexuality is wholly idealised and heterosexuality practically made the source of all evil. Though their arguments have their basis in Freud's theory of infantile bisexuality, they ignore among other things any evidence of the immensely crucial and early nature of gender identification, the evidence that men and women cannot by will change their sexual orientation (homosexuals any more than heterosexuals), clinical evidence (e.g. Masters and Johnson) of the rarity of full practising adult bisexuality, as well as biological rather than cultural reasons for the predominance of heterosexuality. At the same time (like some lesbian critics) they refuse any investigation into the causes of homosexuality, which is either redefined as the essentially natural or as a moral choice which protests at patriarchy and heterosexuality. On the other hand, perhaps the least convincing argument that Freud ever put forward, the idea (in the famous analysis of Schreber) that schizophrenia has its source in repressed homosexuality, is quite uncritically accepted by Wood who (in his most recent book, *Hollywood: From Vietnam to Reagan*, 1986, pp. 253, 258) literally extends the argument to 'most serious mental illness' as well, so that repressed homosexuality becomes the major source of mental illness and civilisation's chief evil. It is all rather like the Poe story *The Premature Burial*, where the narrator is first of all aware that isolated cases of premature burial have occurred, then becomes convinced that many have, and finally comes to believe that the whole of humanity has suffered or will suffer from it. Given the fondness of contemporary criticism for reading Poe's stories as allegories of critical processes, we propose a reading of *The Premature Burial* as an allegory of critical paranoia, of the tendency to move from a true particular to a false universal, and of the belief that only an argument in its most excessive and absolutist form is valid (e.g. Andrea Dworkin's *Intercourse*, Adrienne Rich's 'rapism'). We cannot accept as more than a wish fulfilling fantasy the belief that some blissful Utopia, some higher kind of sexuality, would be brought into existence by a universal release of bisexuality (homosexuality).

The disagreement expressed at length here, and with a certain necessary bluntness which is no doubt open to misinterpretation, cannot be avoided, since the critic who believed Wood (and Britton in the more extreme of his arguments) to be right would find his or her only justification in the examination of texts dealing with heterosexual relations to lie in the exposure of the absolute oppressiveness of heterosexuality and the rescuing of bisexual sub-texts. In protesting at and disassociating ourselves from the logical end of such views we hope that our motivation will not be mistaken. No critic in our field could have failed to learn much of great consequence from the work of Britton, Wood and other gay critics in their investigation of the social creation of absolutes of gender characteristics that are oppressive. Indeed their influence is plain to see in many parts of this book. But inasmuch as our book departs from the most extreme aspect of the radical orthodoxy that they represent, and will be condemned out of hand by some influential critics for doing so, we have to make it clear that – whatever our own particular weaknesses and unconscious evasions – we see ourselves as very consciously resisting a new and influential mythology. To read our criticisms as simply 'reactionary' or the projection of unconscious hostility upon 'the other' would be, we believe, a mistake, as indeed would be the interpretation of a position which by implication accepts the centrality (but not the sole authority or value) of heterosexual experience as in any sense anti the liberation of other sexual orientations, a point which we feel the need to stress, since, while the writers of a book may aim at an audience above the sway of bigotry and prejudice, we cannot ignore the fact that in the present (1988) political climate of right-wing backlash, a critique of theory may be misinterpreted as an attack on rights. Therefore the point bears repetition that what is criticised is a theory that unreasonably marginalises the heterosexual, not alternative life styles. Our argument is against a tendency that is both universalising and unacceptably moralistic, the reverse side, in fact, of the homophobia which produced it.

Our positions, where and where not our critical sympathies lie, will become clear in the pages ahead. For the moment it is enough to signal that a good deal of our theorising about the operation of comedy, jokes and humour (in the Freudian definitions which we accept) has its origins in *Jokes and their Relation to the Unconscious* which, in our view, despite its necessary primitive commitment to structures much more simple than entire works of art, is by far the most perceptive study of the subject ever written, and a constant source of insight.

Besides the psychoanalytic, another obvious area of influence on us has been that of anthropological writing, particularly the works of Margaret Mead (and, to a lesser extent, Bronislaw Malinowski). While noting that, especially in regard to her Samoan idyll, Mead's work has areas of weakness (just as Malinowski's extreme conservatism is open to question), we have nevertheless returned frequently to her books as a continuing source of provocative thinking about the sexes.

In the field of criticism, our profound disagreements with the work of Andrew Britton should not prevent us from acknowledging the thought-provoking force for us of his books on Katharine Hepburn and Cary Grant, and we also wish to acknowledge as a major influence Stanley Cavell's *Pursuits of Happiness : the Hollywood Comedy of Remarriage*. Raymond Durgnat's book on Hollywood comedy, *The Crazy Mirror*, which we read much earlier than the others, should also be mentioned in this context.

As in our earlier work on the Hollywood musical, we have attempted to look at film texts within a wide cultural framework, in this case obviously from the perspective and awareness of contemporary writing on sexuality and its representation (Foucault, Irigaray, Barthes, Lacan, Millett, Mulvey, etc., some named in the text, some not). But we have also tried to place these films within their own historical contexts, preserving them from that terrible undifferentiation whereby they become simple by-products of an unchanging entity called 'Bourgeois Ideology', their original values (and sometimes radicalism) flattened. Richard Dyer's recent *Heavenly Bodies: Film Stars and Society* (1987) seems to us admirable in its ability to discriminate between past and present responses.

Briefly, the structure of this book is as follows. It is subtitled 'The Hollywood comedy of the sexes' rather than 'Hollywood romantic comedy' because although romantic comedy is our main interest, we did not wish to neglect the modes that are closest to it (sometimes operative with it, certainly defining and defined by it), non-romantic sexual comedy and family comedy. The chosen title gives us a broader spectrum to work in, and allows us, for instance, to write about unromantic Mae West, which the other would not have done. Chapter 1 takes a major 1930s comedy, *Bringing Up Baby*, as both a test case for analysis of the comedy of the sexes and as a way of talking more generally about 1930s comedy. Chapter 2 focuses on Ernst Lubitsch as perhaps the major exponent of romantic comedy, certainly its most influential presence. Chapter 3 concentrates on three comedians, Bob Hope, Mae West and Woody Allen, with a consequent emphasis upon the joke. Chapter 4 generalises about 1950s comedy through analysis of three different films (*Pat and Mike, Pillow Talk, The Seven Year Itch*) and a set of related films (Douglas Sirk's family comedies). Chapter 5 theorises about 'post-feminist' romantic comedy, with particular reference to *Tootsie* and *Victor Victoria*.

As with any book on so large a subject there are omissions. Leo McCarey's films, which we have raided for our title, are sadly neglected; we now wonder how we could find no space to write at length about Lubitsch's *The Shop Around the Corner* ; we spent

less time on Billy Wilder than we would have wished; and in our chronological
ordering we certainly neglected the films of the 1940s (most obviously those
of Preston Sturges) for those of the 1930s and 1950s. The only answer we
can make to criticism that fixes on such omissions is that they were necessary
to cover what we did cover. (Also, some of the works of Dorothy Arzner
and Lois Weber which fall within our sphere of interest and which might
have made, alongside newer woman-directed films, another chapter, were
largely unavailable for study.)

For other reasons this book may inevitably displease some groups of readers. Some radical critics will find its emphasis on heterosexuality 'regressive'.
Some 'straight' middlebrow critics will dislike it for even considering the
arguments emerging from sexual–political criticism. Others will duly invoke
the old chestnut about the dullness of analysing comedy at all. Our hope is
that such readers, pressing past the preface to the chapters on the films
themselves, might find that our practice transcends positions with which
they disagree. If the book has an ideal reader, we have imagined one who
wishes to understand the cinema culture that has been our past in the context
of the changes that are making our present and future; someone who might
agree with Virginia Woolf when she writes at the beginning of *A Room of
One's Own*:

> At any rate, when a subject is highly controversial – any question about sex is that
> – one cannot hope to tell the truth. One can only give one's audience the chance
> of drawing their own conclusions as they observe the limitations, the prejudices,
> the idiosyncrasies of the speaker. . .'.

Acknowledgements

We gratefully acknowledge assistance, help and encouragement from the following: John Banks
at Manchester University Press; The Newcastle University Small Grants Research Committee for
a grant which enabled us to see films essential to this study; all the students at Newcastle University's
Adult Education Film classes at The Tyneside Cinema (a course sponsored by the British Film
Institute); The British Film Institute stills library, the Schools of English and Modern Languages
at Newcastle University for their encouragement of film studies; Margaret Jones and Susan David-
son, secretaries of the departments of English Literature and Spanish and Latin American Studies,
who typed and word-processed parts of the book; the UCLA Film Archives for making available
to us *She Done Him Wrong*; Channel 4 for scheduling a whole range of films that are essential
background viewing for the writing of any book of this type; Richard Dyer for help with our section
on Sirk; Chris Perriam for suggesting material for our last chapter; Ron Guariento for stimulating
conversation on film, especially the comedies of Billy Wilder.

Stills from *Bluebeard's Eighth Wife, Design for Living, Belle of the Nineties, I'm No Angel, Pillow
Talk, Meet Me at the Fair, Take Me to Town* courtesy of MCA TV; Stills from *Heaven Can Wait*
and *The Seven Year Itch* courtesy of Twentieth Century Fox; still from *Tootsie* courtesy of Columbia
Pictures Corporation Ltd., stills from *Pat and Mike, Annie Hall, Victor/Victoria, Love and Death*
courtesy of UIP; still from *Carnal Knowledge* courtesy of Enterprise; still from *Bringing Up Baby*
courtesy of Turner Programme Enterprises; still from *The Princess and the Pirate* courtesy of Samuel
Goldwyn Productions; still from *Son of Paleface* courtesy of Bob Hope.

1

'Education sentimentale'

Bringing up Baby
and the golden age
of Hollywood comedy

THE STORY

Do you love her?
Yes, but don't hold it against me – I'm a little screwy myself.
— Clark Gable in *It Happened One Night* (1934)

Bringing up Baby (1938) is well enough known to summarise in the briefest terms. The day before his wedding to the bossy Alice, Professor David Huxley (Cary Grant) receives at his museum news of the discovery of the last bone of the brontosaurus skeleton he is reassembling. Attempting to persuade a lawyer, Alexander Peabody, to advise his client, Mrs Carlton Random, to make a gift of a million dollars to the museum, David meets an independent, wealthy young woman, Susan Vance (Katharine Hepburn). Susan, Mrs Random's niece, falls in love with David and succeeds in making him, against his will, accompany her to Connecticut to leave a pet leopard, the 'Baby' of the title, at her aunt's farm. After Susan has unscrupulously delayed David's return to New York for his wedding day, various complications follow as David is forced to pretend that he is a neurotic big-game hunter. George, Mrs Random's dog, steals the brontosaurus bone and buries it. 'Baby' escapes and becomes confused with a second leopard – a 'killer' – and the odd couple, as well as various other characters, wander through the forest in the night. As confusions multiply, David and Susan are arrested, he as a criminal, she as a lunatic, along with various others, and only after many misunderstandings are they released from jail. In a coda, back at the museum, Alice breaks her engagement to David, and Susan arrives – with the retrieved bone and the million dollars – to claim him.

COMEDY AND HISTORY

An imitation of life, a mirror of culture, and an image of truth.   — Cicero

The comic poet dares to show us men and women coming to this mutual likeness;
he is saying that when they draw together in social life their minds grow liker; just
as the philosopher discovers the similarity of boy and girl until the girl is marched
away to the nursery.   — Meredith

Surprisingly, *Bringing up Baby* had a very mixed response on its first release
in 1938. Its relative failure at the box-office (grossing only $365,000) was
compounded by a surprisingly ungenerous critical response, typical of which
are these dismissive remarks in *The New York Times*:

> To the Music Hall yesterday came a farce which you can barely hear above the
> precisely enunciated patter of Miss Katharine Hepburn and the ominous tread of
> deliberative gags. In *Bringing Up Baby* Miss Hepburn has a role which calls for
> her to be breathless, senseless and terribly, terribly fatiguing. She succeeds and
> we can be callous enough to hint it is not entirely a matter of performance.

Yet *Bringing up Baby* has become almost indispensable not only for an
understanding of the overall careers of its director Howard Hawks (though
we have not chosen to focus on it as a 'Hawks' film), and its principal stars
Katharine Hepburn and Cary Grant, but also for an appreciation of the
development of the whole tradition of the Hollywood comedy of the sexes.
For Hawks, *Bringing up Baby* was an early opportunity to extend his interest
in the portrayal of the independent, strong-minded woman; for Hepburn
and Grant it confirmed their potential for the kind of subversive, unruly,
upside-down roles demanded of the principal characters by the narratives
of 'Screwball' comedy. And in so far as it is a classical example of Hollywood's
own distinctive reformulation of the whole tradition of romantic comedy,
the film is almost a recreation of the Golden Age, that fantasy of pre-civilised,
guiltless and free modes of behaviour still not quite extinct, not even in
Hollywood, in the vaults of the collective modern unconscious. *Bringing up
Baby* is, generically, first and foremost, a Screwball comedy: its principal
characters combining the childish, prank-loving tendencies of the Keystone
Cops with a taste for verbal wit and the anarchy of literary 'crackerbarrel'
stock types; its setting and milieu usually focusing on the high, urban and

country club or estate, life of the upper middle classes; its thematics usually organised around principal female characters acting as redemptresses of a world too long in thrall to the irrationalities/rationalities, largely male-created, of modern life. But, beyond the constraints of Screwball, *Bringing up Baby* is an example of a strain of romantic comedy committed to positive regression and release, however temporary, from the frustrations and repressions of civilised life. In these respects it provides a stark contrast both to Hollywood's own rival tradition of a more satirical, 'Aristotelian' mode of comedy, a mode represented in some ways by Billy Wilder, Frank Tashlin, Preston Sturges and Mike Nichols, and to the patterns and thematics of other contemporary genres – like the gangster or horror film – striving more unambiguously to mirror the harsh realities of modern life.

Yet, while deeply committed to expressing the tensions and incongruities of social structures, sexual relationships and identity and so on, *Bringing up Baby* nevertheless clearly dramatises these issues in a way that is finally more tolerant, more affirmative, and more conciliatory than may be found in a film like, say, *Kiss Me, Stupid* (1964), or Hawks's later *Monkey Business* (1952), both major comedies of the sexes, but in both of which the psychological grotesqueries of the rat-race are far more directly in view. In this respect *Bringing up Baby* belongs to a strain of romantic comedy that Northrop Frye traced back to Greek Old comedy and its prime exponent Aristophanes, a type of comedy that in post-Classical times found its most evocative reformulations in Shakespeare's 'Green World' pastorals such as *As You Like It* and *A Midsummer Night's Dream*. Where Wilder's *Kiss Me, Stupid* is the jaundiced expression of a society in the grip of sleaziness, obsession and neurosis, *Bringing up Baby*, despite its conscious and unconscious inconsistencies, seems to recognise the limits of human potential, to understand the origins of human frailty, and even to remain optimistic not only about a benevolent nature's ultimate triumph over nurture, but also about the feasibility of relationships based on principles of equality between the sexes.

Convincing, all-encompassing, definitions of the comic – the mode as opposed to its techniques – are, not unexpectedly, somewhat scarce. But in addition to Frye's useful distinctions between the satirical, or 'Aristotelian' (comedy as castigation of moral flaws), and the tolerant or romantic strains, Freud's view of comedy as more than a mode of negative comparison, in spite of its formal dependence on victimisation by mimicry, disguise, unmasking, caricature, parody, travesty and so on, seems also highly relevant to the discussion of Screwball. Moreover, Freud's notion of comedy (in the shorter section that follows the large part on jokes in *Jokes and Their Relation to the Unconscious*), as something potentially liberating (a notion Screwball comedies seem themselves to acknowledge in their many direct and indirect allusions to Freud), and his theory of empathetic identification, where he is even prepared to go as far as to argue that 'the feelings of superiority bear no essential relation to comic pleasure', are centrally applicable to the drives and preoccupations of 30s comedy.

Furthermore, if, as successive theorists from Cicero onwards have argued, comedy holds the mirror up to nature, the surface patterns of life's infinite complexities will be its major preoccupations. Not for comedy the ultimate questions of tragedy, horror and other modes. The point is made by Barbara Stanwyck's Jean in Preston Sturges's *The Lady Eve* (1941), where, at an early moment in the film, she takes out her pocket mirror, adjusting it to reflect all the comings and goings around the table in the first-class dining room in the luxury liner where Henry Fonda as Hopsy, the wealthy explorer and heir to millions, is fending off the attentions of a bevy of gold-diggers. Held up by elegant fingers with dark, glossy, somewhat predatory nails, Stanwyck's mirror fills the whole screen and distorts (the mirror can only record sights not sounds) an already distorted reality, to paraphrase Raymond Durgnat's apt remarks in his book on American comedy, *The Crazy Mirror*. As Stanwyck points her mirror at the Human Comedy, her chosen angle and superimposed dialogue persuade us to see that although some of the philosophical implications of idealism may have grown outdated, the notion that reality is inseparable from our apprehension of it is still very compelling, only now the metaphysical uncertainties have yielded to ideological, cultural fragmentations of perception. The mirror here may focus on the cupidities and repressions of life, but as well as highlighting the disappointments, fiascos and traps of personal relationships, the film ultimately belongs to a tradition allowing generous space in its survey of the traffic of everyday life for reconciliations, marriages and even remarriages in recognition of the human instinct, when all argument is done, for forgiveness.

In some films, however, reconciliation will less successfully obliterate memories of pain and conflict, and the happy ending is often little more than a precarious arrangement, as likely to be breached as honoured. On these occasions romantic comedy seems at times to draw very close to melodrama. Just as traditional stage comedy has often seemed like the sunnier complement of tragedy, so it seems to us that film comedy can often be regarded as the lighter side of melodrama. The difficulties of generic classifications are naturally not resticted to comedy (is *Rancho Notorious*, 1952, western or *film noir*?), but as far as comedy is concerned, it is worth noting how far both on stage and on film it relies to a large extent on the same set of stock devices, situations and characterisations associated on stage with tragedy

and, on film, with melodrama, George Meredith, among others, comments on generic cross-fertilisation, and in a discussion of Molière, for
instance, writes of a conception of the comic that 'refines even to pain'.

The pain of romantic comedy in the cinema is perhaps easier to see and
feel in films more overtly addressing the questions of family or marital strife,
like *The Shop around the Corner* (1940), *The Lady Eve*, and *Mr and Mrs Smith*
(1941), than in *Bringing up Baby*, a film cloaking so much of its gravity in
its fondness for disguise, fantasy, farce and tomfoolery. The poignant lonel-
iness of Mr Matuschek at the end of *The Shop around the Corner*, his shop
restored to order but his wife lost to adultery, the destruction of trust in an
essentially well-founded marriage in *Mr and Mrs Smith*, and the discovery
in *The Lady Eve* of duplicity, small-mindedness and pusillanimity as the
sometimes inevitable partners of love, all contribute to the occasionally
sombre and inescapably melodramatic ambience of these films. Yet even in
lighter films like *The Awful Truth* (1937) darkness creeps in, and what at
first glance seems like no more than the painless pain of slapstick turns out
on closer inspection to be the pain of deeper wounds than one is led to
imagine by the distracting antics of its victims and practitioners. Screwball
comedy owes a great deal to silent slapstick, and in that respect revives the
traditions of the Punch and Judy shows (one of which appears briefly in
Holiday, 1938, where the Potters perform a fragment of a burlesque *Romeo
and Juliet*). The legacy of the puppet theatre's stock situations created around
the mayhem of family strife is especially noticeable in *Midnight* (1939), where
the judge, no feminist, proclaims: 'A husband may bring his wife back to
her senses by spanking her with no more than nine blows with an instrument
no bigger than a broom'. In this film the judge speaks bigotedly for Punch,
and with comic myopia misogynistically condones violence against Judy on
the grounds of what patriarchs from the early Church Fathers down to Clark
Gable in *Forsaking All Others* (1934) (when he spanks Joan Crawford with
a brush) take to be all women's essentially sinful natures. On this kind of
reading the whole narrative of *Bringing up Baby* would seem to be organised
around Susan's punishment of David as a reversal of Punch's traditional
persecution of Judy. What is slapstick on the outside is serious on the inside,
and the pain spreads over from farce into metaphor and thematics. Concentration on punishment, conflict, physical ordeals, allows one to see, first, that
these films embody an almost Nietzschean idea of life as an eternal struggle,
a kind of amoral human safari, here emphasised in *Bringing up Baby* by
extensive animal imagery and a near-wilderness setting, a world in which
only the fittest survive; and second, also to recognise that in the social structures of civilisation – economics, law, the family and so on – women have

usually been victimised by men.

Even so, Screwball usually manages to balance disenchantments and sexual revenges with affirmations of human potential, subordinating tendencies towards moral superiority to the predominantly romantic, tolerant, optimistic tone of the narrative, a tone that is far less in evidence in the more satirical, 'Aristotelian' films. If one takes *Kiss Me, Stupid* as typical of the latter, one can see how although an ultimate process of identification, gender differences notwithstanding, is established between the viewer and somewhat shady characters making a fast buck from sexploitation and other dark corners of the American Dream, the major thrust of the film is to make one see clearly through mimicry and caricature (Dino as himself, Dean Martin), parody and travesty (the degradations of American ideals), disguise and unmasking (the husband's plan to 'prostitute' his wife so Dino will buy his songs), how a trio of men on the make are ultimately dehumanised by their quest for fame and fortune. In contrast to, say, *Midnight*, where Plutus, society's ruling deity, is initially revered but ultimately despised by the romantic couple, *Kiss Me, Stupid* allows its characters no such comic *anagnorisis*, though the film's rhetoric makes one realise in other ways that its overall attitude is deeply satirical. In *Kiss Me, Stupid* the mood and ambience are tacky: society has reached hitherto unfathomed depths of materialistic squalor. Though the setting is rural America, Walden is horizons away, and the moral seediness spreading over from the city to the country – in a time-honoured convention dating back to Classical comedy – has even defiled the village setting of the film, significantly deprived of some bucolic and wholesome name like Arden or Westlake, Connecticut, and given instead the more unambiguously Kinseyan and libidinous title of 'Climax' (Nevada).

Bringing up Baby, by contrast, not a satirical comedy, *is* set in Westlake, Connecticut, a place still recognisably sylvan and magical. Romantic comedy, less attracted than the satirical kind to grainy realism, conjures up the worlds of myth and fairy tale: the allusions to Snow White in *Ball of Fire* (1941), to Cinderella in *Midnight*, and to Red Riding Hood in *Easy Living* (1937) tone down realism, allow for release, encourage revelry, fantasy and detachment.

This air of fantasy and detachment is especially pronounced in *Bringing up Baby*. Here Cary Grant's self-conscious acting and Katharine Hepburn's 'breathless' excesses, coupled with the unreality of the events and setting

---

Bringing up Baby (1)
'Bones' everywhere, but Miss Swallow (Virginia Walker) is stirred only by thoughts of academic achievement, while David (Cary Grant) seems ripe for release from the sobrieties of career, status and loveless love.

and the proliferation of disguises towards the end of the film in the jail scene, create an atmosphere of highly-charged artifice, yet not, even so, of triviality. From one point of view, *Bringing up Baby* might be seen as a kind of unconscious, accidental, comic equivalent of Jensen's melodramatic *Gradiva* (1903), the first novel to be given a comprehensive psychoanalytical reading. Like *Gradiva* (the title refers to the hero's fixation with the heroine's walk, as we might feel David to be obsessed with Susan's athletic stride), *Bringing up Baby* is a story of burying and unearthing, metaphorically and literally (for in one the hero is an archaeologist, and in the other a palae-ontologist), and the film comedy, with its dinosaur bone from Utah, reburied in Connecticut, and later unearthed, parallels the novel with its setting in the buried city of Pompeii. In each, even more oddly and suggestively, for there is no point of possible contact between the two texts, a dominant, pursuing young female liberates a repressed scientist male.

The comparison encourages one to take the story as liberation narrative a little more seriously. Seen in this light, too, the bone that is the cause of such a multitude of confusions takes on renewed significance. At once the literal dinosaur bone and symbol of the Reason (archaeology as primarily academic pursuit) from which the liberated characters are ultimately in flight, it is also, through a chain of indirect comic allusions, David's penis: right at the beginning, when he is seen holding the bone in his hand, David wonders about fitting it into the dinosaur's 'tail'. Commenting on *Gradiva*'s hero's obsession with his female statue, Freud remarks: '. . . as we have insisted with admiration, the author has not failed to show how the arousing of the repressed erotism came precisely from the field of the instruments that served to bring about the repression. It was right that an antique, the marble statue of a woman, should have been what tore our archaeologist away from his retreat from love and warned him to pay off the debt to life with which we are burdened from our birth.' Equally, it is 'right' that the dinosaur bone, a constant visual reminder of David's earlier retreat from love and life, should additionally not only be what keeps him away from the museum once he is in Westlake and warns him to pay off his 'debt', but also the instrument – give or take a little polymorphous perversity and pre-genital regression – with which he will pay it.

Bones and erections (so delicately written about by Stanley Cavell), animal intercourse, as George and Baby cavort on the ground, sexual deviation, as Susan and David leave the restaurant *a tergo*, he covering her exposed behind, and so on, remind us of the unshakeability of the body from the spirit's most determined efforts to reach the highest levels of fancy and desire. The film's last moments leave us in no doubt about this: high up above the ground, as near to ecstatic mystical levitation as a Connecticut upper-cruster will ever manage, Susan sways on her unsteady ladder as she climbs up to find David, her New England god of love (in Hebrew, of course, 'David' means 'beloved', working on his dinosaur; her swaying triggers off his rocking, keeping time with hers, and these time and earth-bound mortals now mutually declare their love as a prelude to the dinosaur's (and the rational world's) temporary collapse. The scene once more emphasises their antic harmony and, at the same time, suggests the obvious connotations of rhythmic excitement followed by surrender and climactic fall in the all too familiar patterns and cycles of the act of love itself. If love is the creative ordering of the sexual drive, its partial sublimation into a higher Eros where somehow innocence can be recaptured, we are constantly reminded of the sway of governing sexual instinct, whose power is at once an imprisonment and a release, a flight of the spirit and a bodily *débâcle*.

But alongside areas like these that are especially open to psychoanalytical readings, and others where history intervenes, there are yet more parts of *Bringing up Baby*'s *soufflé* of a narrative that appear at first glance to be by comparison too insubstantial. This is deceptive in two ways. First, the narrative's extreme self-consciousness must mean that its fantasy is playfully self-aware, that its indulgence in wish-fulfilment is not made through ignorance (or rejection) of the laws of reality. Second, just as some of the more brilliant inventions and fantasies are responses to historical reality, so these are paralleled by what we would want to describe as the presence of trace elements of those difficulties and inhibitions which the narrative so easily discards. If we watch carefully enough, the narrative not only delights us because it escapes from the rigours of the real, but delights us even more by respecting our intelligence and the reality principle by acknowledging what it has evaded. This is what makes for the significance of 'light' comedy, or *lightened* comedy as against mere light comedy free of real significance, merely evasive, unconcerned to articulate the values of its freedom.

Bringing up Baby is furthermore a situational as distinct from a 'comedic' type of comedy, relying not on the idiosyncratic persona of a comedian, whose reputation and star status have usually been formed outside film (e.g. radio or vaudeville in the case of Bob Hope), but on film stars whose comic potential is developed and stressed during the course of specific narratives, and whose meanings are formed by a creative interaction between events and issues both on and off screen, and special kinds of romantic empathy discussed in the next section. But these off-screen meanings interact with others. Screwball situational comedy, for all its surface froth and indebtedness to devices associated with the traditions of stage farce and silent film comedy, its most immediate generic predecessor, can only finally be under-stood, like any other genre, within the historical and social contexts of its making. In this case the Depression is quite clearly as crucially inseparable a structural feature of the sub-genre ('*Your* golf ball, *your* car', as the playful accusation of a woman unconsciously reproving what she takes to be the attitudes of an unregenerate capitalist), as of gangster and even musical films, drawing attention to the social injustices of a system serving the interests of a powerful oligarchy. In *Easy Living*, Jean Arthur as Mary Smith peers into an empty fridge, knows she has no dimes for a hamburger and faces starva-tion; down the street, passers-by storm an automat when they hear food is going free there. Even in films where the poor are out of sight, opulence itself becomes a kind of screen dream of an economic utopia. Without wealth, these comedies seem sometimes almost to say, love itself will die: 'When you're poor, love flies out of the window', Tibor Cerny (Don Ameche) remarks in *Midnight*. That may not be saying much for love, but even though, on the negative side, the ideology of the films may be unwittingly or discreetly promoting capitalism – get rich quick so you can find love, and keep it – there are other, more subversive implications pointing out the realities of human relationships on the breadline.

Yet to be too Depression-obsessed, to look only for the literal traces of history, will quite plainly lead to critical and theoretical culs-de-sac. Propp's remarks about 'understanding historicity only as the representation of histor-ical events and personages, whereas works of art aim at transmitting the significance of the event, not just recounting it', are useful warnings to the theorist too content with a crudely mimetic theory of comedy, in which ambiguity, irony, allusion and metaphor are usually missed in the search for a one-to-one correspondence with fact. Flatly sociological criticism that has been satisfied with reductive processes of this kind – that ends up by dismissing Screwball as an evasion of reality – has sometimes also been characterised by a common twofold simplification: an insistence on taking the frame for the whole, whether this means the narrative outline rather than what it contains (so that a romantic comedy ending in marriage is thereby defined as a celebration of 'regressive' values); or whether it means stressing to the exclusion of all else the lowest denominator of audience reaction ('glossy escapism'). In either variant the basic enabling frame is treated as wholly dictating the composition, rather than providing its ultimate constraints.

The way out of this self-created impasse is to combine a realisation of the sophisticated allusiveness and elusiveness of comic forms with an understand-ing that effects in a work of art are neither consistent nor unitary, so that one area of investigation (here the sphere of the relations between the sexes), may be made possible precisely by the exclusion of another. A prime example of this is the case of Lubitsch's early 30s musicals, set in a mythical, chocolate-box Europe at a seemingly irresponsible distance from its Depression audiences. Yet it is this fanciful aristocratic milieu that is capable of being worked to provide images of sexual relationships free from the compromises of social reality, mixing American and European elements in an ideal combination. If on the one hand such comedy fails to reflect the most direct social realities, on the other, through that very omission, it is able to chart rival areas that are equally part of social and historical realities, once we include the realms of fantasy and desire within them.

In *Bringing up Baby* Susan's upper-class origins and wealth will tempt the socio-historical critic to read them simply as cues for the celebration of the reactionary. Yet one could argue that Susan's wealth has much more positive, as well as symbolic, functions. It gives her access to freedoms not otherwise available to her, even if those freedoms are not universally shared, and ultimately based on their denial to others. As Andrew Britton properly notes, one of these important freedoms is that of Susan's not having to think of marriage for economic reasons. It is worth recalling that in his famous treatise on marriage and the family Engels saw such marriages of convenience as the underlying cause of the social subjugation of women. Such motivation, the exchange of sex and wifehood for material security, is an underlying theme, both hidden and overt, of all bourgeois romantic comedy, but it is especially marked in the Depression era. In *Bringing up Baby*, though, Susan is wealthy enough to give away her million-dollar inheritance, and David is also obviously so comfortably off that her wealth is of no personal interest to him. The same is true of the Warriners in *The Awful Truth*, Tracey and C. K. Dexter Haven in *The Philadelphia Story* (1940), and Johnny and Linda in *Holiday*, (1938) though baser comedies (e.g. *Bachelor Mother*, 1939) continue to reward rags with riches.

The inventiveness of 30s comedy, though, does more than sometimes bring into focus golden worlds where economics hold no sway. It also specialises in inventing a scintillating variety of ways, ways other than those proposed by economics, in which the couple can meet as equals, interdependent but independent. In 30s Hollywood comedy of the sexes the question is not whether the hero and heroine will marry, but under what circumstances, terms and safeguards the heroine becomes a wife. If this is a distortion of reality, it is a knowingly utopian gesture, and the wit of such conceits lies in placing in tension the ideal with the real and so being more than a series of fancy 'meet cutes': Rosalind Russell and Claudette Colbert as ace reporters in *His Girl Friday* (1940) and *Arise My Love* (1940), Claudette Colbert as novelist in *It's a Wonderful World* (1939), paralleled by Carole Lombard in *True Confession* (1937); Jean Arthur as test pilot in *Too Hot to Handle* (1938); Irene Dunne as explorer–anthropologist (shades of Margaret Mead and Ruth Benedict) in *My Favourite Wife* (1940); all of these are either the professional equals or superiors of the men in their lives. But whether the heroine is just a lower-class girl struggling to survive (Carole Lombard in *Hands across the Table*, 1935, Jean Arthur in *Easy Living*, Ginger Rogers in *Bachelor Mother* and *Fifth Avenue Girl*, 1939), adventurously and famously employed, like the heroines of *It's a Wonderful World* and *Too Hot to Handle*, a gold-digger like Eve Peabody in *Midnight*, or on the criminal fringes like Jean in *The Lady Eve*, it may be said of all these characters that, though they are placed in narratives all too frequently failing to live up to the promise of their early radicalism, they all in some ways redefine the most common stereotypes of female inferiority. Two of the greatest comedies of this period, *The Lady Eve* and *Bringing up Baby*, almost completely hinge on the nearly total reversal of the male/activity, female/passivity dichotomy.

These are extreme cases, the reduction of the male to a state of almost catatonic incompetence bringing to mind the end of *Jane Eyre*, where the poetic logic seems to be that only through the male's blinding, maiming and emasculating can a relationship of equality be established between husband and wife. In the films, since we are in the domain of comedy, the paralysis of the hero comes as a punishment at the beginning, not the end, its extremity dramatising the ludicrousness of the myths of natural male superiority and female inferiority. Though Claudette Colbert in *Midnight* is ultimately susceptible to materialistic temptations and corruptions, these are as nothing beside the primary effect of her drive, vivacity, style and wit. It is a truly exhilarating moment when we first meet her, dressed in a gold evening gown, travelling as free as any male *pícaro* third-class on the Paris Express, penniless (as a result of gambling debts), parodying the elegance of the Lubitschean comedy with her first remark, 'So this is Paris, huh?' It is one of the limitations of Britton's work on Katharine Hepburn that in defining the radical in female stars in only one direction (towards the humiliation or punishment of heterosexual men by faintly sapphic women), he underestimates the pleasurable subversiveness of all the other great female comic stars of the period, simply because they continue to display signs of unambiguously heterosexual femininity as they invade the masculine world.

As intelligent as they are active, these women are exemplars of comedy's vital intelligence, defining wit and intellect as features of female attractiveness. In both *The Awful Truth* and *My Favorite Wife* Irene Dunne impersonates in devastating fashion other women of a more sultry, intellectually

limited kind to which her husband is attracted, wittily satirising male prefer-
ences in that line, but also showing her own dazzling adaptability. Impersonation, indeed, becomes in these films almost a necessary sign of the heroine's
refusal to play overdefined roles.

Concentration on the heroines of Screwball allows one to see that these
films embrace a belief in a fundamental though contradictory tenet of Western
bourgeois liberalism, that belief in the equality of men and women formally
enshrined in the 1919 Suffrage Amendment, in large part a reformulation
of the thought of Mary Wollstonecraft, John Stuart Mill and Engels. Such
a view may be too extreme, one that fails to take account adequately of the
contradictory nature of an idea in conflict with immemorial views of woman
as inferior, subordinate or other, and a social order based on them. But even
if we admit that this is too exaggeratedly optimistic a view of Screwball's
ultimate allegiance to dominant ideology, we can at least claim that through
the gaps, fissures and incongruities of the films there is a fascinating dramatisation of the culture's unconscious, its instinctual drives, and its ideals of
sexual democracy as well as its shying away from its consequences

The Hollywood comedy of the sexes, a genre escaping no more than any
other the stringent dictates of ideological consensus, takes on by implication
the vast uncanny of desire and prohibition, prejudice and possibility,
romance and rationality, civilisation and discontent making up the terrain
of sexuality. If we pause to ask why in the 30s and early 40s all that talent
– directors like Hawks, Leisen, Sturges, Lubitsch, actors like Gary Cooper,
Fredric March, Herbert Marshall, Cary Grant, Katharine Hepburn,
Claudette Colbert, Ginger Rogers, Barbara Stanwyck – was able to apply
itself so brilliantly to comedies that elevated the role of women, yet out
of that potentially traumatic material was able to make such witty and
intensely pleasureable works of art, the answers are neither self-evident nor
simple. Perhaps we might want to agree, by way of providing a partial answer,
that some sort of truce conducive to positive and experimental images of the
sexes prevailed between the first wave of feminism in the late nineteenth
century and its second wave beginning in the late 60s. Though the statistics
show how little progress was really made as regards employment and pay
equality for women, there was arguably a real feeling of change and development, perhaps based upon very frail foundations, but vividly embodied in
the small yet growing and significant number of women in positions of influence and esteem who were very much in the public eye. The 20s and 30s
are the decades of the emerging sportswoman (the athlete/golfer Babe Didrik-
son, the channel swimmer Gertrude Ederle, and the tennis player Helen
Wills Moody), female adventurer (the fliers Amelia Earhart and Jacqueline

Cochrane), women judges and politicians (Frances Perkins under Roosevelt, the first ever woman cabinet member, at the centre of the drafting of such major legislation as the Social Security Act of 1936, and the Wages and Hours Act of 1938, and, of course, Eleanor Roosevelt herself). In statistical terms these may mean very little, but they were vital symbols, inspirations to women and possibly not too threatening to men, especially since their explicit or implicit rhetoric was one of co-operation rather than of separatism. Perhaps for these and other reasons a relatively untraumatic view of the relations between the sexes is abroad in the 30s films, making for that sense of playfulness and vivacity, not of antagonism and rejection, that is charac-teristically their dominant mode.

Curiously enough, though, few of the comedies discussed in this chapter were written by women, although Hagar Wilde, who wrote the early version on which *Bringing up Baby* was based (she also co-scripted the film), and Vina Delmar, who wrote the story for *Hands across the Table*, were exceptions. In spite of this, it is arguable that Hollywood romantic comedy, whose com-mercial packaging is obviously designed to please female audiences even more than male ones, is very much female influenced. Influenced, that is, in one way by the activity of figures like Virginia Van Upp, who worked on Fred MacMurray/Madeleine Carroll films at Paramount, Bella Spewack, Jane Murfin (*Alice Adams*, 1935), Zoe Akins (the stories of *Morning Glory*, 1933, and *How to Marry a Millionaire*, 1953, and the scripts of *Camille*, 1936, and *Christopher Strong*, 1938, as well as better known writers such as Dorothy Fields (musical comedy) and, perhaps most famous of all, Anita Loos. But influenced also in two other ways. First by the prominence of popular female dramatists and novelists as sources for film treatments (e.g. Vicki Baum, Edna Ferber and Elinor Glyn), and second, by the enormous contribution made by female scenarists in the 20s to the creation of Hollywood genres: e.g. Frances Marion, and perhaps especially Jeannie McPherson, who wrote not only the De Mille epics *King of Kings* and *The Ten Command-ments* but also enormously influential De Mille marital comedies like *Don't Change Your Husband* (1919), *Male and Female* (1919), and *The Affairs of Anatol* (1921). While in itself the presence or the contribution of female writers may not represent any transgression of male-dominated attitudes, since it can be argued that the female in such circumstances will be highly 'colonised', it is probably too narrow to take the extreme view, and more helpful to argue that the innate demands of women-centred melodrama and the couple-centred comedy are the projections of a desire to enforce a respect for the feminine. In this context the historical and contemporary presence of major women writers succeeds in producing discernible influences on the genres. Viewed like this, the Hollywood comedy of the sexes sometimes comes very close to echoing concepts about equality between the sexes associated with a highly influential book published in 1935 by another famous woman of the day, Margaret Mead. In the preface to *Sex and Temperament in Three Primitive Societies*, built around empathetic description of the world-views of three New Guinea peoples (the kindly Arapesh, the warlike Mundugumor and the role-reversing Tchambuli), remotely distant from Hollywood or Middletown, she summarises her belief that the striking difference of role and attributes held by men and women in these miniscule societies suggested the relativity and changeability of the seemingly unalterable ways of perceiving the sexes in vastly more complex Western ones:

> I went to the field in 1931, to study one problem, the 'conditioning of the social personalities of the two sexes'. I found, after two years' work, that the material which I had gathered threw more light on *temperamental* differences, i.e. differences among innate individual endowments, irrespective of sex. I concluded that, until we could understand very thoroughly the way in which a society could mould all the men and women born within it to approximate an ideal of human behaviour which another culture succeeded in limiting to the opposite sex, we wouldn't be able to talk very intelligently about sex differences.

Hollywood's 30s romantic comedies enact a version of what Margaret Mead was coming to elaborate about American society via her ethnographical travels, the release in the female of a more 'masculine' temperament without the loss of the 'drama' of femininity, and in the male of more 'feminine' qualities without the destruction of the 'plot' of masculinity. Despite the readings of these films in terms of the castration of the male, we surely feel that when the hero is made both ludicrous and powerless, suddenly confined in women's clothes, as Cary Grant is in *Bringing up Baby*, or Robert Montgomery in *Forsaking All Others*, these are comic hyperboles which suggest that the adjustments demanded of the male are not traumatising, merely a passing phase on the way to some better, more liberating balance, and not the absolute overthrow of all gender specificity.

In this respect the place of women in romantic Screwball comedy narratives is crucial. For once, women are pushed to the centre of the screen not for the sake purely of spectacle, not even to embody tired fantasies about redemption, eroticism, or paternalism, though these are part of the dialectic through which their social meanings are formulated, but as an expression of the aspirations and betrayals, the ordeals and failures that characterise the lives of all women, both those who accept – to whatever degree – the definitions of a socialised existence, and those who very firmly do not. In this sense the film comedy of the sexes, and particularly the Screwball sub-genre, may be an egalitarian mode, for even where its conclusions sometimes draw a veil of realism over the unrealistic liberation of its middle parts, it continues to be inspired by misrule, rebellion, irrationality, and the topsy-turvy vision of life so well adapted to Katharine Hepburn's Susan and so emphatically, not to say exasperatedly, underlined by Cary Grant's David when he remarks, 'Susan, you look at everything upside down!'

STARS OF THE COMEDY OF THE SEXES: DIZZY DAMES AND SCREWY GENTS

Hey, you ain't no lady!   — Sherriff Slocum in *Bringing up Baby*

I was just wondering what makes dames like you so dizzy?
                        — Clark Gable in *It Happened One Night*

Katharine Hepburn

Critics from the popular reviews of the 30s to the academic journals of the 80s have consistently singled out in Katharine Hepburn's screen presence the irresistible dynamism, assertiveness, WASPish but also college-girl self-assurance of a person in conflict with meanings of femininity created entirely out of vampishness, maternity, domesticity, fatality and other stereotyped distortions associated with the common run of actresses all around her on the studio lots. As a university graduate part of her meaning on the screen is related historically to the idealistic force of the first few generations of women graduates. Of all her apologists Andrew Britton has been most successful in carefully beginning to disentangle the various threads of her conceptualisation, not only its idiosyncrasies of physical beauty, but also the sexual and social meanings attached to her distinctively *gamine*, coltish, and even on occasion (especially in a film like *Sylvia Scarlett*, 1935), androgynous qualities. Britton argues it was especially the 30s comedies that allowed her to release her exhilarating independence of spirit. There is little to disagree with here, but we will have to return in a later chapter to contest his view that her 40s and 50s films with Spencer Tracy were in major respects a capitulation to a demeaning ideology.

In the 30s comedies, where Cary Grant is the partner, Britton persuasively argues that anarchic patterns of behaviour, complemented by the liberation narratives themselves, and in response to Grant's own highly unconventional flourishes and creative unpredictabilities, are what we come to expect of her. Something of the classical stage comedy's wily and witty servant flows over not just into the minor characters of these films, but into their major women stars as well, especially Katharine Hepburn.

While, sexual allure apart, certain other great women stars are more firmly trapped by socialised compromises of gender (Rita Hayworth by fatality, Debbie Reynolds by sisterliness, June Allyson by homeliness), Katharine Hepburn seems more than most to have succeeded in blending conformity with radicalism. Even where the narrative places her, as it does in her first screen role in *Bill of Divorcement* (1932), in a father/daughter relationship (her father, forgotten in a mental hospital, is divorced by her mother, who is planning to re-marry, so begins to rely on his daughter, who eventually gives up her lover to look after him), a vigorous independence and isolation from the more claustrophobic forms of conventional femininity, resisting domination by a benign but potentially infantilising patriarch, is what characterises her complex representation of daughterhood.

Either as an aristocratic English daughter or as an American patrician (with her characteristically Bostonian pronunciations of words like 'dance', 'aunt', and 'ask'), Katharine Hepburn is still a kind of sylvan goddess, especially in *Bringing up Baby* with all its forest fantasies, though not so much shrouded by vows of chastity (perhaps there is a hint of this in *The Philadelphia Story*), as sharing the goddess of the hunt's fearlessness of men. She seems, too, to epitomise Anaïs Nin's conviction that women are closer to the unconscious, and in her affinity with forests, animals and the elements, even though almost invariably an urban socialite (a recalcitrant one, for even in *Alice Adams* (1935) she ultimately recognises the folly of her social pretensions), she embodies the narrative's implicit admission, which she enacts raucously, persistently, bullyingly, that men have lost touch with nature.

What later became a look characterised by frizzy, almost unkempt hair, minimal cosmetics (with occasional lapses into glamour as in *Woman of the Year*, 1942), which in combination with other things suggested an aura primarily of efficiency and the no-nonsense priorities of the professional woman, had originally been a stylish image of sleek *coiffure*, rather heavy make-up emphasising hollow cheeks, chiselled bone contours, dark inquisitive eyes and a generous gash of a mouth – though not as predatory as Joan Crawford's – made not only for kissing but also for a lot of witty talk:

Susan: He also adores music. Particularly that song, 'I can't give you anything but love, Baby'.
David: Oh that's absurd.
Susan: No it isn't David. Really – listen.

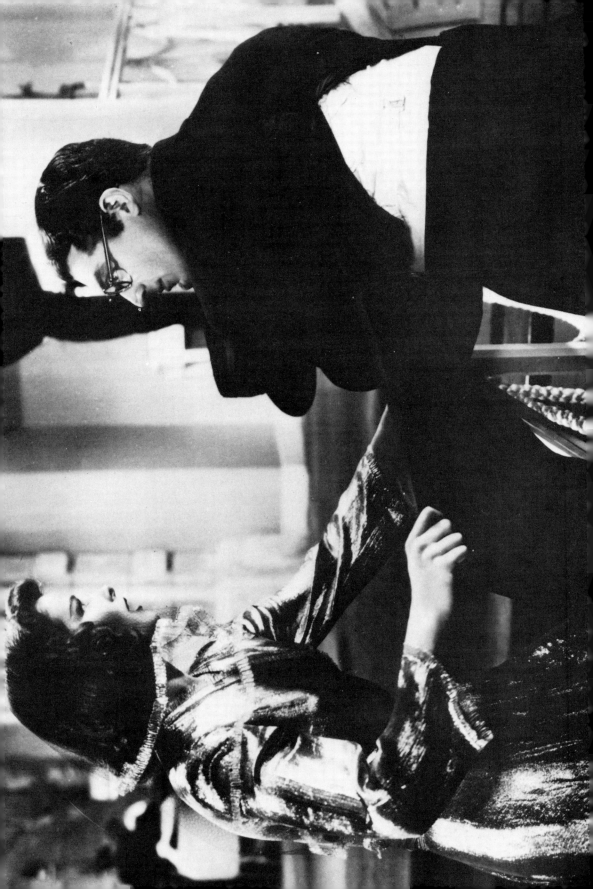

David: This is probably the silliest thing that ever happened to me.
Susan: I know it's silly, but it's true, he absolutely adores the tune.
David: What's the difference whether it adores the tune or not?
Susan: It's funny that he should love such an old tune, isn't it, but I imagine that
down in Brazil they. . .

Katharine Hepburn as Susan never finishes her sentence, but the unspoken continuation of her thought in this speech must run something like this: 'in Brazil they are behind the times with American hit tunes, so "I Can't Give You Anything but Love, Baby" is probably still popular down there, which means that a tame, music-loving leopard might well have heard it a great deal recently'. If we talk of the comic affirmativeness of Susan's freedoms of mind, and as early as *Alice Adams* the Hepburn character is ruled by the imagination ('Oh, Alice! What an imagination!' her mother exclaims), this delicious paradigm of verbal Screwball provides a microcosm of it in the delight released by the way she builds on to the most unlikely and irrational postulate (yet one that is actually true), a superstructure of animated logic – delivered with Hepburn's persuasive simplicity that will turn doubting men of reason into wiser, believing fools – involving considerations of chronology, geography, musical taste and cultural imperialism. Clearly, here we are not just laughing at Susan/Hepburn, but with her as well, enjoying her freedom and play of fantasy.

In the 30s comedy Katharine Hepburn is a screen blend of fantasy, freedom, assertiveness and femininity, sylphlike girlish beauty ('Susan' is an appropriate name for her in *Bringing up Baby*, since its original Hebraic meaning is 'graceful white lily'), genderless athleticism, at ease as much in silky, clingy, silver drawing-room gowns as in tweedy outdoor togs. She was a star dreamy enough for love, yet with abundant self-confidence to risk parody of her own image. Just as Barbara Stanwyck is sufficiently self-assured in *The Lady Eve* to permit herself an unflattering allusion to the size of her own nose (a rather Roman construction, custom-built for those splendid, characteristically adenoidal plebeian vowels), so in *Holiday*, in a remark ambiguous enough to emphasise Screwball's triumph of the primitive, where partial regression to primordial, Darwinian levels of existence is regarded as a sign of progress, Katharine Hepburn as Linda takes pride in noticing how very closely she resembles a toy giraffe: same neck, cheeks, mouth, eyes, and same trailing eyelashes, all reflecting a romantic vision of love through an animal's mask of childish irreverence and play. Not content to be judged

---

Bringing up Baby (2)
The psychopathology of everyday high life. A ripping time is had by all!

by their physical appearances alone, these women can afford to poke fun at blemishes other actressses would waste little time taking to their plastic surgeons. Like the stand-up comedian, with carefree defiance Screwball's women stars draw attention (as Jack Benny drew attention to his stinginess, Bob Hope to his nose and cowardly narcissism, Tony Hancock to his melancholia, and Joan Rivers to her droopy breasts) to what by the standards of the straight society could be considered personal catastrophes.

Katharine Hepburn's relaxed, almost casual attitude to her looks matches the hoydenish instincts of a Jo March (a part she played in the first film version of *Little Women*, 1933). She leaps over barriers in *Sylvia Scarlett*, sits on the backs of settees, not necessarily in them, in *Bill of Divorcement*, and wears trousers, literally in the former and figuratively in the latter. Where her mother in *Bill of Divorcement*, is as her patronising new suitor remarks, 'pure nineteenth-century', Katharine Hepburn both as 'Sidney' in that film and as Susan in *Bringing up Baby*, or any other role in her Screwball films, is pure twentieth-century. These mannish identifications, established from the very outset of her career in *Bill of Divorcement* (1932) ('I'm very like father', 'Father's my job, not yours'), are partly carriers of a traditional wish-fulfilment associated with ideologised fathers incapable of emotionally letting go of their daughters, but they also express a set of contradictorily positive connotations. Above all, they imply a rejection of socialised femininity, for where her 'nineteenth-century' mother – no Dorothea Brooke, the nineteenth century's most shining literary example of (ultimately frustrated) intellectual womanhood – is all lace, soprano trills, softness and frills, an unwitting serf of boudoirs, drawing rooms and kitchens, Hepburn as 'Sidney' is driven by liberating masculine impulses. Refusing marriage, identifying herself with the father, she is at once a hostage to patriarchy and a 30s suffragette of the inner self, seeking sexual equality but, given the infancy of the women's movement, not yet fully able to formulate its clearest messages of protest.

While *Bill of Divorcement* dramatises these issues through melodrama, *Bringing up Baby* returns to them through comedy. Hepburn as Susan merges the traditional subversiveness of all comic heroes and heroines with the more specific demands of a woman's pursuit of equality. Unlike her conformist sister Julia, who in *Holiday* sought after bourgeois comforts, the Hepburn character is still in *Bringing up Baby* the 'mad sister, the family problem, the one they won't speak about', as she herself puts it in *Holiday*. Susan has no blood sister in *Bringing up Baby*, but Miss Swallow, David's fiancée, is a sister-equivalent, a conventional 'other', the Super-Ego to her Id. Miss Swallow is no creature of air, never in graceful flight from the stuffiness of conformist society, preferring instead another element, the barren, gloomy, lifeless life of earth-bound archaeology, its ice and stone-age fixations unrepentantly caricatured by the film to serve as a symbol of all that is inwardly deadly. Miss Swallow is not a woman; she is a doctoral thesis. Her 'other', Susan, has escaped from all peril of being trapped by the Miss Swallow in herself. While Miss Swallow is all conformity, Susan is all independence; while Miss Swallow is an old-fashioned Echo, 'swallowing' the paltry truths of the academic hack, here imaged as the early, as yet unreconstructed Narcissus of a David, Susan's Echo is wholly teasing, mocking, irreverent, her mimicry of David always prompted by a conviction that he can be rescued from his socialised narcissism and desiccation:

David George!
Susan: George!
David: George!
Susan: George!
David: George!
Susan: George!
David: Geor. . . Stop it, Susan. You sound like an echo.

This pursuer of men, with the Gilbert and Sullivan patter-song delivery and the giddy pace of a dizzy dame (nothing here of the sedateness and decorum of another famous comic heroine, *Mansfield Park's* Fanny Price), is fired by a vocation to wholeness, regeneration and creativity. She will be the *anima* to David's *animus*, refusing to be simply the mirror of male desire, and contemptuous of any sister who accepts servility as the price of survival. Neither an obscure object of desire, nor an idol of love, nor an Oedipal memory, Screwball Hepburn strives to be the subject and the controller of her own destiny, that destiny which for a woman, for a change, can include the bewitchment of lovers through instruments and language, ruses and stratagems, laws and privileges, too long appropriated by men.

Cary Grant

I confess I find his whole attitude unAmerican.
— Linda's father about Johnny (Cary Grant) in *Holiday*

Though Cary Grant has himself remarked that the very stylised, self-conscious image – so well adapted to the ostentatiously artificial mode of *Bringing up Baby* – he developed on screen was based on a cocktail mixture of Jack Buchanan, Noel Coward, Rex Harrison and Douglas Fairbanks (the first three for their effortless urbanity, the last for his luxury-cruise tan), it is clear that in Screwball comedy other more anarchic elements of identity play an equally creative part in its genesis.

Like Hepburn's, Grant's image changes and develops and, also like her, he is at his most unconstrained, revelling in pre-civilised energy and release, pursuing the dictates of a primal will in the 30s comedies. In the 50s and 60s his comic roles drive him towards an impassive, invulnerable suaveness, a globe-trotting epicureanism (in both *Indiscreet* (1958) and *That Touch of Mink* (1962) he is a sort of diplomat for American capitalism), and a self-assurance rarely guilty of underestimating its own accomplishments. 'No one speaks like that', Jack Lemmon as Daphne tells Tony Curtis as Josephine in *Some Like it Hot* when he hears his parody Cary Grant accent, that unmistakable blend of gentrified Bristolian vowels and democratic mid-Atlantic consonants, as if not merely to ridicule both Curtis and Grant for implausibility, but also to emphasise that Grant belongs nowhere and everywhere. In these decades only Hitchcock and, to a lesser degree, Hawks in *Monkey Business* would tease out the wild, even satanic streak that is also there. In the late 30s, a decade still very close both in time and in spirit to the great era of film clowns, the cinema, with its ability to combine elegance with an appetite for slapstick and a less sedate, more robust film-making style, was able much more easily to accommodate the persona of a rising star still to some extent drawing significance (e.g. in his somersaults in *Holiday*) from the knockabout fun of his acrobatic past, his earlier self as Archie Leach, tumbler *extraordinaire* in an obscure English vaudeville act touring the United States.

Where among Screwball stars William Powell, say, was one-dimensionally debonair, Ray Milland bland, Don Ameche plebeian and suspiciously Latin, Henry Fonda the soul of uprightness, and Gary Cooper a prodigy of plain-speaking (though in some of these cases they played against type), Grant is marvellously protean, the multifarious embodiment of all these qualities and more. Like the acrobat he had been and still is in *Holiday*, where almost his first act is a somersault, he seems nearly as full of reversals of identity as he had once been of torso and limb. So in *His Girl Friday* he is, among other things, wilful (and deceitful), almost to the point of sadism, in *The Awful Truth* rakish and suave, in *Holiday* striving after virtue and honesty in a world in thrall to cupidity, and in *Bringing up Baby* a wild man struggling inwardly with his civilised self. In all of these roles, the narrative usually places Grant in circumstances forcing him to discover a self through a series of ordeals designed not only to purge him of his own egocentricity, but also through such purification to expose the tyrannies of socially idealised concepts of masculinity, concepts above all associated with sexual stereotyping, hierarchy, and the various other conservative ideals endorsed by capitalism. As Britton further notes, the Grant character is repeatedly humiliated – made to fall (like Henry Fonda in *The Lady Eve*), both physically and morally, to wear women's clothes (*Bringing up Baby*, *I Was a Male War Bride*, 1949), suffer symbolic castration (*The Philadelphia Story*), or woo a bobbysoxer (*Bachelor Knight*, 1947).

Grant's first appearance as David in *Bringing up Baby* pinpoints the tension of the persona. In the first place, Grant wears glasses, which even in the pre-contact lens era are the antithesis of glamour. Here they signify, at best, studiousness and, at worst, academic desiccation (Susan will break them before the end of the film). Secondly, in addition to these deglamourising effects, in relation to a star who in the infancy of his career had already shown signs of a taste for affectations of urbanity, he is made to wear a smock, or apron, here perhaps not necessarily a symbol of domesticity, but, in conventional terms, nevertheless associated with feminisation. So, in the early stages of the film, there is indeed something, as Hawks is on record as wanting, of the Harold Lloyd (both the glasses and the comic, code-breaking zany elements) in Cary Grant. Even when we do see him more recognisably as 'Cary Grant', in top hat, white tie and tails, about to be Buchanan–Harrison–Coward, his suit is very soon in rags, and by the time he has fallen into Susan's Connecticut man-trap, all his clothes are finally taken away from him, and he is forced to wear a selection of items, some belonging to a woman, others to a couple of other men, all to the tune of his characteristic protests of the 'oh, oh, oh', 'mm, mm, mm' kind, and all accompanied by the usual frowns and severe parrot-like inclinations of the head, signs that at once record his fury and register his retreat into the pre-civilised world of animal grunts and irrational instinct.

The ridiculous sight of Grant wearing Susan's flimsy nightgown is compounded by the absurdity of his having to greet Aunt Elizabeth like that. He stands there, the fur edges on the nightie farcical reminders of the film's other animal motifs, unable to convince her of his serious purpose:

David: What do you want?
Aunt: Well who are *you*?
David: Who are *you*?
Aunt: Who are *you*?
David: What do you want?
Aunt: Well who *are* you?
David: I don't know. I'm not quite myself today.
Aunt: Well you look perfectly idiotic in those clothes.
David: They aren't my clothes.

Aunt: Well where *are* your clothes?
David: I've lost my clothes.
Aunt: Well why are you wearing these clothes?
David: Because I just went gay all of a sudden.

The wearing of Susan's nightie, like the fur coat dropped by chance on to Jean Arthur in *Easy Living*, acts as a kind of magic, like the little girl's red riding hood, or Puss's boots and Cinderella's glass slipper in the fairy stories, all objects that transform characters in some ways tyrannised by conformist society. David's transvestism, his 'gayness', may well be, as Britton claims, a comic reference to homoeroticism, but perhaps above all it draws attention, in keeping with all the other implications of the scene, to an educative process of feminisation, David's enforced absorption of aspects of Susan's identity, the discovery of a self through exposure to the 'other', and the gradual erosion of a socially sanctioned male egocentricity. 'Who are you?' Aunt Elizabeth asks. David does not know, and yet knows too well. Too well because he is, after all, 'Cary Grant', epitome of composure, self-consciously playing the fool and yet, not at all known either to himself or to others, through excess of acting, self-projection and a self-consciousness so extreme that the inner self and its meaning become refined to the point of obscurity. In the darkness of his inky hair and hazel eyes, in his somewhat Semitic, Mediterranean good looks, the razor-cut precision of his hair (allowed a degree of scruffiness in Screwball), in the eccentricity of his nasal, cadent tones, in his slightly pigeon-toed stride, his is a persona at once agile, swarthy with sexual allure, yet also uncannily distant, a persona attractive enough for a woman fleeing from stereotype, smart enough to embody ideals of drawing-room elegance, and sexually unthreatening (as Pauline Kael notes), precisely because so self-absorbed in the artifice of the image. This protean self, so self-conscious and aloof, is nevertheless full of sexual promise and (perhaps this is what makes him especially attractive) an appetite for slapstick and antic behaviour, the kind that is ready to mock the solemnest, most sacred values of convention. The hole in his chin and the mole on his cheek, minor blemishes in an otherwise almost flawless physiognomy, are readable perhaps as the signs of an ingrained tendency to sabotage perfection.

Just as David will be made to love Susan for herself, as opposed to his own reflection in her (she is no Miss 'Swallow' and she does not wear, as Miss Swallow does, glasses, a minor clue to the latter's nearly total identification with the unreconstructed David), so Susan will find in David a kindred spirit of comic and sexual refusal, someone irreverent enough to ridicule the sexual/political dullness and conservatism typical of so many other screen partnerships. The primarily ludic, childish side to Grant's 30s persona –

finding a perfect niche here in the part of David, and creating such an effect precisely because it is a feature of an actor so otherwise elegant, beautiful and ideal – is noticeable even when the situation might have tested the spleen of other men. Where in other comedies the ridiculous is a species of the ugly, here it is intended very emphatically to be symptomatic of moral and aesthetic beauty.

THE MINOR CHARACTERS: BLOCKERS, BOORS AND BANSHEES

> I've got to get away from it. I've got to get away from here. Instead of sitting decently at the table eating their dinners, howling and roaring at one another like a lot of Banshees.
> — Gogarty in *Bringing up Baby*

Charles Coburn, gruff, bloated with port, Havana cigars and *savoir faire*, the fat man of comedy, without the innocence of a Sancho Panza or an Oliver Hardy, but with all their undiscriminating addiction to infantile prankishness; William Demarest, all sullenness and cynical humour, a throwback to the wily but caring servant of Roman comedy; Ralph Bellamy, with his wide open face, a mirror of tedium and good intentions; Una Merkel, pert and vulgar shopgirl *soubrette* – these are some of the great minor stars by whom the romantic couple in Screwball are surrounded. Their character-functions in the plots of these films can be divided broadly speaking into four primary categories, although they are all subject to overlaps and reversals. First, what Northrop Frye calls 'blocking characters', those who are opposed to progress, create obstacles for those who are not, and are either bastions of conformity or respectability, or malcontents of one kind or another, sometimes becoming, where the endings are ambiguous, society's scapegoats (e.g. Vadas in *The Shop around the Corner*). Second, the lovers' *confidant(e)s*, maids, butlers, friends and sympathisers. Third, the secondary suitors and lovers, epitomised by Bellamy, the symbol of all that is second best in love. And fourth, bystanders, innocent or otherwise, all with pertinent comments on or contributions to the thematics of the films. These characters belong indispensably to the films' patterns of psychological and social complexity, offering various perspectives of realism, disenchantment, or even cynicism to the higher-flying ideals offered to the audience in the romantic couple.

Sometimes this questioning of the lovers' ambitions becomes, not unexpectedly, the province of authoritarian family figures. In certain 30s comedies family ties are very much in the foreground (*Holiday*, *The Philadelphia Story*), while in others, particularly Lubitsch's films in the 30s, they disappear almost entirely. *Bringing up Baby* largely follows this latter type, but remains nevertheless free of scathing, mocking references to the family, especially those strident, pejorative references to mothers and grandmothers liberally made by Cary Grant in *His Girl Friday*. In *Bringing up Baby* the family is softened and refined almost (but not quite) into invisibility: David's parents are never seen or mentioned, while Susan's family is reduced to her absent brother, Mark (the captor of 'Baby' in Brazil), and her aunt Elizabeth, Mrs Carlton-Random. If specifically patriarchal power is a deeper problem than the matriarchal in most of these comedies, it is interesting that Aunt Elizabeth is Susan's father's sister, standing in (as a sort of reversed matrilineal mother's brother) for the patriarch, though admittedly, a very tolerant one. Aunt Elizabeth – whose Christian name reminds one of the famous virile Queen, and whose surname suggests at least partial affiliation to benevolent anti-authoritarianism – wields the power of the *senex*, initially blocking Susan's marriage to David, but subsequently seen to be hardly serious in doing so. In this film the *senex* is also streaked with a certain harmless madness. The leopard, symbol of an eccentric wildness is, after all, hers; her Robin Hood hat (something, admittedly, very much in vogue in the 30s as may be judged by Ginger Rogers's and Rosalind Russell's wearing of them in *Bachelor Mother* and *His Girl Friday* respectively), cape and scarf identifying her with her 'green world' surroundings.

For all his prissiness, her friend Major Horace Applegate (Charlie Ruggles) is also associated with these positive *senex* values. *Horace* (the poet of pastoral) *Applegate* is in some respects a child of nature, seeking an identity in the wild – big-game hunting, but with a pedant's line in imitating loon and leopard calls – prone to wearing a rather silly but no less symbolically feathered hat, which together with his clipped moustache makes him a comic analogue of Errol Flynn in the great 30s swashbuckler, *The Adventures of Robin Hood* (1938).

Like David, Susan and Aunt Elizabeth, he is not wholly entrenched in the values of the old world associated with the more overtly tradition-bound characters represented by Constable Slocum (the law), Peabody (capitalism) and Lehmann (psychiatry). 'Slow-to-come', 'Lay-man', and 'Pea body (and brain)', these characters all represent hyperboles of the Super-Ego, all typified by the classic Bergsonian flaw of mechanisation and dehumanisation. All three actors (Walter Catlett, Fritz Feld and George Irving) bring an inflexibility of persona, Catlett through cultivated bombast, Feld through sharp punctiliousness – a quality further enriched by his marvellously

Teutonic pronunciations like 'I dizlike ze yooze of zet term' – and Irving through portentousness of expression, to bear on the film's ridicule of authority. So powerful are the values of the old, civilised world they even creep into the consciousness of a minor character who spends his whole life in the country, Aunt Elizabeth's gardener Gogarty (Barry Fitzgerald).

Not only does Gogarty rule over his wife with patriarchal firmness (he threatens to remove her along with his own services if things continue in his view to deteriorate at the estate), but also, being in certain respects a man of tradition, he not surprisingly disapproves of the unruly, what he calls 'Banshee', antics at the dinner table, where Susan and David keep leaping up to chase George whenever they think he is about to lead them to the buried intercostal clavicle, and where Major Applegate insists on showing off his loon and leopard call imitations: 'Well give me patience. No this is too much. I can't stand it. . . And then they say keep away from the bottle. Don't drink. No, not even a wee drop to steady a man's nerves. If one more thing happens I'll quit. I'll quit. And where Aloysius Gogarty goes, Mrs Gogarty goes too.' In *Bringing up Baby* the 'Green World' is not wholly idyll and enchantment; living as close to the land as possible, within earshot of the so-called harmonies of nature and all its bucolic truths, Gogarty can still, for all his endearing humour, find little consolation in the verities of the wilderness, needing even here in Westlake, Connecticut the comforts of the bottle in yet another image of infantile dependency, and not any the less tainted by pretence and a rational kind of lunacy than his social betters.

'THREE LITTLE WORDS' – RHETORIC AND ANTI-RHETORIC

You realise what that means, that you must like me a little bit?   — Susan

We have defined Hollywood romantic comedy, especially its 30s forms, as, among other things, a meditation on equality between the sexes, intuitive rather than didactic, crossed at many points with the contradictions of a specific social ideology. Additionally, as well as restructuring the plots, relationships between lovers and the various other elements of inherited forms, these films sabotage the clichés of literary and film love.

In some of the films there is a more developed negative alternative than *Bringing up Baby*'s Miss Swallow, most memorably the two characters played by Ralph Bellamy in *His Girl Friday* and *The Awful Truth*. Both in what such characters represent – typically, a respect for women too limited by over-protectiveness, innocence and domesticity – and in what and how they use language, they provide us with those deadening images of conformity from which the spirited lovers seek release. Nevertheless, there is enough emotional and moral complexity in these films for us to see the satirised characters ambivalently, to feel that what they represent is not altogether contemptible, indeed that in certain circumstances and in other societies their defects might be considered strengths. But at the very least such characters are guilty of a conservatism and complacency which makes them unfit for these heroines because, in speaking as they do ('Even ten minutes is a long time to be away from you', Ralph Bellamy as Bruce in *His Girl Friday* declares, using all the resources of his Kansas City Idealist school of literary imagination), they offend against one of the most serious laws of the films, the placing of what amounts to a taboo on the clichés of romance. These clichés stretch from linguistic utterances, to action (kissing and so on), to the various forms of cinematic rhetoric (a virtual embargo on, for instance, lushly romantic music, chiaroscuro, and close-up).

The implicit logic of these prohibitions is that if the relationships presented to us are attempts to redefine partially the balance and meanings of contact between the sexes, to escape from outmoded, mutually unsatisfactory ways of saying and doing things, then to fall back into the conventional rhetoric of love is to do no more than repeat the network of suppositions and reflexes for which such rhetoric has become a symbol. Clearly this does not mean that the films are without affecting images of love, but it does mean that they insist on a space in which some degree of reformulation can be imagined outside conventional imagery. It further means that contact between the romantic couple can include gestures to the primarily playful and polymorphous as distinct from the primarily erotic levels of behaviour. The best 30s comedies, rather than portraying – as is the case in the idealism of conservative comedy – the sexual as a realm apart where men and women should meet as equals (whatever else they are outside it), insist on life as a fully shared playful experiment rather than a hierarchically and role-divided enactment of established attitudes. If the 'polymorphous perverse' is what these comedies celebrate, it is less in Freud's sense of literal bi/homosexuality, and more in Marcuse's sense of the eroticising of all activity.

Dr Lehmann's statement that 'the love impulse in men very frequently reveals itself in terms of conflict' might be taken – reading 'men' as 'men and women' – as an epigraph for these films, where sweet nothings and neo-Petrarchan hyperboles are replaced by declarations of love that emerge through hostilities rather than ecstatic rapport. If when David rebuffs Susan's advances by saying, 'Now it isn't that I don't like you, Susan, because after all, in moments of quiet I'm strangely drawn towards you, but. . . well. . . there haven't been any quiet moments', we know that they are meant for each other, it is the vivacity of their antagonism which proves it. Part of the audience's pleasure in seeing a character's aggression revealed as a perverse expression of their love is, no doubt, the comic delight of seeing things overturned, rationality exposed as defenceless before the forces of unconscious desire.

Such transgressions of convention also satisfy what needs to be satisfied in all but the most utopian view of human relationships, the sense that in any conceivable social setting the sexual relations of men and women (or men and men, and women and women), cannot escape the quota of aggression and anxiety that belong to the sphere of sexuality. This is so if only because the needs of the instinct are so basic and their ramifications so many that they are too complicated to be simply and safely organised, and that to blame advanced capitalism for all the aberrations of sexuality (some of which it is, of course, plainly guilty of encouraging and manufacturing on a vast scale), is simply to be blind to the realities of human behaviour as observed in many different social systems. However, even if we do not believe that all aggression, patterns of dominance and subservience, sadism and masochism in relationships are caused exclusively by bourgeois heterosexual marriage, we may still feel that the war fought between the sexes in these films reflects not just 'eternal' differences between them but also the felt injustices of artificial, historically-imposed ones, whose injustice is more obvious to the woman because she is more obviously their victim. We may also feel that the antagonism that exists between the couple is a sort of complex value that symbolises the difference between attraction which fulfils a particular ideological conception of love (conservative, hierarchical, fixated by stereotype), and one that is deeper but which may also be fiercely resisted (hence the displays of conflict), since it is capable of challenging and disturbing those stereotypes so closely bound up with self-esteem. In this sense it is right, symbolically and thematically, that Irene Dunne in *The Awful Truth* should, in staying with Jerry and refusing Dan, keep the name 'Warriner' (with its connotations of creative warfare) and reject the name of Leeson (with its connotations of ownership, property, etc.).

David's speech, quoted above, centres around the word 'like', a word deliberately compared to 'love' in *Bringing up Baby*, for Susan, at the point where David tells her he wishes to complete his forest search without her, begins to weep because he does not 'like' her any more. In the final moments of the film, where the prohibition against the mutual utterance of the words 'I love you' is finally lifted, the release is only allowed via the more neutral, childlike or cautious verbal form of attachment, and even then only in the hectically comic context of the swaying ladder and Hawksian concepts of fun and games.

Occasionally, close-ups give us Susan's enraptured gaze at David, but even here the comic mood is predominant, and more usually the close-up that emphasises romantic susceptibility over everything else is avoided. So when David explains to Aunt Elizabeth, in Susan's presence, that he just wants to get married (the aunt thinks to Susan, Susan dreams to herself), Susan's expression is not allowed the intensity of a close-up to itself, but is placed in shot alongside the aunt's unimpressed reactions, the close-ups being reserved for David's irritation and frustration. The result is that any feelings of romantic rapport are modulated by comedy, just as the comedy is itself softened by those feelings.

Deflections like these are common in 30s comedy. In *Holiday*, for instance, it is the father, the most stifling figure in the film, who makes a speech about 'true love', while the more positive characters speak about love through more oblique, comic language. 'True Love' is also the name of the honeymoon boat in *The Philadelphia Story*, the static ideal of romance embodied in an object, not in the characters' more flexible activity. In *His Girl Friday* aversion to the forms of romance extends even to the gallantry of manners. 'He treats me like a woman', Hildy says of Bruce. 'How did I treat you? Like a water buffalo?' asks Walter. 'I dunno from water buffaloes', replies Hildy, 'but I do know about him. He's kind and he's sweet and he's considerate.' If Walter's off-the-cuff reply, 'He sounds like a guy I should marry', is somewhat limited in its view of gender roles and, additionally, definitely and scornfully unpolymorphous, there is a more interesting point to be taken from the exchange. This is that the codes of manners evolved as tributes by the male to the female may also involve over-protectiveness, condescension and an exploitation of the darker side of gallantry.

This sabotaging of the language of romantic love is matched by a denial of the final kiss or embrace (a point noted by Cavell). In *Midnight*, *The Philadelphia Story*, *His Girl Friday* and *The Awful Truth*, as well as in many others, it is banished completely; in *Holiday* and *Bringing up Baby* it is allowed very fleetingly at the end. There are of course, exceptions, but in, for instance, *The Lady Eve*, or in other films where the hero and heroine kiss in the earlier parts of the films (*Midnight*, *Ball of Fire*), the context will tend to be one of comedy, or of resistance by one or other of the partners. In *Bringing up Baby* the embrace is surrounded by a whole series of displacements and enlargements, games, metaphors, and *double entendre*, so that when it is finally enacted it is inevitably suffused with ambiguity.

Such anti-romantic rhetoric is often paralleled by the gentle subversion of the films' musical scores. Music in romantic comedy is designed most conventionally to express yearning and fulfilment, providing a background of emotion, fading away to silence in scenes of ordinary dialogue, and then swelling up again behind the action at key moments. Thirties comedies, though, tend to use music much more austerely, in the most interesting cases almost avoiding its use altogether. Looking across the whole range of romantic comedy in the period, we can see a spectrum of uses, from the most banal to films where the uses might seem on the surface the same, but are in fact cleverly ironic (e.g. Lubitsch's *Trouble in Paradise*, 1932), to films like *Bringing up Baby* where it is used extremely sparingly. Here, between the energetic rather than sentimental versions of its 'theme' song that mark the opening and closing moments, *Bringing up Baby* is completely without music of any kind, except for the band music playing in the background in the restaurant scene and for the various moments where (without orchestral accompaniment) the characters sing, mostly 'I Can't Give You Anything but Love, Baby' to the leopard, though Susan at one point in the forest hums 'Dixie', and chants 'I Was Born on the Side of a Hill'. In *Bringing up Baby* the song, so important in so many ways, is never sung by the lovers to each other, but only to the leopard. So, for all that it does to define their love, it is never allowed to function as a straightforward sign of their feeling. *Bringing up Baby* breaks the pattern of conventional use of music in the background of romantic comedy (not something that should be regarded as necessarily too obvious or contemptible), even more severely than *The Philadelphia Story*, *Holiday* and *His Girl Friday*, all three of which find ways of insinuating music into key emotional scenes. The least lyrical of these, *His Girl Friday*, eventually allows music its traditional role of underlining emotions, when it is used near the end of the film as Hildy starts to weep. In contrast, *Bringing up Baby*'s final music is only released after David and Susan confess their love for each other, and have fallen into their odd embrace, at which point the music is sanctioned, as celebration, triumphant fanfare, but not, even here, as the embodiment of the lovers' feelings and audience's fantasies.

SIGNS AND SYMBOLS: ANIMALS, IMBECILES, INFANTS, CRIMINALS, FALL GUYS AND RUNNING JOKES

Pussy Galore

Like a leopard, but not a leopard.   — The zoo keeper in *Cat People* (1942)

A married man and scared of a leopard!
     — Satan Synne to Anatol in *The Affairs of Anatol* (1921)

Since comedy is often concerned with the instinctual and irrational it tends to display a fellow-feeling with the animal world (e.g. the feral titles of the Marx Brothers' films, *Monkey Business*, *Animal Crackers*, and *Horse Feathers*). In 30s comedy that connection can sometimes mean the inclusion of animals in the films' *dramatis personae* (Mr Smith, the Warriners' dog in *The Awful Truth*, Hopsy's serpent in *The Lady Eve*, even the mechanised toy Donald Duck that quacks throughout *Bachelor Mother*). And, of course, as well as including a leopard, *Bringing up Baby* borrows George the terrier from the slightly earlier *The Awful Truth* (which in turn borrows him from *The Thin Man* films). These two, like Mr Smith, are leading players, so that cast over everything (we must remember that we are for the most part in a Connecticut forest), is something of the ambience of the wonder tale where magical animals befriend the protagonist. Wilful, unpredictable creatures, they pull the humans this way and that in their 'running wild'.

Who or what is 'Baby'? In the stick-graphics that accompany the film's titles, the leopard is a literal offspring, a changeling, fed, bathed and perambulated like a human infant. At other times he is closely identified with Susan (as when Susan informs the sheriff in the jail scene, 'If I did have an aunt. . .', and he replies, 'She'd muzzle you'). She twice wears costumes that declare her affinity with the creature, first when phoning David to tell him of Baby's arrival, when she wears a spotted negligée, and second, in the film's final scene where she has a spotted veil. At other times, though, the leopard seems to be confused with David. For instance in the forest sequence, when particularly exasperated with Susan, David claws at her as if transformed into a leopard. In the distance, as if to approve the parallel, Baby roars. Elsewhere David wears a spotted tie. Sometimes, especially when his song is sung or played, Baby seems tame. At other times, attracted by the crashed poultry van, or escaping from the barn to roam the New England countryside, his savage nature triumphs over him.

The use of animals as symbolic figures, from cave drawings to bestiaries, Walt Disney and beyond, is as old as narrative art, and takes a multitude of forms. One, though, recurs constantly. The animal as representative of those natural forces in which the human is grounded, but from which he or she is also alienated. On such occasions a real animal, as Ortega y Gasset noted in his essay on hunting, is the human's means of recovery of all but lost primitive instincts and, for all the silliness that is a by-product of such regression in this film, the narrative pleads for the restoration of animal life against, or at least in more equal balance with, the constraints of civilisation. So when the film invokes the call of the loon, it seems to steer a deliberately uncertain course between farce – as the characters strive to make sense of the strange animal noises in the night – and the vital truths of the wilderness. Thoreau's descriptions of the call of the loon – as the sound more of a ferocious predator than a lakeside bird – anticipate *Bringing up Baby*'s interest in loons, especially when they are confused with leopards by the dinner-table guests in Connecticut:

> His usual note was this demonic laughter, yet somewhat like that of a water-fowl; but occasionally, when he had balked me most successfully and come up a long way off, he uttered a long-drawn unearthly howl, probably more like that of a wolf than any bird; as when a beast puts his muzzle to the ground and deliberately howls. This was his looning – perhaps the wildest sound that is ever heard here, making the woods ring far and wide.

After *Walden* and *Bringing up Baby* the loon had to wait until *On Golden Pond* (1981) for an equally faithful representation of its true mysteries. In *Bringing up Baby*, the loon–leopard associations are largely positive. And although the spirit of animal-inspired Screwball survives in films like the Spaniard José Luis Borau's brilliantly inventive and anarchic post-Francoist comedy of the sexes *Tata mía* (1986), other genres dramatise the recovery of the primitive in less positive terms: horror works through animal imagery to dramatise the eruption of dark forces, while melodrama specialises in patterns of insoluble ambivalence. In Powell and Pressburger's *Gone to Earth* (1950), for instance, Hazel's (Jennifer Jones's) pet vixen, Foxy, represents at once her identity with nature and her victimisation by civilising forces intent on seeing her purely in sexual terms as a child of instinct. In comedy, apart from satiric uses which censure excess of animality, animals most often appear as benevolent.

In horror, from Webster's *The Duchess of Malfi* to *An American Werewolf in London* (1981), the animal is often a terrifying sign of the primitive. Irena in Tourneur's *Cat People* is transformed into a leopard when kissed by men, and the comparison of that splendid film with *Bringing up Baby* is too tempting to resist, since in both cases (one comic, and one terrible) the heroine is closely connected with a predator in some way signifying her female nature. 'Like unto a leopard', says the keeper in *Cat People* misogynistically, quoting Revelation. And in *Bringing up Baby*, as the men at the fair discuss the 'bad' leopard, the shadow of a belly dancer plays against the side of a tent at the left of the frame. The logic of the leopard's connection with female sexuality hardly needs underlining. The joke of Ian Fleming's Pussy Galore and Octopussy depends on that identity which Marie Bonaparte writes about in her famous analysis of Poe's *The Black Cat*. The point of this comparison between horror and comedy is that while the former may resort to the same metaphors as an outlet for distorted and destructive shapes, the latter offers a casual psychotherapy, except in satire and black comedy, in which neurosis is defeated, wounds are healed, and mistakes are corrected. Thus, if sexuality, especially female sexuality, or male conceptions of it, at any rate, is a comic problem in *Bringing up Baby*, it is embodied in a beast who retains an unpredictable animal spirit, but whose savage breast is soothed by the love lyrics of a popular song, who may have awesome power, but is also identified with characters as unthreatening as Aunt Elizabeth and Mrs Hannah Gogarty. When, for instance, the drunken Gogarty declares 'Where I go, Mrs Oliver Gogarty goes too', it is the leopard who follows him.

Yet as this 'Baby' is definitely masculine, the animal identifications spread to the male characters as well. To David obviously, but also to Major Horace Applegate, who is by turns inefficient hunter of, expert on and *alter ego* of the leopard, the last in the antic sublimations of his leopard mating calls. Big-game hunting, which figures so largely and so ludicrously in the film (Applegate's expertise, David's assumed persona as the big-game hunter Mr Bone, and so on), was much in the news in the 30s, most of all through Ernest Hemingway, whose famous Tanganyika safari took place in 1933-34, and whose *Green Hills of Africa* was published in 1935. Though there are elements of Hawks's work in general which might make us suspect an attitude more approving than critical of Hemingway, the identification of hunting with heroic masculinity is unquestionably burlesqued in *Bringing up Baby* in the somewhat un-macho Applegate, in David's imposture, and in the ludicrous hunt for the animals and the bone that ensues. But at levels outside burlesque, the leopard's masculinity also works to identify sexuality itself as 'masculine', even where it belongs to the woman, seeing it as an active rather than passive force, overriding the traditional identifications of male activity and female passivity.

Moreover, in the later plot complications Baby is confused with another leopard: one, the tame Baby, the other a killer cat condemned to death in a local gas chamber. This dualism seems designed to impress on us how different versions of sexuality are the product of distinctive preconceptions, or perhaps just to remind us amid the softenings of comedy and romance that sex is still a perilous enterprise, the release of mighty forces.

Even when he is not actually present, Baby travels through the film in minor verbal variations, reminding us perhaps that the words 'cat' (for a female) and 'tomcat' (for a male) were among those specifically forbidden in the MPPA Code. Thus when she becomes 'Swingin' Door Susie', Susan threatens to shoot her 'puss' off, and calls the Sheriff 'Kitty'. It recalls a similar usage in the extravagantly named 'Sugarpuss' O'Shea (Barbara Stanwyck) in *Ball of Fire*, whose ultimate partner, Professor Potter (Gary Cooper), as scholarly, donnish, and repressed as David, has a feline element in him, waiting, like David's, for release, for as he tells 'Sugarpuss', he was known at the age of one to recite 'Tiger, Tiger, Burning Bright'.

Snuffling around Baby's heels is the dog George, the bone thief. It is a fault of Thorstein Veblen's acute analysis of the leisure class that he sees the domestic dog only as another symbol of conspicuous consumption rather than, as in Ortega y Gasset's view, something to be valued as a connecting link between man and nature.

In the image that is the film's paradigm of Screwball, Susan and David (David holding George) serenade the leopard who is sitting on the roof of the Lehmanns' house, with the usual song. This duet becomes a trio, then a quartet, as the leopard roars a third part and George switches from yapping to yowling in what is by now a very elaborate polyphonic motet, as if he too was moving between his more domesticated barking watchdog self and a primeval heritage embodied in his hound's howl. Later in the narrative the strength of the 'bad' leopard is finally controlled by two acts of authority: Susan's as she chidingly drags him into the jail (unaware that he is the wrong leopard), and David's as he defeats the leopard with a chair. The leopard as representation of animal instinct and, more particularly, sexuality, will not be easily accommodated into perceptions that are either too unyieldingly unruly or domesticated. But in the quartet we have for a moment a ridiculous, yet within the context of all the folly, moving version of 'The Peaceable Kingdom', as for a moment the humans and the animals raise their voices together. It is a comic version of Adam and the Lady Eve speaking the original transparent speech with which the mystic philosopher, Jakob Boehme, credited them, a speech closer to the animals' than to the speech of civilisation.

Infantiles, imbeciles, and criminals

Not everybody who acts strangely is insane.   — Dr Lehmann

Ringing the zoo for the second time, to cancel the order to round up the escaped leopard, David picks up the phone and asks, 'Is that [the] zoo?' The unheard answer can be gathered from his reply, which is 'Well, nobody here's talking baby talk'. Delicately fusing the film's several types of babies, children and animals, the comedy here underlines a constant obsession with creative infantilism, itself closely connected with positive forms of folly and animalism. In this context, and perhaps especially with reference to the motivations for the film's title, *Bringing up Baby*, it is worth noting that John B. Watson's behaviourist theories of child-rearing were hugely influential in the mid and late 20s. In *The Perils of Prosperity*, William E. Leuchtenburg writes:

> The Department of Labour incorporated behaviourist assumptions in its pamphlet *Infant and Child Care*, which, with emphasis on rigid scheduling of a baby's activities, became the government's leading bestseller. Watson predicted that the time would come when it would be just as bad manners to show affection to one's mother or father as to come to the table with dirty hands. To inculcate the proper attitudes at an early age, Watson warned parents, 'Never hug and kiss them, never let them sit in your lap.'

Bringing up Baby seems to play against views like these, and Screwball, as we have been defining it, is attracted both to the child and the lunatic (all that verbal play in the film about 'loons'), in a complex version of alienation from the constraints of civilisation, the child not yet fully introduced into civilisation and its discontents, the lunatic remaining outside them. It is not, of course, that the characters and the films seek the literal madness and infancy of the Laings and Coopers of late 60s anti-psychiatry: rather, that the audience is invited to join in a self-conscious and sophisticated play with cradle and straitjacket. 'Except ye become as little children. . .', the films seem to say, exhorting recovery of the childlike, not simple regression.

Positive reversion is a staple device of comedy, but it is especially and very creatively prevalent in 30s romantic comedy. If *Holiday*'s title obliquely indicates the childhood theme (and in that film the children's playroom is at the heart of the action), it is there more explicitly in *Bringing up Baby*. The banishing of the literal child from romantic comedy is an obvious feature of the genre, something that is all the more remarkable in comedies of marriage where the couple (with very rare exceptions like *My Favorite Wife* and *Bachelor Mother*) have no offspring. Though literally absent, the infant is part of the unexplored archaeology of the lovers themselves. In *Holiday* Johnny calls Linda 'child', and he and Linda address each other as 'poor boy' and 'poor girl'. In *Ball of Fire* Sugarpuss's normal mode of address is 'kids'. In *Bringing up Baby* Susan distractedly brushes specks off David's shoulder, remaining nevertheless free of a desire to reshape or mould her 'child' of love.

It is clear that the films make a distinction between two concepts of childishness. In one, 'child' suggests all kinds of positive freedoms, in the other, an improper parental role in the speaker and an improperly dependent one in the person addressed. In *Bringing up Baby*, as in much 30s comedy, the connotations of childishness are largely positive. The child represents energy, from the leopard's conflation with the baby in name, title and graphics, to the many occasions where games (golf, olive tricks played by the bartender and Susan), and pre-adult activities and fantasies are involved: David's assumption when he sees her on all fours that Susan must be playing 'squat tag'; David, on all fours himself, as he pursues George; the various dressing-up episodes; Susan's happy statement to David, 'But this is fun, David, just like a game.'

The feelings produced by these regressions, of the couple reverting from sexual maturity to a kind of period of latency, have already been noticed by Stanley Cavell. Developing his argument, it is possible to maintain that *Bringing up Baby* and its siblings are concerned to dramatise the idea of a second chance given to the characters to undo chronology, to unlearn the platitudes of love and sexuality so that pairing may be approached free from the clutches of the most repressive elements of its ideology. It may be impossible for characters to redefine themselves completely as pre-civilised, but the films suggest that some creative regeneration is possible.

In later comedies these anarchic elements of meaning tend to become faded, even wholly absent: the metaphorical gives way to the literal child in the Day/Hudson cycle; in other cases (*Father Goose*, 1964, *It Happened in Naples*, 1959) the child largely signals responsibility. The theme of infantilism is wholly different in the 30s. Even in the extremely sophisticated milieu of *The Philadelphia Story* the child survives in Tracy's little sister Diana and her embodiment of the characters' inner, pre-socialised selves. As such Diana is closest of all to C. K. Dexter Haven (Cary Grant's ludicrously pretentious name in the film), whose infantilism, which is partly positive and partly negative (his class snobbery, his alcoholism, his desire for Tracy as mother rather than as wife/sister/lover) is expressed through his scoffing freedom from the cares of work. A more powerful version of Diana's role is found in

the Reinhardt/Dieterle *A Midsummer Night's Dream* (1935), that brilliant crossing of Shakespeare with the Screwball sensibility, where Mickey Rooney's whooping, screeching, half-naked Puck is a hyperbole of all the traits we have specified, in a particularly desocialised, Id-like form.

In *Bringing up Baby* the spectacle of the Id-driven childish antics of the 'loonatic' lover David makes everyone except Susan think he is insane. On the one hand this highlights the conventional suppositions of the observers, while on the other it is his punishment to be judged for not being, as it were, mad enough, just as he is arrested as a sex criminal for his asexuality, his crimes against sex.

Regressing to the childishness and madness of this sophisticated figurative structure, David finally accepts the metaphoric role of the criminal, a third form of deviancy from the social order's restrictions. Susan of course, has already been happily disregarding them. In the jail scene, she takes on the role of the moll, the criminal woman; and, following her, David accepts his transformation into a 'wolf', his place at the head of the 'Leopard Gang', and convinces the dull sheriff Slocum that he has been working with 'Mickey the Mouse' and 'Donald the Duck'. In Swingin' Door Susie's claim that he is a regular 'Don Swan', his transition from over-civilised ugly duckling is announced.

Fall guys and running jokes

Similarly, falling, stumbling and slipping need not always be interpreted as purely accidental miscarriages of motor action.   — *The Psychopathology of Everyday Life*

Don't be silly, David. You can't make a leopard stand still.
— Susan in *Bringing up Baby*

In *On Laughter* Bergson's key example of a laughter-provoking situation is this: 'A man, running along the street, stumbles and falls; the passers-by burst out laughing.' They laugh not just because the man has fallen, but also at the combination of the action's involuntariness with its victim's stiffness. For Bergson the fall is the prototype of the comic, the collision of an external reality with an unprepared victim, from which by increasingly complex analogy the external impediment is refined into an inner blockage, absent-mindedness in one form or another.

Bringing up Baby (3)
Following George's lead, Susan (Katharine Hepburn) and David regress on all fours to their wilder, more primitive topsy-turvy selves.

At one end of the spectrum there is, then, a comedy of wholly external accident; at the other, a comedy of internal action and obstruction. The cinema finds particularly congenial that halfway house where physical gesture represents the mind, thus preserving the primitive energies of slapstick, but collapsing them with the psychological. Once attached to the realms of the mind, the simplest physical comedy becomes rich in potential as the basic pratfall is modified not only by the emotional aura surrounding performer and narrative, but also by the creative potential of symbolism and symptomology. The codifications of cackhandedness in *The Psychopathology of Everyday Life* give a systematic coherence to the intuitions of the Symbolists and Realists of fictional and dramatic art. As the dropped glass is the prime sign of stage or novelistic melodrama, so the fall is its equivalent in film comedy. Common usages, taking the literal action as the basis for metaphor, abound in these films: falling in love, falling from grace, falling into reveries, and so on; and the more complex the comedy the more resonances proliferate. If the book of melodrama is *The Interpretation of Dreams*, that of comedy is *The Psychopathology of Everyday Life*.

The traces of popular consciousness of psychoanalysis, clearly present in 40s melodrama, are equally observable in Hollywood comedy of the late 30s and 40s, both in the presence of actual psychiatrist figures (as well as in *Bringing up Baby*, they appear in *5th Avenue Girl*, 1939, *That Uncertain Feeling*, 1941, *His Girl Friday*, 1940, and others), and in frequent references to the hidden meanings of mistakes. *Baby*'s teutonically pedantic, occasionally insightful, finally bemused Dr Lehmann is paralleled by Dr Hugo Kessler in *5th Avenue Girl*, Dr Egelhoffer in *His Girl Friday* and Dr Kolmar in *My Favourite Wife*, among others. These examples tend to be unflattering ones and, as in *Baby*, remembering Lehmann's initially sensible but ultimately loony (or perhaps not loony enough) attitudes, what is said is often saner than the sayer.

David is the most accident-prone of all the comic heroes of Screwball. The narrative of *Bringing up Baby* could be described as a tissue of accidents, punctuated by parapraxes, initiated at the film's very beginning when, preparing to descend from the scaffolding, David bumps his head. Already in this first scene the words he utters have a habit of slipping from the normal securities, mixing names, confusing genders. After the golf course scene, where Susan appropriates both his golf ball and his car, and even his person as he is driven off clinging to her (his?) vehicle, the following sequence at the restaurant has him falling on his top hat when he slips on the olive that Susan has accidentally dropped on the floor in trying to learn the bartender's trick. Following this, she accidentally tears his coat tails, and he reciprocates by equally accidentally removing the lower back panel of her gown. After the scene at Peabody's house, where Susan hits Boopy flush on the head with a rock, a shot meant merely to tap at the window, David – we are still only minutes into the film – getting out of a car, after protesting his essential dignity, pitches over an unnoticed obstacle. This last is as common a comic device as can be found, a classic example of pride coming before a fall, something that is later repeated by Susan when she asserts, 'I can take care of myself', and then trips over a tree.

If David's accidents are the signs of an unconscious demanding liberation, Susan's are less easily fathomable. At one level, they dramatise her creative, careless attitude towards the normal laws of property and division. Clearly, though, inasmuch as we see her as an individual character, neither purely an emanation of David's desires, nor a wholly perfect exemplar of regressive freedom, some of her accidents are less imbued with dramatic purpose, and are principally the products of the 'madness' with which love has inspired her. To take fairly seriously her statement to David at the end that everything happened simply because she wanted to keep him near her does not, though, interfere with the other meanings. Obviously by now we are at a distance from Bergson's simplest examples. We are in a domain of the comic doubly governed by empathy, something produced both by the sympathetic conceptualisation of the characters in the narrative and by the charismatic presence of Katharine Hepburn and Cary Grant. The 'absentmindedness' of love is likely, anyway, to provoke a sympathetic response in the audience, while many of Susan's accidents can be read as being unconsciously full of purpose, and many of David's as expressions of the struggle between flexible and rigid habits of mind and body, so that in most cases the foolish dimensions of their errors are minimised, while their positive features are heightened.

All these falls are given a narrative and structural context of speed, rapidity of events (a motif applied exclusively to the final car chase sequence in Bogdanovich's homage to the film, *What's up Doc?*, 1972), as well as of breathless dialogue and reflex reactions, something it shares with another fast-talking sprint of a film, *His Girl Friday*. *Bringing up Baby* is composed of a large number of often very abrupt scenes, its accumulating, constantly shifting narrative barely punctuated by the most cursory dissolves and fades. As the narrative emphasises movement from scene to scene, and place to place, so within the scenes themselves the characters' movements parallel this haste. Breaking free of the decorum of a restrained social walk, drawing-room glide, or elegant saunter, the characters trot, half-trot, run, half-run. The film self-consciously refers to all this when after Aunt Elizabeth and Applegate have witnessed Susan's and David's latest bout of seemingly inexplicable locomotion, Aunt Elizabeth suggests to Applegate that they take some fresh air. He agrees, and adds, 'Shall we run?', at which point they jog out of the house together, mimicking the younger couple, sharing their comic anarchy and zest for life, rejecting stasis, rather as David stops playing Rodin's immobilised Thinker (our first view of him in the film) and begins to run after and with Susan.

Fast talking is the correlative of fast walking, and throughout the film Susan talks with great speed, while David often fails to get out of the starter's blocks, typically mouthing syllables that fail to emerge, or stuttering and mumbling ineffectually. Another form of language at speed is its 'raciest' form, slang. David's very polite propensities for letting language run away with him are exposed at the beginning of the film when his 'Gee whizz' and 'I'll knock him for a loop' are frowned upon by Miss Swallow ('David, no slang!') while Susan's initially takes the form of expressions like 'Jeepers' but, after various modulations, bursts out riotously in the barrage of mock criminal and erotic slang when she becomes the gangster's moll. Here, however innocently, the forces of the subterranean worlds of uninhibited sexuality and criminality, yet another form of deviancy from convention, comically assault the socialised turgidities of the self. The jail scene is the symbol at once of the straight society's surplus repression and, in this figurative sense, of the lovers' criminal transgressions of desire.

THE END

Oh dear. . . Oh well. . . Hmm.   — David

Comic endings are often ambivalent. True, in *Bringing up Baby* there are no major outsider figures like *The Shop around the Corner's* Vadas whose exclusion from society is enough to stir our conscience, though it is also true, we know, that whatever David and Susan have found, they are the lucky ones, and that Alice Swallow will not find it. Also, whatever Aunt Elizabeth, Gogarty, Slocum and the others represent, it is as much a part of the world as the hero and heroine – what they might have become, what they still might become in the process of ageing. True, comic endings often celebrate luck, suggesting perhaps the futility of agonising about what it all means. There but for the grace of a comic *deus* (*dea?*) *ex machina* goes David married to Miss Swallow. If the characters accept their advantage and run, why should the audience worry unduly? Yet the hesitations at the end of *Bringing up Baby* ought not to be wholly passed over in its embrace of happiness, for it does not altogether dismiss, and might even be seen to consider, some of the questions raised by the narrative as a whole.

When Susan arrives at the museum to see David rush up the ladder to work on his dinosaur skeleton the moment he spies her, she comments on his oddly muted response both to her presence and to the news she brings with her of his million-dollar award and the recovery of the intercostal clavicle. Pressed to explain himself, David admits, 'Well, if you must know, I'm afraid of you.' Not afraid of him, Susan climbs up the ladder, and as she begins to reply, is interrupted by their shared alarm, as the first sign of unsteadiness in the ladder she is perched on becomes noticeable. What she says goes no further than that his being afraid of her is 'the same as'. What she means to say in concluding her sentence remains deliberately ambiguous, though one is tempted to guess that the missing words are 'I love you.' If this is indeed so, in what senses are love and fear compatible? The hypothetical conceit allows one to see that in the first place love is undoubtedly a real power, capable of taking individuals out of themselves, placing them under the control of others and, second, that in this particular case a woman feels safe enough after her lover's honest declaration of an admitted vulnerability to allow herself an uninhibited commitment in return.

As our thoughts trail away over lovers divided by the symbolic hulk of the dinosaur's skeleton, Susan slips, is about to fall, David clutches her hand while she momentarily dangles in air, high above the ground, and then pulls her towards him. In mid-apology, she is hauled by David on to the platform, where they sit. As dejectedly and with weary resignation he shakes his head at the disaster of the collapsed skeleton, he tries unsuccessfully to speak, while on his behalf, asserting his love and forgiveness, she embraces him with an 'Oh, David!' He mutters in reply, 'Oh dear . . . Oh well . . . Hmm', as the music chimes in, his face rather oddly turning away from the audience, hers becoming hidden behind his.

As we contemplate the future of this odd couple, do we simple read this deliberately chaotic ending purely in terms of post-feminism's assault on patriarchy and its inhibitions? Do we take the destruction of the dinosaur (and, by extension, the 'Wall of Jericho' in *It Happened One Night*), the refusal of the recovered bone, and the award, as a rejection of primevally outdated phallocentrism and male/capitalist lucre? Perhaps, but in doing so, in recuperating the radical and polemical potential of the text, we must be careful not to miss, in all the apologies, mumblings, hidden faces, obscurity of embrace, the dinosaur crash itself, the film's indirect but unmistakable and no less troubling questions about the logical outcome of the no-holds-barred assault on the male, here amiably hounded and persecuted into surrender by a woman who knows nothing of compromise. For the film also seems to be asking, innocently and open-mindedly, where the necessary revolutions of sexual politics will ultimately lead, whether things have not gone too far in the female's triumphant humiliation and education of the male, and whether (as having escaped Alice, David prepares to be swallowed up by Susan), total subservience is what all women truly desire in the man they profess to love. In allowing David the opportunity both to rescue Susan from the bad leopard, and to prevent her falling from the scaffold, the film seems itself to want to balance the need for change (a future in which women will have no inhibitions over asserting their equality with men), with a desire not wholly to abandon some of the positive elements in traditional notions of masculinity.

2

'The love parade'

Lubitsch
and romantic comedy

THE COMIC AUTHOR

Her handling of the china has been sinister. . .
— Mr Syrette to Mrs Maile in *Cluny Brown* (1946)

To assert that Ernst Lubitsch invented the Hollywood comedy of the sexes would be an indefensible hyperbole, for there is a prehistory of urbane silent comedy in which as early as *Why Change Your Wife?* (1920) and *The Affairs of Anatol* (1921) Cecil B. De Mille had laid down the outlines of the genre's ultimate complexity, outlines crossed by the influence of Chaplin's melodrama *A Woman of Paris* (1923) and Stiller's *Erotikon* (1929), let alone Wilde, Schnitzler and Pirandello, as they reach Lubitsch. But this much may safely be said. He was its ultimate exponent and influence. He shaped it to the point where it can bear without strain the assertion not only of its predominance over American stage comedy, but its place alongside the classical products of the European comic theatre, for all that it was made as a transient and perishable commodity to be replaced by others in the endless chain of studio production – not altogether unlike the Elizabethan drama in that respect.

The proper suspicion that contemporary criticism has of the tendency to separate the author from the context that, so to speak, authored him or her, also immediately modifies the hyperbole. Structuralism has emphasised the author's place within a shared aesthetic and ideology (aesthetic ideology); that his language is, even at its most original, the inflection of what he has inherited. At the best, autonomy is only relative, especially within the Hollywood industry, with its factory system, its massive capitalist determinants, its rules of what is and is not representable as set down in that lowest common denominator of middle-class morality, the 1930 MPPA self-censorship code.

And yet, clearly, some directors enjoyed an autonomy more autonomous and less relative than others and were, within the confines of aesthetic and ideological prescription, able to make films that evaded such limits. Lubitsch had the historical luck of – but also unerringly took advantage of – a situation in which he could play to the hilt the role which Hollywood at a certain stage of its development needed of him, that part of the representative of European sophistication (on which von Sternberg and von Stroheim played more decadent variations). When in Preston Sturges's *Sullivan's Travels* (1941) Veronica Lake, as an aspiring actress, tells Joel McCrae of her ambition to meet a great Hollywood director, she names Lubitsch, and the allusion becomes comic when the disguised film director pretends that he does not know that name, so familiar to the cinema's public, not to mention his peers.

Never a vast profit-maker, Lubitsch nevertheless retained a position of almost unmatched independence, most obviously in his long tenure at Paramount (1929-38), but also at MGM (1934, then again 1939-40), United Artists (1941-42) and Twentieth Century Fox (1943-47), allowing him to survive the period when, in the most superfical sense, his films in the late 30s and early 40s seemed to have been overtaken by other directors (Hawks, Sturges, Cukor) whose comedies would have been impossible without the discreet revolution in depth and subtlety which he consummated. Comically phallic cigar jutting out, a little gangster-like in the double-breasted suits of his publicity pictures, constantly dealing out opinions to the press, his image was almost as identifiable as Hitchcock's in the next decades. See, for instance, the little cartoon of Lubitsch, complete with megaphone, in the titles to *Cluny Brown*. An act of *hommage* complementary to Sturges's has Ryan O'Neal playing a film scholar with a PhD written about 'the semiological analysis of the sexual overtones in the early films of Ernst Lubitsch'(!) in *Irreconcilable Differences* (1984), a knowing bow to his reputation among *auteurists* (post Sarris's 'Pantheon'), but it was the knowledge of him attributed to Veronica Lake before the birth of film studies that provided the considerable freedom in which Lubitsch pursued his art.

Lubitsch, then, is a label that has to be redefined variously in terms of conditions and collaborators, but there is no reason to doubt the extent of his influence over most of the important areas of the film-making process. Various actors have testified to the creative control this ex-actor maintained over their performances, just as his screenwriters, Samson Raphaelson most notably, have described working with Lubitsch as an intensely collaborative effort. But even without such verification, this is something we would know from internal evidence. His most significant writers, Raphaelson, Ben Hecht, the partnership of Wilder and Brackett, are certainly all writers with very marked individual styles. In concert with Lubitsch these characteristics are to some degree retained. For instance, the visual joke that ends *Ninotchka* (1939) – (the West as corrupt utopia, where one of the three emigré commissars has been ousted from power by his former partners in the restaurant business) – reads to us as very much Wilder and Brackett, as do many details in *Bluebeard's Eighth Wife* (1938). Nevertheless they all – though arguably with Hecht the tensions show more – end up writing quintessentially Lubitschean scripts, accommodating themes, conflicts and verbal motifs that flow across Lubitsch's comedies from at least their early maturity to their end. For instance, the motif of 'Constantinople', Lubitsch's shorthand for fantasies of unmonogamous sexuality, traces its way fascinatingly across scripts by different hands.

Additionally, his short but highly significant term in charge of Paramount production (February 1935 to February 1936) points to the studio's respect for both his financial shrewdness and his artistic taste, and lends credence to Raphaelson's statement that only once, to his knowledge, did any studio insist on Lubitsch's changing a script when he wanted to proceed.

Such uninterrupted agreement might be interpreted less than flatteringly as underlining the essentially conformist nature of Lubitsch's comedy as a skilful playing of both sides, teasing but not offending, unlike the artistic intransigence of a Murnau or a von Stroheim confronting the Hollywood cinema. But this accusation first of all compares Lubitsch with two non-comic directors (von Stroheim being much more a satirist than a comedian), and the comic, which only works at the most primary level by pleasing its audience, tends to insinuate rather than declare its subversiveness. Lubitsch's double-facedness is less the product of shifty compromise than of his tolerant scepticism. While the view in question may see, for instance, *The Marriage Circle*'s (1924) and *One Hour With You*'s (1932) balancing of the sexual freedom of one female character with another's acceptance of monogamy as a compromise with the demands of 'entertainment', it is just as plausible – indeed we feel more so – to see a happy collusion of entertainment and significance, for, after all, in the Lubitschean realm the two positions expressed do not amount to anything so simple as progressive release versus conservative repressions, but are the rendering of a profound tension, not just at the heart of marriage but of much other experience, the pull between the known and the unknown.

The danger of a reputation founded on 'sophistication' in the treatment of the erotic is that it is always likely to be degraded to a smart *boulevardier* cynicism that reduces multifarious effects to the cliché of 'the Lubitsch touch' (more handy as an advertising slogan than an analytical precept), as enshrined, say, in the memory of a 'Do Not Disturb' sign as a metonym for lovemaking, hardly the subtlest moment in *Trouble in Paradise* (1932). Graham Greene's disparaging praise of 'the playboy Lubitsch' hinges on a view of significance that involves an overt commitment to the 'responsibility' which Capra's comedies possess but which Lubitsch's are said to lack. 'Immorality may be fun', as Max Plunkett pontificates in *Design For Living* (1933), 'but it isn't fun enough to take the place of one hundred per cent virtue and three square meals a day', or, he might have added, an overt call upon American socio-political mythologies.

Actually, without prejudice to Capra's very different and not easily comparable art, we may feel that there was a certain steely seriousness in Lubitsch's apparently irresponsible avoidance of American settings for his favoured European terrain, for there were for him undoubted gains in what resulted – a double focus that allowed not only a constant interplay between American and European modes and values (carried through in his mixing of American and European stars as well), but also the making of very American films for – in the first case, anyway – American audiences, but in settings that freed him from a detailed celebration of the society. Because *Heaven Can Wait* (1943), set in New York, is so historically distanced, it falls outside the argument. But it may not be wholly accidental that what we are not alone in thinking the weakest and most compromised of his sound comedies, *That Uncertain Feeling*, is set in contemporary New York, and, in asserting, in its second half anyway, its businessman hero, ends by simply admonishing the un-American as embodied in modern art, the dissatisfied wife, psychoanalysis and scepticism about the status quo.

The urbane, pleasure-loving priorites of his comedies – witty engagements with the problems of sexuality and therefore indirectly with sexual ideology – may cause them to be seen, even from a less moralistic direction than Greene's, as frivolous (if marvellous). For instance, Pauline Kael's contemporary (1983) praise of Lubitsch and Raphaelson is that 'together they made silliness enchanting' and that Lubitsch freed the writer 'from the literate playwright's obligation to have something to say'. This 'praise' – a late variation on the theme of many a 40s reviewer, that Herr Lubitsch has nothing to say but says it delightfully – confuses surface with substance, the lightness of the display with what is displayed.

Though correctives to such views exist, stressing the intellect that directs the comic effects, there is also a curious analytical neglect of Lubitsch's films by the radical wing of film criticism in England and America. Lubitsch is – as he obviously has to be – gestured at as the great influence on Hollywood comedy in the direction of urbanity, but the very real radicalism of his films' portrayal of the sexes is of little interest to these critics. This is, one feels, primarily because of the films' highly heterosexual disposition. A criticism whose motivating force is the detection of sub-texts critical not just of gender conventions but of heterosexuality itself, that undertakes to demonstrate the return of the bisexual repressed (which means in most usages homosexuality), is likely to be ill at ease with Lubitsch. Where the breaking of gender conventions is foregrounded in Lubitsch, there is not – as it might be argued there is in different ways in some of Hawks's films (the product of an excessively 'manly' sensibility) and in some of Cukor's (the products of a homosexual sensibility) – much sense of the fragility of sexual anchoring. Indeed, Lubitsch's occasional homosexual comedy, such as Claudette Colbert's put-down of the mincing shop assistant in *Bluebeard's Eighth Wife*, is both peripheral and conventional.

An important effect of Lubitsch's relative independence was that, after working in various modes in the late 20s – none of his last three silent films were comedies – he was able, with only one exception, the melodrama *Broken Lullaby* (1932), to devote himself to his favourite genre of romantic comedy (crossing in and out of the musical from 1930 to 1934), from his first sound film *The Love Parade* (1930) to his last, *Cluny Brown*. Doing so, he produced an *oeuvre* of vital importance and influence, an anatomy of the possibilities of romantic comedy, marked not only by an ability to transmit delight in sexuality and its vicissitudes, but also by an awareness of the oppressive aspects of its embodiment in certain cultural norms, of sexuality as a site of conflict as well as a source of satisfaction.

For us the obvious comparison for his films is the most significant comedy of the sexes of the European stage tradition, the plays of Wycherley, Congreve, Wilde, Molière, Beaumarchais, Marivaux, Tirso de Molina, Calderón and Shakespeare. Tracing back the metamorphoses of Lubitsch, from the master of Hollywood sound comedy to the master of American silent comedy (*Lady Windermere's Fan*, 1925, *The Marriage Circle*), from the exponent of the fluid rhetoric of late silent cinema (*The Student Prince of Old Heidelburg*, 1927) to the maker of historical epics with a psychological slant (*Madame Du Barry*, 1919), to his earliest incarnations as actor, then actor-director in the ethnic Berlin comedies of 'Meyer', we find him an actor in Reinhardt's company, playing Shakespearean clowns. Like the great dramatists above, Lubitsch found a mode that combined affirmation with scepticism, surface vivacity with more troubling speculations. In what we might see as a master metaphor in his comedies, his early musical *Monte Carlo* (1930) has a play, or rather an opera, within the film, that traces to a negative conclusion the love/class/identity problems of the main plot. While in the world of comedy Jeanette MacDonald and Jack Buchanan are allowed to resolve the problems that are unresolvable in the opera, Lubitsch reminds us that there are other perspectives than the wish-fulfilments of comedy, at the same time as he does not withhold from us those satisfactions.

Placed against the other major comedies of the 1930s, Lubitsch's films, caught up with them in a profound give-and-take relationship, are both similar and different, most crucially as they touch on Screwball. Though a case might be made for *Design for Living* as the first Screwball comedy, Lubitsch's world is incorrigibly one of codes and self-consciousness, never really of innocence, allowing little space for the return of the pre-civilised Arcadian. So afraid is Leon, in *Ninotchka*, of appearing direct and unsophisticated that, in explaining his love for Ninotchka to the Countess, her rival, he has to preface his confession with the words – 'I know you hate the obvious. Would you mind for a moment if I'm not in the least subtle?' Though his characters constantly struggle against imposed social roles ('That's very interesting,' says Belinsky to Cluny, 'you don't seem to be inhibited'), they can only escape to other ones. This is why Miriam Hopkins, in Lubitsch at least, is a great actress.

To escape consists in mastering the games of social life, not in dreams of evading them. Accordingly, what we have defined as the master metaphors of Screwball, the animal, the insane, the childlike and the criminal, have, though occasionally employed, much less (or a much more constrained) force in Lubitsch. Criminality, for instance, in *Trouble in Paradise*, is not, as it is in *Bringing up Baby*, a metaphor for unspecific urges towards transgression, but Monescu's and Lily's career: not an escape from the unjust social world but a manipulation of its prejudices and deceits. Lubitsch's characters fairly revel in the corrupt sophistication of the urban bourgeois life, that Scylla and Charybdis of ensnaring pleasures and enchantments. Moscow in *Ninotchka* may have the moral advantage, but Paris has all the fun. Particularly noticeable is Lubitsch's temperamental swerving away from the pastoral so common as the place of love's rejuvenation in 30s comedy, which lends autobiographical resonance to Belinsky's statement, 'I'm a city man, I love cars and traffic lights, smoke in my lungs. What have I got? A bigmouthed nightingale under my window!' In the same film Cluny's momentary 'Persian cat feeling' and Belinsky's trick of ringing Wilson's doorbell briefly activate the classic Screwball metaphors, but we are at some distance from the leopards and loons of Connecticut.

What follows is organised so that parts 2 and 3 approach general problems and thematics of the films, while parts 4 and 5 are readings of individual works. The more general discussion centres around some of the best known of the films, *Trouble in Paradise, Design for Living* and *Angel.* In choosing the films for more particular analysis we have turned to two works that for various reasons have had little attention, *Bluebeard's Eighth Wife* and *Heaven Can Wait*, but which have every claim to be seen as major films.

PHYSICS AND METAPHYSICS

Sights and Sounds

Spend in pure converse our eternal day.   — Rupert Brooke

How I'd enjoy one hour with you.
   You silly boy. Just what would you do?
Leave that to me.
   Now I see what champagne can do.
No, No, honestly, I'm tipsy for you.
       — Colette and Adolphe in *One Hour With You*

When Lily in *Trouble in Paradise* angrily rebukes her partner-in-crime, Monescu ('Come on! Be brilliant! Talk yourself out of it! Bluff yourself in!') for a glibness that enables him to slide out of difficulties with a smart turn of phrase, her remark is not just a comment on Monescu's character, but a self-conscious allusion by Lubitsch and Raphaelson to the film's, and, more generally, screen comedy's preoccupation with the nature of film dialogue.

Thirties sound comedy, where the wisecracking of the popular tradition crosses with reminiscences of the wit battles of Elizabethan, Restoration and classical European comedy, could be defined as the kind of film where dialogue is most indulged, the most talking kind of talking picture. This, though, is not so simple as it sounds; witness the extremities of the rewriting of Noel Coward Ben Hecht did, with the director, for Lubitsch's *Design for Living* where, putting it shortly, a form of words ill-adapted to the cinema is replaced by an (at the time iconoclastic) other, well adapted to it. Witness also that 'rightness' in such matters may vary from the languorous poetic speeches of Herbert Marshall to Gary Cooper telling Fredric March 'I oughta bust you right in that ugly pan of yours.' Effectiveness is contingent upon context, too variable to be theorised, though able to be defined after the event.

Trouble in Paradise, like all of Lubitsch's sound comedies, reminds one that untutored responses to film dialogue are often in danger of prompting a dismissal of the apparently thinner lines given to film characters as inferior to the richer resources of stage dialogue, particularly the expansive speeches that in poetic drama are the life blood of the action. It is an obvious point – but one still worth making – that in a film speech exists in relation to a network of gestures, intimate facial kinesics, music, augmented sound, camera-directed expressivities of costume, décor, movement and montage beyond the possibilities of theatre. When, in Molière's *Dom Juan*, Donna Elvira remarks 'Your expression when you first saw me told me more than I ever cared to admit', her words, beyond the particular force they have in the particular context, point to where the dramatist is conscious of a lack in the theatrical art itself, its inability to communicate to a distant audience the minutest nuances of the human behaviour which is its subject, those nuances which can be taken for granted when film actors speak.

The opening of *Trouble in Paradise* can be looked at as an example of the way in which words that are relatively threadbare on the page become, in relation to all the other agencies of cinematic meaning, enormously rich in effect. And since this opening presents a microcosm of the world of attitudes contained in Lubitsch's comedies, the beckoning but problematic world of the erotic for which *Trouble in Paradise* is so apt a title, it is worth considering in some detail.

The film opens with credits appearing against a visual background of nocturnal clouds and sky on which a double bed is superimposed, a juxtaposition which puts together both the spiritual idea of Paradise and a much more secular one, something doubled and further exploited by the title song whose leisurely lullaby cadences and teasing lyrics are sung by a cross between a Venetian tenor and a Rudy Vallee soundalike. As the voice that sings is that of a counter-tenor in its high floating register, and thus sexually ambiguous, the film makes an early intimation of its sexual egalitarianism, an announcement, through a voice representing Eros itself, and neither definitely male or female, that it will be interested in female as much as male sexuality, and not just female sexuality seen through the demands of the male. Likewise, more obviously, the opening of *Design for Living*, through its insistence on giving Gilda as well as Tom and George, the authority of the gaze, proclaims that the woman is as much subject as object. The song goes:

Most any place can seem to be a paradise,
While you embrace just the one that you adore;
There needn't be an apple tree with magic powers,
You'll need no garden filled with flowers,
To taste the thrill of sweet, sweet hours.
Gentle perfume
And cushions that are silk and soft;
Two in the gloom
That is silent but for sighs –
That's paradise
While arms entwine and lips are kissing,
But if there's something missing,
That signifies Trouble in Paradise.

As prologue to the film (and we would wish to give it the force of a metalogue to Lubitsch's comedies as a whole), the lyrics with their sensuous musical setting lull the intellect with promise of the fulfilment of desire, but, in the same breath, shed dubiety over such hopes. The bed, close, tangible and real, is a more actual paradise than that of the religious pastoral, but what it brings may also be illusory ('seems') and is certainly circumscribed temporally ('while'), reminding us of the implication of the mutability of love in the title and title song of another Lubitsch film, *One Hour With You* ('how I would love *one hour* with you'). The 'something missing', the unspecified absence that brings trouble to paradise is *lack* itself, the impossibility of desire ever attaining and resting with its object (in the Lacanian inflection of Freudianism, the mother's body to which we can never be reunited and for which only endless substitutions can be found). Such intimations as these play about Monescu's opening remarks about beginnings, which seem to betray a history of mistaken paradises.

Waiter: Yes, Baron. What shall we start with Baron?
*Monescu:*Mm, Oh, yes, That's not so easy. Beginnings are always difficult.

The softly melancholic tone of the song, the cut at its completion to more mundane levels of existence as the Venetian dustman collects refuse in his gondola and sings 'O Sole Mio', a glimpse of a couple of gaudily dressed and harshly spoken call-girls unable to get into M. Filiba's room (where the robbery has been committed), a shot of the criminal in silhouette that suggests a thematic preoccupation with shadowiness and insubstantiality, and finally the long tracking shot which ends in the location of the hero, the paradise-seeker himself, Monescu, fallen angel, criminal, lover, impostor, epitome in Herbert Marshall of urbane elegance – all these prepare the ambivalent context for his remarks about beginnings and, alas, we must assume, endings.

These remarks, hinting at the fragilities and disappointments of romantic love, seem all the more convincing in being associated with Herbert Marshall's playing of Monescu with its mixture of well-bred charm and matured sensibility tinged with melancholia. As we first see him he stands on the right of a balcony on a still, dark night, his right hand at ease in his tuxedo pocket, his left holding a cigarette whose trail of smoke adds to the atmosphere of dream and unsubstantiality. While, in the left-hand side of the frame, slightly out of focus, in the room itself and under the light of a chic chandelier, a portly and, as we find, benign waiter (not altogether unlike Lubitsch himself in appearance and an ultimately earthbound character, promoting, but at the same time deflating the high-flown attitudes of the paradise seeker) is setting dinner. Monescu's posture is languid, his head bowed in reverie as he looks away from life's realities into the mysterious void. As he is transported back to earth by the waiter's question, his words, spare though they may be by the standards of dramatic poetry, reverberate with connotation.

Monescu: If Casanova suddenly turned out to be Romeo having supper with Juliet who might become Cleopatra – how would you start?

Waiter: I would start with cocktails.

Monescu: Mm. Very good. Excellent . . . It must be the most marvellous supper. We may not eat it, but it must be marvellous.

Waiter: Yes, Baron.

Monescu: And Waiter . . . You see that moon?

Waiter: Yes, Baron.

Monescu: I want to see that moon in the champagne.

Waiter: Yes, Baron. (Writes.) Moon in champagne.

Monescu: I want to see . . . uh (a pause; he gestures vaguely at some indefinable concept) . . .

Waiter: Yes, Baron?

Monescu: And as for you, Waiter . . .

Waiter: Yes, Baron?

Monescu: I don't want to see *you* at all.

Waiter: No, Baron.

All through these exchanges, which in Monescu's case are a sort of distracted monologue barely addressed to his interlocutor, the gentle lullaby with its dominant mandolin continues to play, offering an illusion of paradise like a siren's call against Monescu's acknowledgement of the principle of the mutability at life's core. But it is an illusion that Monescu is about to grasp again in his dinner date with the Countess. A shot shows him waving at Miriam Hopkins as she floats towards him in her gondola. Whatever philosophy says, life is only tolerable through the pretence that the marvellous is within one's reach, that it can be captured like the moon in champagne on occasions like the one he is awaiting. The waiter's repetitions of the prosaic phrase 'yes, Baron', a response only to his practical meanings, emphasise the dreamy, metaphysical qualities of Monescu's meditations. As the two converse, Marshall in moody condescension pronouncing his vowels fully, his 'r's fricatively in a style associated with Noel Coward (but with a deeper note of troubled desire invading the *ennui*), the camera position changes. Now inside the room, it photographs Monescu against a background of Venetian buildings and canals as he still looks away, refusing to take full account of the waiter's presence. Then finally he turns to him with aristocratic brutality and tells him, 'I don't want to see *you* at all.' Spoken almost through the nose, the sneering dismissal seems aimed less at the unfortunate servant than at mundane reality itself.

Monescu's fantasies belong to the plane of (romantic) comedy concerned with the illusory and the evanescent (*The Tempest*, *Life is a Dream*, Troilus's complaint that 'the desire is boundless, and the act a slave to limit'). A tendency of radical sexual–political criticism is to reject this whole area as a mystification of the social nature of desire. But the 'common sense' that knows that what is said here is equally part of the real, can find support in the discourse of psychoanalysis, in what Freud and his reviser, Lacan, have to say about desire, that endless series of attempts to recapture a primal unity that can never be regained. This does not mean that any critique of the organisation and ideology of sexuality should cease, just because perfect satisfactions are impossible. After all, there are degrees of imperfection. But it does suggest that we should be more cautious than some schools of criticism which lay on specific forms of sexual relations – the bourgeois couple, the institution of marriage, even heterosexuality itself – a totality of blame for sexuality's tensions and contradictions, some of which only the most naively utopian thinkers can imagine wholly disappearing in a world of post-patriarchal relations. Such criticism is no longer talking of possible, if difficult, movements towards change – Engels's insight that true sexual equality could only come with economic equality: Freud's hope that certain degrees of sexual repression might be dispensed with; later realisations that conservative and degrading ideas of sexual differences are massively grounded in ideology – but of a Paradise without troubles, wholly idealised and removed from the realm of the problematic. Before *Trouble in Paradise* passes from the balcony of speculation to the hotel room of reality where the 'Baron' and the 'Countess' meet and fall in love, it chastens such vanities – or, if you like, covers with mystification the real conditions of sexuality.

The frame that Lubitsch gives his narrative plays with images of desire irreducible to social forms, though of course given expression by them. The scene that hinges on to it, where Gaston and Lily dine together, plunges us back into the world of contingency. This moment of love, away from the balcony, wholly inside the room, is very significantly not allowed to proceed uninterrupted and aloof from the actions happening around it. Instead it is intercut with various scenes of the hotel's chaos after the discovery of the crime – the police interviewing Filiba, the hotel telephonists at the switchboard, a farcical babble as the Italian police conduct their questioning bilingually. It is a love scene that is also, in its supremely elegant way, an assault on the myth of transparency in love, since the courting of the 'Baron' and the 'Countess', carried out as the ritual seduction of the quavering female by the courteously dominant male, is a self-consciously ironic playing-out of conventional roles that both parties are free enough to know as conventions. Their encounter is not one of desocialised essential selves, but conducted under aliases. The 'Baron' and the 'Countess', are, of course, nothing of the kind, only a self-appointed aristocracy in the world of confidence tricksters. Meeting predatorily, they fall in love, but it is not the traditional perception of the truth beneath the mask that enraptures them. Rather it is the attractions of the mask itself. Not for a second is it suggested that love redeems the criminal in them. In a moment that reminds one of the association of love and the unlawful in Grace Kelly's erotic excitement over the ex-cat burglar, Cary Grant, in *To Catch a Thief* (1955), Gaston addresses Lily lovingly as 'My little shoplifter, My darling.' And later in the film Lily chastises Monescu when he shows signs of recidivism, saying, 'Remember you are a crook, I want you as a crook, I love you as a crook, I've worshipped you as a crook, Steal, swindle, rob . . . oh, but don't become one of those useless, good-for-nothing gigolos!'

Their exchanges are shot through with duplicity, Lily's first words as she rushes in breathlessly are, 'Oh, my gracious, the Marquis de la Tour . . . he almost saw me.' Her phone call from the so-called 'Duchess of Chambreaux' is revealed to the audience as emanating from an enormous, tough-speaking, exasperated-looking woman in a tent of a floral dress, ringing from a mean room. Lily makes a virginal pretence that she shouldn't be there – 'Baron, I shouldn't have come.' Monescu caps it with an elaborately gentlemanly gesture of believing her and being willing to let her go, followed by her pretence of believing his pretence, and so to infinite regression. (Lubitsch's and Raphaelson's attraction to such truth-in-mask situations can be further illustrated by the end of the wholly uncomic *Broken Lullaby* (1932) where the lovers decide to live a benign lie rather than destroy the parents with the truth that Paul killed Walter in the war). The highlight of the scene comes when, during the meal they eat together, each of them reveals to the other what he or she has stolen in their brief encounter – his wallet, her pin, his watch and, finally, her garter! If this display of the authentic as inauthentic, the inauthentic as paradoxically authentic, isn't enough, there are suggestions of a certain sadistic enjoyment in Monescu and (worse, from the point of view of the purity of sexual politics) of a certain masochistic satisfaction in Lily when, in a moment of sudden tension with undeniably sexual overtones, Monescu locks the door and almost savagely shakes her, though only, as it turns out, to dislodge the wallet she is carrying in her dress. It is a little like the unregenerate incident in *Angel* (1937) where Maria tells her husband of a supposed and, we gather, not disagreeable dream in which he has beaten her. Lubitsch's view of sexual relations is too realistic to ignore its more curious and darker areas, though we may note that the power relations here are reversed in other films, so that there are more than traces of sadism in Gilda's and Angel's control over their men, and more than traces of masochism in the men's submission to the woman's will.

A love begun under aliases, with criminality and competitiveness as its provocation, then continues as the partners, joined in a bond of hyper-capitalist duplicity, live off the brilliant but rotten society (perfume and rubbish heaps in the film's early metaphors) which they inhabit. We are a long way from moons in champagne. But it is a paradox that the film delights in. Being diagnostic rather than directly reformist, its comedy exposes the contradictions and absurdities of the status quo, but knows that its lovers will try for what happiness they can within it, with most audiences' approval. At least within their world, then, Lily and Gaston are pointed to as a (very flawed) ideal of the couple, as equal as any relationship can be between unsentimentally-conceived egotists (which in Lubitsch's world we all are). Here, admittedly, the balance of power is with Monescu, the male, as is the social norm, but again we should remember that it is far from invariably so in Lubitsch's films.

The relationship with Mariette (Kay Francis) that tempts Gaston away from Lily enacts the truth that no one person can offer everything. For most people, as for Monescu, there is an irresistible 'bouquet' in the unknown. Apart from her money and the restful stasis that she symbolises for Monescu, her attraction is a wholly different, much more passive sensuality than Lily's attractive audacity. Though Gaston's desire for Mariette is shown as real enough to provoke a sense of true reluctance as he parts from her, she is too much his victim for the film, in the last instance, quite to want them to be together. As her secretary/manager/lover he controls her life, her finances, the programme of her day, even supervising the shaping of her body as he denies her potatoes and puts her through her paces in the gym. Though her awakened sexuality starts to express itself in a flirtatious dominance towards the end of the film, this quality belongs exclusively to the sexual realm. Elsewhere she is still his victim. Lily, by a contrast as striking as that of her quickness and blondeness against Mariette's darkness and languor, is never that, being as self-aware, as protean, as tainted with the predatory as Monescu himself. In a way that we might find too fluid to tolerate in ordinary life, but which stands as a complex, demystifying almost-ideal of relationship, their provisional coupling is minute by minute kept alive by their proving to each other that they are indispensably brilliant. Domesticity finds them sitting reading the newspapers and discussing the opera reviews, but a huge trunk dominates the *mise-en-scène*, reminding us that at any moment they might have to leave, or that one might want to leave the other. The actressy mannerisms, darting movements, constant hand gestures, petite melodramatic moues and mock-gauche eye-widenings of Miriam Hopkins are used by Lubitsch to signify a constant sense of a self-conscious intelligence searching through forms for some adequate embodiment of her feeling. This contrasts very sharply with a later role expressing a typically more limited response to Hopkins such as Millie in *Old Acquaintance* (Vincent Sherman, 1943) where the same gestures betray superficiality. There, in a scene based on a memory of *Trouble in Paradise*, Bette Davis, as the audience's surrogate, shakes her as Herbert Marshall did, but with violent anger. In the scene where she and Monescu plan their escape, Lily is brilliantly quick and hyperbolically capable, surprising him with her knowledge of train timetables and passport details, her efficient, if atrociously accented, Spanish and, finally, her bantering German to match his own. When they are together she and Monescu even dissolve some of the most deeply-rooted conventions of gender attribution, so that while she is seen in terms of restlessness, activity and speech that often erupts in staccato brusqueness, he is languorous, self-pampering, possessed of a feline moodiness, a Dietrich among men, yet at the same time their sexual identity remains pleasurably reassuring for the audience.

Monescu's wavering between the two women, two visions of desire and two kinds of relationship, is marvellously caught by the words spoken by Herbert Marshall (and above all by the way he speaks them) when his hectic banter with Lily is immediately followed by his phone call to the florist for flowers as a farewell gift to Mme Colet, a gift to make another ending rather than a beginning. 'I want you to take', he begins in those tones of Noel Coward crossed with Byron, 'five dozen roses – deep red roses – and I want you to put them in a basket and to send them to Mme Colet.' But here reality asserts itself, the room takes precedence over the balcony for a while, there is an unacknowledged conviction that romanticism itself is a kind of predatoriness, and the realist adds: 'Charge it to Mme Colet.'

Marriage – singles, doubles and trios

I've always heard that the ideal marriage should be something of a mystery.
— Jane Baker in *That Uncertain Feeling*

Oh, she worships me sir, but it was by no means an easy conquest. The young lady didn't believe in the institution of marriage.
— Wilton, the butler, in *Angel*

As Monescu stands on the Venetian balcony, poised between the mysteries of the night and the social microcosm of the hotel, the amorous thief indulges a fragmentary fantasy, a hypothesis that trails away into ambiguous irresolution. 'If Casanova suddenly turned out to be Romeo having supper with Juliet who might become Cleopatra . . . How would you begin?' It is a question that releases, to use the Monescuan terminology, the philosophical 'bouquet' of Lubitsch's comedies, their pervasive sense of individuals, both male and female, not as simple essences, but compounded of contrasts, conflicts and contradictions.

Turned about, Monescu's statement reveals different facets in different lights, like the lampshade with which Sir Frederick and Anthony image Maria in *Angel*. From one angle it is a statement of romantic disillusionment, despairing of the desired transparencies and symmetries promised by the myths of love. Thus the ageing roué, Casanova, dreams of innocence recaptured in Juliet, and himself turns into Romeo, only to find that Juliet (more complex as a subject with her own desires than she is simply as the object of his, and so enacting the Lacanian drama of the impossibility of love) has metamorphosed into Cleopatra, ironically a match for Casanova's surface self, but not for the desires which sent him in pursuit of Juliet. Adjusted slightly, it might, however, be taken more serenely as an assertion of psychic multifariousness, pointing past simplification to the Cleopatra in every Juliet, the Romeo in every Casanova, and vice versa. And yet again, from a different position, it seems to read as the comic artist's dismissal of the more sentimental symmetries (young love, tragedy) for the more mature, ironic and anti-absolutist positions represented by the older lover–libertines. The connotations of the riddling words within their full actorly and visual context are hardly encompassed by such a brief explication – the various strands of which coexist rather than cancel each other out – but those traced suggest that perspective of psychological fluidity and complexity with which love (an ideal, but not an essence) is treated in Lubitsch's films.

Of the two overarching forms that comic love narratives take in Hollywood and the wider culture, *courtship* plots (for which marriage is the reward) and *marriage* plots (which deal with the actual facts of living together only gestured to hopefully in the former), Lubitsch is unusual in his preference (which, however, De Mille also shared) for the latter. These (e.g. *To Be Or Not To Be*, 1942, *One Hour With You*, *That Uncertain Feeling*, *Heaven Can Wait*, *Design for Living*, *Trouble in Paradise*, the last two dealing with marriage-like relationships as distinct from marriages) predominate over courtships (e.g. *Monte Carlo*, 1930, *The Merry Widow*, 1934, *Ninotchka*, *Cluny Brown*, 1946), reflecting his interest in the relatively mature rather than the youthful, in desire in the context of experience rather than innocence, and in the complications of love in its most socialised form. Like most other films of the genre, Lubitsch's exclude children from the scene, annulling or at least delaying the productive function of marriage which will inevitably alter the romantic love celebrated in the couple by making demands beyond them. Only once, at the close of *Cluny Brown*, does Lubitsch end a narrative with the (imminent) birth of a child, and only once, in *Heaven Can Wait*, do children appear in a marriage. In this purified, childless space the biological function of pairing is attenuated and we are given disquisitions on the most refined epiphenomena of the reproductive function, sexuality as it is involved in the search for identity, needs and satisfactions linked to, but not defined by, the biological. If the couple are attracted to each other and stay together it is for the other reasons than 'for the sake of the children'.

Marriage in Lubitsch is at once the object of romantic desire (perfect union), its regulator (since, having found the perfect object, desire should cease, except for that object) and, inevitably, its ironiser (desire, sadly, fades, the overestimation of the love-object, to use those stern Freudian terms, lessens as the object is possessed, and desire for a different object springs to life). The general sense of the instability of monogamy in his films is no doubt in part prompted by the great increase in divorce in the USA; by 1914 the figures reaching 100,000; by 1929 over 205,000; something reflected in the De Mille comedies as well as the later films which Cavell alludes to in his sub-genre of 'comedies of remarriage'. Nevertheless, Lubitsch's attitude is more the European one than the American – marriage with all its complications rather than serial monogamy. Mariette, talking to one of her suitors in *Trouble in Paradise*, defines it as 'a beautiful mistake'. The conceit that ends *The Merry Widow* encapsulates this – the drive to unity expressed by the romantic sweep of the great walz, uncertainty by the idea of a wedding in a prison cell. Differently, but similarly, Klara Novak in *The Shop Around the Corner* waits idealistically for her unseen lover in the café, but carries with her as an (unconsciously ironic) mark of identification a copy of *Anna Karenina*. At the very least, or perhaps at its best, marriage means coming to terms with change and movement in the other, Juliet having to comprehend Romeo ageing into Casanova, Romeo watching Juliet turning into Cleopatra. In *The Shop Around the Corner* the elderly Mr Matuschek (played by the enormously sympathetic Frank Morgan), says that his adulterous wife didn't want to grow old with him. We sympathise with Matuschek as the film does, Emma Matuschek never being seen, simply an off-screen character. But had Lubitsch made her a central presence we can be sure that he would, as always, have made us feel the force of her desire (which in Lubitsch's characters always has a tinge of narcissism about it), that desire which in the films is again and again expressed by the configuration of the sexual triangle.

Two major overviews of Lubitsch have foregrounded the use of the erotic triangle as more than a *donnée* for the mechanical complications of marital farce. Carringer and Sabath, abstracting a model for the typical Lubitsch comedy, write:

> A man and a woman are perfectly suited for one another. They have a potentially ideal relationship, but time has slightly taken the edge off their romance and they have both begun to settle into the routine of taking one another for granted. A third party enters the scene, a sexual rival. One of the partners is lured into a flirtation and possibly a sexual dalliance. The original relationship is threatened. But only temporarily: the interlude of infidelity turns out to be a catalyst to self-awareness and psychological renewal.

It is not that this model is simply wrong. Obviously it responds to something present in many of the films, showing insight into the qualities forgotten in a partner that may be positively 'estranged' again because they have been perceived by a third party, and into the role that sexual competition may have in even the most stable relationships. In a highly refined version it is even working at the back of the love plot in *The Shop Around the Corner*, where it is the shadowy real/unreal presence of competitors who are in fact idealised versions of themselves that in the end pushes the misapprehending lovers together.

Not wholly wrong then, but it is certainly too reductive and optimistic in that 'perfectly suited'. If we take two films that the model might seem to describe – leaving aside a third, *Design for Living*, to which it is wholly inadequate – we can see that with *One Hour With You* it works fairly well, but that in *Angel* Lubitsch has used only the outward form of the model, investing it with dubiousness at crucial points. In *One Hour With You*, Dr André Berthier (Maurice Chevalier) is lured by the vampish and dissatisfied Mitzi into being unfaithful to his wife, Colette (Jeanette MacDonald). There the brief relationship ends, with the couple back together and the implication that relationships which last a lifetime have to admit minor infidelities from time to time. This is the European 'cynicism' and sexual wisdom that Carringer and Sabath are quite correct in interpreting as much more meaningful, in its socio-sexual reverberations, in the more puritan public moral framework of 1930s America than in Europe. But with *Angel* the model leaves out more than it contains. Though Maria stays with her husband rather than eloping with Anthony, the treatment of the situation is weighted so as to resist both the simplest readings – either a resurrection of the Barkers' marriage, the disappearance of Maria's opaque disenchantment, the re-awakening of Sir Frederick's passion, etc., or the one that is its obvious replacement, the shadow of Anthony Halton coming between the couple.

Molly Haskell, one of Lubitsch's most subtle analysts, sees the role of the triangle more subversively.

> The triangle permits us to see a person being seen by two different people, being interpreted like the proverbial glass of water as half-empty or half-full . . . No one person is the complete complement to the other; the side of the person exposed by the triangle continues to exist, even where the triangle has been superseded by the pair.

There are different ways of reading the implications here, depending on one's optimism or pessimism about the institution of marriage, whether as the unavoidable complications of the choices most people have to make (i.e. no one can have everything; every choice means something not chosen), or as contradiction that might point the way to different and better modes of organising sexuality. But clearly, while Carringer and Sabath's model is one that privileges the couple, making any intrusion only the catalyst to renewal, Haskell's emphasises conflict and fragility. This triangular situation has many manifestations in Lubitsch's films – André, Colette and Mitzi in *One Hour with You*; Josef, Maria and Lieutenant Sobinsky in *To Be Or Nor To Be*; Monescu, Lily and Mariette in *Trouble in Paradise*; Gilda, Tom and George in *Design for Living*; Sir Frederick, Maria and Anthony in *Angel*; Henry, Martha and Henry's many women in *Heaven Can Wait* – but we shall examine it as it appears in two films, first *Angel*, then *Design For Living*.

In *Angel* a mysterious woman (Marlene Dietrich) meets Anthony Halton (Melvyn Douglas) in a *salon d'assignation* in Paris. That night he falls in love with her, begging to know her name, which she withholds. She promises, however, that she will think about returning to him if he will let her go. Only later does the narrative establish that she is Lady Maria Barker, the Russian wife of Sir Frederick Barker (Herbert Marshall), a major figure in the British Foreign Office. Whereas her meeting with Anthony is all romance and mystery, her marriage seems to lack that dimension. At various points

in the narrative she seems to will her husband to spare time for their relationship from his all-consuming work, but on each occasion foreign affairs (via
telegrams and phone calls) punningly intervene. By a coincidence, Sir Frederick and Anthony meet and discover that, though they have never come
face to face, during the war they shared the same mistress in Paris. As
unaware as Frederick of the ironies involved, Anthony tells him about the
woman he has christened 'Angel', and he is invited to the Barkers' house.
The ensuing complications culminate in a scene in the *salon* in Paris where
both men are present as Barker discovers Maria's second identity, as 'Angel'.
She chooses, in a moment that is ambiguous at every level, to follow her
husband.

The evasive camera rhetoric of the closure, which (as happens in crucial
earlier scenes) denies one expected views of the characters' reactions, is far
from exceptional in this film, in fact only the last item of a systematic play
with secrecy and withheld revelation. Conversations typically proceed up
pre-Pinterian culs-de-sac ('How's Rome?' 'I haven't seen Rome for years');
shot and reaction shot are subtly loosed from expected patterns in an unsett-
ling, momentary unhinging from within of the classical Hollywood style;
and some scenes take place wordlessly, as if to heighten problems of interpretation through the removal of verbal clues or from a viewpoint so external
(e.g. the tracking shot from outside the building where we first see the
activities of the *salon*) as to become enigmatic. And where the many-sidedness
of Lily in *Trouble in Paradise* and Gilda in *Design for Living* is conveyed by
the actorly *tours-de-force* of Miriam Hopkins's highly-wrought extroversion,
with Maria Lubitsch utilises, for the portrayal of an equally complex woman,
the mysterious stasis latent in the persona of Marlene Dietrich, emphasising
– in a context far from the exotica of Sternberg – her facial inscrutability and
aura of irony. At first glance this opacity might look as if it signifies the
rather clichéd 'otherness' of the *femme fatale* (a view of herself that Maria
sometimes seems to share, as when she says to Anthony, 'But it's a privilege
of a woman not to make sense. Men who expect women to be logical are apt
to be failures in love'). But the narrative progressively reveals itself not just
to be structured around the men's attempt to grasp the obscure object of
their desire, but shifts so that her reactions and desires, her subjectivity as
well as her objectivity, move to the centre of the film's thematic enigmas.

The narrative seductively offers a number of simple unifying operations,
ways of clearing up the problems on screen, which it simultaneously undermines. In the Barkers' living room the unknowing male rivals discuss their
opposing philosophies of love. Anthony in the role of Caesar, Frederick as
Brutus and 'Angel' as Cleopatra (not Juliet). 'One says the shade is blue.

The other swears it's green', says Frederick. 'But one hour with "Angel",' sighs Anthony. 'Sixty minutes', replies Barker. 'Three thousand six hundred seconds' is Anthony's counter. What do the events of the narrative do with this antithesis? Do we read them as positively offering Maria romantic love with Anthony, an offer she fails by her inability to dare the unknown in more than the fantasy of her secret trips to Paris? Or do we read them as giving a hopeful answer to Maria's question to her husband, 'It's true the dream is over. But does it have to be?' Both choices, though at moments presented so as to stir unambivalent sympathies, are, however, less than fully underwritten. For instance, Anthony's status as romantic lover is somewhat undermined by his visit to the brothel with the entrée from Captain Butler, as is Sir Frederick's understanding as a husband by his refusal to accept not knowing whether his wife is 'Angel' or not. The lovers' night in Paris veers disturbingly between moments which straightforwardly invoke romance and others that are pressed to the point of parody, as when the cloyingly suave violinist who plays a romantic solo at their dinner table, asked the name of the tune, replies with glib implausibility, 'It has no name, I just made it up for you, Madame' (and then, quickly, as he receives Anthony's tip), 'and for you, M'sieur.'

The violinist's answer might also be read as parodying Maria's persona of secrecy in Paris, where we first see her calling herself 'Mrs Brown' and then refusing to give her name to Anthony. But before asking the point of this parody, there are more positive aspects to be considered. Her evasion of her name at the hotel and refusal to give it to Anthony can be interpreted past her caution, and her delight in mystery, as a perhaps only haltingly understood refusal of a nominalisation which symbolises a definition, or series of definitions, resistance to which she nowhere articulates, but which is embodied in those of her actions that are never overtly explained (e.g. the visit to Paris, calling on the Grand Duchess/procuress).

As the film explores 'Angel's' hesitations between the two men and what they represent (the evenness of the battle reflected in the very different but equal charm of Herbert Marshall and Melvyn Douglas), there are hints that her problem may not simply be which of two lovers to choose, identified as they are with romantic wildness and stability, but may arise from the social conventions which associate women only with the paraphernalia of the private life, but men with the public world. An apparently throwaway line has characters at the *Club de la Russie* joking about having to work for one's living under the Bolsheviks. The speaker here is male, and the immediate reverberations are of class rather than of gender, but the film will introduce the latter as a consideration. As Kate Millett (*Sexual Politics*) and others have noticed, this division of labour has a venerable ancestry. It is one of the great themes of the nineteenth-century novel where, for instance, Levin in *Anna Karenina* condemns his wife to trivial chores, or where in *Middlemarch* George Eliot decries woman's restriction to menial or domestic work, however much sanctified by the rhetoric of female service, as found, say, in Coventry Patmore's Victorian erotic–domestic glorifications of *The Angel in the House*.

And still with favour singl'd out,
Marr'd less than man by mortal fall,
Her disposition is devout,
Her countenance angelical.
The best things that the best believe,
Are in her face so kindly writ,
The faithless, seeing her, conceive
Not only heaven, but hope of it.

Not quite an 'angel' in Patmore's sense, though not, either, its melodramatic or comic antitheses, Dietrich's previous incarnation as 'The Blue Angel' or Mae West's declaration 'I'm no angel', Lubitsch's Maria shows none of the thwarted ambition of a Dorothea as she elaborately dresses to meet her guests, goes to Ascot, or attends the opera. But it is surely aspects of this life, exaggerated by Sir Frederick's constant calls of duty, from which she is consciously or unconsciously in literal flight (by plane, in the angelic element of air) in the first moments of the film. When her husband, after she comes back from Paris, startles her by also calling her 'angel', his use of the epithet places her on the domestic pedestal which is also a cage of entrapment. Ironically, escaping to Paris in an action that in some dim way is connected to self-definition, she is swept up in Anthony's elevating concept of her as the 'angel' of love, rather than of the house, but it is a concept which is, in a different way, equally limiting.

As Maria her name is of some significance. Lubitsch's concerns are not religious and, as a Jew, he is doubly distanced from Christian symbolism (as is Raphaelson, his writer), but the story of Mary and Martha in chapter ten of the Gospel according to St. Luke is part of the fund of meaning available in a culture derived dominantly from Christianity. Martha, it will be remembered, complained to Jesus that she was left to do the serving alone, while Mary 'took her place at the Lord's feet and listened to his words'. Jesus's reply was that 'Mary has chosen for herself the best part of all, that which shall never be taken away from her.' The analogy takes on further meaning, becomes indubitable, when we consider that the most conservative, the most traditionally domesticated and ideologically complying of all Lubitsch's heroines is Martha in *Heaven Can Wait* (see the last section of this chapter). Indeed, she is the only one who could be described in such terms. Mary/Maria, unlike Martha in the last film, seems obscurely aware of some better part, some 'angelic' knowledge (to use the terminology of mystical writers). This knowledge has to be conceived of in a secular sense rather than a wholly metaphysical one, 'angellic' perhaps in its ability to look past dominant social forms and expectations. It is only a fleeting presence in the film, expressed by negation rather than concrete embodiment, playing between the interstices of Maria's ambivalence about the two men and the fictions of her that they offer.

Finally, the waiter's parody of Maria's divesting herself of her identity is accurate inasmuch as, in a comedy of culs-de-sac, it gets her nowhere, or if somewhere, to Paris, the city of love, which offers her ecstasy (apparent 'angellic' knowledge as deception?), but at the price of Anthony's misperceptions of her.

In the end the film is too allusive to yield tightly unambiguous meanings, a trait that will annoy the literalist, but delight others. Does Maria reject Anthony because, as she tells him, she never loved him? Or because of her habituation to the material and social status she has as the wife of Sir Frederick, a more comfortable version of the 'place' from which Cluny is able to extricate herself in *Cluny Brown*? Or is it because she loves her husband? Or because – wary of the supposed paradise of romantic love – she draws back from the excess of trusting in the force of romantic passion to dissolve problems, some of which may have a specific social cause, some of which may reside in the nature of desire itself? More conservative, more constrained, perhaps wiser than Emma Bovary and Anna Karenina, 'Angel' follows her husband out at the film's end, and as she does so, these various possibilities play against one another. Certainly they do not fade away unquestionably as she makes her decision, a decision which, for all that it partly satisfies the ingrained wish for a closure that asserts dissatisfaction's end in the couple, is also part of the more troubling comedy of dissatisfaction that pervades the film.

Angel ends with the resolution of a triangular relationship back into a couple, but the resolution is ambivalent on several counts, not least in the sense that prevails that neither Anthony's nor her husband's definition of 'Angel' can be experienced by her as adequate – though she is obliged (or feels she is obliged) to choose one of them. It is the most disquieting, the most 'Pirandellian' of Lubitsch's films, the material of melodrama refined into the coolest comedy (too cool, in fact, for 1930s popular taste). By scrupulously avoiding making husband or lover more sympathetic or to embody more or less desirable values, it pushes one to suspend sympathies and produces conflicts more interesting than the divided sympathies of the usual intractable romantic triangle. Ultimately, it suggests that the object the self chooses to reside in will always be unsatisfying at some level – but for women even more than for men, since women, in the world shown by the film, have for the most part only the realm of love as their source of self-definition, while men – though through it they risk, like Sir Frederick, the loss of the personal world – have at least the realm of public affairs.

Design For Living (1933), following the Noël Coward play which it controversially rewrote and re- (at the time it was very much thought mis-) cast, deviates from the norm by finding an unorthodox solution to the triangles. It reverses the movement of other films by working through various non-sexual and sexual couples (i.e. Max and Gilda, Tom and George, George and Gilda, Gilda and Tom, Gilda and Max consolidated as marriage), to a final marriage-like *triangle*, Gilda, Tom and George, of precariously sublimated sexuality.

At the centre of *Angel*, Maria is the object of the other character's desires, but her control of events proves to be largely illusory. Gilda (Miriam Hopkins) in *Design For Living* has, however, the force to break with the status quo, leave her husband Max (Edward Everett Horton), the great advertiser, and live with both Tom (Fredric March) and George (Gary Cooper), converting them both to her point of view. As in *Trouble in Paradise* Lubitsch is again able to deploy positively qualities in Miriam Hopkins that later in her career tend to be used very unsympathetically as she is typecast as the self-dramatist of superficial emotions. Here, as in *Trouble in Paradise*, the relentless self-projection of the star generates sympathetic engagement, as it will do again in Mamoulian's Lubitsch-influenced use of her as anti-heroine in *Becky Sharp* (1935), since we, as spectators, perceive through the miniature melodramas she suffers and enjoys the force of her dilemma, as enunciated in that pleasurably shocking moment when she confronts both Cooper and March:

> A thing happened to me that usually happens to men. You see a man can meet two, three or four women and fall in love with all of them, and then, by a process of – er – interesting elimination, he is able to decide which he prefers; but a woman must decide purely on instinct, guesswork, if she wants to be considered nice . . .

And then, in reply to Tom's question, 'Which *chapeau* do you want, Madame?' her answer is 'Both', so that the dilemma is redefined as not merely being the desire to 'try on' both men before making her decision, but the desire for a decision by which she can have both.

A significant piece of comedy is pursued when, straight after Gilda

addresses the problem of sexual economy just created by saying, with topical reference, 'Now let's talk it over from every angle without any excitement, like a Disarmament Conference', the men then rush off to the nearby restaurant to order '*trois* frankfurters'. These they are seen finishing off as the solution occurs to Gilda – 'Boys, it's the only thing we can do. Let's forget sex!' Clearly part of the wit is that the invention of the sublimatory solution somewhat collides with the suggestive, as well as indigestive, meal, but it is surely the subtler part of the comedy that here the frankfurter-as-phallus is shared out to all three, including the dominant woman, without any overtones of castration or denigration of the woman as too masculine. The original Gilda of the Noel Coward play tends to think with hostility of her femininity, a view shared by Leo and Otto, the prototypes for George and Tom. For instance, she describes herself 'Squirming with archness, being aloof and desirable, consciously alluring, snatching and grabbing, evading and surrendering, dressed and painted for victory, an object of strange contempt!'. It may be that the Gilda of the play's antagonism to her femininity is not to the feminine itself, but to the particular embodiment of it that she feels to be demanded of her. But it is noticeable that no anti-feminine statements at all are attached to the screen Gilda, so that the film's project seems to be to allow the woman to 'possess the phallus' as far as equality, decisiveness and outward-lookingness are concerned. At the same time she retains what are conceived of as pleasurable gender differentiations, in the case of the more outwardly excessive ones required of the female (embodied in the kittenish qualities of Miriam Hopkins), with the self-conscious understanding that they are arbitrary. And, of course, the audience's perception of a relatively unambiguous masculinity in Cooper and March is likely to work to make more acceptable the 'feminine' position in which they usually find themselves as regards Gilda. Perhaps any lingering feelings that their masculinity is in danger is hived off on to the rather effeminate Max Plunkett, played with Horton's usual fussy sexual ambivalence.

Perhaps we should also see in this light the off-screen brawl at the end of the film in which Tom and George, invading the Plunkett household, destroy Max's party by fighting with the guests. Corliss, in his book on Hollywood screenwriters, sees it as Hecht's laying one on the effete Englishman, Coward, but equally it might be seen as a last-minute, and rather crude reminder that the men have not lost their conventional manliness. It is undoubtedly the

---

Design for Living
Well, who would you choose? Gary Cooper or Fredric March? Lubitsch has Miriam Hopkins say both, of course.

least subtle moment in the film but, typically, Lubitsch is able also to make
it the vehicle for more resonant meanings. When Tom and George enter the
Plunkett house, they casually and jokingly take on the personae of policeman,
Inspector Knox (!) and Sergeant O'Toole (!). As laughably literal exemplars
of the phallic law, they are also its parodists and overthrowers, the 'hooligans'
that Max calls them, breaking up the party of businessmen and punishing
Max for upholding an ethic of capitalism, 'normality' and containment, and
undermining both the law of monogamy (since they both come for Gilda)
and the rule of masculine dominance (since in the triangle Gilda is the leading
party).

The ending, like most of Lubitsch's closures, cultivates ambivalence. Coward's play ends with Leo, Otto and Gilda hysterically laughing at themselves
and their situation, with their fate uncertain, but their situation clear. They
will live as a sexual triangle, two men with one woman. William Paul has
outlined very well the significance of some of the profound changes in the
film from its source. The most important of these is the shift from characters
who are viewed, and view themselves as fascinating exceptions – (Otto: 'We
are different. Our lives are diametrically opposed to ordinary sexual conventions') – cosmopolitan and androgynous, to characters who are firmly American instead of ambiguously international (as Lily's 'Aw, nuts!' and the men's
rendition of 'Oh Say Can You See?' at their first meeting immediately underlines), and not only firmly heterosexual, but highly interested in sex. In a
way that has no trace in the film, the play's Leo, Otto and Gilda really seem
to find sex a messy business that disturbs more important matters. To the
contrary, Tom, George and Gilda, grounded in the physical appeal of charis-
matically sexy stars, constantly suggest the strong libidinal drives shared by
most of Lubitsch's heroes and heroines.

So what are we to make of the ending as 'The Three Musketeers – Athos,
Porthos and Mademoiselle D'Artagnan' reassert, with a mixture of excitement and resignation, the condition of their pact – 'No sex'? As they do so,
they repeat the action at the institution of their agreement when Gilda, as
'Mother of the Arts', checked their desire to kiss her on the lips and offered
them her brow. But there is a significant difference here as the men in turn
kiss her on the lips. The gestures, far less sublimatory than the first, must
cast some doubt on the viability of their agreement.

Diverting an answer for a moment, it is perhaps salutary to bear in mind
the problems that a fairly sophisticated contemporary Hollywood comedy,
Michael Ritchie's *Semi-Tough* (1975), full of gestures towards a new 'laid-
back' morality, has in handling the same situation, the triangle made up of
the professional footballers played by Burt Reynolds and Kris Kristofferson

and the woman played by Jill Clayburgh. The film is aware of, could even be seen as a rewriting of, *Design for Living*, down to the image of the Three Musketeers (Bobby-Jean to Billy Clyde: 'Still all for one and one for all, huh?') and the same-sex declarations of love. It is, as we might expect, much more open in its talk about sex, with Jill Clayburgh even outdoing the men in profanity. But in spite of the change of profession that makes the men irreproachably macho as footballers rather than as artists, the closure here can't think for a moment of even approaching the (albeit conditional) radicalism of its distant source. When Billy Clyde talks enough doubts into Shake for him to balk at the altar, he himself is there to take Bobby-Jean off to Hawaii to begin a new life 'living in sin'. Significantly, all the film feels it can do is totally expel Shake from the narrative, with a last sequence in which the couple walk along the beach. Finally, only the slightest deviation from the norm of the couple and the ironies of 'I'm Back in the Saddle Again' try to hide the betrayal of the intractabilities of the source – Gilda telling Tom what she felt about him when she was with George: 'You haunted me like a nasty ghost. On rainy nights I could hear you moaning down the chimney.'

For all its fashionable contemporaneity then, *Semi-Tough* is unable – even at the most superficial level – to follow its source's outrageousness, an instance that might cure naïve thoughts that contemporary comedy, because it can profanely articulate things about sex forbidden by earlier codes, is necessarily more, or even as radical as earlier comedy.

Doubtless a straight version of the end of the Coward play would have run foul of even the relatively liberal censorship code of the year of the film. Do we then unhesitatingly read the tension signified at the end (will they, or won't they, in either sense, make it?) as a joke, signalling to the knowing the inevitable return of the repressed? It would be difficult to argue that that isn't part of the effect, but it is also arguable that, as he often does, Lubitsch makes a lot out of his constraints and, given the choice, he might not in the end have altered his closure. The same can be said of the ending of *Angel*. At the simplest level there things are constrained by the impossibility of Maria's walking off with Anthony happily, but such an ending would hardly have carried the multiple possibilities the one created within censorship constraints enacts. So *Design for Living*'s ending, apparently pulling back from the brink of the radical, dramatises by implication problems and pos-siblities that would be cancelled out by the more obviously shocking finale, questions that tend to be more social than the ones of *Angel*, which embrace that area, but slide away into the metapsychology or metaphysics of desire, since we are never quite allowed to fix 'Angel's' unspoken needs and desires to any precise 'objective correlative'. The perfect, but precarious, balance of the triangle, existing only in celibacy, expresses the knowledge that in the present ideology of monogamy (to which Tom and George really belong) this is the only way the three can be together. Thus the ending preserves a realism about the power of sexual ideologies and even, it may be, from the anthropological perspective, the power of pairing as the basis of all known social life, while wondering if some other kind of arrangement is possible. It perhaps also embodies our knowledge that, though the celibate situation involves losses (even the going against Nature that George complains of), it enacts the cross and the same sex affection of a less than wholly sexual kind that are lost in the prevalent, competitive way of viewing sexuality. 'Playing tricks on Nature' may be too great a price to pay, but at least, temporarily, we see three relationships flourishing rather than one, a final image reminding us of the disparate, inexhaustible and often duplicitous demands of love.

WHY CAN'T A MAN BE MORE LIKE A WOMAN?

> *Nicole:*   Here's to our agreement. No love-making, no quarrels.
> *Michael:* Just like an ordinary married couple.
> *Nicole:*   I said no quarrels.
>
> — *Bluebeard's Eighth Wife* (1938)

Bluebeard's Eighth Wife (1938)

Like many other Lubitsch films *Bluebeard's Eighth Wife* develops the complexities of romance beyond the thrills of courtship and into the troubled serenities of marriage. But where most of those films are characterised by a generally tolerant understanding of human frailty, *Bluebeard* has the more frantic pace and tone of 'Screwball' comedy. Where *Angel* and *Trouble in Paradise*, in particular, play on the emotions, gently troubling as well as pleasing, *Bluebeard* – at times veering into farce – demands a more detached attitude. Even if we wouldn't want to go as far as to say with Bergson that 'Comedy can only begin at the point where our neighbour's personality ceases to affect us', we can still agree with him that much of this film's comedy derives from exposure of the socialised rigidities of human behaviour. The straitjacket in which Michael Brandon is confined near the end of the film so that Nicole, his ex-wife, can talk to him, kiss him and propose marriage to him without resistance, is the film's most extreme symbol of such rigidity.

The narrative (a Paramount property, made into a silent film starring Gloria Swanson in 1923) is a reformulation of a play by Alfred Savoir, which in turn depends distantly on a tale by Perrault about a man who marries and murders seven women. When he attempts to inflict the same fate on his eighth wife who, during his absence has discovered a room housing the corpses of her predecessors, her brothers arrive in time to kill Bluebeard, whose estate and wealth she consequently inherits to live happily every after. In Lubitsch's film there is a comic undertone of violence retained from Perrault, overt when Michael struggles in the straitjacket, or husband and wife slap each others' faces, or when the boxer, 'Kid' Mulligan, is around; covert when Michael Brandon, the film's Bluebeard, asks his eighth bride-to-be, Nicole, whether she has heard of Henry VIII, a remark designed to conjure up images of beheaded wives. But that and the latent aggression of his whole approach to women apart, Michael's usual way of ridding himself of his wives is by a much more modern means of disposal, divorce.

The film tells the story of a young American millionaire's (Gary Cooper) desire to make an impoverished French aristocrat's daughter (Claudette Colbert) his eighth wife. She is also courted by an effete, virtually penniless and incompetent aristocratic admirer, Albert (David Niven), who also happens to be an employee of Brandon's in France. But she falls in love with Brandon, ignorant of his previous marital history. Nicole discovers with horror, almost on the eve of their wedding, the full truth, including the revelation that, anticipating speedy divorce, he invariably settles an annuity of $50,000 before the nuptial vows are taken. She reacts by deciding – partly spurred on by her avaricious father who has already spent a fortune, mainly on himself, in anticipation of the marriage, and partly from her own desire to (to use her own term) 'break' Michael down – that she will still marry him, evolving a plan by which they will eventually meet as equal partners on equal terms, thus ensuring the survival of this marriage. So, demanding that the annuity be stepped up to $100,000, she marries him in a calculated alliance between marriage and wealth that echoes in reverse *The Taming of the Shrew*, which the film in several ways resembles, and to which there is one direct and several indirect references. As Nicole clinches the deal, the inner family group of herself, her father, her aunt (the head of the family), plus Brandon, stand beneath an oval portrait of a demure eighteenth-century girl holding a rose, a composition that comments on innocence and experience by reminding us that however idyllic such ladies look, their fate was to be the subject of patriarchal alliances much less to their advantage than Nicole's.

But when Brandon expects to enjoy the fruits of his solemnised union he discovers that his wife has become a Lysistrata, refusing to 'be nice'

As we argue elsewhere, Lubitsch was perpetually fascinated by the conflicting demands of plurality and exclusivity in sexual relations. Gilda in *Design for Living* cannot decide between Tom and George, while, for all her 'angellic' beauty, Martha cannot wholly satisfy Henry in *Heaven Can Wait*. Lubitsch seems to feel or at least to accept as his culture's basic ideal, that life's rewards are richest in the shared intimacy of an exclusive relationship. But this is checked by the recognition that, in practice, the all-embracing nature of the exclusive relationship sometimes, or often is too claustrophobic to satisfy the needs and cravings of husbands, wives and lovers. In Lubitsch's films this recognition is sometimes playful, even cynical, and sometimes melancholy (regretful of the gap between ideals and reality). The recognition of some people's needs for multiple relationships balances or rather unbalances the others' needs (often the same psyche's needs) for monogamy. The former are, however, far from being presented programmatically as a radical, universal solution to psychosexual problems arising from the conflict of a need to explore the unknown with an equally powerful drive towards exclusivity.

Though there is something to respect in Lubitsch's misanthrope's dedication to sexual honesty, it is also, as he practises it, absurd, and infected by a kind of emotional laziness in a man too 'busy' to get to know his partners. As he later aggressively declares: 'I hate overtures. Lovemaking is the red tape of marriage. It doesn't get you anywhere. I could take you out for three months and send you flowers and all that flapdoodle, and I wouldn't know any more about you than I do now.' More and more, his virtues are seen to be comically retarded and dehumanised by the armament of aggressive 'business' values in which he imprisons his inner self. Business and its attendant values are, not unnaturally, recurring concerns in Lubitsch's films, and in Hollywood comedy as a whole, reflecting more generally the ambivalence of a culture practically founded on business values but also holding ideals in conflict with those values. Lubitsch, both outsider–satirist–artist and insider–producer–businessman, feels, and gives expression to this ambivalence as much as any Hollywood film-maker. One pole of his approach may be seen in Max Plunkett in *Design For Living*, so much the slave of his advertising business that he is called by the other characters 'Plunkett Incorporated'. For all his determined chasing of Gilda he is really much less interested in her than in advertising, unable to attend to her as she leaves their marriage because he is talking to his client Mr Egelbauer on the phone. But, secondly and antithetically, criticism of the business ethic may be as muted as in the gentle *petit-bourgeois* celebration (a kind of nostalgia for Lubitsch's own origins) of 'Matuschek and Company' in *The Shop Around The Corner*. And in *That Uncertain Feeling* (which we have already noted as the most conventional of Lubitsch's films) the modern businessman (insurance executive), in Larry, is the hero, and the situation of *Design For Living*, where the 'Bohemians' defeated Plunkett, is reversed in Larry's defeat of the artist figure, Alexander Sebastian.

But in *Bluebeard* there is a view of capitalist activity producing a distorted individual, ossifying him to the degree that he becomes an epitome of the Bergsonian notion that comedy arises from inflexibility – 'A flexible vice may not be so easy to ridicule as a rigid virtue. It is rigidity that society eyes with suspicion.' Part of this inflexibility is his archaic attitude to women, an attitude shown in the film as pervasive, for on both sides of the Atlantic there is evidence that cultures both old and new find ways of keeping women down. For all its advanced civilisation, European society treats its women as chattels, property for barter in marriages of convenience, despite centuries of European literary works warning their readers or audiences aganst the dangers and injustices of such practice. In such unchanging circumstances only strong, wily women can escape their destiny, women such as Claudette Colbert's Nicole, using her sexuality self-consciously as the instrument through which she can achieve the equality she desires in marriage. As she launches her campaign for imposing her will on her as yet unreconstructed husband, Nicole personifies in comic terms Angela Carter's proposition that 'a free woman.in an unfree society will be a monster', a monster here of sexual abstinence and symbolic castration, though so graceful and witty a 'dark lady' that she delights as she transgresses.

In persevering with Michael's socio-sexual education, Nicole is Lubitsch's image of the feminist who has not given up on men by exclusively pursuing her own and her sisters' destinies, preferring instead the prospect of reconciliation on an equal footing in a world remade with no regard for hierarchies based on gender.

Beneath the businessman's carapace of values that has smothered him, Nicole recognises in Michael a lovable man with inner qualities of sensitivity, honesty and ruggedness that in more auspicous circumstances could produce a far more attractive partner than any she is liable to find in the genial, but ultimately tiresome and archaic European milieu to which she belongs. Albert's neighing pusillanimity (a beautiful use of David Niven's crisply supercilious qualities) makes him no rival at all of Michael's strength which, put to better uses, Nicole knows would be a thing to admire, not fear.

It is clear that Nicole, a modern woman contributing her own share of effort to the overthrow of patriarchy, seeks an equally modern partner, what Anaïs Nin calls the 'sensitive man'. Such a woman cannot be satisfied by crude male power, but neither will she be content with a castrated lackey like Albert whom she would only vilify and abandon, as Anthony Storr plausibly argues in *Human Aggression*: 'By irritating a man, making unreasonable demands and criticising, [a wowan] is really trying to evoke a dominant response by attacking him for his lack of virility. Her aggression is fulfilling a double purpose, both protecting against male dominance and, at the same time, demanding it . . .'. Storr's remark may seem outdated by the standards of modern feminist debate, particularly in his crude references to female demand for male dominance, but the point about male servility is worth preserving. The desire for a servile man can only be associated with feminists whose aim is invertedly to engross, rather than either dismantle or redistribute patriarchal power, and Nicole (a redistributor rather than a dismantler) isn't to be suspected of this.

In romantic comedy's most familiar way of imagining the reciprocal meeting of minds, the partners eventually partake of each other's worlds and as Michael, to please Nicole, learns some facts about Louis XIV, so she matches him by acquiring knowledge of how many cents oil has risen or fallen on the Stock Exchange. If, as the European, she is associated with art (his idea for the evening out is to go to a prize fight, hers to go to the Russian ballet), she can also tease its dullness by threatening him with that ominous dance programme consisting of 'Cupid and Psyche', 'A Toyshop in Old Moscow' and 'The Glow Worm's Birthday', and looks pleased by the closest he can come to *Lieder* or a love serenade – his surprising at-the-piano rendition of 'Looky, looky, looky, / Here comes Cooky'.

The matter of Nicole's growing interest in the Stock Exchange bears some examination. It is not just academic, or to please Michael, for by the end of the film (with the $100,000 from the divorce) she can buy up the sanctuary–asylum where he is sheltering. What should we think of this where elsewhere the film argues that the world of high finance is one of madness, turning normal people into imbeciles (e.g. one of the inmates of the asylum, who imagines he is a chicken after crashing on the market)? For a moment the film hovers over a profound question facing the critic of the patriarchal capitalist system. Does the gaining of true power consist in seizing equal power within that system or in dismantling it? Nicole and the film are too pragmatic to think other than the former. At least with her $100,000 (which we could read as a hyperbolic version of the famous £500 a year Virginia Woolf sought for the independent woman artist) she has financial independence, and the sense to use, and not be dominated by, business. Touching the question for a moment, Lubitsch's comedy, firmly anchored for better or worse in what is near at hand, then leaves it to be disagreed upon by the reformist and the revolutionary.

Michael's problem is less the usual Don Juan syndrome, even though he has been married seven times, than a confusion of love with business. As he says, 'love and business are just the same – you have to gamble, you have to take chances; only yesterday I took a chance with oil'. But the parallel has more than gambling to it, for, though as a self-respecting puritan he has to be in love to purchase his women, he runs through them like commodities, dispensing with them if they drop a point or two on the index for another rising stock. Stood up to by Nicole he can only play the part of Petruchio, trying to tame and turn a wild Kate into a Kate 'comfortable as other household Kates' ('cookies' in the Elizabethan pun). Of all the 'classics' he is given to read for relaxation, *The Taming of the Shrew* is the single one that seizes his attention, but only to engender identification at the crudest level with its hero.

Some literary works (Jacobean city comedy for example) make a causal link between business obsessions and sexual impotence, where the unnatural getting, spending and breeding of finance are punished by a bankrupting of the erotic drive. A less extreme and more plausible equation is dramatised in *Bluebeard* which underlines its interest in sexuality by an opening scene built around the joke about pyjama tops and bottoms. Michael will only purchase the tops because he says he never wears pyjama bottoms, a trait that clearly indicates his unimpaired virility. (The same allusion occurs in *One Hour With You* where Mitzi approvingly notes that André wears only the upper half.) Performance, then, in the crudest sense, is no problem for Michael, yet problems associated with the sexual keep him awake at night, his recurrent sleeplessness often referred to in the early part of the film. Obviously this is in part because he sleeps alone and his sexuality protests at it, but a complex piece of visual wit suggests more.

Nicole, as a cure for his sleeplessness, has recommended spelling 'Czecho-slovakia' backwards. However, tossing and turning in his newly bought pyjama top (the vibrant stripes of which Nicole has suggested rather than his choice of a conservative dark blue), he finds that it fails to work. Unsure of the spelling, he switches on the light to look at the large capitals he has written up on the mantelpiece. At one point, however, in the close-up of the word, our attention is wholly fixed on the letters 'CZECH'. Backwards it is meaningless, but read forwards it may suddenly overflow with meaning – (i) as in mid-European; (ii) as in balked or obstructed, or even as in 'checkmate'; (iii) through sound similarity, softening 'cz' to 'sh' or 'c', where it invokes sex and its lack; and finally (iv) as in 'cheque', the means by which Michael thinks he can obtain what he lacks, a significance underlined when Nicole says to here father 'that cheque' (Michael) 'is a down-payment on me'. That for a moment a pre-Godardian multi-levelled punning with graphics (think, for instance, of the way a 'DANGER' sign in *Une Femme Mariée* (1964), closed in by a camera shift, becomes 'ANGE') takes over the narrative is an instance of the cinematic awareness at work within the decorum of Lubitsch's Hollywood sound style, and reminds us of the formal experimentalism of the German comedies *Die Puppe* (1919) and *Die Bergkatze* (1921), still visible in the dance montage in *So This is Paris* (1926) and aspects of *The Student Prince of Old Heidelburg* (1927), which Lubitsch gradually dropped in favour of more discreet subtleties in tune with the dominant Hollywood sound style and approach to comedy. Interestingly the conceptual montage at the beginning of *Broken Lullaby*, which has the licence of melodrama, is more excessive and even confusing than anything in the comedies.

The cascade of puns draws attention to the great flaw in the potent man's deification of women in the pursuit of his sexual desire. Neither Nicole – a passionate heterosexual woman – nor Lubitsch, whose constant theme it is – is hostile to sex. What they define is that quality attacked by some radical feminist writers, such as Adrienne Rich (though obscured in the tendentious desire to brand heterosexual sex *per se* as violation), of treating women in and out of marriage as exploitable objects. 'Rapism' is a term that short-circuits too much thought to be used here, but behind it lies a protest at a phallic domination of female, and a misuse of male energies, particularly fostered and encouraged by business capitalism's ethic of domination and exploitation. The pattern and progress of the film is a comic ideal of one woman's resistance to this ethic and her comic breaking-down of her partner's commitment to it.

In the film's last scene, Nicole, her ex-husband in a straightjacket, confined as a lunatic, attacks Michael with a mixture of reason and sexual persuasion. Several times her father the Marquis (played with a typical nervous incapacity by Horton) intrudes, looks bewildered and says only the word 'nothing'. Again the word may signal possible different meanings: that he has nothing to say because the avaricious principle that he represents has been defeated by a true sexuality (he, it will be remembered, is the only male character in the film who sleeps in pyjama bottoms as well as tops); or that the fruits of her labour of love will eventually come to nothing. Uncertainty surrounds even the best relationships in Lubitsch's films, but the last scene gives at least present fulfilment. In a complicated image that fuses binding and chastening of aberrant masculinity with the release of renascent, redefined male power, Gary Cooper's legs are seen in close-up relaxing ('femininely') to Claudette Colbert's (agressively 'masculine') wooing. Then, suddenly, they tense and kick and he bounds to his feet, now in full shot, where, like Samson facing Delilah, he breaks the bonds of his straightjacket and moves, it may seem threateningly, towards her – only to fall, all aggression vanishing, into her arms. It is the pattern of romantic comedy to tell us, with Simone de Beauvoir, that 'the balanced couple is not a Utopian fantasy; such couples do exist, sometimes even within the frame of marriage . . . a combining of two whole, independent existences, not a retreat, an annexation, a flight, a remedy'. The film can't pretend to tell us how this – and the necessary equality in economic terms of the partners Engels proposed as essential – will materialise, but it presents an ambitious (also strained, farcical) image of it. 'If I take you now, you can be sure I love you', Nicole exclaims, 'I'm free, independent. We're on equal terms, Michael.'

'AS A MAN GROWS OLDER' – *HEAVEN CAN WAIT* (1943)

Yes, that's the trouble with mothers. First you get to like them and then they die.
— Marianne in *Trouble in Paradise*

No, no one can be old like that to himself in his feeling. No it must be always as grown and young men and women that we know ourselves and our friends in our feeling. We know it is not so, by our saying, but it must be so always to our feeling.
— Gertrude Stein, *The Making of Americans*

Where *Bluebeard* is up-to-date, brittle, farcical, openly if antically invoking matters of socio-sexual debate, *Heaven Can Wait* is backward-looking, nostalgic, so gentle in its humour that its significances may at first evade the observer. While the earlier work wittily feeds off *The Taming of the Shrew* and Perrault's grotesque fairy tale, the later glows with the tones of perennial popular sentiment, songs like 'By the Light of the Silvery Moon' (very much the film's theme tune) and 'The Sheik of Araby'. *Bluebeard* surprises by placing the primary insights and activity with the female (in the tradition of another Shakespearean comedy, *All's Well That Ends Well*), but *Heaven Can Wait* is very much male-centred, an emphasis compounded by a narrative form unique in Lubitsch's output – a subjective memoir, given wholly from the hero's viewpoint in the posthumous review of his life as the *histoire des amours* of 'a retired Casanova'.

Made within the vogue at the Fox studio for nostalgic Americana, *Heaven Can Wait* (also Lubitsch's first colour film) is as ornately elaborate in décor as its predecessors tend to be stylishly spare. The weightless whites and geometrics of Art Deco (an architectural echo of the characters' contemporaneity in modes and manners, something played on in the title taken from Coward, *Design for Living*), are replaced by the comfortable conservative beauties of Victorian and Edwardian interior design, lounges, libraries, conservatories laden with *objets d'art*, mock-classical pillars, wall niches holding portraits, lamps and vases prolific with flowers. Though the narrative travels from Henry's birth in the 1860s to his death in the 1930s, the New York greystone in which most of the action takes place shows changes only within the same comfortable oldfashioned style. As conspicuous consumers the van Cleves belong to the past even in their day. The fact that the ante-room to Hell in which the prologue takes place is highly modernistic in design underlines how little new styles, let alone events, impinge on the old New York family. Henry's narrative provocatively (though provocation isn't the well-mannered Henry's aim) neglects any mention, even in passing, of events such as the First World War or, despite the date 1932 being stressed, the Depression (which has its reflection in such films as *Trouble in Paradise*, *The Merry Widow* and *The Shop Around The Corner*). The realities of the business that is the source of Henry's family's wealth hardly get a mention, only a passing reference to its being an importing company founded by Grandfather van Cleve. The film's view of sexual relations may seem equally conservative, dominated not by the voices of the interacting couple but by one male voice from the leisure class, whose woman-centredness, while courteous and chivalric, sees the female in an extremely limited way, as sweet sexual creature on the one hand and maternal redemptress on the other. Women who fit neither pattern (the formidable Dr Blossom Franklin, writer of *How to Please Your Husband*, and the unattractive middle-aged nurse who enrages Henry by arousing him from a pleasurable dream on his death-bed) evoke wry horror. 'Well, it's all Martha, and only Martha', Henry says humbly, or smugly, in tribute to his wife's goodness, conversing with his mother on the tenth wedding anniversary.

Henry has more than his share of those strong libidinal drives which the best writers on Lubitsch have recognised in his characters, female as well as male. That last point, that Lubitsch is interested in and gives vivid expression to female desire (sometimes unconventional) in other films, is important, providing a perspective that helps to unravel the mixture of celebration and critical detachment at work in this film. Celebration of the hero's vitality and determination to pursue erotic happiness without too much guilt to the end of his days, but parallel to that – subsidiary but within – a more critical meditation on the social ideologies and restrictions that govern erotic experience.

Henry van Cleve narrates his history in the flashback structure popular in the 1940s, with the difference that his memoir is not only delivered post-humously, but to a sophisticated, large-mannered Satan (Laird Cregar). Having just died on his seventieth birthday, Henry (Don Ameche) introduces himself as an obvious candidate for Hell. *He presented himself where innumerable people had told him so often to go*, reads the opening title, thus introducing with a euphemism a film that structurally, visually and verbally takes euphemism and polite ellipsis as its basic tropes. Required to provide evidence of substantial sins, Henry is at a loss, but replies that at least he can 'safely say my life was one continuous misdemeanour'. Searching for a narrative focus, he decides 'perhaps the best way to tell you the story of my life is to tell you about the women in my life'.

So the narrative unfolds out of the framing device, its sections introduced by Henry's reminiscing overvoice, from infancy to old age and death; short scenes introducing Henry as baby and boy, followed by a sequence of longer episodes attached to the hero's birthdays – Henry at 15, at 26, at 50, at 60 and at 70 – and attached to them a series of women, first of all mother and grandmother, then a nursemaid and little girl neighbour, then Mam'selle who brings advanced sexual fashion from France to the puritan New World. A decade later he meets his wife (Gene Tierney), provincial heiress of the Strabels, Kansas meat packers, stealing her from her fiancé, cousin Albert. At which, with elliptical obliquity typical of the film, the narrative jumps to Henry's 36th birthday, and their 10th wedding anniversary, where he is left by Martha as a result of his infidelities. Henry and his Grandfather (Charles Coburn) persuade Martha to return from Kansas to New York. At 50 Henry uses his past experience to buy off a gold-digging chorus girl who has been involved with his son. At 60, now a widower, he seeks female comforts even younger than his son, now a conservatively married man. At 70 he dies, overexcited by the presence of a beautiful night nurse. The epilogue re-enfolds the narrative as Henry is judged by Satan who sends him not 'Down' but 'Up', to an annexe where we understand various young ladies, Grandfather and Martha (the last hushfully, almost idolatrously invoked as 'She' and the 'Dear One') will successfully intercede for him.

Though reviewing opinion (paralleling good audience figures) received the film favourably both in America and England, it was largely seen in those familiar terms of brilliant confectionery whipped up by the master chef. Bosley Crowther is typical, liking the film but concluding, 'This picture has utterly no significance. Indeed it has very little point, except to afford entertainment. And that it does quite well.' Lubitsch himself, in a letter written at the end of his life, gives some encouragement to this kind of view,

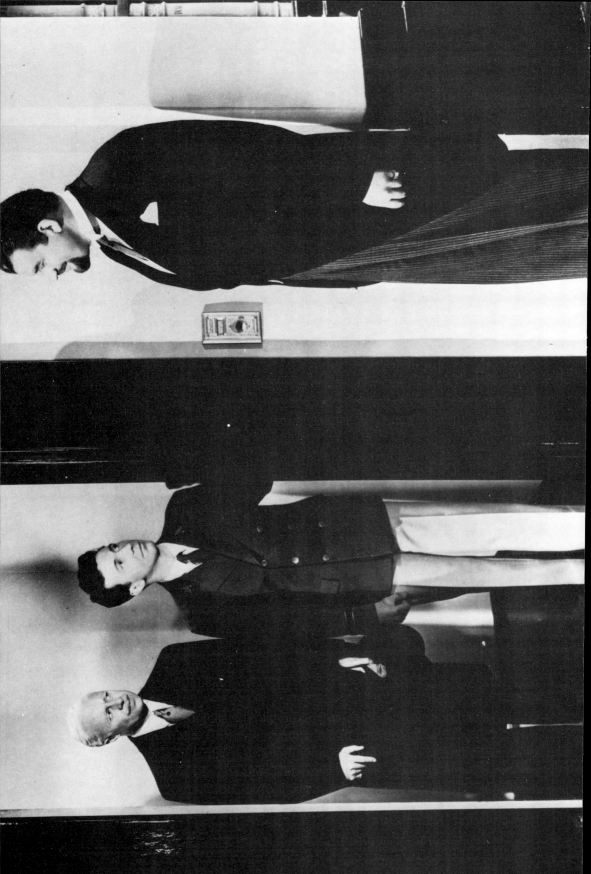

for though he says of *Heaven Can Wait*, 'I consider it to be one of my major productions, because I tried to break away in several respects from the established moving picture formula', he follows it up with a less than interesting definition of what those respects were, 'I encountered partly great resistance before I made this picture because it had no message and made no point whatsoever. The hero was a man only interested in good living with no aim of accomplishing anything or doing anthing noble . . .'. Clearly this begs any number of questions that the film politely, but on reflection, inevitably raises. What meanings, as distinct from the crassness of Front Office messages and points, are made? What attitudes does the film present towards a man who wishes to accomplish nothing or do anything noble? In what sense can such living be good? If the benign Devil is the audience's surrogate as judge, for what reason will they approve of his sentence?

The narrative of *Heaven Can Wait* is given through Henry but is not limited to Henry's account (as is the case in many sophisticated modern literary narratives in the first person, though fewer films). Henry, by his lights, is telling us and the Devil the truth. He is convinced that he deserves Hell, so his account is not to be deconstructed as a pack of lies, neither (as in Nabokov's *Despair*) does the teller reveal himself unwittingly as a fantasist, nor (as in Schnitzler's *Lieutenant Güstl*) as a monster of convention and prejudice. Rather, pervasive hints amidst a climate of sympathy reveal limitations in Henry's account, not disqualifying it as a version of experience, but placing it within a context that raises questions of which Henry is scarcely aware.

While techniques of implication rather than overt statement are of the essence of Lubitschean comedy, *Heaven Can Wait* takes them further than any of his films by applying them to the narrative stucture as a whole, to the extent that (though with its discreet charm it feels anything but radical, formally or otherwise) it is in many ways an advanced experiment in elliptical, implied narration. But manner here is not divorced from matter, for the narrative's euphemistic way of progressing – which lends it much of its charm but also makes it an object of suspicion – is quintessentially Henry's mode of telling, and that of his class and upbringing. The number of major events decorously omitted is startling. The deaths of Henry's father, mother, grand-father, Martha and Henry himself all take place off screen; and in the first three cases the event only becomes clear through a later passing reference

---

Heaven Can Wait
The way of all flesh. After a life in thrall to the libido, Henry (Don Ameche) sentences himself in death to the infernal company of His Excellency (Laird Cregar).

or simply from the character's absence from the scene. And equally, the
central matter of Henry's infidelities has no actual dramatisation, so that we
never see him coming out of a stage door with a Follies girl on his arm, or
champagning a debutante, let alone entering a boudoir. No scene shows
Martha's learning of his infidelity; the information is only relayed to the
audience through such means as Grandfather's comments, Peggy Nash's
remarks to Henry about his reputation, and Martha's comments on two
occasions, first in Kansas after she has left Henry, and then much later as
she reminisces about the moment in middle age when his growing stomach
made her realise that her 'little Casanova' was hers alone. 'But you didn't
want to make me uncomfortable, even for one second', she says on the first
occasion, pre-empting Henry's predictable excuse, and we may apply her
remark to Henry's telling of his story as a whole, for his well-mannered
recounting which spares the audience any discomfort (we remember Peggy
Nash's mock complaint at the forthrightness of her modern admirers – 'How
crude! How crude!') spares him, truthful though he is, from articulating
anything too gross. Also, all but hidden in Henry's account is the source of
his financial independence in the family firm which (we glancingly learn) is
mainly run by other male members of the family, Grandfather, Rudolph,
Henry's father, and Jack, his son. Telling his mother about first meeting
Martha, he surprises her by suggesting that he will get a job, but later
evidence suggests his place and salary in the firm are purely honorary. Such
ironies as his finding mundane commercial and professional metaphors to
express his love for Martha, as in 'If you'd walked into a restaurant I would
have become a waiter; if you'd walked into a burning building I would have
become a fireman', and his taking on the role of a bookseller in Brentano's
for a moment in order to court Martha, escape him. In three consecutive
early middle sequences there is an establishing shot of Fifth Avenue with
the van Cleve house and an overvoice commentary linking Henry's life with
the changing face of the city. But what has been strongly established as a
recurring symmetry then drops away from the film, suggesting that the
privileged Henry's reality is becoming more and more interiorised. The
various sources of Henry's freedom to live a life so materially and erotically
sweet that, in one of the senses the title gives rise to, Heaven can indeed
wait, are typically concealed from him, but not quite from the viewer.

Henry's narrative of his life begins with an old-fashioned novel's complete-
ness in his babyhood. But biographical totality, or the 'kidded clichés' James
Agee responded to, are not the only logic here. For the child is posited as
father to the man in two ways: firstly in the narrator's wit in pointing to his
future in the sight of women (mother and grandmother) already fighting

over him, and an early lesson that women may falsely cajole when the nurse-maid who, in front of the family, calls him 'honeybunch', calls him 'you nasty little brat' as he interrupts her courting in the park, and secondly in lingering close-ups at the end of each episode. These close-ups are of 'His Majesty the Baby' in crib and carriage, expressing in the first case narcissistic satisfaction, in the second a tantrum of rejected rage. 'His Majesty the Baby', it may be remembered, was the title of an English cartoon that amused Freud and which he quoted when writing on infantile narcissim, in which a baby, being pushed in a pram, causes the traffic to halt in a busy street. These close-ups of the infantile Majesty (who at 50 is to be associated with another absolute Monarch, 'The Sheik of Araby', via the Follies spectacle featuring Peggy Nash) begin a chain of allusions, grounded in Don Ameche's softly bewildered charm, that establish Henry as a perpetual child throughout his life. For instance, the 26th and 60th birthday episodes echo each other closely, despite the protagonist's being in one a young man and in the other approaching old age. In the first, the playboy son, returning after a night out, suffers his mother's gentle rebukes and then cajoles $100 from her which she has already (as if leaving her little child the gift of the tooth fairy) left under his pillow. In the second, dressed in much the same night-clubbing gear as 34 years before, a white-haired Henry creeps in in the morning, the father as errant son pursuing a second adolescence, to be paternalistically upbraided by his son Jack, reversed into the role of stern but finally indulgent patriarch. Before this we have just heard Jack's secretary telling him that the old man has been writing to the Board of Governors asking for a raise in his salary. The repetition of situation shows him to be incorrigible.

Henry's initiation into the moral philosophy of a new permissive age ('Kiss is like candy. You eat candy only for the beautiful taste and this is enough reason to eat candy') comes through the agency of an older woman, the vivacious Mam'selle, engaged by his mother as his French tutor. Her status as a mixture of sex object and mother-figure underlined by the way she addresses the adolescent young master as 'little boy' and 'little fellow' and (to his mother) 'your babee'. Aware of this chain of meaning, we may also recall that when, in the prologue, Henry meets one of his old lovers, Edna Craig, they remember Marmaduke Harrison's fancy dress party where all the guests went dressed as children, Henry as Little Lord Fauntleroy! Henry's death, in the company of Nellie Brown is a final variation on the theme, not just in the involuntary infantilism attendant upon old age, but in the mordant wit of a death at the hands of a voluptuous night nurse (sex object *and* ministering angel) who pops a thermometer in his mouth, like a mother attending her sick little boy, and even recalling the primary erotics of a more basic nurturing. Thus there may be more than appears on the surface in the circumstances of the first meeting between Henry and Martha Strabel in Wanamaker's where, as Henry relates it, 'Here was a girl lying to her mother. Naturally that interested me at once.' The lying phone call excites him because it suggests a girl available for amorous adventure, but we may also feel that Henry is unconsciously interested in a girl who lies to her mother precisely because Martha's action parallels his own situation of lying to *his* mother, evading her authority in his transgressions with younger women, yet ultimately dependent on her love and forgiveness. Eluding her own mother, the formidable Mrs Strabel (Majorie Main), Martha is, ironically, destined to become less Henry's *dis*placement of his mother than her *re*placement, at first the sole object of his desire, but then lied to in his many unseen amours, while at the same time endlessly available for forgiveness, eternal understanding and indulgence.

Particularly interesting in this light is the conversation where Henry (trying to persuade her to come back from Kansas to their marriage in New York) plays quite consciously upon a governing element of their relationships. He tells Martha how their son has got himself into trouble by giving ice-cream promised to one little girl to another, extracting from Martha (Martha/Mother, almost a homonym) laughter at 'the stories' 'the little devil' has told to get himself out of the impasse. As it dawns upon her that her husband has tricked her again, she can't deny her fond, familiar response to him, and the relationship resumes its old course.

From Henry's point of view Martha is the perfect woman, the 'angel' (again!) he apostrophises when he proposes – 'charming', 'young', 'beautiful', 'adorable' – swearing to make her happy and hold her in his arms forever. Only once do we have an overt glimpse of a disjunction between Henry's view of their marriage (corroborated by Martha late in the film when, near her death, she tells Henry she is 'the happiest woman in the world') and any other, when she leaves him on their 10th anniversary. But this gap is rapidly closed and elsewhere we tend to see her in her appointed role, charming, tolerantly superior to Henry's deceits and foibles, and apparently contentedly habituated to it. Of all Lubitsch's heroines she is the most passive and conventional – indeed she is the only one who could at all be described in such terms. The active, combative intelligence of Sonia (in *The Merry Widow*) or Gilda or Lily is held in check, all but concealed in propriety, so that it is only many years after the event that she tells Henry that she was an active, passionate agent in their courtship, not the frightened *ingénue* he presumed.

The film's most subversive viewing of her is through the submerged but reiterated parallelism it makes between her and the famous other Strabel offspring, Mabel the Cow, heroine of the advertising jingle that runs:

> To the world my name is Mabel,
> You may see me on the label,
> I was packed by E. F. Strabel
> For the pleasure of your table.

The opening and closing shots of the section of the film based on Martha's return home dwell on the bovine icon. Furthermore, as the trio escape for New York, Grandfather triumphantly recites

> And so farewell, dear E. F. Strabel,
> We'll take Martha, you keep Mabel!

itself a variation on the variation of ten years earlier:

> She was packed by E. F. Strabel
> To be served at Albert's table,
> But that Henry changed the label . . .

'That's poetry!' he adds, the transfer from dull Albert to attractive Henry elevating the base jingle. But though one part of the Martha/Mother equation made here is laughingly incongruous, posing Martha's grace against Mabel's lumpish image, it is also readable in more subversive terms. Following an equation of female flesh and meat active in works as far apart as Middleton's Jacobean comedy, *A Chaste Maid in Cheapside*, and the recent film thriller, *Prime Cut* (1972), both are slaughtered, packed and labelled to grace the tables of the metropoles, while celebrated in sentimental images.

And yet Henry is so charming we cannot quite end there. The duality and difficulty of the film is that in at least two (compromised but very real) senses he *is* presented as a hero, his childishness as a virtue as well as an obvious vice. We have already briefly suggested his status as a hero of the senses and cultivated pleasure, high values in all Lubitsch's romantic comedies. Such values are kept more or less in tension with the social and moral interests of the films. If Henry in his elegant way is self-centred, then so are all of Lubitsch's heroes, and heroines too, the vital women as much as the fascinating men, without distinction of gender. If we do not accept that as the way of the world, the films accuse us of a utopian sentimentality in the sphere of human relations. Devotion to self, commitment to interior fantasies and desires, precede commitment to others in any world that the films are cognisant of. As we recognise that, we see Henry in one light, and as our gaze shifts to the demands of the social order, we see him in another.

Further, Henry's refusal to accept the withering of desire into the proper behaviour of old age, though it compromises him and makes him in obvious respects ridiculous, also makes him the bearer of the poignant insights alluded to in the epigraph from Gertrude Stein. This is especially dramatised in the photo taken on Henry's 60th birthday where he is surrounded by hundreds of years of antiquity in his older relations. If on the one hand (the social, the responsible and, in this case, the feminist) we see Henry's devotion to the fulfilment of his desire as immature, unreasonable and dependent on the subservience of women, on the other we see why Lubitsch indulgently allows him to die, if not in the odour of sanctity, at least to the strains of 'The Merry Widow Waltz', full of positive connotations from an earlier film.

Within the framework of the society portrayed in the film and the (almost exclusively male) choices of contrasts it offers, Henry's (flawed) superiority is not hard to find. His father Randolph, his son Jack, and above all his cousin Albert (from whom he rescues Martha) are all products of a puritan business ethic from which all trace of sensuous pleasure has been expunged. Henry's father, as his mother unwittingly discloses, has certainly never had 'a spark', while Jack, after a short run in his father's footsteps chasing Follies girls, now hardly has time to eat his breakfast, owing to business preoccupations. Albert (whom Henry calls 'a neutral subject') is prissy, pompous, industrious without passion and, as corporation legal advisor, the standard-bearer of an anti-sensuous law. E. F. Strabel (Eugene Pallette), the Kansas patriarch, and his wife sit at the distant ends of the Sunday breakfast table, like a mid-western version of Orchardson's painting of the desolation of Victorian wedlock, *Mariage de Convenance*, conducting their quarrel over who should have the newspaper comics through the butler.

Grandpa's role in the film (one of Charles Coburn's most memorable) shifts between criticism and celebration of Henry, but largely expresses love for him. The founding father of the business dynasty, Grandfather is conscious of what he has lost through his devotion to industry. Convivial but lonely, he often sits or stands apart from groups, something of an alien in his own social matrix. He openly expressses his unforced love for Henry (in contrast, both his son and Albert must make do with brusque recognition, a gesture purely to family obligation) and does not hide his fantasy-investment in Henry as a surrogate self that has not placed business above Eros, though ironically, it is only business that has made possible his nephew's flagrantly unindustrious lifestyle. His flamboyant baiting of the beef-baron Strabels at Henry's 26th birthday gathering seems as much flaying of himself as of that pair. Freed from responsibility, he can act like a gleeful child (though he is enough of the patriarch to order Mam'selle to go), pouring water over Albert and acting out his fantasies of a fuller life by speeding Henry on his honeymoon and helping the re-elopement from Kansas. In the other characters such positive suggestions of childishness take stunted or negative forms – E. F. Strabel's desire to know the fate of the Captain, stuck in a barrel in the *Katzenjammer Kids* (echoing Michael Brandon's sending of a cable to America to find out whether Flash Gordon has escaped a burning submarine), and Henry's father's infantile lack of knowledge of sexual and social realities which provoke Grandfather's outburst to the 43-year-old, 'Well, I think you are definitely old enough to be told the facts of life . . . I'll have to shatter your illusions, Randolph, my son, there is no Santa Claus.'

In some senses Henry never learns of the non-existence of Santa Claus. Early in the film he jokingly recounts his introduction to the economic laws governing the distribution of female sexuality, when the little girl demands not one but two beetles before allowing him to walk with her. 'If you want to win a girl you have to have lots of beetles.' As Henry phrases it from his posthumous vantage point, he does not seem to have progressed beyond the boy's conclusion that the girl's demand comes from the settled nature of girl/woman who has something to sell (though typically, charmingly, he finds a pleasant euphemism) and will get the best return for it she possibly can. In Henry's and his culture's scheme of things the female is illusorily seen as an equal, indeed superior party in the bartering game of sex, since she possesses the femininity men seek and pay for. This condition – in reality not a 'free market' at all – is hidden in the love match Martha makes with Henry, but its reality can surface, as for instance in Henry's crass attempt to win her back with a $10,000 bracelet, just after she has told him of her discovery of a receipt for a $500 one (presumably given to one of Henry's mistresses). His interview with Peggy Nash, the chorus girl who has been seeing his son, is full of related ironies, for this hard-bitten, cheating veteran of the extra-marital world of the Follies and Scandals really exposes the myth of the *süsser Mädel* in her American or any other inflection. Peggy Nash may be more openly grasping than the girls of Henry's youth, but she is really no different in essentials, swapping her assets, while they are still able to be traded, for beetles. In this society Henry's sexual freedom is bought at the expense of others both inside and outside his marriage, though a wily campaigner like Peggy can do very well from the status quo.

The Devil, listening, forgives Henry, perhaps taking the view that on the one hand his sins of commission and omission are the sins of a patriarchal structure rather than those of an individual, and on the other that he has virtues which partly redeem him. There is room for caution here. 'Who is the Devil to forgive anyone?', one might ask, but even audiences steeped in the theologies of sexual politics might absolve Henry from perpetual damnation. In the film only the bustling Edna Craig, battle axe of cocktail parties, is trapdoored to Hell by His Excellency. Satan – himself a once youthful, dashing rebel – very naturally sympathises with Henry's plight, recognises the young spirit in an old body, or as Mam'selle puts it, the soul too big for his pants, but is unable to indulge the same when an old woman shows her knees, an action which draws from him a distasteful look and comment, 'Some things are better left to memory.' Yet as Henry makes his way out of Hell we suspect that even the Devil may not have appreciated all the nuances of his confession.

3
'Joking apart'

Three comedians
Bob Hope
Mae West
and Woody Allen

BOB HOPE

Performer and persona

Like many major creations of popular art the Bob Hope persona tends to be under-read even where it is most applauded, an effect of the widespread prejudice that resents the analysis of the popular and, above all, the comic. Doubtless another contributory cause is a three-way confusion between the cinematic mask, the persona of the extra-filmic entertainer, and what we think of as knowledge of the man himself – a failure to recognise that the Hope character on film is twice removed from the real-life figure, once from the stage, radio and TV comic, US troop entertainer, chat show perennial, charity worker and golf tournament sponsor. Such distinctions are especially important since we claim the cinematic persona is significantly more subtle and even subversive than that of the famous extra-filmic entertainer, so that the two – though they share many traits – should not be confused. In reality the ageing off-screen celebrity has increasingly tended to stitch his gags around a series of predictable jibes against right-wing targets of ridicule that have embarrassed many of his once more committed devotees: outraging Thais with jokes* about their big feet in 1972, scoring the weakest points

---

* For the sake of economy throughout the three essays on Hope, West and Allen the term 'joke' is used, though in some instances comic saying or humour might be the more accurate category, if we follow Freud.

off protesting feminists at a Miss World contest, or, in 1971 as Richard West reported in the *New Statesman*, getting laughs at homosexuals in front of GIs in Vietnam:

> The jokes and the display of girls are meant to remind the soldiers that they are red-blooded, virile, heterosexual, 100 per cent Americans whose only desire is to get back home and bed down a fine big-busted American girl. But don't they know that already? This audience did not want or need assurances of its virility. There was a frozen, even embarrassed silence at two Hope jokes against homosexuals . . .

As is the case with another great actor of a very different kind but of rather similar political views, John Wayne, there is a temptation for any critic to the left of Ronald Reagan to simplify his art out of a dislike of his political tendencies. An image from Coppola's *Apocalypse Now* (1979), of the flamboyant grotesquerie of a troop entertainment in the Vietnamese jungle, parading Playboy bunnies (though the frenetic younger compère is not in the same league with Hope even at his weakest and most reactionary), might seem to justify such a prejudice. But we have only to remember the old adage to trust the tale and not the teller or, in this case, the joke and not the joker, to take the point that the artistic product may speak with a more complex voice than the most overt ideology of its speaker. It may seem a long way from Balzac to Bob Hope, but it is relevant to recall Georg Lukács's exemplary examination (via Engels) of the way that, in the former's novels, a radical analysis contradicts its maker's known social attitudes.

We may note, too, that when in interviews and profiles the persona is described and defined by its inventors the descriptions tend towards the obvious. Hope thinks of the character as 'full of lust and never getting the girl', and in terms of the continual put-down of the hero's 'big front'. The most inventive of his directors, Frank Tashlin (a writer on *The Paleface*, director of *Son of Paleface*), emphasises the character's bragadoccio, but also points to his incorrigible resilience, detecting a curious resemblance between him and another star: 'There is a startling similarity between Bob Hope and Donald Duck. Both became immensely popular during World War II. Both were braggers who backed down in a pinch but somehow prevailed.'

Such definitions are adequate up to a point, emphasising as they do major facets of the persona that will be taken up below, but on the whole they state the obvious without illuminating it. It is as if the makers are too close, too familiar with their work to be able to articulate (perhaps even to recognise) its more subversive resonances. It is not too surprising that Hope in interview skates over the surface, though we might have expected Tashlin to indicate more of the perverse and even disturbing elements he so brilliantly develops in his films, since his work – particularly the use of Jayne Mansfield – is drawn to such areas.

Coward, braggart, survivor – we can clearly see the lineaments of Shakespeare's Parolles and Falstaff in contemporary form – but whatever the anti-heroic shallows of the parts he plays ('Men run in my family'), Bob Hope is always, if no other kind, a linguistic hero, fast and accurate on the draw for release of pleasure from verbal wit. His films, like his stage, radio and TV acts, are driven by a perpetual motion of wisecracking. Often this is, to use Freud's teminology, predominantly 'innocent', a play with words for its own sake, without giving rise to 'tendentious' sexual or aggressive meanings, or indeed much that approaches paraphrasable thought. A typical instance might be the moment in *The Road to Morocco* (1942), where, banishing his side-kick Bing Crosby from his presence, he says with that typical bland insolence and self-satisfaction that marks his delivery, 'I don't dally much with riff-raff these days, and he's a pretty raffy type of a Riff.' Inspecting this we find that the pleasure produced – incidentally fulfilling one of Freud's descriptions of the major joke techniques in being based on the economic double use of a single word, 'multiple use of the same material as a whole and in parts' – comes from the playful fabrication of an etymology for 'riff-raff', made by breaking it up into constituent parts, a 'raffy' (raffish?) 'Riff' (kind of Arab as in *The Desert Song*), with the extra bonus of the musical meaning of 'riff' cleverly attracting itself to the crooner Crosby. Ultimately the joke is a means of aggression since it exalts Hope and puts Crosby down, but some large part of the effect comes from the release of a sophisticated form of childish word play, regardless of the temporary end it serves. A second joke, again of the predominantly 'innocent' type, illustrates further related apects of Hope's joke-making art – Hope being here defined as the film persona created by the comedian and his various writers and directors, Elliot Nugent, Don Hartman, Frank Butler, David Butler, Melvin Frank and others. In *The Princess and the Pirate* (1944), a sinister thug intones (of someone who has just been murdered), 'this unfortunate dog has done a very bad thing. He has cast his shadow upon him.' Hope replies, 'Bad casting, Huh?' which, while allowing him that typical exclamation ('Huh?') of breathy, cockily aggressive paralinguistic superiority, pivots on the double meaning in 'casting', of both throwing and picking for a part in a film. The joke conflates two characteristic Hope techniques, anachronism and meta-cinematic/theatrical reference: the first, overturning grandeur, gravity or the exotic by couching it in slang or local contemporary terms; the second, disrupting the homogeneous narrative by exposing and joking about the conditions of its making. Hope's films overflow with both techniques. In

of comedy in the extract quoted. Briefly, though, we might note the following as central. Replies 1, 2 and 4 employ the deflationary anachronism that we have already underlined (while 1 and 4 have elements of the meta-cinematic/theatrical features also referred to). Replies 1, 4 and 5 are primarily based on Sylvester's boasting about his sexual interests and appetite. Reply 3 hinges on Sylvester's unwitting exposure of his own ignorance, for in spite of his know-all air he fails to grasp the meaning of 'accoutrements', but it also has a sexual drift since, given a libidinous nudge, 'accoutrements' can suggest sexual equipment. Reply 2 exposes – very interestingly – a strong suggestion of fear of being branded effeminate or homosexual, while 5 is an involuntary admission of sexual inadequacy that contradicts the previous boasting (he is apparently used to chickens fighting back, i.e. girls refusing his advances). Reply 2 also highlights one of the absolutely central aspects of the Hope persona, his indefatigable, massive and inalienable narcissism (for here, with more understatement than usual, he simply refrains from negating the governor's mock compliment to his beauty, in a way not dissimilar to Mae West). And the whole sequence is suffused with comedy emanating from Sylvester's self-confidence in a situation that is, unbeknown to him but known to the audience, a threatening one, a situation that promises to enact that typical comic *peripeteia* of the Hope films, for which we as audience wait expectantly, the disintegration of the jaunty façade and the revelation of his cowardice, followed by the undaunted reassertion of his complacency.

We shall develop the various elements discovered here a little later on, but at this juncture pick up an earlier point, the pervasiveness in Hope's comedy of meta-cinematic/theatrical transgressions of illusion. In fact the greater part of the very small amount of serious analysis of Hope has concentrated on this area, defining a particular filmic mode of 'comedian comedy' (Steve Seidman) which exploits a pre-established (vaudeville, radio or TV, or all three in Hope's case) comic performer wholly identified by the audience as comedian rather than as actor. Both 'play' a character, but we might say that while the actor tends towards the dissolution of him or herself within the part played, the comedian pays much less attention to such rules, since the display of the comic persona takes precedence over everything else. In this mode the character in the film flagrantly retains the theatrical stand-up comic's relationship with the audience, not wholly subjugated like the other characters in the story to the rules of ordinary narrative coherence, but able to address the audience directly, to make jokes about the conventions of films and film-making, to refer openly to other films and performers, to attempt (unsuccessfully) to persuade the audience to accept a substitute ending as Hope does in *Casanova's Big Night* (1954).

Crudely speaking, then, the protagonist here is a double character, half anchored in the narrative world (as 'Painless' Potter in *The Paleface* (1948), say), but half over and above it (as the comedian Bob Hope, expected to produce jokes in a ceaseless flow irrespective of the rules of narrative and psychological probability). This is something quite different from our apprehension of the usual kind of performance in a comedy, for instance any one of Cary Grant's, discussed elsewhere in this book. There part of our response is certainly to the star who exists beyond and in a certain sense overrides the particular character he plays. But the difference is, firstly, that this is wholly implicit, readable but not underlined, since the shell of characterisation is never broken by the film articulating it (or if it is – as when in *The Front Page* Grant makes a reference to Archie Leach, or Ralph Bellamy – only glancingly and exceptionally, as it were, subliminally) and, secondly, because he is usually the victim of the comic situation, only rarely the conscious joke-maker, and then always 'in character'. That is, if he does tell a joke it is told either to another character or to the self, not delivered straight to the audience in the mode of the stand-up comedian.

For anyone else to usurp the comedian's privilege and tell a joke is to infringe the rules of the mode and (Crosby as co-hero apart) there are few exceptions in the Hope films. One occurs in *The Princess and the Pirate* when during the quick-change act in front of a literally dangerous audience, Sylvester imitates very badly an old man, quaveringly declaring that he has 'seen much of life'. An aggressive patron shoots at him, quipping, in a modification of Al Jolson's boast, 'You ain't seen nothin' yet!', a transgressive play of wit which depends on the audience's apprehension of the rules of the game as outlined above. In this instance the rule-breaking has the comic justification that Sylvester's act is so atrocious that the comedy has to be provided by the audience, reminding us of another running constituent of the Hope persona, references to the fabled bathos of his act, references which are appreciated only within the context of an acknowledgement that only the very good can play at being very bad. (A splendid example of this is found in *The Cat and the Canary*, 1939, in the quip about not being afraid of big empty houses, because he has played on the vaudeville circuit.)

Such conventions operate in much the greater part of the output of films in Hope's long cinema career, stretching from *The Big Broadcast of 1938* to the 1972 *Cancel My Reservation*, a career both preceded and succeeded by his longer activity as an entertainer. After early tentative experimentation a basic mode and character were established, broken only very rarely and then only partially, as in the conventional Biopic *Beau James* (1957), based on the life of Jimmy Walker, the mayor of New York, though even here a consistency of another kind can be found in the hint of narcissism in the title, and Walker, the politician as songwriter and quipping entertainer, is in the end a pseudo-Hope rather than the other way around.

This effect of duplicity created by conventions which hold together both the off-screen comedian and the fictive characters ensures that the operation of comedy is never simply that we laugh at the deficiencies of the Hope character as we laugh at the witless fops of Restoration comedy or dullards in more modern works, such as Edward Everett Horton in many of his doltish film roles. To adapt to Hope a statement William Paul makes of another great comedian, Jack Benny, he is an *alazon* who is also his own *eiron*, both gull and ironist, exposed and exposer. Thus, if 'Painless' Potter is the object of ridicule, he is also the knowing director of the comic effect both on himself and others, not a naïve character in the simplest country bumpkin sense but a naïve puppet presented by a ventriloquist who is himself far from naïve. When (to take a simple example from hundreds) the newly married 'Painless' is asked by the hotel clerk if he wants 'a boy' (meaning someone to take his belongings to the bridal suite upstairs), he misinterprets it as a question asking whether he wants to produce a son, an act which must involve sexual intercourse. His response is a bravura exhibition of the semiotics of bashful lust, but, as ever, in a kind of quotation marks, for though our laughter is directed *at* a character whose libidinousness is so puritanically socialised that he confuses sexuality with reproduction, we also laugh *with* the worldy-wise intelligence that denies the automatic connection between the two. (Probably, too, considering the homoerotic element lurking in some of Hope's jokes, part of 'Painless' interprets the joke even more scandalously.)

In moving to analyse in greater detail the content of Hope's comedy below, we contend that there is a radical tendency in his comedy or, it would be more accurate to say, a tendency – regardless of the star's political and politico-sexual views – to make comedy out of the material of problematics attached to gender divisions and sexual roles which has radical potentialities. There is nothing programmatic in Hope's play with them. Indeed, the comedian's intuition is, we feel, as unanalytic as it is profound in searching out his comedy. And, as we would expect of a hugely popular star, the most successful comedian in the history of the sound cinema (listed by Pirie as the top box-office star of the years 1941-45, second in 1946-50, fifth in 1951-55), the persona and the films featuring it combine subversion with conservatism, allowing his appeal to cut across all kinds of political, gender and class demarcations. Thus Hope as a comedian is simultaneously and paradoxically on the one hand safe and likeable, and on the other disruptive and perverse. His film persona has far more of the latter than his off-screen roles and the comic narratives into which he is placed may be divided into those which allow the subversive elements more play (e.g. the two *Paleface* films, some of the *Road* films, *The Princess and the Pirate*, and those that allow it less by emphasising conventionalities). Musical numbers (for Hope has the skills of a song and dance man) often become a focal point for conventional sentiment and affirmation of mainstream 'American' institutions. 'Our cheque-book is minus /But when our arms entwine us / Gee, lucky us', he sings in *The Great Lover* (1949) and the Christmassy titles in *The Lemon Drop Kid* (1951), 'Silver Bells' and 'It Doesn't Cost a Dime to Dream', speak for themselves.

By contrast, the Tashlin films censor the sentimental and romantic potential of Hope's musical numbers. The best known of them, 'Buttons and Bows' from *Paleface*, winner of the song Oscar in 1948, may have the lilt of a love song, but is primarily a *tour de force* of foppery and fetishism: 'East is East and West is West / And the wrong one I have chose / Let's go where you'll keep on wearing / Those frills and flowers and buttons and bows / Rings and things and buttons and bows!'. Another indication of the tensions between radical and conservative elements in his material and narrative situations is the degree of conventionality in the closure of the hero's sexual relationships, for whereas in *The Lemon Drop Kid* and *They Got Me Covered* (1942) he has a long-suffering girlfriend waiting for him, and in *The Great Lover* will marry the Duchess, in *The Princess and the Pirate* he loses Virginia Mayo to Bing Crosby and the improbable marriages to Jane Russell at the end of both of the *Paleface* films are undermined by gags. *Son of Paleface* is also an example of the way the narrative's conventional drift towards the assertion of a moral principle in the hero can be subverted even as it is stated, since Junior's conversion to selflessness and heroism, the result of being instructed by his father's ghost, has its source in his father's assurances that death and Hell have compensatory pleasures – she-devils with Southern accents – and are therefore to be embraced rather than avoided by the heroic hedonist.

Heroic masculinity

That's not me folks, I play the coward   — Sylvester in *The Princess and the Pirate*

The recurring narrative of Hope's films sets down the inveterate coward and dandy, the corrupt innocent crassly crossing the ambitions of a Horatio Alger and Hugh Hefner, in an environment that would be testing for an authentic hero, and is potentially disastrous for one who is nothing of the kind. The backdrop varies place and circumstances but is constant in its test and dangers. In *The Lemon Drop Kid* (1951), it is the minatory world of the mob. In *They Got Me Covered* (1942) Nazi espionage threatens. *The Princess and the Pirate* (1944) takes place in the sadistic world of the buccaneer. *The Cat and the Canary* (1939) takes place in the 'old dark house' of the Horror film. In *Casanova's Big Night* (1954), Hope as Pipo Pippelino is required to impersonate not only the world's greatest lover but also the greatest duellist in Europe.

And in *The Paleface* (1948), the setting forced on the effete Easterner is the violent Western frontier. This generic anti-hero character is perhaps most perfectly moulded in 'Painless' Peter Potter in *The Paleface* whose answer to a tendentious question is to seek definition in an unusual third category: 'I'm not a mouse and I'm not a man, I'm a dentist.' As quack dentist it is as if the required, culturally sanctioned sadism and aggression of the warrior have been diverted into the inept oral torturings we see him practising at the beginning of the film, practised moreover in an adjunct to a ladies' bathhouse, so that we immediately meet him in a woman's sanctum rather than in an environment belonging to the male group, the opposite of the 'long-house' world of the warrior. We might remember too that both Freud and Otto Rank suggested unconscious equations in *The Interpretation of Dreams* between dreams of tooth-pulling and auto-eroticism. If 'Painless' signifies Potter's inability to direct aggression on the outside world as demanded by society's interpretation of the male role, the epithet is also attached to his Christian name which in its conventional symbolism suggests rockiness or sturdiness, but which in its slang usage denotes the male member, so that (with sexual prowess linked to an aggressive concept of masculinity) the phallus is an inept weapon, 'painless' in the sense of un-aggressive, not giving hurt, and unable to conquer.

We hardly need to consult exhaustively such compendia of the heroic – whether in semi-divine or purely human manifestations – as Joseph Campbell's *The Hero with a Thousand Faces*, Jung's *Man and His Symbols*, or C. M. Bowra's *Heroic Poetry*, to take the force of the Hope character's dissolute burlesque of cultural archetypes. What property of the noble man of action and his quest remains intact in him? Where the traditional hero stoically accepts his often youthful death, Hope, in *Son of Paleface* (1952), cries to Jane Russell when under fire, 'Let me in, you're too young to be a widow.' Note the typical self-aggrandising switch of emphasis in his state-ment (she will miss his life even more than he will). The epic hero's great skill with weaponry is reversed. In *The Paleface* 'Painless', who, as ever, is blissfully confident of his abilities until they are put to the test, imitates the most surface and most flashy skills of the gunfighter by ritually twirling his six-shooters, only to jam his trigger finger humiliatingly. In Hope the classic hero's characteristic 'dunamis' (force, dynamism), loyalty, integrity and 'centredness' (Bowra's term for his essential selfhood) collapse. The narrative of the films in its presentation, ultimately, of the anti-hero as hero, the schmuck as survivor, often has a penultimate motion that more or less half-heartedly pushes him towards moral conformity and the discovery of hidden courage. But the Hope of the main part of the text contradicts this, though it may be that the carnival dissolution is dependent for wholesale audience approval on the safety-net ideal that a bedrock of conventional virtue can be discovered underneath it all. (The huge popularity of Hope in the years of the Second World War, when audiences must have sought release from the stern ethos of war and yet found dramatisations of the anti-heroic tolerable only to a certain point, argues this.) Essentially Hope is loyal to no one but himself. Rather than stand and declare himself, he is always on the run, evading capture through loss of identity in protean if inept disguise. The epic hero's dominating presence is a physical embodiment of his inner qualities. Hope's physical appearance, which, as we shall see, is a problem raising complicated questions, typically provokes only derision. An ingenious piece of comedy is built into Junior Potter's entry into the narrative in *Son of Paleface*, where instead of arriving like the traditional Westerner on horseback (like Alan Ladd in *Shane*, 1953), he drives up in a primitive automobile. Before the car appears there is a burst of explosions on the soundtrack, suggesting gunfire let off by a stranger heralding his deadly approach. But *visual* evidence redefines *aural* evidence and shows it only to be the vehicle sarcastically backfiring. In *The Paleface*, 'Painless', spuriously thought to be an Indian fighter, swaps his Eastern duds for the uniform of the gunfighter. This metamorphosis is accompanied by the laughter of the real gunfighter on whom the dentist has used laughing gas as a persuader, functioning chorically beyond its local cause.

The western setting of the Paleface films – 'Paleface' here functioning with a double meaning, i.e. pale in the sense of white man, but also pale in the sense of bloodless through fear – demands what is perhaps the last major inflection in Western culture of the epic hero. The pattern for this is Fenimore Cooper's Natty Bumpo, the 'Deerslayer', 'Hawkeye', in the *Leatherstocking Tales*, taciturn, at one with nature, ascetic and unflinching. The Potters, father and son, are his parodic inverse: garrulous (Junior, the Harvard student with a tiresome habit of correcting his interlocutors' grammar), mourning the loss of the corrupt East rather than looking Westward (the subject of 'Buttons and Bows' – 'Ma bones denounce the buckboard bounce

/ And the cactus hurts ma toes'); in the case of Junior not only disliked by
but outwitted by 'Trigger', the Bucephalus of Western stallions; seeking not
to escape the temptations of the flesh, but to embrace them; and wholly
lacking in fortitude (compare the almost supernatural calm with which Natty
returns to the Indian camp to accept torture and death in *The Deerslayer* with
'Painless's' hysterical protestations when about to go to the stake). Hope is
not just city man side-tracked into Nature, he is corrupt city man dreaming
nostalgically, reversing the pastoral tradition, of fleshpots and rackets,
chizzles and five-star hotel rooms and, if he has to embrace the wilderness,
it will be to help himself to its grapes and wines on silver salvers, 'sashaying'
around like-minded ladies – keeping well away from the heat or toil of their
cultivation.

If there are any heroic values pursued by Hope they are those only of a
degraded contemporary version of the hero in which action as spiritual force
is diminished to mere machismo. But even the fulfilment of these debased
codes proves too arduous. Hope attempts to assert his masculinity by drinking rituals, but lacks even the most elementary knowledge, let alone ability
with alchohol. Given a huge tankard of beer, the fraudulent cowboy dips
his whiskey chaser glass into it and pails himself without embarrassment the
miniscule drink he can cope with. Offered a 'Horse's Neck', he declines it
in order to avoid needless equine slaughter.

The other proof of the hero's machismo is his sexual prowess, something
constantly and smugly asserted as an apparently eager libido expresses its
intentions in a ceaseless lubricious discourse of glances, smirks, animal
growls and suggestive (yet innocent) comments. Told that 'California Rose'
(Jane Russell) is 'tops in California', he replies that 'her North and South
Dakotas aren't bad either'. He specialises in knowing remarks about 'it' – the
mysteries of female sexual allure. Forced in *The Great Lover* to take a vow
of abstinence by the prudish Boy Foresters (a variation of Boy Scouts or
Junior Woodchucks) in his charge, he reluctantly swears, 'no women', adding
sotto voce 'over sixty'. But this apparently irrepressible desire tends to falter
at the point of enactment. For instance, when Freddy Hunter (another ironic
surname for one far removed from hunter–gatherer origins) is taken by the
Duchess (Rhonda Fleming) to her cabin in the same film, she wants to stay
in the dark, but his response – both sexually regressive and typically meta-
theatrical is 'Lights! Lights!' A splendid running joke in *The Paleface* has
Jane Russell knocking him out with a pistol butt while kissing him, provoking
a swoon the naïve sexual adventurer confuses with erotic euphoria, 'Boy,
can you kiss!'

The only conventional aspect of the hero that Hope undeniably shares is his self-assertion, a quality downgraded in Hope's hands to boastfulness. 'I who am praised, / I who do not despise myself' orates the speaker in an East African 'praise poem', the product of a still extant heroic culture. (The second line has almost the ring of an African inflection of the Hope character.) But the difference here is that no irony surrounds the speaker who can clearly back up his assertions with actions whereas our constant comic expectation – very seldom denied – is that events will deflate Hope's boast without harming his incorrigible overestimation of himself.

The constant jokes about the protagonist's heroic and sexual ineptitude culminate in a series that confuses sexual roles and actually types him as feminine, that is, in the mainstream view of the culture, more extreme in the 40s and 50s than now, conventionally passive. In the joke repeated across several films he announces to his partner on the dance floor, 'I'll lead', with the superfluous directive suggesting some doubt as to who really should take the male and female roles. Similarly, in *The Paleface*, he introduces himself and Jane Russell as Mr and Mrs Potter, qualifying it, as if to allay confusion, with 'I'm Mr'. Such moments, as we shall see below, can be read in terms of Hope's pervasive narcissism, the character's more complicated desire to be like a woman, that is, to reverse cultural roles and himself be the object of the gaze and of desire. But at a simpler level they embody his wish to share the female's exemption from the more dangerous masculine roles. In *The Princess and the Pirate* the point is made quite clearly when Princess Margaret asks 'Why don't you die like a man?' and Sylvester, disguised as the old gypsy woman, replies 'Cos I'd rather live like a woman'. The element that adds the crowning and rather disturbing touch to this is the precise way he then caresses the long hair of his wig, seriously, meditatively, as if he has already half crossed the gender boundaries into cultural femininity, a region he finds very much to his fancy. In this instance verbal wit has been objectified in the assumption of female disguise, a fairly common transformation in the narratives. Later in the same film gestures rather than costumes produce further startling possibilities. The treasure map tattooed on Sylvester's chest makes him desperately reluctant to expose himself in the Governor's pool. Urged not to behave like a 'coy wench', he accidentally loses his covering and falls into the water where, as he bobs up and down, he frantically tries to conceal the map with his hands and arms. But, guided by the Governor's reprimand, another action can be read into the flurry of activity, the 'coy wench's' hiding of her breasts from a stranger's sight.

The most bizarre extention of the displacement of conventional male/female roles takes place in the two Tashlin-influenced films, *Paleface* and its offshoot, where Hope's playing of the timid 'feminised' hero is opposed in an excessively heightened way by Jane Russell's 'masculine', aggressive role as Calamity Jane and the outlaw 'The Torch', alias 'Mike', a 'pretty masculine handle for such a feminine pile of goods', as Junior chauvinistically remarks. Despite her excess of obvious femininity – it will be remembered that there were well known censorship problems in the 40s over her 'mean, moody and magnificent' role in *The Outlaw* (1943), with much crude publicity focussing on her impressive breasts – Russell has, it may be felt, something in her image that threatens the idea of natural female passivity, to which even the alliterative hype of the famous adjectives attests, since in themselves they might as easily be attached to the persona of, say, Robert Mitchum. Such intimations are taken up by both Tashlin and Hawks. In *Gentlemen Prefer Blondes* (1953), for instance, whatever else is going on in the film, her more phallic presence is played against the softer, giddier stereotype invoked by Marilyn Monroe. In the Tashlin films it is she – often dressed like a gunfighter – rather than Hope who has mastery of the gun (which, as the worship of the sharpshooter by the women in the films makes clear, is equated with the phallus), shooting down various dangerous assailants in the prologue section of *The Paleface*, killing the thirteen Indians attributed to 'Painless', acting as Liberty Valance to Hope's Rance Stoddart when she kills his opponent in the duel where he forgot to bend to the East, move to the Right and crouch on his toes, and knocking out the saloon girl 'Red' Pepper for making a pass at her man. Her appropriation of the male role in *Son of Paleface* is equalled by the Potters' failure in it in both films, a minor instance of which is Junior's failure when he tries to lift her on to the bar counter before Roy Rogers, the ludicrously straight hero, once he has decided in favour of women rather than horses, does it with ease. (Here too, in Hope's fascinated inability to leave alone the subject of Roger's attraction to his horse, the jokes threaten an even greater perversity – bestiality.) Again it is not just that the Hope character fails in his task, but that an identification with the female takes place, for in the same film a careful set of parallelisms echoes one of the softer, more securely female views of Jane Russell, soaping herself in the bath while singing 'What a night for a wing-ding', as Junior later bathes and sings the same song and the camera observes even the traditional coy leg shot – indicating total nudity – as he prepares to get into the bath.

Bob Hope in **Son of Paleface**
All for Jane's buttons and bows, Junior looks worried by the prairie troubadour's *aubade* to Trigger.

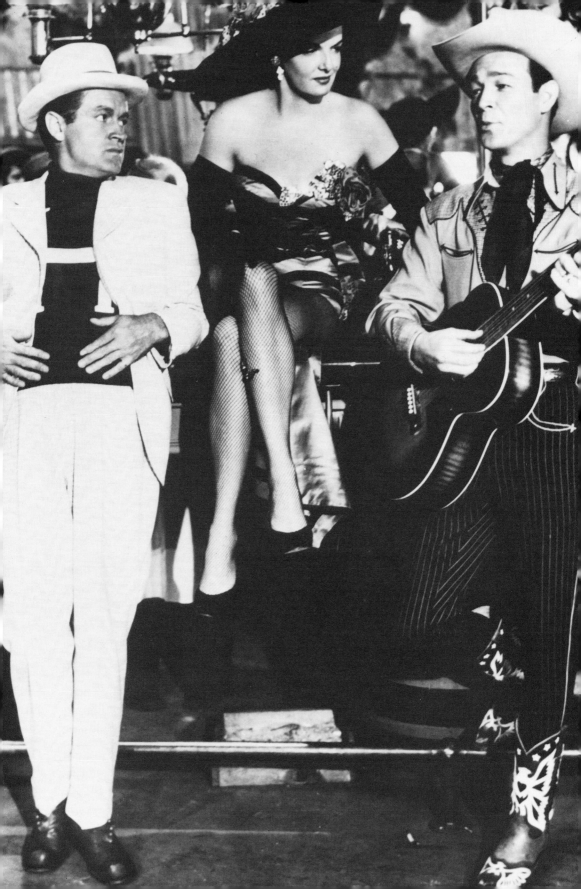

Narcissism

It's only me – that must be the understatement of the year!
                          — Hope in *They Got Me Covered* (1942)

Prithee, Dorimant, why hast not thou a glass hung up here? A room is the dullest
thing without one.   — Etheredge, *The Man of Mode*

In his richly evocative extension of the social implications of Freud's work
Herbert Marcuse argues in *Eros and Civilization* that the history of Western
cultures hinges on three archetypal myths, the myth of Prometheus, and the
related ones of Orpheus and Narcissus. And in fact, just as Hope is part
Prometheus, labouring (fitfully, incompetently, with conventional last-reel
success) against various modern Titans of social oppression, tyranny or criminality – merely impersonating in the process, and that wholly unsatisfactor-
ily, 'the culture-hero of toil, productivity and progress' – he is just as surely
part Orpheus/Narcissus, overwhelmed by a desire to lose the self in the
sensual and sensuous beauties of nature, as it were, to forego the thrill of
the chase, the duel, the tournament, for the self-indulgent pleasures of
nature's riches and consolations. As Narcissus/Orpheus, Hope strives not
to be a culture-hero but (though no doubt those profane eyes would widen
to have it defined so) to find, though in a very impure inflection, 'joy and
fulfilment; the voice which does not command but sings; . . . the liberation
from time which unites with god, man with nature . . . a freedom that will
release the powers of Eros now bound in the repressed and petrified forms
of man and nature'.

And while it is true that Hope, like Orpheus, is capable of lyricising the
beauty of women – he even sometimes, as we have seen, stretches to a song,
though admittedly its mood is usually equivocal, as in 'What a night for a
wing-ding' (*Son of Paleface*): 'I love coffee, / I love tea, / I love the girls /
And I love me' – he is much more comfortable when eulogising his own. In
certain respects his self-admiration is part of the staple diet of many a comedian's range of comic devices. From Malvolio's yellow garters to Don Quixote's irascibility and inflated sense of his own chivalric reputation, the comic
tradition is full of writers who have used variations of the *miles gloriosus*'s
boastfulness as ingredients of their comic heroes' personalities. In film history
the actor who comes closest to Hope in this respect – particularly in Lubitsch's
To Be Or Not to Be – is Jack Benny. But where Benny is corruptly insinuating,
precious, mincing, Hope is almost guilelessly, innocently and immaculately
narcissistic. From his casual quips ('Did she get me?', in *They Got Me
Covered*'), to his perpetual self-pampering ('At least wrap me up as a gift'

in *The Road to Morocco*), to his entranced, rapturous self-adoration in mirrors, Hope's pure and innocent dandy is a brilliant incarnation of Freud's primary narcissist, childishly self-absorbed to the point of latent homosexuality.

In *On Narcissism*, Freud comments significantly on the narcissistic tendencies of all comedians: '. . . even great criminals and humorists, as they are represented in literature, compel our interest by the narcissistic consistency with which they manage to keep away from their ego anything that would diminish it.' And, while discussing the salient features of male narcissism (something he distinguishes in various ways from its female counterpart, whose incarnation is, as we shall see, Mae West), Freud further points out the childish nature of narcissism's dedication to self-contentment and inaccessibility. The child, he argues, behaves in this respect rather like primitive man in overvaluing the magical power of thought and the 'thaumaturgic force of words', both as a way of providing himself with protection and as a means of counteracting or anticipating the hostility of all rivals. Thus the Hope character consistently uses words as jokes to impose himself on the other characters, so that in this sense even the most innocent of his jokes have an aggressive function. In the child this is a form of megalomania (resurfacing even in normal adulthood, when parental loving is seen in some senses to be a reproduction of the child's original narcissism) which in its extreme form fails to choose the mother as a love object, preferring instead the greater comfort of the self. The narcissistic tendency, though present in everyone, is exaggerated in some individuals and, where it occurs, according to the psychoanalytic theory, indicates latent homosexuality.

Freud's remarks on narcissism almost seems to have been written with Hope in mind, for though much of the Hope persona relies on the effects of witty allusions to topical situations and events – the fortunes of the Republican Party (e.g. in *Call Me Bwana* 'What shall we tell the President (Kennedy)'?, officials ask Hope before he lands in the tribal area of man-eating savages, and Hope replies, 'Tell him I voted for Nixon'), and his friendship/ rivalry with Crosby, but also with Jack Benny, Milton Berle, and Martin and Lewis – its cornerstone is the much more universal and timeless psychological complexity of the tensions raised by the conflict between self-denying heroism and self-preserving narcissism.

The triple ingredients of Freud's theory of narcissism – childishness, self-love and latent homosexuality – surface abundantly in the Hope persona, contributing enormously towards the verbal and visual comedy engendered by the narrative structures of the films.

His childishness is brilliantly drawn out, for instance, in a significant number of films. There is an infantile element in many jokes and much comedy (Freud in fact greatly stresses this), and it is obvious in the comic character created for Hope who is actually called 'Junior' in both *Son of Paleface* and *The Road to Morocco*. In *The Paleface* Jane Russell as Calamity Jane calls him 'son' and 'kid', while in *My Favorite Brunette* (1947) his career as a baby photographer can be read as a displacement for his infantilism. In *The Road to Morocco*, after being callously sold into slavery by Bing Crosby, characteristically indifferent to his partner's fate until his higher conscience is pricked by Hope's aunt's ghost, we discover Hope reclining on a luxurious bed of satin and silk, surrounded by voluptuous slave-girls, some manicuring him, others soothing his brow, and cradled by Dorothy Lamour herself, the sultry Arabian princess who has purchased him – though we are expected to wonder why – for her private gratification and dalliance. Not content with such enviable adult pleasures, he holds up a yo-yo in his hand and orders lollipops, both symbols less of his phallic capabilities than of his ultimately regressive, childish, pre-adolescent emotional retardation. This scene of predominantly innocent debauchery naturally satirises Hollywood's most sybaritic genre – the Eastern – but while the sets, with their Moorish curves and arabesques, the costumes, with their billowy trousers, plunging *décolletés* and choking jewellery, and his dialogue, with its fruity vulgarity, 'I'm gonna be a pasha, with the accent on the 'pash'', are designed to remind audiences playfully of the rather less tongue-in-cheek atmosphere of Yvonne de Carlo frivolities, Hope's incorrigible ineptitude and immaturity are further comically exposed. We know that despite his trademark growl (more an absurd gurgle than the desired canine ferocity), that despite the boastful litany of his prowess, and that despite an immodest evaluation of his own varied attributes, Bing Crosby will more often than not get the girl. Even where Bing does not, Bob and Dorothy's son in *The Road to Utopia* (1945) looks very suspiciously like Bing. In *The Princess and the Pirate*, a film like many other Hope vehicles where Crosby is not the co-star but in which there is the odd aside about his absent partner, Crosby actually appears at the very end to whisk away the heroine (Virginia Mayo), whose cause Hope had been championing. Where in other circumstances, with other actors, one might have objected that this was unfair, here we more or less share Hope's implied consolation in feeling that he is left with the greater reward of his own self.

He does not get the girl because, as ever, he is too self-absorbed: his persona is ruled by an addict's need for applause, and to that end all is sacrificed, even the fantasy of romantic union with an idealised woman. The audience expects as much, anticipates in a sub-genre committed to transgression of the normal audience/character relationships the relegation of expectations of wholeness, order, or romance to the necessities of the comic persona. In any case how could any woman match the devotion lavished on the persona by Hope's own limitless idolatry? How could anyone rival his own extravagant self-wooing? The most brilliant example of this self-courtship, a widely recurrent feature of all the films, occurs in *The Lemon Drop Kid*.

The film is ultimately disappointing. Starting promisingly with a situation ripe for the exploitation of Hope's idiosyncrasies, it degenerates into a limp sentimentalism that debases the spirit of the Runyon story on which it is based. A $2 tout, earning his living by persuading gullible punters to back horses with no chance of winning, Hope as the 'Lemon Drop Kid' (the title again suggest the 'childish') convinces the moll of mobster Moose Moran – without knowing her identity – to back a horse that eventually comes in last. When Moose discovers what has happened he gives the Kid until Christmas to find the money he would have made on the horse had the original bet been placed. At first the only solution Hope can think of is to touch his long-suffering sweetheart 'Brainy' Baxter (Marilyn Maxwell) for a loan, instinctively feeling that the way to her heart and to her purse is through his looks and charm. So on a blustery, snowy New York night Hope blows out of the gale and into her apartment building. Impoverished to the point of having to hock his coat even in such intemperate weather, he has been driven to steal the flea-infested coat off the back of someone's pet dog, but as he comes into the warmth of the building, he begins to thaw out and to restore his weather and gangster-beaten poise and dignity. Setting the pattern for successive sybarites – Marilyn Monroe in *The Seven Year Itch* (1955) and Kelly Le Brock in *The Woman in Red* (1984) – he at first treats himself to a warm air bath by standing over the central heating grille on the ground floor. As the air shoots up his trouser legs he lets out ripples of sensual delight, and ready now for further pampering, he makes his way to his ubiquitous Mecca, the ever-faithful mirror, here considerately placed for its worshipper near the letter boxes on the ground floor. The comedy now flows from the visual antics and gestures of an exaggerated narcissism. Hope is prepared for any eventuality: his inner resources and sustaining powers in the face of all adversity are his self-idolatry, the praise of his own beauty, an open secret of a weapon to disarm his enemies and charm his friends.

Dotted about his clothes is the arsenal of tools necessary for all his campaigns. His jacket is a coiffeur's stockpile containing not just a comb, but also a razor, a toothbrush, and after-shave lotion, all of which are now ritualistically applied before the kill. Yet the real source of the comedy is not simply that a man in a society ideologically committed to a polarisation of the sexes on the grounds of strictly conformist notions of role and gender is seen to be transgressing limits in male attention to appearance. Rather, that as he begins to apply what by contemporary standards would have seemed an indiscreet dose of attention to the self by a man, he should reveal himself so absorbed in his preparations that his aim of overwhelming a love object – 'Brainy' Baxter – is almost lost from sight as the narcissist begins to revel in his own perfection. As he studies himself in the glass while the cosmetics are applied and the grooming is under way, the eyes grow rounder not just in idolatry but also in amazement that they had seemingly and unaccountably somehow forgotten quite how magnificent and ravishingly beautiful the image really is. The lips stretch into a knowing smile, complementing the sentiment of the eyes, the famous nose is checked to see if it has suffered an act of sacrilege, and the soft panegyric whistling that has accompanied the performance suddenly gives way to the voice's additional approval in this courtship of the self: 'What a crime if you had to die . . . Oh! Dandy! . . . I hate to leave you, but that's fate.' These remarks (reformulated in a multitude of different ways in many films, such as in *Call Me Bwana* (1963) where so devastating does he feel his appearance to be on women that he decides he had better invest in some ugly pills) at once satirise the mock heroics of the melodramatically intense lovers of screen romances and reveal Hope's limited self-conscious insight into the fop's disruptive radicalism.

Hope's dandyism and narcissism take to an extreme a tendency latent and exploitable in his appearance. He is surely the most complacent looking of all well known comedians, blissfully untouched by self-doubt, and certainly among the more conventionally handsome. It is only a touch of caricature, of overemphasis in his features that separates him from say, Robert Montgomery in *Mr and Mrs Smith* (1941). Looks only slightly more charismatic might have disqualified him as a stand-up comedian on the grounds that, occupying such a privileged position in the world of the erotic, he has little reason for comic dissatisfaction, which in large part revolves around sexual themes. Today, where the erotic is an ideological minefield, such a distinction possibly no longer holds, since the possession of sexual allure allows entry into a realm no longer pastoral but political and may therefore be part of a comedy of misfortune. Thinking of Hope singing 'Thanks for the Memory' in *The Big Broadcast of 1938* reminds us of his near-miss romantic status and how hard screenwriters and the comedian himself strive to elucidate the potential for caricature in his face, above all the famous nose. 'That scoopnose' is the term used by one of his adversaries in *The Paleface*, an epithet varied throughout the films, but again it is Tashlin, in *The Son of Paleface*, who gives the joke its most excessive, and in this case, purely visual form, with a cartoon-based gag in which when 'Junior' is lying hiding under a plank, Trigger walks over it, depressing the 'scoop' sideways as if it were as malleable as Daffy Duck's body. It may not be too fanciful to read this and other indignities heaped on the organ as symbolic castrating, given the often-made equation between nose and penis.

But it is an essential part of Hope, no mere Cyrano in looks, that he is not simply totally miscast physically as the sexual *arriviste*. The unswervable fixity of self-regard, the healthy glow, the infantile eagerness for praise, the surface aggression are in complete contrast to, say, the spiritualising tendencies to other-worldliness in the looks of Chaplin, and, above all, Keaton. There is in Hope not an ounce of conscious or altruistic rebellion. Every lineament of the visible persona, from the slightly receding, impeccably combed and brilliantined hair, to the squarely-fed chin, the slight chubbiness of body, the candid egotism in the glance avidly searching for confirmation and applause, speaks of a socialised, ideologised being within a culture of unflagging materialism. Hope is, firstly, a narcissist; secondly he is also a representative of ideologised capitalist man, but the point is that it is precisely this ideology of capitalism that encourages to excess the ineptly competitive, childlike Hope characteristics. (The typically mirthless grin, thrifty substitute for the giving of the self to laughter, seems vetted by some interior accounting system limiting exterior investment.) Inasmuch as we wish in maturity to escape the chains of narcissism we deplore him, but inasmuch as we harbour the incorrigible narcissist (predating any socialisation, capitalist or otherwise) within ourselves we applaud not his downfall but his indefatigable assertion of self, thus giving rise to a complex identification, half celebratory, half critical. Moreover, as the gangster is the hyperbole of capitalist industry, so this narcissist, paradoxically both a-social and socialised, is the *reductio ad absurdum* of capitalist self-centredness, the two-way mirror of our own irreconcilable contradictions.

Equally, one should be careful to note that Hope's dandyism is neither a simplistic assault on effeminacy in a society constantly on its alert against the threat of ideologically undesirable male feminisation, nor a radical critique of the extreme masculinity that conventions of gender create. As we have argued, it is probably unhelpful to draw parallels between Hope's off-screen conservatism and the ideological expectations that his on-screen persona, largely the creature of writers and directors, is capable of arousing, but in a genre that is not ultimately disposed to subvert all social conventions it is nevertheless legitimate to note the contradictions in conformist definitions of role and gender that the Hope persona and its attendant situations inevitably raise.

Hope repeatedly uses costume as a comic prop in this muted unconscious critique of social conventions. In *Son of Paleface* the outsize ten-gallon hat and boots, spurs and waistcoat he assumes in his spurious ascent to gunfighter hero are primarily intended to expose the inadequacies of a self ill-suited to the rigours of the manly life out West. Yet whatever the original intention of the idea may have been, their effect is actually also to cast doubt on machoism itself. In other films, where his clothes are not caricatures of ethnic, group, or regional practices, but merely the carefully, only slightly dandified versions of what the ordinary well-dressed man in the street wears, his preoccupation with dress makes of him, borrowing Angela Carter's terms – which she uses *à propos* the dandyism of Hell's Angels – an 'outlaw of the social order'. Significantly Hope's fate for long stretches of screen time is frequently to live like an outlaw, crook, pirate, or to be associated with marginalised characters, and this life of social ostracism which the middle part of the comedy condemns him to succeeds in highlighting the extent to which he is also unconsciously an outlaw of sexual conventions as well, a marginalisation in fact that extends even as far as an unarticulated, but nevertheless unmistakable, though indirect, admission of latent homo-sexuality (something glancingly picked up by Parker Tyler in his *Screening the Sexes*).

Freud states in his major essay on narcissism that in what he regards as 'people whose libidinal development has suffered some disturbance' – among whom he includes homosexuals – the mother as love-object has been supplanted by the self. So it is highly appropriate that the comic cinema's greatest male narcissist should not only reveal himself obsessed with his own appearance, something the culture preaches as being largely associated with women (Freud himself defines female narcissism largely in terms of preoccu-pations of this type), but even be eternally ready to use the clichés of socialised femininity, willing to slip into women's clothes whenever necessity demands it of him (Dorothy Lamour even accuses him playfully of wearing a girdle under his male clothes in *They Got Me Covered*). Further, when he does disguise himself as a woman, he frequently chooses to be a mother figure: Aunt Lucy in *The Road to Morocco*, a homeless old lady in *The Lemon Drop Kid*, a gypsy bawd and fortune teller in *The Princess and the Pirate*, and so on. Not fixing his love in the usual way on his mother, this narcissist loves the mother in himself. In *The Princess and the Pirate* Sylvester is attempting to evade 'The Hook' who, played with literally castrating power by Victor McLaglen, shoots a victim in the groin in the film's prologue. To do this he takes on the disguise of an old gypsy hag who he claims to be his mother. This advances the extraordinary Oedipal convolutions of the earlier scene which introduces Sylvester, at first as an off-screen voice heard by Princess Margaret, practising his act and playing all three parts (father, son, mother) in a melodrama where a mother is attempting to stop a duel between antagonists who do not know that they are father and son. Sylvester plays all three parts, but the first and last voice he assumes is that of the mother, and he plays most of the following conversation with the Princess in a skirt.

Hope has it each way in loving both the undisguised male youth he sees in the mirror – the sort of male beauty Hollywood quietly admired in such mildly feminised stars like Tyrone Power, James Dean and Montgomery Clift – and the inner doting self no mother could rival. The simple quip Hope makes to Crosby in *The Road to Morocco* when he imagines at first that a man has bought him, 'Why would a guy buy a guy?', makes one aware of ambiguities which reformulate Freud's recognition that the narcissistic ego is composed of libidinal elements of a basically homosexual type (and many of the films occasionally put Hope under homosexual threat, such as when in *The Princess and the Pirate* Featherhead claims him as a bride) – as Hope not only loves what he himself is, was, would like to be, but also invents the absent mother that his narcissism craves.

Quite clearly there is – once again, beyond conscious intentions – a level of significance to his cross-dressing lying outside traditional expectations. In addition to the rudimentary needs of his desire to display his talents for impersonation, and beyond patriarchal culture's almost ubiquitous taste for satirising female mannerisms and idiosyncrasies, Hope's preference for the boudoir and its promise of rituals of toenail-painting in nightingale blush (*The Road to Morocco*), to the male changing room and its certainties of jockstrap sweat and ribaldry splashed with after-shave lotions, is a sign of his discomfort in the company of more or less straight men. Even though he is frequently partnered by Crosby, he is always critical of him, fears him even, seeks out Lamour as soon as possible, or, at any rate, is ready to abandon Crosby for her at the drop of a hat, never conscious of the act of disloyalty he commits in leaving a friend, knowing full well that this friend is even capable of cannibalism when the food is low and the ship has been wrecked. In *They Got Me Covered* he goes as far as to think Crosby a haunting phantom, whose crooning 'boo-boo-boo-boos', drifting out of a musical cigarette case, are read by Hope as the menacing sounds of a hostile ghost, while in *My Favourite Brunette*, in which Hope tells his story in flashback as a prisoner of the state, Crosby is revealed, right at the very end of the film, as the executioner. In the Crosby/Hope films, Crosby is the more conventional, the more conformist of the pair. He sings romantic songs, he is a plausible suitor, and is much more acceptable to women than Hope, who remains unpredictable, farcical, ill-at-ease in love, more childlike and narcissistic. While Crosby's persona is straight (crooning, smoking pipes, etc.), Hope's is farcical. Even though the double act differs from other comedy teams in that neither Hope nor Crosby is wholly either a straight man or a fall guy, Hope is so absorbed in his narcissism that no normal sexual relationship is ever finally and enduringly possible.

So with all its narcissistic implications – rather than more straightforward sexual ones – women's company is what Hope seeks. Though the *mise-en-scène*, costume, cosmetics and scents of his sexual paradise are centrally, almost clichéically feminine, it is noticeable that while, as the narcissist must (because at all times he seeks to impose his own will on others), he frequently infantalises his women by patronising them, he usually falls for women who are in one way or another quite powerful, a characteristic feature that naturally appeals to the narcissist who projects his own introverted notion of beauty and allure on to the image of his partner. Jane Russell, Dorothy Lamour, Rhonda Fleming, Marilyn Maxwell, Lucille Ball and many others are hardly fragile, virginal, 'Victorian angel' types. If Hope suggests a male child veering between the demands of cultural masculinity and escape back into the irresponsibly infantile, Jane Russell's role in the Western comedies could be described as clitoral, like that of the pregendered female child whose sexuality and behaviour are, in the Freudian reading in his discussion of 'Femininity', still masculine and active. The nursery ambience of the films, full of childish jokes even where Hope is not at their centre (e.g. the title 'night fell' that falls in *The Paleface*), regresses to a stage where gender roles are unhinged and even reversed. These women in some way or other display reserves of masculine strength, and sometimes even dress like men, so that though occasionally he is in awe or even afraid of them, like Ovid's Narcissus Hope is the 'fondly foolish boy who beholds but the shadow of a reflected form' on the masculinised women he woos.

MAE WEST

The star

While female comedians do exist – Vesta Tilley, Marie Lloyd, Nancy Walker, Sophie Tucker, Bette Midler, etc. – there are notably fewer of them than male ones. Why? Clearly, historically, in our civilisation and its origins, there have been more restrictions imposed on female behaviour and its representation in art, largely as a result of the symbolic roles women are expected to play, especially those expressing purity and domestication or display. Thus the comedian who is critic, celebrant of the id, the anti-social, the mocker of forms, is more acceptable when male, and especially so as regards the subject of sexuality. In *Jokes and their Relation to the Unconscious* the obscene joke is treated solely as a male phenomenon – made by the male to another male, its object the woman. The obscene parts of a contemporary act like Bette Midler's, for instance, gain their effects from the shock of a gross articulation, normally acceptable only from the male. The movement away from polarised sex roles (male: dynamic, female: passive) is reflected in the greater number of contemporary female comedians and their use of obscenity as part of their acts. Many of them, in this and other respects, are indebted to Mae West.

Neither innocent, like most female comic actresses (e.g. Clara Bow, the seemingly hard-boiled but really vulnerable Jean Harlow, Judy Holliday), nor too solemnly vampish like other (non-comic) actresses trading on sexuality (e.g. Joan Collins, Theda Bara), Mae West is the female comedian who *par excellence*, in her own words, seems to have been born to 'kid sex all along'. Simultaneously a paean to sex and a self-conscious parody of it, she is a knowing indictment of predictable dreams of erotic fulfilment. At times visually almost phallic-shaped (sometimes, in *She Done Him Wrong*, stressing the point by carrying sticks), to remind us of her appropriated masculinity, she is nevertheless also exaggeratedly feminine, dressed to kill in satins, silks, *crêpe-de-chine* and furs; furs on her body, around her shoulders, in muffs, on her head, all signs of her 'conspicuous consumption', but, additionally, warnings of her predatory instincts and, perhaps above all, an unconscious gesture to Freud's notion in the essay on fetishism that, like velvet, fur is a 'fixation of the sight of pubic hair'. But where at other times, in other ages, fur might have reflected the status of a husband, proudly flaunting his sexual conquest, here it stands for a woman's triumph, in career and personal terms, an equivocal apparition of aggressively mocking femininity. Mae West as Venus in furs is a comic, somewhat implausible memory of Zola's description of Nana (who, it will be remembered, is first seen, as West often is, as a stage performer) and of her power over men: 'A whole society hurling itself at the cunt. A pack of hounds after a bitch, who is not even on heat and makes fun of a pack of hounds following her. . .'.

Kidding sex, though, is a notion whose simplicity of expression is belied by complexity of conception. There have always been women who mock passion: recently Joan Rivers, invoking almost Augustinian revulsion against sexual appetite through her painstaking descriptions of the ins and outs of

E

menstruation; Karen Finley, hardly mediating shock with comedy at all, sticking her bare backside out at the audience as she continues to chat to them. Mae West's use of sex, by contrast, is a very elaborate variation of a venerable device relying on failures of perception. Her act, never in the least scatalogical, is basically an illusion of concupiscence, not its reality, a dream of sex whose essence is in fact ultimately banal. The point is neatly made in *Every Day's a Holiday*, when she arrives at an elegant house dressed as usual as flamboyantly as a peacock, opens her handbag and takes out not some dainty cosmetic box, but a grim set of burglar's tools. As Alison Lurie notes in *The Language of Clothes* 'the most universally recognised sexual indicator in women . . . is the purse or handbag. Freudians may have been the first to state the connection directly, but the use of the word 'purse' for the female pudenda dates from the early seventeenth century. . .'. So gold, platinum gold, she may be on the outside, but on the inside Mae West is made of the baser metal of a literal and symbolic thief of love and wealth. The point is not moralistic, just a small comic reminder of the inner limits of any mortal paradise.

Paradise of a sexual kind is what West promises, an empire of the senses at the 'Sensation House' of her sexual charms, constructed around her various ideas of male needs and susceptibilities. She plays on contradictory desires for subjugation and domination, fantasy and reality, extreme femininity and masculinity, passivity and aggression. This 'Sensation House' of the libido (Ace La Mont's establishment in *Belle of the Nineties*, but also the objective correlative of the West persona) is typically associated in setting with the 'Gay Nineties', a psycho-sexual *mise en scène* that can be read in several ways. Above all, perhaps, the primary effect is of making the men in her 1930s audiences revive their slumbering oedipal traumas and longings. Mae West dressed in nineties style is, for mature male audiences of the Depression, a half-remembered image of their own mothers. In all her staged routines on film she sets herself up as a *prima donna assoluta*. As *Screenplay* (November 1933) put it, she is 'Broadway's hottest Mama'. Her slightly overweight porportions, reminding one faintly of those squat, paleolithic statuettes of fertility, the special attention to her breasts (making them appear far more ample than in reality they were), all in symphony with her period costume, serve to emphasise the maternal, matriarchal or what Graham Greene called the 'stout matronly figure' of a woman already forty by the time of her first film.

Yet this *prima donna* is of course neither immaculately conceived, nor in any sense a *mater dolorosa*. This 'mama', the antithesis of spare, classical ideals of female beauty, and less normal, much wilder than Sophie Tucker (another 'red hot mama' of the day), is a *pot pourri* of carnality, a paragon of venal beaty, a comic throwback to the Delilahs, Sphinxes and other *femmes fatales* of nineteenth-century paintings (Moreau's *Cleopatra*, Fernand Khnopff's *The Caress*), a courtesan feeding off the carrion of all gullible libertines of love. Or, like some overdressed Rubens nude, without the unself-conscious rapport with nature, she stands there full of knowing sexual mischief, an Irish/Catholic matriarch who is also a Bacchante and a Spider Lady, exploiting her male exploiters by making them regress to their infancy, turning them into 'suckers' in this literal infantile sense as well as in the more ordinary one of being gulls. Though the costume is all 'Gay Nineties', the dialogue is pure Brooklynese 30s. Nothing here either of the courtesies of the 90s, or the flappers' frivolity of the 20s; she is the epitome of 30s streetwise toughness looking the Depression straight in the eye.

So neither a petite Correggio nymph nor a D. W. Griffith waif, Mae West refuses to be a voluptuary, preferring instead the less psychologically and emotionally vulnerable calling of the confidence-trickster, a shrewd operator exploiting the weaknesses of male debauchees by offering them regressive visions of nostalgia and eroticism too irresistible to their collective unconscious, in the knowledge that for the sake of sexual gratification some men will gladly make chumps of themselves. 'Find 'em, fool 'em and forget 'em' is her motto in *I'm No Angel*, as she steers wealthy, middle-aged Romeos from the Bowery to the Klondyke, to the tomb of love. Her comic revenge is partly aimed at the whole tradition of female victimisation by the male arts of love. Reversing dominant patterns of wooing, where the individuality of maidens, goddesses and mistresses is obliterated by the indiscriminate applications of conventional images of love, Mae West treats her male victims to the same aesthetic pap women have endured for centuries. Her almost monotonous assortment of dupes are only given the illusions of privilege and distinctiveness while in reality they are all part of a dragoon of ultimately nameless male victims valued only in terms of their expendability. When she enlists the aid of a 'sucker' in *Holiday*, the telling scene where he stands beside a shop window dummy during the course of a robbery she has masterminded crystallises the metamorphoses by which, through her influence, all libertines turn into chumps. Falling for her charms means being a 'dummy', just one in a series of victims who have been slipped a mickey of empty desires: 'no one loves me like that Dallas/Frisco/Kansas man'. The man is the same, only his name and place of origin distinct, as in the collection of gramophone records she keeps for every geographic possibility in *I'm No Angel*.

This urge to discipline men for their wickedness towards women extends

even to giving mischievous schoolboys – embryo patriarchs – a lesson in obedience in *My Little Chickadee*. When the official schoolmarm resigns – defeated by the unruliness of her all-male class – West steps in and whips them into line, not so much taking advantage of an unexpected opportunity to show off her intellect (her maths is corrected by one of the boys), as relishing yet another occasion for caning today's callow bucks for committing tomorrow's adult sins of the flesh. The sexual effect she has on the pubertal thugs is unmistakable, their regimented rise and fall as they answer her questions a deflected means of drawing attention to the stirring effect her presence has on other parts of their anatomies. Taking no notice of their adolescent sexual excitability, West in front of the class is as expert as 'Tira', the 'incomparable', the 'marvel' of *I'm No Angel*, fearlessly coping with the savage beasts in the lions' cage.

West is leonine, in fact draws attention to her own sun sign, Leo, the 'king of the beasts', in *I'm No Angel*, though part of her deception is to make men believe they are lions while she is turning them into lambs. On the one hand yielding to male fantasies of extreme femininity, on the other adopting attitudes of unexampled aggression, she marshals her purblind admirers – as we might expect from her militaristic uniform of the lions scene (peaked cap, trousers, doublet with brocade) – into the sweet oblivion of erotic surrender. She is as soft as a flower (Florabelle in *My Little Chickadee*, a 'euphonious appellation', as W. C. Fields so felicitously notes in characteristic mock-approval), yet as tough as a diamond 'Tiara', 'tirin' men out as 'Tira' with her sexual prowess, or as regal as Ruby (*Belle of the Nineties*), a jewel symbolising royalty, dignity, power, and a mockery of Proverbs and its reference to the Good Woman's worth. In *Every Day's a Holiday*, she is 'Peaches O'Day', her Christian name fulfilling conventional expectations of stereotyped female banalities ('Peaches' as in a still life, or 'peaches and cream' complexions), her surname bristling with connotations of suns, light, virile sources of energy (the sun is the male god, Apollo), and female sexuality ('O' as in the famous pornographic novel, *The History of O*, as in all those 'Os' and 'Mms' punctuating her songs and snatches of dialogue, all of which signify sex and more sex – even her telephone number in *Belle* is Davenport 7-Oh-Oh-Oh!).

The composite image of allure, control and mockery rests, as it does in the case of all stars, on complex processes of interaction between looks, posture, delivery, setting and function. This 'dynamite dame with a wicked

Mae West in *I'm No Angel*
The Sensation House Aphrodite attended by her New World Graces.

wit' as the *Picture Play* hack of April 1933 defines her, relies heavily on shaded eye make-up, giving her an almost Oriental aura, very suitable to the *bain turc* ambience of her persona. The effect is lewdness: her eyes are only half-open, suspicious, concealing their truths, preferring to keep the promise rather than to expose the reality of her desires. Her mouth is stretched almost into a sneer, teeth sufficiently bared to suggest sensuality accentuated by rapacity, a nose perfectly moulded for all those nasal 'mms' and throaty 'ohs', so full of phoney sexual enticement, so empty of genuine ardour. The platinum hair, squeezed into tight curls low on the head, is an image of composure and, especially, of inviolability, not a strand loosened by lover or confidant. This is the face, she boasts in *I'm No Angel*, with which she struck oil. Her height is exaggerated by heavily platformed heels and soles, stressing her queenly aura, as well as by constant ingenuities of framing, and her posture is invariably frozen into an hour-glass shape by the impossibly tight *fin-de-siècle* creations of her designer Travis Banton. One hand is on the hip – with all the swagger of a saloon bravado – the other behind her coiffure, softening the aggression with a reminder of her femininity. When she walks, this low-life cocotte's famous 'swivel-swing' captures even here the ambivalence of her male/female persona, drawing attention at once to her female treasures below the waist, and to the reserves of strength she can rely on against any male who tries to steal them. Though corseted in with all the violence neces-sary to create the writhing, wiggly shape ('next to her a wiggling worm looks paralysed', an aficionado in *I'm No Angel* affirms), her walk has nothing in it of the dainty prissiness of period stereotypes. Her stride is characterised instead by the very freedom such wrappings are designed to suppress. In motion she reminds one of John Wayne swaggering into a saloon; in repose she has the stance of a hip-jutting Aphrodite painted by Ingres.

This unmistakable ability to slide across the bounds of convention is given a crucial structural function in the films. Steve Seidman has already pointed out how comedian-based comedy can sometimes match the more overtly Brechtian or 'alienating' techniques of a Godard where comedians speak directly to the audience, play on the idea of the audience's inscription in the text, and create a possible subversive pattern of dynamics between audience and actors. As we point out, much of Bob Hope's humour, for instance, depends on a direct relationship with the audience. There is no direct com-munication between the real audience and West, for it would be somehow unlikely for her to allow such intimacy, but her connection with her fictive audience – during her stage numbers – is designed to question our own (the real audience's) complex responses to her. The stage audience becomes our alter ego, on both of whom the tables are turned.

West's performance is not only a spectacle but also, fascinatingly, a response to the spectacle her audience, greedily taking their fill of her carnality, make of themselves. Baudelaire, in an inspired essay on comedy, the grotesque and laughter, argues that laughter is in many respects 'satanic' and therefore ('our faces distort in laughing as they do in pain'), because 'fallen', profoundly human. West's act, it must be remembered, is designed to make sex 'laughable', as if in making them laugh at her, following Baudelaire, she plunges her audience into ignorance and weakness. This kind of laughter, the kind the sage avoids (Christ never laughed, Baudelaire reminds us), manufactured by a highly self-conscious artist turning punters into suckers, is radically different from another kind inwardly enjoyed at their (and our) expense by the comedian herself, as she counts the rewards ultimately reaped for her through her skills in peddling illusory sex, oedipal nostalgia and dreams of a libidinous paradise. The comedian becomes the audience, serious, superior in the knowledge that her act has worked its magic on us. And just to emphasise the point, the camera is frequently placed behind her so we can see the effect her jokes, singing, and sexual presence have on the audience's faces. At times, too, the camera tracks along the ranks of male admirers, in close-up rather like the lust-crazed characters of a Bosch painting, identifying itself with the comedian, signalling her as audience now scrutinising the performance of her foolish playthings. The male gaze is thrown back upon itself, not so that the film becomes wholly radical, just so that some of its frames of intelligibility become focused. The conservative and capitalist strains of the film are there, clearly in evidence in *Belle of the Nineties*, as when Ruby is made to agree to the Tiger Kid's release from her clutches so he can pursue his career as a boxer undistracted by her sexual allure, and in her endless quest for material luxury. These films, it should be remembered, were made at Paramount, the studio of Lubitsch and the Marx Brothers in their early phase, so the more questioning, more subversive elements are not completely overshadowed. West uses some of the conventional assumptions about women (seductiveness, glamour, etc.), but not in the ways that mean she is either male-fixated, domesticated, or in need of rescue from the various perils of her threatened existence. The erotic archetype of the *femme fatale* may indeed be softened to fit into the rough and ready patterns of popular culture through an injection of certain enervating virtues. Yet Mae West ultimately triumphs over all around her as the woman who not only laughs at sex but who also, somewhat like Maureen O'Hara in Dorothy Arzner's *Dance, Girl, Dance* (1940) turns the focus on her male patrons, and in so doing becomes the object who becomes the subject of desire.

Left-handed Orlando:
Mae West and the comedy of androgyny

Mae West: Maybe I ain't got no soul.
Cummings: Oh yes you have, but you keep it hidden under a mask.
                                        — *She Done Him Wrong*

There have been many stars whose tendency is to throw into confusion the boundaries of sexual roles and identities. Different though she is from the Garbos, the Hepburns, the Clifts and the Deans in being a creature neither of mystery, sublety, passion nor torment, West shares with them a capacity which brings absolute fixities of sexual definition into doubt. Her adoption as an icon by the camp-loving element in homosexual culture (she was herself fascinated by homosexuality, going so far in her pre-filmic days as to write a play, *The Drag*, on the subject), the 'Mother Superior of the faggots' in Parker Tyler's gaudy phrase, is a response to part of these meanings. There is an often-remarked suspicion of the female impersonator in West, springing from the sense of a phallic will directing the pose of the visibly overstated qualities of her femininity, so swaggeringly exaggerated and begartered in quotation marks (to use Susan Sontag's term) that they appear unnatural, assumed, like the mocking mimicry of the Drag Queen.

For some feminist critics her main interest has been less her theatricality than those elements in her which can be seen as celebrating female sexuality. Professionally independent, refusing in all but the formalities of narrative closure the role of monogamous dependence, she appropriates dominant male roles and subverts passive female ones. Yet comedy is essentially a labile mode, setting off a constellation of effects that may be variously interpreted. Nowhere is this clearer than in the sometimes negative view of her put forward by other feminist critics who reject the 'positive' view of West parodying the female star and her spectacle of femininity. The contrary view sees her as part male Oedipal fantasy of the mother and part fetish, a phallic replacement for the woman feared by the male spectator. In either case, for all the veneer of subversive words and actions, she is seen as essentially a projection of male as opposed to female fantasies.

Are these two positions irreconcilable? Susan Sontag's famous meditation on 'camp' in *Against Interpretation* includes specific reference to West's film performances and 'successful camp'; qualities of 'artifice' and 'exaggeration'; the mode that sees everything in quotation marks; *double entendre* and flamboyant gestures; all these and other related flourishes accurately evoke the excess of her persona, the equivocal filter through which any meanings she creates emerge. Where such ornate deformations so tightly surround the persona there is hardly space for the kind of straightforward decoding desired by the unswerving critic of ideology. 'Camp' as defined by Sontag is a mode that 'even when it reveals self-parody, reeks of self-love', a remark that underlines the curious way in which West's irony, although constantly revealing the artificiality of the image she projects, is also a technique for self-admiration. At the same time, though, the fact that this irony never turns on itself critically does not dissolve away the attendant possibilities of meaning, though they arrive through a haze of impurities which make them somewhat different from the straightforward exposure of satire. On the other hand, to take the comic viewpoint, one should remember that the meanings created would be of little interest to audiences, or even critics, stripped of the often irresponsible impulses of comedy. The unregenerate qualities of West are so intimately bound up with the more regenerate ones (critically ironic of the most unyielding conventions of gender) that it is impossible to separate the two. So attempts to label her as either wholly progressive or fundamentally regressive are too naïvely extreme.

While her partisan apologists, Angela Carter among them, can be seen to fall too easily into the traps of heroine-hunting in the thickets of patriarchal culture, her ideological critics, widening the debate to take in the whole question of female representation in the cinema, conceal flawed arguments in the absolutist rigours of a tendentious methodology. Their view that she is nothing but a fetishistic projection of male fantasies far too crudely simplifies her effects.

The fetish, as Freud analyses it, is a possible development of the male infant's initial refusal to believe that the mother has no penis, since such an admission would suggest his own castration. While the majority surmount this trauma, accept sexual difference, and are able to enjoy normal heterosexual relations, a minority develop an aversion to women which results in homosexuality. But a third group are only able to have heterosexual relations by means of a fetish (typically a shoe or underwear), which has the unconscious role of standing in for the lost penis and thus making female sexuality tolerable.

What is typically done by contemporary film theorists with this formulation is to amalgamate it to a sense in which film itself is a sort of metaphorical fetishism, in other words the psychological mechanism of the viewer who both believes in and does not believe in the illusion he sees, resembles that of the fetishist who both believes in and disavows that for which the fetish stands. But certain critics wish to do more than this, arguing that since all patriarchal thought about women is governed by unconscious factors, all patriarchal representations of women are the product of castration fears. In some versions of this argument fetishisation seems to mean only an unreal glamorisation, since it is not easy to argue persuasively that Rita Hayworth, say, or Dolores del Rio are marked by masculine characteristics. But with West, where it has been noted that there are 'many traces of phallic replacement', 'phallic dress', and a voice that is 'strongly masculine', the argument is that fetishism is literal, that what we watch in West is not a woman pirating certain characteristics classified as male, but a woman who in a profound sense is male and whose actions, rather than subverting male power, support it, since they show that it is only a male, or a male disguised as a woman, or a woman whose femaleness has become ludicrous, who can carry them out.

Not only does this generalising use of the concept of fetishism flatten all representations of women into simple, inescapable formulae (all female stars, all male representations of women are fetishes) that are little more than dogma, but it also, while basing itself on Freud, ignores Freud's interest in the fact that most men do not become fetishists but, having surmounted the original infantile trauma, need no such absolute escape from the terrors of femininity as the argument supposes. However, the view that West has various phallic characteristics is by no means as strained as the one that would ask us to see Betty Grable's legs or Monroe's breasts as penis substitutes. The point about West, however, is surely the disturbing juxtaposition of male and female characteristics in the persona, and the view of her as wholly a male fetish must find a lot about her hard to explain, in particular the various female revenges she exacts on males, and the castrating edge to many of her jokes. We might well argue that certain of her male characteristics (as does her middle-age) soften the jokes, make them easier to take because they do not come from an unambiguously desirable female source. But the existence and activity of such masculine traits hardly overwhelms all traces of femininity and female viewpoint. To so withdraw from the impurities of the persona that one no longer sees the traces of the usurping female, the deflator of hyperboles of female (and male) sexuality, the witty Amazon, but only the male fetish, is to make one point but in the process to lose many others.

We have spoken of the disturbing mix of male and female elements in West. This demands some final definition. At the Romantic pole of the comedy of the sexes the blurring of male and female characteristics into an image of bisexuality is presented as a thing of delicate mystery (Viola/Cesario's masculine/feminine youth – 'For they shall yet belie thy happy years / That say thou art a man'). It centres around images of youth, either a girlish boy or a boyish girl. Some of its most profound expressions are found in Virginia Woolf's *Orlando* where, it will be remembered, the hero wondrously becomes the heroine, and is thus uniquely placed to experience and comment on the separateness and togetherness of the sexes. This is the passage where Orlando, still a he, first sees his love, Sasha:

> . . . a figure, which, whether boy's or woman's, for the loose tunic and trousers of the Russian fashion served to disguise the sex, filled him with the highest curiosity . . . A melon, an emerald, a fox in the snow, so he raved, so he stared . . . Legs, hands, carriage were a boy's, but no boy had those breasts; no boy had eyes which looked as if they had been fished from the bottom of the sea . . . She was a woman.

In this description we seem to see Garbo's Queen Christina as glimpsed by John Gilbert's Don Antonio, the youthful Katharine Hepburn, whether in the male apparel of *Sylvia Scarlett* (1935) or otherwise, even the virile, hoydenish beauty of Jean Peters in *Anne of the Indies* (1951). But at the other, satiric, pole of the comedy of the sexes, rather than that blurring of masculine and feminine into an intermediate state possessed of the graces of both (the younger Alain Delon as a male instance?), we find imaginings that, though they join masculinity and femininity together in the same figure, rather than dissolving the separate characteristics, heighten and exaggerate them to the point of parody. And so we have in Mae West a femininity compounded of a series of blatantly overwrought and banal signals, parts, too, so artificial that they seem easily dismantled, as in the famous life-jacket or Dali's couch and room in the shape of her lips or face, placed in conjunction with a masculinity that selectively consists of its least graceful cultural characteristics, aggression, egotism, dominance. Both, rather than fluidly merging, coexist in a hypertrophied excess, evoking laughter rather than the wonder or 'delight' of older comic theorists. But it is a complex laughter that can be seen to ridicule both, in the knowing, if complacent irony of the performer, producing effects far more ambiguous than simple satire of the masculine woman or the feminine man.

The comedy of anatomy

West in close-up: the opening of Belle of the Nineties

'You don't have to have feet to be a dancer.'   — said of Tira in *I'm No Angel*

The opening of *Belle of the Nineties*, suffused with nostalgia for the 1890s, shows titles and cameos of the leading players presented as the pages of an old-fashioned album and accompanied by the music of 'And the Band Played On', and 'My American Beauty'. The high-level shot that initiates the narrative encompasses a crowd below and, above it, the banner that signals the presence into which they have gathered: 'HERE! HERE! HERE! RUBY CARTER THE MOST TALKED ABOUT WOMAN IN AMERICA'. As the shot cranes closer we pick out among the crowd various posters of Mae West wearing the gown in which she will be seen a few moments later, and near the centre of the screen an advertisement made up of two newspaper front pages which read, '1892 GRAND JURY TRIES RUBY CARTER: 1893 RUBY CARTER INNOCENT'. We register the typical motifs: the 1890s as a time of heightened sex differences; West's self-aggrandisement; the heroine as stage entertainer, Nana-like exhibitor of the self, irresistible flame of desire to which men are drawn to destruction; the ambivalence stated by the juxtaposition of the two front pages, the earlier one highlighting Ruby as criminal, as callous exploiter of men, the later one imaging her as the exploiter of the exploiters. The time is actually 1894 as the bottom of the billboard informs us, without comment, as if demanding synthesis from the thesis and antithesis embodied in the other two dates.

Inside, a female chorus line, more than a little frumpy and buxomly over-blown in 1890s postcard style, performs a clumping song-and-dance routine: 'Here we are, the beauties of the town / the suckers buy us wine / In cabarets, we dine / We sip and chat / And walk on back to back. . .'. Full of gestures that show them to the least advantage, cross-stage movements, characteristically inelegant hops and over-winsome poses, their performance is further compromised by costumes that manage within the bounds of decorum to suggest provocative revelation (they all wear a kind of body-stocking), yet at the same time are wholly unflattering (their seeming near-nakedness is only pathetic). This sense of exposure is accentuated by the little pom-poms that decorate their costumes around the genital area, front and back, a significance underlined by the refrain of the male singer who joins them. The nonsense phrase 'pom-tiddley-om-pom-pom' of their song (somewhat similar to the more familiar 'Ta-ra-ra-boom-de-ay'), functions as a euphemism for sex generally, and the female genitals particularly. With the arrival of this equally cretinous male performer their galumphing progress gives way to his memorably foolish lyrics:

> Ha, ha . . . Oh you chicken, oh you kid,
> Pom-tiddley-om-pom-pom,
> I've gone loony in my lid,
> Pom-tiddley-om-pom-pom, etc . . .

Whatever other functions it has, this opening number works as a foil to the delayed entry of Ruby/West. The girls, wholly unlike Ruby in their dowdiness, are, however, like her in exhibiting their bodies for men, an exhibition (as the lyrics indicate) that is not only aesthetic but also a prelude to material rewards earned from the granting of sexual favours. But though they insultingly objectify the male audience who buy them wine and dinner as 'suckers', it is the defensive pretence of the victim, not, as is the case when West uses the same term at the beginning of *I'm No Angel*, the scorn of the manipulator that gives it meaning. Patently inferior on stage, these women are also immediately placed as inferior to her in the world of sexual competition when they run off stage and peer longingly at Ruby's lover, the Tiger Kid, sitting in the audience with his friends. Envying Ruby's possession of him, two of them begin to quarrel and even come to blows, an inversion of the more usual fictional commonplace in which men fight over women. From this image of frustrated, inferior women, fighting, out of control, the narrative cuts to Ruby herself, in contrast to all this futile activity, statuesquely poised and posed, serenely transfixed in self-absorbed contemplation of her face in a hand-mirror, a middle-aged maid kneeling at her side.

The gesture tells us that though she will parade herself for the watchers, her true audience is the image she reflects back to herself. Milton's Eve in *Paradise Lost*, waking into existence, is only unwillingly weaned of the image that, Narcissus-like, attracts her as she peers into the water, by the superior, other image of Adam. Transferring the accusation of narcissism across the sexes may seem merely an unfair patriarchal manouevre to make women bear the guilt of a tendency deep in the constitution of both sexes, but we might feel that both in the high puritan view of Milton and the plebeian glamorous–grotesque of West, this narcissism unconsciously punishes the male prohibitions that have cultivated it, by turning women further in on themselves, anchoring them more firmly to a view of themselves as objects of desire. One of the insights of Freud's essay on narcissism, an insight that binds together the primary elements of Mae West, comedy and the flaunting of female sexuality, is the implicit comparison between the desire of many men for such self-centred women and the attachment of the voyeur–audience to the 'great criminals and humourists as they are presented in literature'. The suggestion is that over and beyond other motivations, such a woman is attractive because she has maintained 'an unassailable libidinal position which we ourselves have long since abandoned'. But as the essay further notes, 'the great charm of narcissistic women has its reverse side; a large part of the lover's dissatisfaction, of his doubts of the woman's love, of his complaints of her enigmatic nature, has its roots in this incongruity between the types of object-choice', something most of the men in West's films find out soon enough.

Where the chorines' costumes only expose them and make them defenceless to the view, West's is, in total contrast, a full-length gown – so full that
it has a sort of mermaid's tail to it – body hugging in its blatant outline and
improbable hour-glass figure. Attracting, yet at the same time defeating all
more intimate voyeurism, seemingly metallic, it is an impervious armour, a
costume that is both an invitation and a defence, an image of fecundity and
sterility, a promise and a cheat. The obvious necessities that govern the
presentation of her body by a middle-aged performer may be the most basic
reason for the care West takes to hide and buttress her body, but in the
elaborated ironic contexts of her film performances this modesty takes on
further meanings. Her carapaces of lace and satin take on the quality of
fetishes and metaphors for the sought-for mystery and nullity at the centre
of desire, that fascination out of the understanding of which she wields her
power over men. This particular gown, renouncing flounces, and without a
hat, makes West as implausibly smooth as the classical nude female statuary
that is sometimes positioned in shot with her.

The middle-aged maid engages her in conversation, or what passes for
conversation in West's films, that stylised process of feed-line and riposte
enacted so well here:

> *Maid:* You know, honey, when I did my act and had a figure like yours, every
> man in town was at my feet.
> *Ruby:* At ya feet? I'd rather have 'em round my neck. [joke 1] Got me hooked
> up? I feel a draught. [joke 2]
> *Maid:* I've never known a woman who had so many gentleman friends. You cer-
> tainly know the way to a man's heart.
> *Ruby:* Funny too, because I don't know how to cook. [joke 3]

Two of these three jokes, the first and the third, follow a pattern of statement and riposte. In the first, pretending to take literally rather than
metaphorically the men 'at your feet', the joke places the men's arms where
they belong, around the neck, as a prelude to intercourse. Abstract devotion
is worth less than physical fulfilment to West in her more appetitive moods,
and the joke also asserts what so many of her utterances express: physical
satisfaction with not one but a plurality of men, thus reversing aggressively
the norm dramatised in the preceding number, the dandified Lothario's
pursuit of the multiplicity of chorus girls. Alternatively, for the wit is ambiguous, and during the scene she fingers a necklace (thus recalling Diamond
Lil from *She Done Him Wrong*, the prototype of all West's gold-digging
heroines), having men at your feet should translate into men's wealth around
your neck. The ambivalence of the joke corresponds to an ambivalence in
the essential persona whereby at different times West presents herself both

as the gold-digger sleeping with men only for their money, like the Eartha Kitt character, and, contradictorily, as the active pleasure-seeker taking men only for the sexual satisfaction they can give her. What is consistent is the structure whereby she is the aggressor and the male the passive, used object, with the 'wicked' lady as the director of comic meaning rather than the representation of the melodramatic temptress.

In the third joke the maid's praise of her mistress is turned into a salute to Ruby's knowledge and worldliness, since the core of the joke is the over-turning of the cliché about the way to a man's heart being through his stomach into Ruby's knowledge that male hearts are governed by other appetites. Anti-domestic, the reply is that of a sexual adventuress rather than a wife. Having no desire for men longer than they can satisfy her either sexually or materially, and having no weakness of sentiment, she has no desire for a man, as distinct from men. Consequently, she can mock the folk-wisdom postulating that after the transitory ecstasies of passion have vanished other qualities will be required of the wife.

Unlike the other two, the second joke springs solely from Ruby. The first layer of significance plays against the overwhelming artifice of the West image, revealing it as a complex fabrication, but there is a second layer where, pretending to reveal herself, this bride is seen never to be naked, but eternally clothed, something that gives a further twist to her role-playing function and image.

At various times in her films, and in addition to her other transgressions, West is a breaker of class barriers in the democratic insolence that is a favoured (often complacent) form of American comedy, making her way from the lower rungs of the social ladder into the 400. But her proletarian qualities ('At ya feet' is delivered in choicest Brooklynese) have another significance too, connected with the sexual, since the visible artifices of femin-inity (manners, deportment, ways of speech) are predominantly codes of the middle and upper classes. Though it may be that the lower-class woman's structural role is ultimately the same, and even in many ways more con-strained, certain fixities of behaviour – the female as repository of the polite, the repressed, the pure – are less heavily impressed on her. At times in the films jokes are constructed around the West character's lack of education (she commends someone's 'conversatory') but in many cases this lower-class status, always announced by her voice, frees her from feminine constraints.

As Ruby converses with the maid, four gestures predominate. The mirror raised in one hand to reflect her face back to her; a hand running its touch along a string of pearls at her neck; an arm bent behind her head as she parts the artificial clusters of her blonde curls; and an arm bent at her hip. Narcissism, materialism, parodic femininity, masculine aggression are all embodied in these gestures, presided over by a look of ironic self-content, a raised eye, an over-langorous and studied smile, a minute bounce of the hip as if motivated by some mechanical spring of incessant sexual stimulation. As she listens to the maid and replies to her we note that Ruby – who will not differ in this when she is with her lovers – if she looks at her, does so formally rather than substantially, occasionally, as it were, acknowledging the direction from which the remark comes, but turning away in her addressee's mid-speech or her own, here never, elsewhere hardly ever making eye contact, treating her interlocutor as an audience rather than an intimate (so that just at the cut which ends the scene Ruby turns smiling to her again, but clearly not for further communication, only to gauge the comic effect of her final remark). These three jokes possess an absolute self-regarding typicality, in every case focusing the attention solely on her. And unlike the masochistic narcissist (e.g. Woody Allen) whose preoccupation with his image is neurotic and negative, or the insecure narcissist (e.g. Hope) expert in devices to rescue a constantly collapsing image, West is of all comedians the least assailed by doubt, never victim. With heroic discipline her jokes (unlike Allen's and Hope's) resist almost every temptation to draw in material from the larger world outside sex relations and herself. The least monologue-oriented of comedians, her jokes never take on the kind of autonomy which, however marginally, displaces the teller.

The finale towards which the backstage scene has been building surprises by putting West on stage neither as teller nor singer, but as the tale, the wholly mute and apparently passive object of a serenading stage-door Johnny's song. Like 'A Pretty Girl is Like a Melody' (from *Ziegfeld Girl*, 1941) or 'The Girl on a Magazine Cover' (from *Easter Parade*, 1948) his 'My American Beauty' is a number that calls up a series of tableaux offering literal equivalents of the lyrics, though Ruby alone, rather than a Ziegfeldian bevy of girls, will take on all the roles. In the serenader's song (a clumsier version of Andrew Marvell's poem *The Gallery*, where the male speaker expresses the wholly conflicting views he holds of his mistress – beatific and witch-like – in terms of the various portraits in a picture gallery), these amount to a catalogue of conventional similes and metaphors, both positive and negative, of womanhood brought to bizarre life by the kitschy cheapness of the concepts and designs and Ruby's own silent wealth of commentary on them.

Mae West in **Belle of the Nineties**
'Don't know what to call her, but she's mighty like a rose.' Queen bee, phallus and John D. Rockefeller's American beauty rose of Social Darwinism in one.

Her first appearance is as a butterfly: 'Sometimes you are like a gorgeous butterfly, / Sturdy hearts are shattered as you flutter by.' Then, antithetically, she becomes a vampire bat: 'They say you're a vampire / Playing at love's game.' Then, with alternative symmetry, a rose: 'You may have too many beaux, / But to me you're a beautiful rose.' Penultimately, a spider poised in its web: 'You're the spider, I'm the fly / That's caught up in your web.' Then finally, a replica of that 'monumental maiden', the Statue of Liberty: 'North and south and east and west / The country proclaim / My American beauty / Sweetheart of the Red, White and Blue.' The minutely syncopating shoulders, head and hips, mockingly contradicting the statue's passivity, the arms spread away from the body in various attitudes denoting defencelessness and surrender but negated by the body's imperviousness and the patent insincerity of the open-lipped smile of vulnerable desire presented to the audience, dictate that the images should be read with the fullest irony, and Ruby's collusion in them as knowing and mocking. Seemingly placed as object simply to be viewed, Ruby is attended by the camera in a sequence of semi-close-ups and close-ups and positioned so that she looks straight out at the audience as if it is they who are the vaudeville audience for her spectacle. Not only can they then register every detail of the kinetic commentary she makes on the images she has assumed, and the singer's description of them, but the voyeuristic economy is subverted since the film turns back on them in Ruby's gaze. Yet we may feel that there is something in West which makes all this profoundly ambiguous, part at least unabashed self-celebration, with the image of West as 'American Beauty Rose' reminding us of John D. Rockefeller telling a Sunday School class, 'The growth of a large business is merely the survival of the fittest . . . The American Beauty Rose can be produced in the splendour and fragrance which bring cheer to its beholder only by sacrificing the early buds which grow up around it.'

West as narcissist, West as conscious celebrant/unconscious critic of capitalism, West as Social Darwinist, intersect with West as critic of sexual ideology, the same ambiguities accompanying the final image of the presiding female genius of the Republic, the Statue of Liberty (Statue of Libido, in the famous joke): at once an image of West's hubristic libertarianism holding aloft the phallus-torch for the United States of desire, the uncritical prophetess of sexual consumerism, and the iron-ised, ultimate burlesque representation of woman as 'monumental maiden', statuesque allegory, symbol and object.

The anatomy of comedy – eight typical jokes

What kind of men do you like?
Just two, domestic and foreign.
— Belle of the Nineties

What follows is a shorthand listing of the most characteristic and most consistent of her jokes. These types have been established in terms of subject
matter rather than of more abstract joke technique, so that the verbal skill,
sometimes of a high order ('It's better to be looked over than overlooked'),
is taken for granted in a primary emphasis on meaning.

1. Jokes of the objectified male. This set of jokes is the verbal equivalent
of the scrutinising gaze the West character turns on the men who approach
her, as for instance when she first meets the handsome Brooks Clayborne
in *Belle of the Nineties*. When he gallantly suggests, 'Perhaps I can do something for you sometime' she drops her eyes from his face to his crotch before
replying 'Yeah'. In this paradigm the male is inspected and judged not as a
person, but solely for his sexual endowments. In the simpler form of the
joke these endowments are only material (West as businesswoman), as where
in *I'm No Angel* Tira's point of view from the stage takes in the ring on
Ernest Brown's finger rather than the man. Where, though, material considerations are not paramount, the most developed form of the joke has West
choose for herself in the end the male with the grossest physical attributes.
Thus the hero of *Belle of the Nineties*, the ultimate winner of Ruby, is a
boxer, the Tiger Kid who is, as the closing wedding joke has it, 'the best
man' because as a primitive athlete he should be the most potent of men (as
she has said to him earlier, 'I like a man with masculine supremacy'). In
both *She Done Him Wrong* and *I'm No Angel* Cary Grant is a more suave,
more civilised prize (in *Angel* from a higher social world), but the force of
the joke in *Belle of the Nineties* seems refuelled by personal obsession: we
remember that her father, 'Battling Jack West, was a prizefighter, and her autobiography recounts both a meeting with Jack Dempsey ('a shy-looking, tough
young man, solid but graceful, and his muscles appealed to me'), and with
the world heavyweight wrestling champion Vincent Lopez ('I looked and
touched those shoulders and we became romantically interested in each
other'). In *I'm No Angel* Charles Atlas is one of her pin-ups, and in her
private life, whether as reality or carefully constructed myth, the parade of
muscle men on stage or in personal attendance suggests an uninspected
obsession. But in the context of the films – as in *I'm No Angel*, where she
fondles the body of the amorous acrobat ('Don't worry, I ain't gonna hurt

him. I only wanna feel his muscles') – the preference becomes more a meaningful sign than a psychological oddity, readable as the revenge of the objectified female who is only judged in terms of her sexuality and who insolently
turns the tables on the male by viewing his muscles as the equivalents of her
hips and breasts.

   2. *Jokes of the unsatisfied female*. Closely related to the joke above,
these work to defeat any surviving male self-esteem. Here the man who is
wholly sure of his potency, who identifies himself with the sexual athlete
demanded by the heroine, is subjected to the insinuation that even the 'best
man' could never hope to satisfy her.

> *Tiger:* Promise me that you'll never think of another man.
> *Ruby:* That depends on you.   *Belle of the Nineties*

Or again her answer when he asks her to give up her 'art' for him:

> *Tiger:* Well, you will if you love me enough.
> *Ruby:* If I love you enough, I'll have to.

The surface manouevres of the jokes work, in the case of the first, on the
reversal whereby the woman's fidelity, rather than being absolutely assumed,
is redefined as (in the most innocent interpretation) depending on the man's
attitude, or (in the least innocent) on his sexual performance. In the second
it works on the cynical taking of the word 'love' not as a spiritual essence,
but as a bodily act, so that Ruby's implicit argument runs: 'If my body is
so constantly employed in love-making that I cannot follow my career,
because, literally, I can't move, then I will have to give it up.' But both
replies are formally hypothetical, and therefore expressions of doubt, the
sneering delivery leaving no question that the condition (repletion, satisfaction of the heroine) is impossible.

   Another major version of the joke is constant reference to the multiplicity
of the heroine's lovers, past, present and future.

> *Ace La Mont:* (meeting Belle at the docks with a large crowd) Take care of these
>   men.
> *Belle:*   Yes. Give them all my address.

In its various manifestations the joke deflates pride in male potency by claiming infinite, inexhaustible receptivity for the female, with West as a sort of
Queen Bee endlessly serviced by her colony of men, but always on the lookout
for a new opportunity. She is unconcerned with questions of quality or
psychological, as distinct from purely physical, capacities. Legman, in his
Rationale of the Dirty Joke, claims that the hidden matriarchal joke goes

'unerringly to the essence of matriarchy . . . the relationship to the child
. . . and pays little attention to the stud-male's moment of usefulness in
intercourse'. Since West is a childless, parody matriarch, a barren earth-
mother whose offspring is herself, the joke dispenses with the child and only
the female's inexhaustible receptivity remains. Because the joke in its various
forms finally makes even the most potent male impotent, it is ultimately a
castration joke. If we speculate about why it gives pleasure, our answer will
be complicated: first, the joke is distanced by being made at the expense of
another man (in the narrative), who becomes the scapegoat for any fears
aroused in the male viewer; second, it might well be argued that such jokes
stir up masochistic, secretly pleasureable feelings in the male viewer; third,
the anxiety the joke produces is mitigated by the ludicrous features of the
West persona, features which deflate the seriousness of what is being said,
but, crucially, are the preconditions of the utterance, since a joke that fails
to give pleasure is not, in fact, a joke. Finally though, we should consider
not the victim but, gender-specifically, the aggressor. Through West (though
identification with the comic monster has to be devious, playful, partial),
the female audience is offered the enjoyment of comic revenge on the dominant male. This might be read either as sadism or a feeling justified by social
circumstances.

   3. The comedy of female calculation. The comedy here depends on the
belief that women, being more susceptible to passion and softer feelings than
men, subdue themselves more willingly to the demands of love and lover.
The barker touting for custom at her carnival performance in *I'm No Angel*
promises that 'with the right kind of encouragement she throws discretion
to the winds', but if we know Mae West, we laugh at the unlikelihood of
the promise and the naïvety of the customers. Some of the most striking
examples are primarily or wholly visual. In the familiar iconography of the
romantic film the female shuts her eyes when kissed by the male, as if to
assert that the deeper meaning of the proverb 'Love is Blind' is that female
love is and should be the blindest of all. On the rare occasions when Mae
West is embraced or kissed, she goes in literally with eyes open and, typically,
just at the discreet cut or fade on the embrace, her eyes (or perhaps the single
eye visible over the lover's shoulder) roll upwards, signalling the opposite
of absorption. Verbally the same point is being made when she says to the
masked bandit in *My Little Chickadee*, 'You're the one man in my life . . .
right now.' In a different inflection, when asked in *Belle of the Nineties* if
she was nervous about receiving so many presents, she replies in one of her
most formally perfect ripostes: 'No, I was calm and collected.' As a catch-
phrase may be recycled, so a proverb may be given a twist as in 'A man in

the house is worth two in the street' (to Ace in *Belle of the Nineties*, with its suggestions of rates of payment for high and low-class prostitution). The idea of a woman as naturally selfless, endlessly giving, is shattered in a number of quips, perhaps most memorably in Tira's jarring response to Ernest Brown's compliment 'You're certainly givin' me the time of my life'; 'Don't say givin'. I don't like that word 'givin'.' And the comic blasphemy of woman as detached observer and collector has its apotheosis when, in reply to Ace La Mont's importunate catalogue of her charms, 'Your golden hair, your fascinating eyes, alluring smile and lovely arms, your form divine', Ruby queries 'Is this a proposal or are ya takin' inventory?'

4. *The comedy of female helplessness*. Here in sardonic contradiction to everything else about her, West acts out the traditional female role of helplessness, an act, however, characterised by all her usual irony and insincerity. When Ace La Mont, meeting Ruby on her arrival in New Orleans, asks 'Shall we go?', her reply is 'Why sure, but you'll have to show me the way, because I'm just a Babe in the Woods.' The unlikeliness of this is recognised by the crowd of men who laugh at her remark. Neither Babe, chicken nor kid (remembering the dandy's song in *Belle of the Nineties*), she clearly does not need to be shown the way by anyone. Moments later, when Ace shows her round his establishment, the 'Sensation House', there is the following exchange:

> *Ace:* It won't all be work. You will have moments of your own.
> *Ruby:* Well, I do have my moments.
> *Ace:* You have?
> *Ruby:* Yeah, but they're all weak ones.

The wit depends on two meanings of 'moments' and two meanings of 'weak'. If to a male-centred Victorian view of things woman's sexuality is viewed as the product of her weakness, thus conflating the two meanings, West's pretence of accepting their identity actually forces them apart again. Her weak (sexual) moments are ones where she pretends to be weak but is really strong. As she says to a suitor in *My Little Chickadee*, 'Funny. Every man I meet wants to protect me. I can't figure out from what.' For West (unlike Sophie Tucker, who celebrated the sacrifices of her 'Yiddisher Momma'), attachment to the mother, the representative of female self-sacrifice, is a sign of weakness. In a significant moment in *Belle of the Nineties*, Ace's mistress, Molly, advances on her usurping rival, Ruby, uttering Ruby's name. Ruby's reply is that this (the name) is the only thing she ever learnt from her mother. Properly parthenogenetic, the reply, allied to her complete absence of interest in children, underlines the character's absolute detachment from the roles of succourer or succoured. Cuthbert J. Twillie's (W. C. Field's) inability to perceive this in *My Little Chickadee* leads him to misapprehend the cry of the goat Florabelle has placed in their marriage bed as her cries for her Mama ('Mah-Mah').

5. ***The comedy of masculine traits***. In West's films the appropriation of masculine roles is often literal – Tira as lion-tamer, taking on the gangster's role of fight-fixer in *Belle of the Nineties*, shooting down marauding Indians in *My Little Chickadee*, etc. It can occasionally take the form of violent behaviour – actual or verbal – as when Tira spits a mouthful of water at her upper-class rival Alicia, or when she makes the threat 'A better dame than you once called me a liar and they had to sew her up in twelve different places.' Moreover, given the typical period setting of her films, West's smoking has an important meaning, disregarding its status as a masculine trait banned to females. Sometimes the use of an exaggeratedly long cigarette holder underlines the phallic exclusiveness of the ban and the significance of her disregarding it. Another reversal is implicit in the famous line 'C'm up 'n see me s'm'time' and its variations, where it is not only she who offers the sexual invitation, but the invitation is to her place. This demand that the male visit her establishes an actual and symbolic matrilocality, breaking the rule that the female lives in the male's house (if they are married) or visits him (if they are not), so that place becomes an expression of his economic power to support her and her status as appendage. In *Belle of the Nineties*, for instance, in the second scene the Tiger Kid visits Ruby's apartment and sets the tone for the rest of the film, so that later, when the plot requires her to go to New Orleans and live at Ace La Mont's place, we still feel the environment to be hers, and the 'Sensation House' becomes a kind of baroque metaphor for Mae West herself. Where the plot's vicissitudes (and perhaps unconscious censoring mechanisms, alongside the conscious ones of the later 30s films) dictate a departure from this pattern, as in *Every Day's a Holiday*, where Peaches is mostly in the van Doon mansion, there is a resulting tameness in much of the film. We cannot simply call this matrilocal tendency the assertiveness of the matriarch, since West is wholly self-orientated, largely uninterested in other women, wholly unreproductive and completely uninterested in children. But within her comic monstrousness such connotations – the comic film's version of the horror film's monstrous 'return of the repressed' – obliquely abound.

Pervasive as the confusion of male and female traits is in the persona, it takes many forms, both obvious and displaced, in the films. In *I'm No Angel*, before Tira performs at the carnival we are made aware of a competing attraction, the 'Turtle Boy', half boy, half marine creature who plays the zither, in complex analogy to Tira, part 'male', part 'female' and her music. In *Every Day's a Holiday* the corrupt police commissioner Quaide is angered when Peaches has a poster for Mlle Fifi's show put on his billboard, creating a composite image of his head sitting on a cartoon of Mae West's body. In *Belle of the Nineties* there are many examples of West's masculinised aggression, here over a boxer, the most masculine of men, as she asserts her predominance verbally and physically, first putting the manager down with a quip, then keeping the man standing in the rain and finally getting him arrested. Then she tells the Kid, 'I could manage ya, honey.' In the lead-up to this, as she spars verbally with the manager over the Kid on the steps outside her apartment, she is characteristically positioned above them both, one of many instances of placing and framing that assert her dominance.

   6. *Jokes of narcissism*. Like the play with masculinity, this is a pervasive verbal and visual element of West's persona, constantly interacting with the others. As comedy it might equally be said to conform to conventional expectations both in asserting that women are naturally more narcissistic and by moralistically blaming them – i.e. women should not be so narcissistic. But equally it involves the more complex consequences already noted: admiration for the unregenerate narcissist and punishment for the patriarchal world's cultivation of female self-centredness. One notable form that such jokes take is West's habit, when praised excessively by an admirer, of simply accepting the hyperbole as if it were a neutral description:

> *Kirk Lawrence:* I'll never forget you.
> *Tira:*   No one ever does   — *I'm No Angel*

> *Tiger:* If I catch some other guy foolin' round with you I'll bust him in half.
> *Ruby:* Hmm. I couldn't blame ya.   — *Belle of the Nineties*

   7. *Jokes of insolence*. Much comedy hinges on insolence, insolence of the small against the great, the lower against the upper class, and part of Mae West's function in the films is to suggest a proletarian revolt against authority. But more primary with this comedian is insolence directed against the male, as overbearing suitor, as audience of the female spectacle, and as figure of authority (voyeur, saloon owner, criminal, judge and court of law).

> *Judge:* Young lady, are you trying to show contempt for this court?
> *Tira:*   No, I'm doin' my best to hide it.   — *I'm No Angel*

In a specialised variant she pretends that she does not understand the codes of masculine gallantry when they are offered to her, thus leaving the profferer up in the air.

Van Doon: Won't you sit down?
Peaches: What for? I ain't tired.
Van Doon (offering his arm): My arm.
Peaches: What's the matter with it?   — *Every Day's a Holiday*

8. Obscene jokes. West's wit is constantly libidinous and as such plays against ideas of female purity and passivity. The demands both of the satisfactory joke and censorship make for that certain indirection of statement that can just be taken in two different ways, one innocent, one not.

Maid: I've been married four times.
Tira: Yeah? You ought to do well in the wholesale business.   — *I'm No Angel*

An important variant crosses with another major type, and might equally be classed as narcissistic. Here West's typical forcing of an 'innocent' term into sexual meaning is specifically directed towards her own body, as are so many of her gestures:

Man (of Brooklyn Bridge): What a beautiful structure!
Peaches: Hey, cut that out! People'll think you know me!
                                                        — *Every Day's a Holiday*

Ace: Great town, St. Louis. You were born there?
Ruby: Yes.
Ace: What part?
Ruby: All of me.   — *Belle of the Nineties*

As is often the case with her jokes of insolence, some of West's quasi-obscene jokes have no real content, but exist almost solely by virtue of a generalised aura of suggestiveness. As she remarks in one of the more soberly analytical moments of her autobiography, 'I had learned by now that I could say almost anything on stage if I smiled and was properly ironic in delivering my dialogue.' A simple, blatant instance is the wiggle that accompanies the last word when she tells a crowd of admirers in *Belle of the Nineties*, 'I'm sorry, gents, but I have to retire.'

The songs

He was her man,
But she done him wrong.   — 'Frankie and Johnnie'

As they do in fully-fledged musicals, though in a somewhat looser way, the songs in a Mae West film comment on and help explain the interrelationships of form and theme in the narrative (here *Belle of the Nineties*, the film we have chosen to concentrate on most). Moreover, they also serve as important agents for the promotion of the persona, a litany to her *outré* status as a turn-of-the-century divinity of love whose outsize libido is in its boundless cupidity and brio matched only by the devotion of votaries worshipping her at the profane vaudeville or roulette-room shrines of mortal desire. Within the all-engulfing egocentricity of these constraints the songs divide roughly-speaking either into those focusing primarily on the men in Mae's life (or the life in her men, all men, that is: 'some like short men, some like 'em tall, I'm funny that way, 'cos I like them all', *Belle of the Nineties*), or on those celebrating her own endowments and accomplishments, either rousing men to feats of sexual prowess, or else relieving them of their fortunes. In each case the lyrics, melody, orchestration and thin, bluesy delivery are given a camera style and a *mise-en-scène* perfectly fitting their mood, creating a sense of aesthetic and thematic continuity between the self-conscious theatricalisation of the musical numbers and the very slightly more muted self-conscious fulfilment of the persona in other non-musical periods of the narrative.

In these non-musical sections the settings of West's work choke with statuettes of near-naked women, vases filled with flowers, and salons and boudoirs bedecked with voluptuous drapery. And so, in *Belle of the Nineties*, as she takes the stage in New Orleans under the rakish management of Ace La Mont, with his pencil-thin moustache, seedy gentility and unctuousness, a comic throwback to melodramatic villains of the bayou, the proscenium arch is decorated at each end with stucco cameos of nymphs, naked from the waist up, apparently supporting the entire edifice. On the stage itself the only decor in the 'St. Louis Woman' number is a huge vase filled with sumptuous roses, the flowers and statuettes emphasising in their orchideous-ness her confected femininity. And yet these symbols of art and nature hold in tension, no less here in 1930s Hollywood than in sixteenth or seventeenth-century Europe, contradictory values of life and death. The roses are, as they are in metaphysical poetry, a *carpe diem*, while the statuettes of near-naked women are, typically, both marvels of art and nature, and handmaidens of the devil. As if to emphasise the latter point, West draws near, prior to taking the stage for the 'Memphis Blues' number in *Belle of the Nineties*, to one of the sculpted nudes in her apartment, and strikes a match against it, a gesture which provides the cue for the overture of the number. We take the semi-nude statuette as a symbol both of West's ivory-clad sensuality and of mock-serious associations with the devil. Yet, though hard-edged, self-seeking and sensual is what she plainly is, whatever infernal elements (she is a 'devil in disguise' as Sister Honkytonk in *I'm No Angel*) she possesses, they cannot be taken too seriously. To the League of Decency she probably did seem unmixedly diabolical; to the chumps she was a crucible of their

own fantasies and lusts; to anyone else, though we note with Hamlet that
'. . . the devil hath power / T'assume a pleasing shape', and from Marlene
Dietrich that the devil is a woman, she was as Mephistophelian as the goat
who replaced her in the nuptial bed by W. C. Fields's side in *My Little
Chickadee*. Though he took the point of the goat's traditional symbolism,
and in exclaiming 'Beelzebub!' used the most appropriate oath in the circumstances, Fields naturally only emphasises the parodic mood.

The fire motif is pervasive in the 'My Old Flame' number of *Belle of the
Nineties*:

> My old flame.
> I can't even think of his name.
> But it's funny now and then
> How my thoughts go drifting back again to
> My old flame.
> My old flame.
> My new lovers all seem so tame.
> Oh there never was a gent
> More magnificent
> Than my old flame.

The whole film trades on traditional images mirroring the representation of
sexual passion and its cultural taboos and repressions. New Orleans or St
Louis: each has a veneer of civilisation, but beneath the mask of their sophistication, a set of moral codes stifling the drives of the libido. Even New
Orleans, with its 'Frenchness' (and therefore clichéd sexiness) and Negro
roots, is not spared the rigours of the Superego's laws. When we see the
blacks dancing their voodoo rituals at the end of the film, the native rhythms
and values have been sabotaged by spiritualist hymns about guilt and mortification, but not before this (as sung by most singers, e.g. most recently
Linda Ronstadt) sentimental song, turned wholly libidinous in its performance by Mae West, has left us with the memory of a woman so preoccupied
by promiscuity as to become uninterested in the names of the men she has
seduced. (As she passes down the row of prison inmates in *She Done Him
Wrong*, she responds to them all in a way that suggests she's had relations
with every one of them.)

West's 'fire song', 'My Old Flame', is superseded by 'Troubled Waters'.
The fires of sex, not their life-giving, healing warmth but, in social terms,
their demonic and destructive properties, are eventually doused by the waters
of a New Orleans River Jordan:

Oh, I'm gonna drown,
Down in those troubled waters
That creep in round my soul.
They're way beyond control
And they'll wash my sins away
Before the morn . . .

The den of vice itself, the devil's own palace, secularised in Ace La Mont's decadent lair of gambling tables and lewd cabaret acts, eventually goes up in flames, its ashes representing a collective social desire to purge not only more self-evident evils like gambling, deceit, treachery and the self-seeking wickedness that leads to murder, but also the whole spectrum of sexual desire itself. After the fire, West is united with the boyish, even somewhat childish Tiger Kid, more a kid than a tiger ('I can always manage you honey'), a competent aggressor in fisticuffs, but in sexual terms probably as ferocious as the miniature animal figurines on display beside all those photographs of the men in her life this mock-Circe has shipwrecked over love in *I'm No Angel*. We know Mae West will survive the fire and all its temporary guilt-healing energies, that she will banish or ignore all thoughts of remorse and mortification, forget the Tiger Kid as easily in her next film as in this she has forgotten the name of her old flame. Resilience and inviolable egocentricity are the primary drives of the persona, and these will resurface to turn the temporary wastelands of erotic defeat into the jungles of regenerate desire.

So 'My Old Flame', 'Willy of the Valley', 'Frankie and Johnny' and other songs about exaggerated specimens of male virility turn out, on closer inspection, to be either elaborate excuses for a display of West's repertoire of imaginative verbal, kinetic and other talents, or else camp jokes about the priapic rituals of sex. Whatever the focus of the lyrics, the promotion and self-engrossments of the persona remain primary, and a whole range of devices ensure that this is so. Not even an edict of banishment in *Every Day's a Holiday* manages to quell this paranoiac obsession for self-display, and she returns to the New York stage to sing as 'Fifi', a supposedly renowned French chanteuse.

You got to click ze heel,
You got to kiss ze hand,
If you want to make ze hit wiz Fifi.
You got to buy ze sparkling jewel,
And be prepared to fight ze duel.
You got to own a creek or a well,
And say 'oui, oui, mam'selle'.
If you want to make ze hit wiz Fifi,
Why don't you come up and see me?

The disguise, the masquerade, the lyrics and production of the number, clarify some of the essential features of her aura. Frenchness of course well suits the 'Gay Nineties' connotations, not only because of the Toulouse-Lautrec inspired ambience of demi-monde eroticism, but also because of the exoticism that is also usually her hallmark: Frenchmen imaged as Montmartre artists, flower-sellers, toffs in evening dress, *flics*, and waterfront Johnnies in striped T-shirts, neckerchiefs and berets, prepare the sacred ground for the White Goddess's arrival. She enters in a horse-drawn carriage as 'Fifi', looking every bit like the whorish Madame the name, when it is not given to poodles, inescapably suggests. As she begins to sing, at first in French and then in English, a huge drape, studded with jewels and frilly patterns, rises up behind her like some enormous eiderdown quilt, a suggestion, in a parody of Venus's rising fom her watery bed, with the eiderdown here as conch, that 'Fifi's' song comes straight from the boudoir, from the very cradle of desire. Wherever she is, West is never without her aura of the boudoir, always beckoning studs to 'come up' and see her, like Cary Grant as Captain Cummings in *She Done Him Wrong* and the unnamed lover who has to climb all of six flights in the St Louis Woman number when he 'comes' to see her.

Everything here is covered in winks and nudges in a play-acting, oblique response to real sex, but in 'Fifi' the joke is taken yet another stage, into the realms of sado-masochism. Though the whips and bare buttocks are missing, the song's evocations of the folly of desire bear comparison with Buñuel's comic obsession with the Marquis de Sade. Discipline, obedience, subservience and pain – these are the qualities men must value and practise if 'zey are to make ze hit wiz Fifi'. But perhaps, after all, we know they will never make 'ze hit' in whichever part of her anatomy she means, because as she sings, here as on other occasions, her eyes roll around, her sidelong glances find no fixed target, her hips constantly move in a gesture at once sexual (flaunting her concealed genitalia) and political (trying to evade the kind of man who would like to make her, as Cummings in *She Done Him Wrong* puts it, 'my prisoner, and I'm going to be your jailer for a long, long time'). In 'Fifi' we see only the empty verbal husks of the Sadean ideal; West is only playing; it is all an act, as full of serious intention as the curling cigar smoke that drifts across the screen and into her stage space from the tables and bars crowded with men who have come to worship at her shrine of love. 'I've never seen anyone like her. She's simply divine', an admirer in *Belle of the Nineties* comments, apparently totally unaware that Mae West is above all an ironic image of the fictionalisation of experience, testimony to a conviction that the imagined delights and thrills of sexual desire are far more reward-

ing than their reality. She is the Don Quixote of the libido (not simply in
her daring exploits, like the Don's, in the lion's cage), in love with a self-image
created entirely out of sensual fantasies and erotic utopias.

The narrative

> Are you in town for good?
> I expect to be here, but not for good.   — *Belle of the Nineties*

Theorising the role and functions of the protagonists in comedian–comedy,
Steve Seidman argues that in its initial stages at least the structural formula
of the comedic persona succeeds in posing a dynamic, sometimes subversive
threat to the established order and moral certainties of conventional society.
The disruption of the ideological certainties is mirrored by a transgression
of formal constraints, so that, typically in a way that bears some resemblance
to more obviously code-breaking narratives (Godard, Buñuel, etc.). a rapport
is established between comedian and audience that very much recalls the
'alienation technique' of Brecht's plays, especially in the assertion of the
text's (here the film text's) fictionality that such subversions of realism, of
the very conditions of illusion, usually achieve. It also mirrors the audience's
own desires for transgression against the constraints of civilisation's restraints
and orders. Comedian comedy seems to stress the imaginative qualities that
such transgressions encourage, for as Brecht wrote, 'There is a vast difference
between somebody's having a picture of something, which demands imagination, and an illusion, which demands gullibility.'

What Seidman further claims, however, is that this healthily disruptive,
even necessary questioning of the conventions of narrative, the overthrowing
of the authority of mimesis, has only a limited, circumscribed licence. On
this reading the revels, the formal and ideological insubordination of the
beginning and middle sections of the narrative, will finally be overshadowed
by the restored conservatism of the finale. The *rites de passage* of the typical
comedian–hero/heroine are from a state of uncivilised, unruly, anti-social
behaviour to a wholly socialised, integrated, and therefore deradicalised identity no longer a threat to the status quo.

The first part of the theory is more easily acceptable than the second. Mae
West can indeed be seen, in the early and middle sections of the films as a
disruptive, marginalised figure, frequently associated, like Hope, with low
life and even, on occasion, crime. With the singular exception of her double
act with W. C. Fields in *My Little Chickadee*, she stands alone – tall, dark
and handsome men like Cary Grant notwithstanding – as the scourge of

convention. Such low-life or criminal associations make of her an enemy of form, a loner in the narrative. But her relationship with her 30s audience is also deliberately and creatively embedded in alienation since, of course, she is a character out of her time, the *Belle of the Nineties*, a *fin de siècle* Bowery-style courtesan.

Yet neither in the case of West nor in that of Hope, Benny, Lewis, or for that matter any of the great comedians of the Hollywood tradition, is disruption quite so easily confined by the closure of the narrative. As we have already seen in the discussion of Hope, the ambiguities of the persona tend to override the pointed conventionalities of closure, and the same is clearly true of West. Despite the conventional drive of the narratives, the endings of her films usually reaffirm the unpredictability and the outrageousness of a persona that is admittedly very prone to contradiction, both of gender and ideology. This is so even in the case of narratives where marriage is her ultimate destiny. Of course, in narratives where marriage is deliberately avoided – e.g. *My Little Chickadee* where three men (if we include Fields / Cuthbert Twillie among them) are left dangling on her whimsicality – the radical potential of the persona is very clearly left intact. If marriage is the lot of many a Clara Bow, a Lilian Gish or even a Jean Harlow, it is certainly not that of a Mae West as Florabelle. The film (made later than those in the middle and late 30s most affected by censorship) is set on frustrating all pious, hypocritical attitudinising towards marriage of the kind so brilliantly satirised in Margaret Hammeton's turn-of-the-century representative of the League of Decency or Moral Majority. Florabelle is banished (yet again) from the town at the beginning of the film, told not to return until married. She does return, under the pretence that she has married Twillie – the ceremony having been carried out by a liquor salesman on a train – and by the end of the film she is still refusing to take the sacrament properly. (But equally, dressed to take it in *I'm No Angel* in a white wedding gown, the vision of the lasciviously bobbing mock-ingenue is as subversive in acceptance as refusal elsewhere.) While *My Little Chickadee*'s moral majority are implicitly siding with St Paul, whose line on marriage was, of course, 'I say therefore to the unmarried and the widows it is good for them to abide even as I. But if they cannot abstain, let them marry, for it is better to marry than to burn', Mae West knows in the depths of her heart that marriage for her – and for many women (or men, for that matter) – can easily become, if entered into with hierarchical expectations, an imprisonment of heart and mind, as well as of body. So when in *I'm No Angel* Tira is asked, 'I don't suppose you believe in marriage', her quick-witted answer is almost predictably, 'Only as a last resort.'

Naturally, her films are not overtly diatribes against matrimony, only against marriages with shaky foundations, for West does marry in some films. Yet even here, convention is quite clearly at her mercy: will the Tiger Kid be a patriarch, limit her taste for independence, play-acting, diamonds? Hardly. He has already been – despite all his boxing triumphs – her dupe. He is no Tiger, only a kid in her hands, a phallic toy, to be played with and, ultimately, like all toys, ignored or discarded. The final narrative union of West and the Tiger Kid is as much rooted in contradiction, tension, ambiguity as has been their development up to this point in the narrative. The closure of the film unites two characters with all these idiosyncrasies left intact, in a way that deliberately asks us to speculate on the unlikely prospects of their union. Even when she marries the strong ex-policeman in *Every Day's a Holiday*, we know she will get the better of him, as of all men, because whereas all the good guys ultimately fail in their plans to outwit the bad guys in the film, West's is the only plan that succeeds. And even where, in *I'm No Angel*, the prize is Cary Grant, the ending still manages to hint at extracurricular activities.

Contradictions, of course, abound in the West character, sometimes in surprising ways, typically where marriage is concerned: the films expect to be anti-marriage on the one hand, but, on the other hand, sometimes steer her conventionally towards it. ('Marriage is a good enough cause for any-thing.') Whereas the persona, the songs, or the jokes seem primarily intent on promoting the sense of an individual ruled unswervingly by egocentricity, it almost comes as something of a shock to find, in *Belle of the Nineties*, for instance, that she is prepared to sacrifice her own selfish interest in the Tiger Kid for the altruistic purpose of allowing him to pursue his career undis-tracted by her allure. A pseudo-redemptive side to her nature is also a feature of *Every Day's A Holiday*, where she acts socially, in concert with van Doon and the other anti-corruption citizens who oppose Quaid and his cronies; in *I'm No Angel* we find her acting towards an unhappy girl in a sisterly fashion; in *My Little Chickadee* she cares enough about Fields to rescue him at his execution; in *Belle of the Nineties* she dissociates herself from La Mont as he becomes more ruthless and criminal. The plots rather unconvincingly push her towards monogamy and true love and in the process she is asked implicitly to take leave both of her criminality and her sexual predatoriness. So in *Belle of the Nineties* her release of the Kid is an ideologically-motivated gesture of Camille-like proportions, the act a repetition of the tired association between, on the one hand, women and the snares of voluptuousness and, on the other, between men, innocence, sexual vulnerability and the primacy of career.

As she veers between predatoriness and heroism, her behaviour is judged by all around her. Her detractors are on the side of the law, all Pharisees under the skin, deriving guilt-bred satisfaction from banishing, jailing or vilifying her as an adultress or Jezebel of the New World. When they are not agents of the Law (*Every Day's a Holiday*) her opponents are still making use of her, either as sinister male villains, pimp figures from whom she struggles to be free (*I'm No Angel*), or as wives and spinsters, the former envious that anyone should have somehow escaped the enslavements of bad marriages, the latter enraged and frustrated by the lubricities from which they appear to have been excluded.

Her partisans, not less numerous, are with one exception (Fields) usually less interesting; aside from the tall, dark and handsome, yet somehow bland leading men (this is even true of Cary Grant, early in his career), the unnamed chumps in the audience, the managers, or agents who promote her act, all of whom, of course, have their moments (as when a nameless spectator at the circus in *I'm No Angel* comments, 'say, if those lions don't show some sense I'm going down there and bite her myself!'), perhaps the most interesting members of her entourage are her black maids, sometimes appearing as a group, sometimes, as in *Belle of the Nineties*, restricted to the solitary presence of Beulah. Though West is often less than sisterly to other women (an exception already noted occurs in *She Done Him Wrong*, where she helps comfort Sally, a girl who has tried to commit suicide over a man), the maids are curiously indulgent towards her in ways that seem to go beyond purely material considerations, suggesting even a kind of vicarious pleasure in West's career, as it were on behalf of the gender, especially in *I'm No Angel* where they form an appreciative audience to her manipulations of the males. The black maids, though, are ultimately a sort of unconscious parody of the three Graces in Classical or Renaissance art. Where, say, in Botticelli they represent different strands of the beauty of Aphrodite herself, here their devotional, friendly uncouthness is designed to provide a marked contrast to the lustrous beauty of their own divinity of love, Mae West. West's pearly, ivory whiteness is set in relief against the background of these unself-conscious racist images. These jovial, and by the standards of the film's own reactionary rhetoric, somewhat cretinous picaninnies may be the hand-maidens of a vulgar Aphrodite as she prepares herself for her own Primavera rituals of stage and boudoir, but they are also a constant reminder of the grace by which she and, through her, all white women have been spared the socialised, racial humiliations of being black. That is the ultimate set of connotations associated with Beulah and her sisters. But whereas it was left for other comedians (e.g. Richard Pryor and Bill Cosby) and other film-makers (e.g. Mel Brooks) gradually to question and then reformulate images of blackness in the comic cinema, here, despite all the contradictions of the West character, there was little to be done for a topic whose radical interrogation could add nothing to the all-embracing project of promoting the ineffable qualities of a persona hermetically sealed in the conviction of its own Olympian stature.

WOODY ALLEN

The analysis of comedy, the comedy of analysis

I haven't seen my analyst in the last 200 years. He was a strict Freudian, and if I'd been going all this time I'd probably almost be cured by now.
— Woody Allen in *Sleeper*

Exteriors

In his fastidiously casual uniform of sports jacket, open-necked shirt, Oxford bags, middle-class NHS-equivalent spectacles (half symbolising myopic weakness, half superior insight), and a do-it-yourself coiffure which pays tribute to the hair-thinning climate of the hectic urbanised life of downtown Manhattan, Woody Allen is a mirror of the American new man, struggling in a pre-Yuppie world to detach himself both from Madison Avenue taste and the traumas of an ethnic minority childhood, while adapting himself to the demands of a deconstructionist, post-feminist, post-Vietnam culture. Immitigably Manhattanesque in sensibility, his films, with their New York settings and satire of California lifestyles, are only technically Hollywood comedies. Both on and off screen, Allen is the confused prototype of the new 'feminised' man: off-screen, admitting that Mia Farrow, his post-Keaton partner, mends the TV and drives the farm tractor while he devours the fashion pages and confesses, in childhood, to having dressed up cut-out Deanna Durbin paper dolls; on screen, constructing narratives which more than incidentally represent the struggle of women for emancipation both from cultural stereotyping and from lovers not yet wholly free from tradition. Beneath the unmistakable idiosyncrasy, a persona making it no longer *de rigeur* for screen lovers to look like Cary Grant or Tyrone Power, Allen is also of course, as comedian, not merely a limited 70s and 80s barometer of the times, independently measuring the changes in attitudes towards relations between the sexes, the meaning of life, and so on. He is also a fragmented author, a de-*auteur*ising *auteur* (unlike Allen, Hope is not an *auteur*, for his

vehicles are written and directed by others, while West is a limited kind of
auteur, having written and semi-directed her films), someone who within
his immediately recognisable persona at times even seems to acknowledge
the post-structuralist principle of the author's de-centred contribution to a
tissue of multiple voices and writings, as he consciously or self-consciously
(and sometimes unconsciously) refers in the films to, among others, Bob
Hope, Charlie Chaplin, Groucho Marx, Lenny Bruce and Philip Roth, fel-
low-travellers all, as well as primary ingredients of the comedian's persona,
on the journey through self-mockery, the irrational, and the irreverent, to
the complicated truths of self and society. Commentary on Allen's films has
been extensive. But no serious book on the film comedy of the sexes can
afford to ignore his centrality in the genre. As we look at that centrality, we
shall concentrate primarily on narrative strategies blurring divisions between
autobiography and fiction, between text and audience. And as we relate
Allen to the specific contexts of the 'narcissism culture', the 'sexual fix', and
the new consciousness *vis-à-vis* questions about gender and the relations
between the sexes, we shall listen out for the background voices that help
create the idiosyncratic end-product of the Allen persona, leaving the last
stage of our analysis for a closer look at some of the visual effects of his art,
something that is all too frequently and perhaps understandably neglected
under the force of the relentless, attention-stealing verbal wit.

Terms of endearment

Ariel (Mia Farrow):   How's your marriage?
Andrew (Woody Allen):It's fine. It's not working but it's fine.
                              – *A Midsummer Night's Sex Comedy* (1982)

The difficulty about discussing Allen's films, though, is not just that he has
been the target of so much analysis and commentary but that as the primary
comedian of the last twenty years, pre-eminently the age of deconstruction,
he has made his terrain, above all, a comedy of analysis. This is not something
restricted to processes of psychoanalytic introspection (the many jokes about
Freud and analysis), embracing as it does the equally important related
meaning of a comedy acutely conscious of the deconstruction of the discourses
making up individual and social reality. Even comedy itself – not just the
material of comedy, but the meaning and role of comedy and the comedian
himself – becomes the focus of his attention as he highlights the process by
which he and his works are received, analysed, praised, damned in the
complex system of cultural production and reception of art and entertainment. In this respect, of all the films touching on this subject, *Stardust*

Memories (1980) is the most extreme, with its shadowing of Fellini's *8½* (1963) in the form of a fantasy-ridden Allenesque figure, the comic film-maker Sandy Bates, attending a film-weekend showing his work in progress, where he is surounded by fans, groupies, buffs, academics, studio personnel, psychoanalysts, all in some ways obsessed by or involved in his work. At one point, trapped by an old boyhood friend, tormented by his own failure in the face of Bates's success and fame, he attempts to placate his envious persecutor with an answer that at the same time is a partial rationale for the place and relative value of comedy itself:

> I was the kid in the neighbourhood that told the jokes, right? So . . . so . . . we . . . you know we live in a . . . society that . . . yes, puts a big value on jokes, you know . . . if . . . think of it this way . . . if I had been an Apache Indian . . . those guys didn't need comedians at all, right . . . so . . . so, I'd be outa work . . . Look, I was lucky. I'm the first to admit it. I was a lucky bum. If I was born in Poland or Berlin, I'd be a lampshade today, right?

The core of Allen's comedy is to be found here, much of it embodying Freud's distinct notion of 'humour', something different from comedy and jokes: '. . . as a means of obtaining pleasure in spite of the distressing affects that interfere with the comic . . . one of the highest psychical achievements [which] enjoys the particular favour of thinkers'. Thus the comedy (humour) here not only invokes the horrors of the Holocaust, but also the aleatory as the comic (and tragic) law, while, in the interaction of Bates and Jerry Abraham, dramatising both the crassness of the culture in which the artist/ comedian finds himself and his own guilt as star commodity in that commodity-conscious society. But what is equally striking is the cross-cultural reference which so unexpectedly undermines the notion of comedy as a unified, inevitable, unchanging force, and places Bates's/Allen's desire to make laughter very specifically as a mode for achieving the complex needs for dramatisation and release of a sophisticated, neurotic, contemporary society.

These considerations lead at once to two complications. Firstly, that Allen's own self-conscious interest in analysis, that subversion of the usually separate roles of unself-conscious comic performer and detached critic–observer that characterises his comedy, seems to have as one of its effects, desirable from the point of view of the joke-maker (constantly in need of keeping one up on the audience), an undermining by pre-emption of the critic's procedures. The second is that even while Allen discourses (as above) on the relativity of comedy and on the importance of considering it with the eye of anthropology, the very terms he uses, that verbal/visual confection of anxiety and arrogance, hedonism and guilt, self-abasement and complacency, confidence and hesitation, are so much the mirror-image of his critics that they see in him too absolutely and seductively the reflection of their own exposed and redeemed selves for any sort of detachment to take place. By comparison Hope and West, by virtue of their historical distance, extreme stylisation and marvellous shallowness, repel such identification. Whereas very few watchers could ever have actually wanted to be the Mae West character, as distinct from possessing certain of her effects and powers, clearly many have taken Woody Allen as their role model of humane scepticism and anxious reconciliation to the contents and discontents of civilisation.

To note that Allen's huge minority audience is largely college-educated, mainly urban middle-class, is also to draw attention to fundamental changes in conditions and audiences that have made his films possible. Firstly, there is the enormous growth in college and university education in America, producing an audience for a comedy laden with cultural allusion, able to take the point, say, when Marshall McLuhan (standing in for Buñuel) is happily available for questioning in the cinema queue sequence from *Annie Hall* (1977), or recognise the various pastiches of the staple Arts Cinema or Campus European film nights that Allen himself, like many of his audience, first saw in the late 50s and early 60s. Secondly, there is American cinema's drift away from the idea of a universal audience to one of several large minority audiences who may only meet in the exceptional movie (in Allen's case *Annie Hall*, 1977, as distinct, say, from *The Purple Rose of Cairo*, 1985). This fragmentation is related to the ideological splintering of American society in the 60s and 70s, the increasing pessimism, powerlessness, and alienation from traditional native optimism and idealism – prominently featured in the cheerfully materialist assumptions and incorrigible individualism of both Hope and West – of the liberal intelligentsia, though an alienation muted into ambivalence by the freedom and material rewards enjoyed by that class and the perceived failure of a Marxist critique against the generative mythologies and spectacular productiveness of that society.

If in addressing a specific audience his comedy concentrates on certain areas at the expense of others, this is not simply an evasion of reality. For one thing, issues that originate – like feminism – in the middle class might eventually be of the greatest ultimate concern to the working class. For another, the concerns of love, in some form or other, are universal. Moreover, a radically politicised reading of Allen's films is as likely to neglect the realities of 'love and death' as a liberal criticism is the social infrastructure of the world he depicts. It is not to discredit or minimise the importance of Allen's themes – as we move to his specifically sexual comedy – to note that one reason among many for his complex appeal to his audience is the creation,

under the aegis of the great bourgeois dramatists Strindberg, Ibsen, O'Neill
and Ingmar Bergman, of a kind of pastoral of Love and Death (the 'straight',
darker side of which in Allen's *oeuvre* is *Interiors*), unsurpassed in its comic
insight which, pitted with despair though it is, escapes the mundane pressures
of the socio-political except as an antic realm of inauthenticity or madness
(the collection of jokes about committed radicals going mad and dribbling
saliva, turning to pornography or performing with pinwheel hat and roller
skates in Central Park).

Terms of enslavement

Love is everything, Boris.   — Sonia in *Love and Death*

I never want to get married. I just want to get divorced.
                                                         — Natasha in *Love and Death*

Perhaps the most typical Woody Allen joke incongruously places a vulgar,
low-order item against a higher one (or series of them): 'Modern man is here
defined as any person born after Nietzsche's edict that "God is dead", but
before the hit recording "I wanna hold your hand".' Freud's categories of
'degradation', 'unmasking' and 'revelation of physical automatism' in *Jokes
and Their Relation to the Unconscious* are called to mind here, but Allen's
jokes are usually more ambivalent than straighforward unmasking of
metaphysical pretensions by the drives of the body. Here Nietzsche and a
banal pop song, in other jokes Tolstoyan emotions and embarrassing sores,
jostle for prominence in a comedy of contradiction, the essence of which is
its unresolvability. Frequently the joke is structured around a clash of mind
and body, love and sexuality: 'I was seized with an urge to love. All I could
think of was Sonia. I wanted to hold her close to me, to weep tears on her
shoulder and engage in oral sex.'

Boris's joke emerges out of the paradox of a simultaneous affirmation and
denial of the identity of love and sex. Romantic sexual love, felt to be the
highest, most absolutely desirable human experience, cannot exist without
sex, yet cannot simply be identified with it. Sex is clearly not love, but love
without sex is not love in the truest sense. As it is for Sonia, 'love is everything'
to Boris and other Allen heroes, even when they deny it or defensively label
it as 'fun'.

But even if it is difficult to know what love and sex are, the only imperative
is that they must be known, since the most fulfilling experiences seem to
depend upon them. So Boris and Allen's other characters, both male and
female, are the mirror of his sophisticated audience's confusions over the
erotic and its meanings, like them jaundiced captives of Eros, sceptical,

compulsively-joking prisoners of the discourses of love and sexuality that are the day-to-day mythology and even, as Foucault argues in *The History of Sexuality* (Vol I), the tyranny of contemporary Western society.

As lover, Allen moves from sexual loser in the early films to sexual victor in the later ones, but even in the second state of the persona (e.g. in films like *Annie Hall, Manhattan, A Midsummer Night's Sex Comedy, Stardust Memories* and *Hannah and Her Sisters*, 1985) he remains prey to bafflement and indecision, though now more in a context of choice than lack, the question not so much whether he will be loved but whether he can ultimately commit himself to anyone.

Where the mood is one of scepticism, the comedy, built on the possibility of sexual failure, physical inferiority to other men, and overwhelming inferiority to women, extracts humour from situations and anxieties not ultimately different from those catalogued in Michel Leiris's confessional autobiography, *Manhood*. There the hero is tormented by an acute sense of his unprepossessing qualities, his sexuality so ruled by anxiety that the sexual act has become a 'relatively exceptional event', and his inferiority and passivity in the presence of women unconquerable. Each of these traumas, not in the least comic in Leiris, has its analogue in a basic Allen joke: in the first case, paralleled by the grotesque mime sequences in *Bananas* (1971) and *Play it Again Sam* (1972) where the hero, caught up in a frenzy of self-preening, is nearly exterminated in an eruption of talcum powder designed to erase all undesirability and inferiority, a comic scene that perhaps plays on gentile mythology accusing the Jew of unclean odours; the second, in *Bananas*, where Fielding Mellish's honeymoon night is treated by the media like a world championship bout, but whereas his wife is clearly ready for a rematch, Fielding can only declare, 'I think we will probably do this again next Spring'; the third, Allen's cry of despairing subjugation to a blonde girl dancing in a disco in *Play It Again Sam*, 'I love you, Miss, whoever you are, I want to have your child.'

There is no absolute break between the early Allen heroes and the late ones, for the earlier are allowed in most cases an eventual triumph, mitigating the comedy of sexual failure with wish-fulfilment, while the late ones reverse the situation, presenting a sexual affluence which still has its difficulties. These tend to begin rather than end with the possession of the woman, as when, for instance, Sandy Bates in *Stardust Memories* asks, 'How can I fall in love? or why can't I fall in love, more accurately?' These more subtle preoccupations centre on fear of commitment, the complex pressures on the individual of modern attitudes to sex, and the fear of being in some way inadequate to – rather than simply being denied – the rewards that a sexually

liberated society promises to grant the lover through passion and desire.

It is a key factor in much contemporary 'comedian comedy' that the distance between comic persona and author behind it is broken down, and that the autobiographical, confessional elements are increasingly highlighted. In the case of Lenny Bruce, the narrowing of the gap between persona and self became so extreme that the excitement of his performance depended on the audience's sense of his *spiel*ing as the relatively unfiltered material of his life, the performance becoming a dangerous extrapolation of the self rather than a more distanced comic mask. Allen, more discreet, more tasteful, as well as far more protean than Bruce, seduces rather than bludgeons his audience into an ambiguously intimate autobiographical relationship with himself. Beyond his more generalised play on the confessional mode, he clearly invites his audience to identify themselves with him through his creations, and to read these as more or less distanced versions of his own personal desires, difficulties, phobias and triumphs, a process which validates both the art and the comic artist as personal and 'authentic' in a way quite irrelevant to the perception of either Hope or West, with whom the comic mask is all-embracing and in whose comic personae inauthenticity grows to heroic proportions. The confessional book that Isaac Davis's lesbian ex-wife (Meryl Streep) is writing in *Manhattan, Divorce, Marriage and Selfhood*, raises the same unanswered question: a valid work of self-exploration, or feminist sloganising, more trapped than liberated by the confessional ritual?

Films like *Annie Hall*, *Manhattan* and *Stardust Memories* raise the autobiographical issue in an extreme way: Alvy Singer, Isaac Davis and Sandy Bates are all comedians, with Bates additionally a film-maker, and in two of the three films Allen casts his real-life lovers opposite him. In these respects Allen's comedy should be viewed within the larger perspective of what Lionel Trilling has defined as the tradition of 'sincerity and authenticity' in European culture, a tradition particularly concentrated in the confessional autobiography and autobiographical novel from Rousseau onwards, but especially pronounced in post-war America, most noticeably in the degree to which the cult of the artist as angst-ridden expressionist prevails in the legends of Rothko and Pollock in the visual arts, and elsewhere in different inflections the autobiographic rules, as in Norman Mailer's *Advertisements for Myself*, the school of 'confessional poetry', and the feminist confessional, e.g. Kate Millett's *Flying*, and the personalised 'herstory in history' element in some

---

Woody Allen in **Love and Death**
The New York Jewish hero of post-Freudian, post-feminist consciousness has trouble unsheathing his virility.

current feminist criticism. Allen picks up and consciously shapes these influences, worrying as he does so whether the self-reference which he cannot escape and which seems the necessary validating factor in his comedy reaches some real truth or is merely another aspect of the culture of narcissism he satirises. Characteristically, then, Sandy Bates's self-exploratory art may just be narcissistic self-indulgence, or it may be the royal road to contemporary truth. Like Philip Roth with *Portnoy's Complaint*, Allen on the one hand pushes the audience into accepting a quasi-autobiographical intimacy but, on the other, condemns them for their crudity and prurience (the grotesque portrayal of his fans and critics in *Stardust Memories*), both enforcing and condemning his own autobiographical flagrancy, particularly in its re-enacting of romantic/sexual triumphs to a mass audience positioned as so many Jerry Abrahams.

The theme of authenticity and the confessional mode converge on the 'sexual fix' for, as Foucault argues, it is precisely in the realm of sexuality that modern men and women seek some absolute hidden knowledge and definition. Beyond the simpler oppressions of modern sexuality (group sex, mechanisation – the 'orgasmatron' machine – satirised in *Sleeper*), lies a deeper issue created by the 'austere monarchy' of sex, 'so that we became dedicated to the endless task of forcing its secret, of exacting the truest of confessions from a shadow . . . We expect an intelligibility from what was for many centuries thought a madness.'

Pulled this way and that by the various codes of sexuality that haunt and shape him, the Allen hero finds himself above all caught up between two controlling perceptions of the erotic: one, scientific, value-free and behaviouristic; the other, humane, moralistic and intuitive. In collision they baffle him; separately each oppresses him. The authority of the former derives from the Kinsey Reports (1948,1953), Masters and Johnson's *Human Sexual Response* (1966), and the proliferation of contemporary popular sexology (e.g. the Hite Reports). Yet in their very processes of liberation – the saying of the previously unsayable, the admission of the previously inadmissible, so amusingly catalogued in *Everything You Always Wanted to Know about Sex but Were Afraid to Ask* (1972), bestiality, transvestism, fetishism, etc.) – these gospels of sexual liberation bring with them, as Stephen Heath in *The Sexual Fix*, for one, has noted, a new set of tyrannies and anxieties in which performance almost becomes the *sine qua non* of the truly fulfilling life. So when Allan Felix eventually gets Linda into bed in *Play It Again Sam*, he expresses his sense of overwhelming success by joking that he 'never once had to sit up and consult the manual'.

This liberation sexology that is also a tyranny is a recurrent feature of Allen's comedy. Like several other elements of the comedy, or rather 'humour' of sexuality in Allen, it is something equally available to women, and indeed the Diane Keaton character frequently acts out bravura versions of them: for instance, her monologue about marrying or not marrying Boris in *Love and Death*, swinging between desires for commitment and fears of suffocation. Such jokes cross gender lines without difficulty, but even more specifically male-orientated ones are given contexts that are equally applicable to female and male audiences, the former, it may be, empathising with the hero's sexual difficulties while enjoying their dramatised power over him.

Cross-gender issues are given a highly problematic context through Allen's interest, via the new sexology, in the question of female sexual pleasure. One result of this has been to produce a scientifically-based inflection of older fears of the devouring, insatiable female in the clinician's multi-orgasmic woman whose capacities exceed the male's. These demands, in part an overdue emphasis on female pleasure long denied by phallocentric attitudes, but in some of their manifestations another efflorescence of the culture of narcissism, merely the obverse side of the instrumentalism feminist critics have criticised in male sexual attitudes, constantly harass Allen's heroes, though sometimes we may feel their fate is deserved. Fabritio (Allen) in the 'Why do some women experience difficulty having orgasm?' sketch of *Everything* is driven frantic by his wife's inability to come, but his worry seems entirely self-orientated, more concerned for his reputation as a lover than for his wife. Moreover, his frantic search for sexual knowledge of the cause of her frigidity is conducted only among his male acquaintances whose advice about gratifying females is transparently influenced by their own self-serving fantasies of masculinity.

In further developing a comedy of male insufficiency before the aggressive female, Allen veers away from clear-cut jokes about impotence (just as the residually romantic side of him scrupulously avoids jokes about *female* masturbation, seen also perhaps as a threat to the male's sexual role), which might be too traumatic, instead perfecting a type of joke about infrequent and/or unremarkable performance: as when the countess asks Boris how long it is since he last made love, he replies, 'Let me see . . . Monday . . . Tuesday . . . um, two years'; or when in a spate of Grouchoesque word play after the countess's jealous lover, intent on a duel, directs him to instruct seconds, Boris protests, 'I never gave her seconds.' The whole relationship with the insatiable countess in *Love and Death* is a site for jokes inspired by the 1953 Kinsey Report's and Masters and Johnson's focus on the multi-orgasmic nature of female sexuality.

Perhaps, though, the prime example of Allen's comedy of anxiety is the 'What happens to the sperm during ejaculation?' sketch in *Everything*, where fascination with and fear of the ethos of sexual engineering, of the image of the body as computerised laboratory, is hyperbolised in the conceit whereby the audience gains entry into Stanley's nervous system and finds it to be the exaggerated décor of a behaviourism that has literally invaded the self, a control-room stocked with flashing panels and staffed by a white-coated retinue of experts handling the cause and effect, stimulus and response mechanisms of mind and body. The disturbances plaguing Stanley's promiscuous relations with his predatory university graduate dinner date (in whom female intellect and sexual aggression combine threateningly) are eventually overcome, but before this happens the episode seems almost to illustrate Freud's forbidding dictum: 'The normal performance of the sexual function can only come about as the result of a very complicated process; a disturbance may appear at any point in it.' Within the structure of a comedy of eventual success (Stanley's repeated intercourse) there is another extended hyperbole in which – just as the hero's body is taken over by the regime of therapeutic behaviourism – the 'free floating' anxiety transfers itself from the hero to his sperm (via such literary sources as John Barth's *Night Sea Journey* and Kafka's *Investigations of a Dog*), as if to suggest an anxiety so deeply-rooted that it invades the most blindly insensate elements of the sexual act. While his gung-ho marine colleagues long for action and death in the ovary, one sperm (Allen himself) fantasises nervously about what awaits him, an onanistic expulsion on to the ceiling in an act of masturbation, or, worse, involuntary participation in a homosexual encounter.

This comedy of the traumatic invasion of the self by the forces of sexology – desirable in allowing the hero freer sexuality, but undesirable in both reducing sexuality to the mechanical and to a mechanism which self-consciousness seems, especially in the male, to render fragile – is paralleled by an opposite set of pressures, no less stringent in their demands: a set of assumptions that sees male-female sexual relationships as the privileged site of the most intensely self-defining expectations, which modulate the ideology of romantic love into a more morally strenuous form of the phantom of absolute authenticity. When Felix utters the word 'relationship' it prompts Bogart to snarl in *Play It Again Sam*, 'Relationship! Where did you get that word? From one of your Park Avenue head-shrinkers?'

The language of 'relationship' – a vulgarisation of such liberal/moralist texts as Fromm's *The Art of Loving* – constantly fascinates Allen, paralleling as it does the language of existential ethics, itself signalled as a powerful discourse, via Sartre and Heidegger, over Boris and Sonia in *Love and Death*: 'an abstract and empirical concept such as being or to be or to occur in the thing itself or of the thing itself'. Most of all, perhaps, this alludes to the 'I and thou' questions, though here subjected to eroticisation, of the Jewish philosopher Martin Buber. The transference of such a weight of transcendent expectation on to the realm of the sexual creates further problems for the Allen hero, sceptical but not free of its claims in a climate that not only encourages expression for every drive likely to disrupt the ideal, but in which the suspicion arises that, as Luna says to Miles in *Sleeper*, '. . . meaningful relationships between men and women don't last. You see there's a chemical in our bodies that makes it so that we all get on each other's nerves sooner or later.' Caught in the grip of the ideal proposed, Allen and his female alter egos frantically discriminate among the forms of love in an attempt to find their essence, as when Sonia tells Boris as she gets into bed with him on their wedding night, 'Boris, I just don't love you. Oh, I mean I love you, but I'm not *in* love with you.' But the process can easily slip into a demonstraton of the lure of the perverse as the voyeuristic disrupts Sonia's highmindedness when she starts to instruct Boris in the various kinds of love:

> *Sonia:* There are many kinds of love, Boris. There's love between a man and a woman, love between a mother and son . . .
> *Boris:* Two women, let's not forget my favourite.

Equally, when in *Annie Hall* Annie asks Alvy if he loves her, instead of answering absolutely directly, he goes into a routine which, based apparently on a flattering conceit of the inadequacy of connotations surrounding the overused word 'love', consists of a kind of parodic estranging of the word, distorting it into a series of exotic aural shapes: 'Love . . . Lov. . . Luhv', as if trying through this deformation to catch at some essence for which the word is merely the worn-out sign. It may also be that there is an element of aggressive parody here, a mocking of the ethical/existential demands of love, made to carry the burden of desire and feelings (for non-existent social coherence, for lost religious faith) which it cannot possibly satisfy. The idea which Allen's characters half perceive as flawed, which they constantly mock but yet from which they cannot escape, of self-consciousness–denying authenticity in sexuality, is given an exquisite formulation in the moment in *Manhattan*, where having made love to Mary for the first time, Isaac jokes that he felt for 'two seconds' during their love-making that she might have been 'faking'. The joke pivots, firstly, on the audience's equally ambivalent response to their surrogates' mirroring of their own hesitations between belief and scepticism, and, secondly, on their perception of the irony of precisely these characters, irredeemably self-conscious and self-regarding, sceptical in every other element of their psychic constitution and behaviour, imagining the sexual realm as somehow the one place they are truly who, as distinct from what, they are.

Instincts and their vicissitudes: regression

Virgil tries to join the navy, but is psychologically unfit.
— Commentator in *Take the Money and Run*

Yet alongside the overwhelming importance of women to the Allen character, and exacerbated by the absolute demands made on the male both by the cultural mythicisation of women and by the new consciousness of sex and gender, various forms of regression beckon, even bestiality, a running sub-theme throughout the films, as when Boris has his experience of the divine in the death-cell of *Love and Death*, and in a parody of *Leviticus* 20 denounces those who indulge in 'fooling around with barnyard animals'. At the very least, bestiality comically beckons because the partner makes absolutely no demands. If, despite the psychiatrist's asking him in *Stardust Memories* whether he has ever had intercourse 'with any type of animal', such temptations are too *outré* to be pressing, masturbation is a more regular comic preoccupation, with *Stardust Memories*'s Sandy *Bates*, the most seriously autobiographical character, constantly being associated with the habit through the surname's coupling with 'Mister' and, in one instance, 'Master'.

Masturbation in Allen's jokes means many things: a normal, if rarely acknowledged outlet for sexual urges (Kinsey again); a shameful admission of sexual solitariness or inadequacy; an unadmitted but sought-for release from the pressure of relationship and the female's escalated demands for five-star orgasms (when Count Libedikov accuses Boris in *Love and Death* of insulting the honour of the countess, he denies the charge, claiming that he 'let her finish first'); a regression to narcissism (variations on the joke that masturbation is doing it 'with a person I love'); a boast of libido unsatisfied by the relative infrequency of intercourse (when the countess in *Love and Death* tells Boris he is the greatest lover she has known, he says he practises a lot on his own); an act of rebellion against his upbringing, very much like *Portnoy's Complaint* in this respect, so that even if he is not, as Portnoy was, actually fucking the Sunday lunch, he is still through this act rejecting the strict sexual ethics of his Hebrew culture; and finally, most complicatedly in *Stardust Memories*, equated with the controlled onanistic perfections of art: 'You can't control life. It doesn't wind up perfectly . . . only . . . only art you can control. Art and masturbation. Two areas on which I'm an absolute expert.'

Allen is as compulsively drawn to homosexuality as to masturbation. The prominence of homosexual jokes – not so much aimed at homosexuals as at expressions of the hero's own self-centred nervousness about homosexuality

– generates meaning from the extraordinary charisma and over-determined significance that women have for his heroes. Homosexuality constantly lurks as a feared abyss, the worst of all possible states, since it would exclude the hero from all the meanings of heterosexual love, yet possibly half-desired since it would release him from its conflicts and obligations. The prevalence of so many jokes about homosexuality ('I cannot suck anybody's leg that I'm not engaged to', Fielding, in a typical example, tells a wounded male comrade suffering from a snake-bite in *Bananas*) may derive consciously or unconsciously from a repressed homosexuality, something that would be at one with a Freudian reading (see the Schreber case) – notoriously, monolithically homosexual – of the paranoiac strains in Allen, so beautifully illustrated in his manic exegesis of the words 'D'you?' as 'Jew' in *Annie Hall*. But, even more so, it seems to be the product of a heterosexuality so anxious about the ideals of masculinity it feels it has to live up to (emphasised most dramatically through the presence of Humphrey Bogart as Allan Felix's sexual coach in *Play It Again Sam*) that, failing to reach such standards, the hero has no option but to identify himself with the reverse of masculinity, defined by the dominant culture as homosexuality.

Allen's homosexual jokes range from the very simple ('My sweetheart's married. I got a lock of her husband's hair. It was the best I could do' – *Love and Death*), to the brilliantly complicated: in another example from *Love and Death*, Boris, standing over the unconscious Napoleon, hesitates over killing him, stricken with philosophical doubts:

> But murder? What would Socrates say? All those Greeks were homosexuals. Boy, they must have had some wild parties! I bet they all took a home together in Crete for the summer. A. Socrates is a man. B. All men are mortal. C. All men are Socrates. That means all men are homosexuals. I . . I . . once . . . some . . . some Cossacks whistled at me . . . I . . . I . . . happen to have the kind of body that excites both persuasions.

Initially, the comedy here derives from the incongruity of the displacement of thought patterns fixed on ethical questions of murder. Socrates is first invoked as part of this debate in his role as ethical philosopher, but becomes more interesting to Boris in his secondary role as famous homosexual, a subject for the rest of the monologue pressing enough wholly to expel the original and urgent moral dilemma. The swerve from Socrates the philosopher to Socrates the homosexual is pursued in details (wild parties, house in Crete), which gain some of their effects from witty anachronisms and our doubt as to whether to attribute Boris's fascinated interest merely to excited prurience (pre-*Aids* homosexuals are reputedly more promiscuous than heterosexuals and are therefore to be envied), or to a deeper identification. Boris's sketchy memories of Freshman logic lead him to argue that all men are homosexuals, something that additionally may well be echoing Kinsey's emphasis on the homosexual experiences of primarily heterosexual males. The logical outcome of his reasoning is quickly and strenuously rejected, but then, with his recounting of the Cossack episode, which reasserts Boris's ungovernable narcissism, the opposition between heterosexual and homosexual threatens to collapse.

An extremely interesting case of both a conscious foregrounding of this material and a simultaneous masking of it occurs in *Stardust Memories*, where Sandy converses with Daisy's boyfriend, a film teacher who asserts his theory of comedy as aggression:

> *Sandy:*   Whad'ya saying? Are you saying that someone like myself or
>   Laurel and Hardy or Bob Hope are furious?
> *Daisy's Boyfriend:* Furious, or latent homosexuals – it's hidden beneath the joke.

Elsewhere, in one of the sequences shown from his movie-in-progress, there is a moment that seems to stress Sandy's acknowledgement of the at least partial truth of the notion of comedy as aggression: Sidney Findelstein's hostility is unleashed as he begins to commit various murders and is pursued by the law. The homosexual implications, though, are never given the same dramatic expression. Is this due to an unconscious act of camouflage, a psychoanalytically learned comedian's pointing to a character's veering away from such issues, a desire not to alienate many of his audience, or simply a rejection of a silly theory? The question is one of considerable complexity, made even more so by Allen's knowledge of and ability to use comically the modes of critical and psychoanalytical analysis with which the critic interrogates him. Where with Hope and West one invokes with little hesitation the unconscious as explanation for their constitution and behaviour, with Allen the process of scrutiny has to take into account the comic dramatisation of the unconscious, so that, as it were, the analyst seeks not the unconscious within the conscious (as with Hope and West), but the unconscious within the consciously dramatised unconscious.

Such questions could also be applied to a series of jokes about the Allen character's pre-pubertal heterosexuality, a childhood deprived, as Alvy Singer claims, or rather boasts, in *Annie Hall*, of a latency period. Over-assertion of his unflagging desire is so strong – or the anxiety surrounding it so strong – that there is a claim there never was a time when it was inactive, as if the existence of the slightest fissure, such as a period of childhood latency, might bring the whole edifice tumbling down.

Now about these women

> If you lusted after me why weren't you also in love with me? Can the two feelings
> really be separate? — Ariel in *A Midsummer Night's Sex Comedy*

As someone whose heterosexual orientations developed in an age beginning
increasingly – in radical circles at least – to equate heterosexuality with
phallocentrism and the subjugation of women, Allen structures his comedies
around tensions between what have traditionally been identified as the
normal, healthy sexual desires of the male for the female, and the reorientations and reassessments of such desires demanded of him by the post-Vietnam, New York Jewish culture of heightened radicalism and feminism. But
the call of radicalism – with all its attendant intellectualism, vegetarianism,
organicism (he is surprised to hear in *Sleeper* that death has not spared the
friend who ate organic rice) – is counteracted by the appeal of more traditional
values: Manhattan (as distinct from Greenwich Village), Broadway hit tunes,
Borscht-belt humour, Gucci/Dior styles, for instance, compete with Bob
Dylan, esoteric or minority group ethnicity and the counter-culture, and for
every studenty Carol Kane (*Annie Hall*) there is someone to speak for the
mainstream (Maureen Stapleton in *Interiors* or Marie-Christine Barrault in
Stardust Memories).

Though a certain kind of tradition is sometimes satirised directly – as
represented, for example, by the WASP families in *Interiors* or *Annie Hall*
– another kind is often enthusiastically celebrated. Counteracting the effects
of the colourless world of the high bourgeoisie in *Interiors*, where the
matriarch's fondness for white roses (echoes of Bergman's *Cries and Whispers*,
1972) symbolises a declining oligarchy, there are the life-affirming middlebrow traditions of the 'vulgarian' Pearl, with all her gaudy scarlet dresses,
minks, jewellery, card tricks and passion for dancing, the antidote to an
ailing culture too often embarrassed by its highbrow legacy. In the long run,
for all her loudness, creative sentimentality and disregard of form, Pearl is
an ambivalent character, someone whose limited intelligence will ultimately
exhaust the tolerance of her staunchest devotees, but any life failing to
embrace some of the interests and passions that motivate her runs the risk,
in the film's view, of being doomed to the inner emptiness created by values
too much in thrall to elitism.

Pearl belongs to a series of women characters playing a crucial part in
Allen's films by creating images of tradition, something kept alive in songs
with evocative titles like 'Someone to Watch over Me' (played during the
couple's romantic stroll at dusk near Brooklyn Bridge in *Manhattan*) or 'It

Had to Be You' and 'Seems Like Old Times' (*Annie Hall*), rooting a part of the Allen character in fantasies and illusions of the past, where women are associated with life, are the *raisons d'être* of all men, are synonymous with all the vitality and creativity of culture, while the modern male struggles to take on board and to make sense of modernity and its insistence on the deconstruction of the old.

Traditional women remind him of home, childhood, uncomplicated sexuality, so although radical chic attracts the Allen character, he seems also very troubled by it, sometimes going so far as to pursue virginal women who have not as yet been corrupted by what to him are the equivocal liberations of post-feminism: in *Manhattan*, for instance, Tracy (Meriel Hemingway) is pure, still a schoolgirl ('I'm dating a girl who does homework!'), someone unlikely to irritate him with either pretentious party talk or women's libber patter (his lesbian ex-wife is writing a book called *Marriage, Divorce and Selfhood*). It is a perception of women designed perhaps to seem as naïve in its narcissistic quest for purity as the distortedly innocent utopian vision of Manhattan itself: a world of Gershwin songs and chiaroscuro photography, totally free of ghettoes, Blacks, Hispanics, squalor, drug addiction (as distinct from trendy grass-smoking) and poverty. In due course, the Allen character naturally tires of the illusion, even if only temporarily; he is eventually back on the streets looking for a woman to whom he can talk as well as make love, though by the end of the film he is pursuing Tracy again. The fascination of a woman existing solely to celebrate the superiority of the male – as in the flashback childhood sequence of *Stardust Memories* where a little blonde girl plays the traditional role of assistant, presenting and aggrandising the male, Sandy Bates, as he performs his magic tricks at the Brooklyn Boys' Club – soon loses its hold over the Allen character, but not quite totally, as his ambivalent feelings about the New Woman usually show.

To keep up with his intellectual, philosophy major girl friend (Louise Lasser in *Bananas*), Fielding Mellish claims, with self-conscious one-upmanship, he has dabbled with Kierkegaard, but when asked to say 'I love you' in French, asks in reply, invoking an older, more traditional, authority, whether he can do so instead in Hebrew. Tradition dies hard even when one is trying to live up to the ideals of a girl friend of seemingly alternative, radical views, for even though the Allen character tries to fit into the new radical ethos by becoming politicised, taking part in the revolution of a Latin American banana republic, he finds himself still overwhelmingly attracted not so much to the political credentials as to the outsize bust of a fellow guerrilla.

Notwithstanding all efforts to embrace the ideals of the new, Allen remains wedded in crucial ways to many of the values of the old. In one of his wittiest short stories, *The Kugelmass Episode* (1980), the hero's idea of womanhood veers between Madame Bovary and the 'Monkey' in *Portnoy's Complaint*, and his dream of voluptuousness only ends when Emma, a character who comes to life to gratify his sexual demands, starts to assert herself. And even though the major women characters in the films are usually allowed a more protean nature, some of the minor characters, not the more overtly tradition-bound relatives, but the subsidiary girl friends, friends' lovers and so on, are grim visions of the New Woman; for instance, Shelley Duvall's rock reporter–Maharishi groupie in *Annie Hall*, or Meryl Streep's humourless lesbian castrator in *Manhattan*. Once again, it is difficult to know to what extent these are self-conscious caricatures of male fears about the New Woman, and to what extent a reflection of his own real anxieties. The question becomes even more difficult when one considers how the old and the new merge together in the creation of the major women characters, all of whom are to a certain extent, as representations of the new women, targets for different types of satire.

From Louise Lasser to Diane Keaton to Mia Farrow, Allen's principal women stars in some ways represent a consistent desire to visualise a new, reconstructed woman, someone who could not only approximate to the European cinematic tradition of Bergmanesque and Antonioniesque heroines, but also distance herself from the Hollywood norm, where even in the supposedly more mature post-Vietnam culture of the early 70s a Raquel Welch could continue to sustain the Oedipal tradition. Keaton and Farrow are the intellectual, professional middle-class answer to Raquel Welch in clothes (rather tweedy, with sensible shoes, woollen stockings and jumpers), cosmetics (the bare minimum), coiffure (sometimes permed, sometimes unfussy, shortish, medium-cropped styles), physique (except on very rare occasions, eschewing voluptuousness). But though epitomising the celebration of the cerebral, the intelligent, self-liberating alternative to the Oedipally-fixated, objectified, conformist woman of the straight cinema, they themselves are subject to contradiction both in terms of looks and narrative function. The paradox of the intellectual's anti-intellectualism is turned in on them, as they, in addition to the Allen character himself, are sometimes satirised for pretentiousness, both sexes accused of narcissism: Diane Keaton's New Womanly absurdity in *Sleeper* even stretches to the composition of a poem about a butterfly who turned into a caterpillar.

The major women characters are also sometimes distorted to mirror Allen's own social or existential angst: 'I'm trouble' say Diane Keaton in *Manhattan* and *Annie Hall*, and Charlotte Rampling, the most extreme example of the neurotic woman in the Allen range, in *Stardust Memories*. At times as in the case of Keaton, the woman even mirrors the Allen look: men's jackets, trousers and a replica of the famous spectacles. Sometimes women are used as ways of expressing the contradictions of his own muddled attitudes towards them (the very floosyish, almost criminal look of Mia Farrow in *Broadway Danny Rose*, 1984, or the pre-Raphaelite fantasy of a totally misjudged sexual innocence in *Sex Comedy*, a film like *Stardust Memories* most systematically placing different choices of women before the Allen character). Among the films offering a variety of women types, *Hannah and Her Sisters*, like *Interiors*, *Sex Comedy* and *Stardust Memories*, seems especially intent on dramatising these conflicting responses.

Here, Mia Farrow as Hannah plays someone whose emotional difficulties and career ambitions are offset by those associated with her sisters; one, Lee (Barbara Hershey), maturing from father-fixation (her lover is a split-off of the serious, metaphysical Allen, a father-figure of an artist played in another act of *homage* to Bergman by Max von Sydow), to self-confidence and marriage. Another, Holly (Diane Wiest), progressing from inner frustration, career disorientation and drugs (she is still the questing woman in *Radio Days* (1987) but there, in an earlier time, the quest is wholly male-orientated), to a more settled life both as a writer and as Allen's lover, in the process becoming a kind of female double, mirroring his own emotional, intellectual and artistic odysseys. Yet in spite of superficial differences created by the necessities of plot and characterisation, all of these women are linked together through the desire for self-improvement, knowledge and a career rewarding in more than purely material or aesthetic terms. Lee is taking courses at Columbia, Holly finds some fulfilment through writing, a way of coming to terms with herself, even if the writing is not Emily Dickinson or Philip Roth; and Hannah herself, perhaps the least intellectually curious, is nevertheless significantly appearing as Nora in *A Doll's House*. The winner of the August Strindberg award for relationships with women (*Manhattan*) here deliberately makes Hannah star in the by now almost clichéd play about a woman's subjugation by patriarchy. Even if the committed art of high seriousness can all too frequently lead to futility, art for art's sake, without awareness, something done primarily for show, leads only to futility and unhappiness, as Hannah's gin-sodden mother (her real mother, Maureen O'Sullivan), bringing with her a whole intertextuality of reference to 'entertainment' films like the Tarzan series, is there to remind us.

Hannah's mother is a survivor from the old days, pathetic as well as resilient in old age, and, in one of the film's more negative views of tradition, a representative of the traditional star who has lived only for glamour and for men. The modern generation has outlived all that, yet for all the drugs, Californian laid-backness, and passivity, has even so failed in Allen's view to solve the problem of sexuality, for in *Hannah*, as in other films, people are still being compromised by their sexual instincts, still betraying others through adultery, still feeling humiliated by it in spite of the supposedly more relaxed attitudes of the new permissiveness. A more radical, more austere artist might have punished Michael Caine's Eliot for his deceit of Hannah: Allen's decision to let dogs who sleep around lie, to prevent Hannah from knowing the truth, is the product of a deep-seated tolerance. He celebrates the possible, refuses to ask too much of individuals, urges his audience to be thankful for what in spite of all the odds has been achieved. Significantly, this film ends with a symbolic ritual of togetherness and reconciliation over the Thanksgiving meal. Since we only go round once in the fair-ride of life, we are urged to accentuate the positive, eliminate the negative, and wherever possible take the in-between road to reconciliation.

And if the real grimness and misery of divorce, the sadness of children caught in the crossfire of the sometimes openly warring, sometimes discreetly vindictive strategies of separating parents is ignored by Allen as he either defuses the poignancy of these questions through the usual jokes, or else ignores them altogether, it is all part of a view of life dominated by the feeling that if relationships are henceforward to be in flux, ruled by experiment and uncertainty, flexibility and reorientation, we should all agree that traditional instincts towards pinning the blame on easily-identified scapegoats is no longer to be in touch with one's humanity. When the Allen character marries Holly, he moves back into the family he once belonged to, no longer now married to Hannah, but once again becoming a part of her, reinstated in her extended family, seeking through this act of reconciliation (with its obviously negative as well as positive overtones) to cling back to some of the good things that brought them together in the first place, even if the original relationship can never be recaptured, even if he must make do, at this second attempt, with a second-hand, second-choice woman. Moving back into the family also means that for all his Jewishness, Allen is catholic enough to embrace the wider ethnic and cultural values of the *shiksas* he so compulsively pursues.

What follows is a more detailed look at a sequence from *Annie Hall*, picking up some of these women-related issues, injected with Allen's usual wit and ambivalence. We have chosen to concentrate on *Annie Hall* for many reasons, but perhaps, above all, because in its attempt to be female-centred it nevertheless manages to remain a resiliently subjective impression of a view of women that for all its vaunted modernity expresses the nostalgia of a man still not prepared entirely to resist celebrating women for what are in some senses their more traditional virtues, attributes and meanings.

Annie Hall

Synopsis

It Had to Be You.   — Sung by Annie in *Annie Hall*

Following a somewhat trying visit to Annie's parents' home where over dinner he meets her WASP parents, Jew-loathing grandmother, and speed-crazed brother, Alvy (Woody Allen) is seen back in New York, agitatedly walking down a street, in heated conversation with Annie Hall (Diane Keaton), Annie accusing Alvy of following her, Alvy trying to explain himself. Having in the first place encouraged her to take adult education courses, he is now beginning to regret this act of consciousness-raising, not having anticipated the threat to his masculinity by the availability of attractive male tutors. The scene shifts in mid-conversation to their apartment where, perhaps a day or so later, returning to find Alvy at the kitchen sink, Annie tells him all about the session with her analyst. He had read her dream – in which Frank Sinatra is suffocating her – as her fear that Alvy is placing intolerable constraints on her emotional and intellectual development: since his name is 'Singer' he has been displaced on to the real singer in that dream. We cut to another street scene where in a typically self-conscious sequence Alvy first appeals directly to the audience for sympathy, and then asks passers-by how they manage to sustain their sex lives, finally approaching a horse (ridden by a policeman), to explain to it how throughout his life, from infancy, he has always fallen for the wrong woman. The scene gives way to a Disneyesque cartoon sequence in which Woody and his friend Rob (Tony Roberts), whom Alvy will also later call 'Max', a name Rob has already been calling him, appear as themselves, Annie taking the part of the wicked step-mother in a witty, overtly Oedipal update of *Snow White and the Seven Dwarfs*.

Stitched together almost seamlessly, as dialogue drifts across from one scene to another, as topics are picked up and developed from frame to frame, the sequence is a succinct exposé of some of the key elements of Woody Allen's ultimately more than slightly ambivalent conceptualisation of women, and the traumas and exhilarations to which they subject the heterosexual hero.

The Conversation. 1

You followed me! I can't believe it!
　I didn't follow you.
You followed me!
　Why? 'Cos I was walking along the block behind you, staring at you? That's not following.
Well what is your definition of following?
　Following is different. I was spying.

This is the moment where the physically alluring but callow middle-class woman whom Allen has rescued from trivia begins, inspired at first by him, to flex her wings and, gaining confidence, to find her independence and destiny without him. The transformation from gauchely-mannered Chippewa Falls socialite to whom almost everything is 'la-de-dah' (if not actually, as Alvy mockingly accuses her, 'peachy' or 'keen'), to assertive, post-feminist torch-bearer of the career woman's cause, is signalled in many ways here in the sequence, not least by dress. Significantly, the Annie Hall Look that, as Alison Lurie notes, so dominated women's fashions after the film's release, is based on the clothes Annie wears in her as yet unreconstructed, empty-headed identity of her first appearances in the film (though it is interesting to see that in yet another self-incriminating moment Alvy himself compliments her on her dress, part of him attracted to her original hollow-headed identity). By the time this sequence begins, that look of male waistcoat, hat, tie and tweedy trousers, has disappeared, giving way to a much more liberated outfit, one that combines a reasserted femaleness (the skirt she now wears is readable as rejection of her pre-Alvy taste for the trappings of masculinity) with the academic's single-minded and, in Allen's view, frequently misdirected pursuit of truth. As always, though, the point is surrounded by contradictions: Allen is the intellectual hero who argues against intellectualism in the knowledge that he will never be able to dispense with it, however unliberated crash courses in 'Contemporary Crisis in Modern Man' or 'Existential Motifs in Russian Literature' will ultimately turn out to be.

Annie carries a bag over her shoulder, her clothes no longer fashion-fixated or trend-setting, but practical, summery, loose-fitting, and female. This is the woman his intellect tells him he should pursue, even if his mind is still cluttered up with images of busty nurses (*Sex Comedy*), romance (*Hannah and Her Sisters*) and mystery (*Stardust Memories*), and it comes as no surprise to find that even though it is offered to her as a joke the present he gives Annie for her birthday is an item of gaudily red and black see-through sexy lingerie straight out of the Sadean, as opposed to the consciousness-raising, school of modern love. Not even when Annie casually refers to her tutor by his first name, 'David', can his tradition-obsessed mind prevent him from thinking of her as Bathsheba, a symbol from the Book of Samuel down to Rembrandt and beyond, of adultery and desire.

Life is a Dream

The remarks made by Annie, following her visit to the analyst, about watching her parents make love when she was a child, coupled with references to guilt about marriage and children, are the clichés of the 70s narcissism culture. Even so, in so far as they relate to Allen's attempts to come to terms with the internal conflicts faced by women in decisions over choices between career and family life, Annie's expressions of anxiety are far from trivial indications of her private torment.

These Freudian jokes (two thirds committed, one third sceptical?) play with dream analysis, since in a Freudian slip, one that Alvy shares directly with the audience, Annie is made to say 'Will it change my wife?' Annie is imaged as a woman whose sea-change from pretty object to thinking, knowledge and career-seeking individual is in danger of making her usurp roles and status usually reserved for men. Though the comparisons are of course exaggerated, Annie is in certain ways becoming masculinised: in this section of the sequence her hair is up, her clothes are executive-style, both visual signs, among many, of her rebellion against her 'second sex' status, with all its implications of subservience and domesticity expected of women in a conformist society. In such circumstances, as in some senses Annie takes over conventional masculine roles, she may well feel she needs a wife, someone to play a stereotypical part in looking after her domestic needs now that she is going into public life. Elsewhere in the film she confides, 'Sometimes I feel I should just live with a woman.' The confession is partly designed to reactivate male fears about lesbianism, but there is the additional point, made in self-defence by a working male, that if women work they will see how working men's needs for conventional wives are not exclusively male-specific. This is something rather different from a plea for equality between the sexes, the sort of equality based on mutual respect, inseparable from ideals of independence and wholeness.

Annie Hall

Allen and Keaton. 'In one class of cases being in love is nothing more than object – cathexis on the part of the sexual instincts with a view to directly sexual satisfaction, a cathexis which expires, moreover, when this aim has been reached; this is what is called common, sensual love. But, as we know, the libidinal situation rarely remains so simple.' (Freud, 'Being in love and hypnosis'.)

The implications of complex issues like these are nevertheless an inseparable part of the mass of contradictions raised by the scene. An assertive woman, seeking liberation for herself and, implicitly, all women, is nevertheless, as she finds freedom, seemingly in pursuit too of the traditional gender-specific consolations of domesticity. As the contradiction is formulated we have to ask whether Allen's dramatisation of the paradox of the tradition-seeking feminist is something born of observed experience, theory, or male prejudice, a way of discreetly vilifying women through their representation as a sex no less ruled by ideologically unsound impulses than the arch-enemy himself, the threatened, embattled male, readjusting himself in the fictionalised Woody Allen comic hero, characterised by baffled emotions and urgent libido, to the demands of the sexual revolution. Yet, of course, only the most refined man-haters are going to refuse to allow any criticism of female characters, and Allen himself is quite determined to show that selfishness, narcissism, ruthlessness and contradictoriness are as much part of a woman's make-up as a man's. Ultimately, though, the film's images of women are inescapably the fictions and perceptions of a male, someone consciously responding to the new climate of sex relations, yet who, unconsciously, may well be nevertheless, in spite of everything, in spite of all statements to the contrary, a kind of Frank Sinatra figure, in the negative senses of the analogy. For however strenuously he may in theory be a supporter of women's liberation, in practice Woody/Alvy seems to be something of a (failed) tyrant. In terms of glamour, of course, Woody/Alvy is the antithesis of Sinatra: the Sinatra of shiny Italian suits, sleek grooming, hair transplants (in the prologue to the film he admits he won't in years to come be the distinguished grey, but more the bald virile type), suave mannerisms, hardly finds its reflection in Allen's casual, tie-less, stuttering style and gestures. On the other hand, Woody/Alvy may well be as impenetrable, as much in steely control of his life, as Sinatra the heavily body-guarded and very private friend of the mighty. In this respect, as the Sinatra allusions allow readings that encompass unconscious as well as conscious motivations, the scene becomes highly self-reflexive and autobiographical. As Allen gives the Sinatra references to his female star, someone who was, moreover, his real-life lover, it is not difficult to see at the edges of the joke, a hint of self-doubt, perhaps even of mild self-disgust in the recognition of an unshakable conservatism, however rudimentary, in his complex, contradictory attitudes to women. As Philip Roth, that other angst-ridden comedian of sexual consciousness, with whom Allen has much in common and from whom he occasionally borrows, puts it in *The Anatomy Lesson:* 'This is what you know about someone you have to hate: he charges you with his crime and castigates himself in you.'

The Conversation. 2

Alvy is still spying on Annie, and as she drives off in a taxi, once again accusing him of harassing her, he is at his most vulnerable, first asking the audience where he went wrong, and then questioning passers-by on their recipes for sexual and emotional happiness. 'Love fades', an elderly woman informs him bluntly, her brisk stride signifying an age-old sublimation of desire; by contrast, an elderly man claims, having clearly abandoned love for lust, the only way to keep a relationship alive is through the use of vibrating eggs; while even more comically depressing, a young couple suggest mutual shallowness of mind is love's only guarantee of durability.

Though the *schlemiel* is finding greater confidence in himself as lover, the Allen character remains characteristically depressed by the transitoriness of what had once seemed the most firmly fixed of relationships. Refusing merely to view as a law of nature the mutability of all human relationships, Alvy pursues a dream of eternal sexual fulfilment, seems to be constantly driven, even in a post-Kantian world, by an impossibly idealistic mission in quest of a magical formula or elixir that will keep love eternally aflame, even when his reason tells him no such thing exists.

The tensions between idealism and realism, mind and body, promiscuity and fidelity, experiment and consolidation, all these and more – perhaps even bestiality – torment the mind of the observer and analyst of the 70s sexual fix as, in this scene, he finally walks up to the police horse in downtown Manhattan to unburden himself of his emotional anguish. The approach to the beast, an image here of law, order and tradition, too, of course, as well as of virility, recalls Bob Hope's suspicions of Roy Rogers's true designs on Trigger in *Son of Paleface*, and leads into even more self-conscious animal imagery in the following scene, where Woody Allen becomes Walt Disney, Alvy Singer a caricature of himself, and Diane Keaton the Wicked Step-mother in the New York Jewish Liberal version of *Snow White and the Seven Dwarfs*.

Obscure object of desire

In the cartoon, Annie, the 70s middle-class, extra-mural classes student of raised consciousness, is transformed into a sultry, voluptuous Wicked Queen. Her hair is draped with an ominous black shawl, making her a truly dark lady of desire. She wears a clingy, body-hugging orange gown made of satin fine enough to expose her belly-button and nipples (if she won't wear sexy clothes in real life, she will wear them in his fantasies). Superficially, this is a satire of Disney's demure sexiness (the nymphs in *Fantasia*,

Tinker Bell in *Peter Pan*). But the heavy symbolism of a Poe-style black raven perched on the queen's shoulder, its sombre feathers matching the dark sexual aura of the cartoon *femme fatale*, suggests that its creator is someone probably at the deepest levels left unsatisfied as much by Snow White equivalents as by cerebral East-Siders. The Wicked Queen is not Annie Hall. She has her voice but not her look. While her voice defines her as the New Woman, liberated from cultural stereotyping, her look visualises her as all she rebels against in her reconstructed self. The Woody Allen character here is now part Alvy, encouraging Annie to struggle against stereotype, and part 'Max' – who is also in the cartoon – the overtly satyric, priapic side-kick (looking out at parties for VPLs, visible pantie lines, he tells Alvy at a Hollywood soirée), of this and many other Allen films. Max (Tony Roberts) has actually been calling Alvy 'Max' all along, in spite of Alvy's resistance, and as Alvy seems finally to become 'Max' in the cartoon, turning his new woman into a traditional *femme fatale*, we are shown a comic image of the new man tormented by lusts his civilised self has taught him to control, disguise or sublimate.

In these scenes the subjectivity of women, their 'interpellation', is clearly what is of crucial importance. What to Alvy is the real issue – the point at which relationships begin to founder – is for Woody Allen, above all, a comic meditation on the narcissist's love of the self in his beloved, here the Galatea/ Annie Hall he helps create. But it is also a meditation both on recidivist yearnings for more traditional images of female sexuality and on the melan- cholia setting in when the creature betrays the creator once she glimpses the route to her own, independently pursued self-discovery.

4

The fifties

A meditation on comedy in the age of conformity, via Pat and Mike, Rock and Doris, Wilder and Marilyn and Douglas Sirk

A BRIEF OVERVIEW

I'm old-fashioned. I like two sexes.

— Adam (Spencer Tracy) in *Adam's Rib* (1949)

Seen in many summaries only as the age of conformity, the 1950s now appear Janus-faced. 'Yet at this very moment the same economic changes [that promoted conservatism] were creating the two new 'classes' that were to challenge the philosophy of abundance in the late 1960s: the new students and the new blacks' (Godfrey Hodgson). We might add to the two a third, the contemporary inflection of 'the New Woman'. Two recent studies of the cinema of the period show the newer, more complex view clearly. Brandon French's *On the Verge of Revolt: Women in American Film in the 1950s* (which begins with a covering quote from Molly Haskell – 'It was as if the whole period of the fifties was a front, the topsoil that protected the seed of rebellion that was germinating below') and Peter Biskind's *Seeing is Believing: How We Learned to Stop Worrying and Love the Fifties*. Biskind's approach is too mechanically schematic and not sufficiently interested in the specifically filmic to appeal to us greatly, but his view of the time and its films as not just 'an era of political and cultural uniformity' but 'an era of conflict and contradiction in which a complex set of ideologies contended for public

allegiance' is helpful even where the actual application of his initially attractive concepts of conservative, liberal, centrist, etc., films makes too crude a
grid to be persuasively applicable. The comic output of the 50s is significant
enough to benefit from a model of multiple contradiction within texts rather
than simple commitment of each film to a single reflective position.

Like the term 'thirties' the term 'fifties' is stretched here beyond its exact
chronological limits, a looseness we justify by appealing to pragmatic usefulness and common usage based on a perception of chronological relation,
shared tendencies and attitudes even where the decade is overstepped (as,
say, with *Lover Come Back* (1962), or, looking at the 30s, *Ball of Fire* (1942)
or *The Lady Eve* (1941)). Our view of 40s romantic comedy as distinguished
by lingering affiliation to 30s modes, or prefigurations of 50s ones, is doubtless in some ways reductive and ripe for revision, yet 1940s comedy seems
to us transitional overall, less rewarding for analysis than either the 1930s
or the 1950s.

No small group of films could cover every major trend of an era like the
50s, but the ones chosen here justify their abstraction from the mass not
only by their own significance but also as pointers to the larger currents of
which they are part.

Thus *Pat and Mike* (1952) is an example of the way themes of overt
egalitarianism, so common earlier, survive in the 50s; *Pillow Talk* (1959)
traces a more glossy pattern of consumerist comedy which, however, appears
more complex and riven the more it is looked at; *The Seven Year Itch* (1955)
represents the marked urge to satirise the conformist society of the 1950s;
while the collection of small-budget 'B' comedies directed by Douglas Sirk
at Universal (1951-53) provides a retrospective on the highly family-orien-
tated 50s through the most domestic of genres, the family comedy.

Apart from the growing teenage movie market (the mostly conservative
aspects of which have been noted by Marjorie Rosen), the only major stream
of 1950s romantic comedy that the selection does not substantially touch is
the lushest form of romantic comedy represented by films like *Three Coins
in the Fountain* (1954), *Indiscreet* (1958) and *An Affair to Remember* (1954),
usually set in a glamorously European location and dominated by unconstrained visual production values. The opening sequence of *Three Coins in
the Fountain*, that stunning extravaganza of Roman fountains, statuary and
location shooting, the *Eaux d'artifice* of the mainstream cinema, is the
apotheosis of this tendency. Besides advertising the film industry's superiority over television, with its four-wall sitcoms, in the realm of romance as
elsewhere, these values function as metaphors for an unabashedly romantic,
and usually conservative view of love. The title/theme songs that are often

a feature of these films (Frank Sinatra singing 'Three Coins in the Fountain', Vic Damone 'An Affair to Remember') underline their affiliation with melodrama, e.g. the song 'Love is a Many Splendoured Thing' that surrounds William Holden's and Jennifer Jones's doomed love in the famous film. It will be remembered how sparsely many 1930s comedies use music, in contrast to the metaphysic of love, set to a voluptuously orchestrated adagio, which is more yearning and oceanic than anything in the earlier comedies:

> A love affair is a wondrous thing
> That we'll rejoice in remembering.
> Our love was born with our first embrace
> And a page was torn out of time and space.

In their greater or lesser aspiration to the condition of melodrama (*An Affair to Remember* with its patterns of fate and redemption through suffering is the supreme example) these kinds of comedy touch on desires and feelings of great importance – love as fate, as suffering, as truth, as mystery – less tapped by less lyrical films, but because their vision tends to be of love as an essence, dissolving all differences, rather than as something socially regulated, they tend to have less impetus to negotiate the social problematics of maleness and femaleness, though they do other things. *Indiscreet*'s final image of Ingrid Bergman's masochistic smiles amidst tears (she has earlier said that it was specifically seeing *Camille*, 'that poor frail woman', that turned her to acting, so that even her career seems an effusion of female masochism) when Cary Grant finally agrees to marry her, fully illustrates these conservative potentialities.

TRACY AND HEPBURN: *PAT AND MIKE*

In the Name of the Father:
the good, the bad and the not so ugly

He has usurped the prerogative of Jehovah himself, claiming it as his right to assign for her a sphere of action, when that belongs to her conscience and her God. He has endeavoured in every way that he could to destroy her confidence in her own power, to lessen her self-respect, and to make her willing to lead an abject and dependent life.
— The First Women's Rights Convention, Seneca Falls, New York, 1848.

Pops.
   — Kay (Elizabeth Taylor) to her father (Spencer Tracy) in *Father of the Bride* (1950)

To speak of fathers here is not necessarily to be literal, to invoke Leon Ames, paterfamilias of MGM smalltown or the benignly crusty authority of C. Aubrey Smith as perennial grandsire. The last part of this chapter deals specifically with family comedy, but for the moment we want to think of the father in his essence, as he who holds power – as contemporary criticism puts it, he who possesses the phallus (actual and symbolic) and the law – in which sense the great male stars, the Gables and Coopers, the Grants and the Waynes, whether film narratives endow them with offspring or not, are all his representatives.

If in the overarching reign of cinematic patriarchy certain eras have been freer (e.g. 30s comedy), others especially the 1950s, have seemingly been obsessed with representations consolidating patriarchal power. The father as unconscious topos is inescapable in 50s romantic comedy (and other genres too). When we think of 30s comedy, we think of Cary Grant or Gary Cooper as roughly the same age as Katharine Hepburn, Marlene Dietrich or Irene Dunne, yet we cannot but feel that as John Wayne embraces Maureen O'Hara in *The Quiet Man* (1952), as Humphrey Bogart pairs with Audrey Hepburn in *Sabrina Fair* (1952), as Clark Gable closes with Doris Day in *Teacher's Pet* (1958) or with Sophia Loren in *It Happened in Naples* (1960), and as Cary Grant is endlessly involved with most of these youthful female stars, a greater than usual conflation of lover and father figure, of wife and daughter, is made. (In *How to Marry a Millionaire*, 1953, an aged William Powell nobly bows out, leaving Schatzi (Lauren Bacall) to a younger millionaire, but this generosity is unusual.) It might be said that this extreme inequality of age is merely historical accident, Hollywood's inheritance of a now ageing generation of great male stars of the 30s that has to be used until the day when they became biologically unlikely. But, true as that may be, it seems symptomatic of something more, the image of a more conservative time which sees men as fathers and teachers, women as mothers/daughters and pupils. As an instance of this, think how much that witty liberal comedy *Born Yesterday* (1958) is based around tutor and tutee, father and daughter. When Billie (Judy Holliday), initially the dumbest of dumb broads, rings Paul Verrell (William Holden) near the end of the film, she confuses his name with that of Thomas Jefferson, one of the stations of the liberal education Paul has given her in art, politics, the Declaration of Independence, the Bill of Rights, the Gettysburg Address and the Constitution. Billie's actual father, with whom she has quarrelled over her not living 'ethical' in her liaison with the gangster Harry (Broderick Crawford), has written to her again. Harry is the bad patriarch who may, in a way not devoid of pathos, eventually admit his love for her, but it is in terms we have to remark as comically regressive – 'I love that broad. Do you think we could find someone to make her dumb again?' A relatively youthful William Holden, who releases her, may be at this time almost filial as Hollywood patriarchs go, but he has her literal, and the Republic's founding, fathers behind him. Judy Holliday's strangulated voice, as odd as a Chinese coloratura and as significant of cultural estrangement as bound feet, is a kind of hyperbole of female underprivilege and stifled resistance. That the film releases her through a man is hardly surprising, but the intensity of the father-fixation in such a liberal film is notable and in some ways representative.

Of all Hollywood's great patriarchs, Spencer Tracy is the star whose later career was most characterised by roles written around narratives attempting to come to terms with what were, by 1930s Hollywood standards, the somewhat faded issues of the equality of the sexes. These are kept alive as the overt subject matter of the comedies with Katharine Hepburn (the early *Woman of the Year*, 1942, which sets the pattern, *Adam's Rib*, 1949, *Pat and Mike*, 1952, and *The Desk Set*, 1957), all of which foreground the clash between Hepburn's championing of the New Woman's demand for equality with men, and Tracy's mixture of egalitarian receptiveness and defence of more traditional values associated with masculinity and fatherhood. Here the issues are overt and articulated rather than metaphoric and concealed. Three illustrative moments come to mind. In *Woman of the Year* in a remarkable scene touching, as that film often does, the melodramatic, the viewer is concentrated on Hepburn's ecstatically tearful face as she watches the marriage of her feminist aunt and listens to the preacher's homily about marriage – 'Believe in the ideal. You saw it once. It is the final truth.' If this points to the film's emotional–philosophical investment in matrimony, Amanda's (Hepburn's) angry musing to Kip in *Adam's Rib* (a provocative, myth-searching title) investigates and restates this 'ideal' and 'truth'. . . . 'Balance, equality, mutual everything . . . Equality, mutual everything or nothing.' And a third moment from the same film, as Amanda defends Mrs Attinger, has her invent an anthropological allegory of unbenign matriarchy to point out the flaws of patriarchy: 'A people known as the Locaniarnos . . . descended from the Amazons . . . members of the female sex rule and govern and systematically deny equal rights to the men made weak and puny by years of subservience.' Here not only are wit and playfulness, the ability to change perspectives (as will indeed happen visually when, at Amanda's courtroom command, the audience sees the sexes of the Attingers and Mr Attinger's mistress transposed) assumed, but also a certain mythic serious-ness – a transhistorical perspective on the struggles between matriarchy and patriarchy – is encapsulated in the reference to the Amazons and the cross-cultural discoveries of the 20s and 30s.

It is, then, a 'feminist theme' questioning 'bourgeois marriage itself' that the Spencer Tracy character is called upon to face. From the early 1940s on he is the image of the father as this society would like to conceive of him, in Aristotelian terms perhaps not as he always is, but as he should be. It is not accidental that around the time of *Adam's Rib* and *Pat and Mike* he played the epitome of idealised suburban fatherhood in *Father of the Bride* (1950). There he was literally a parent (as he also is in the melodramatic *State of the Union*, 1948), but, as mostly happens in romantic comedy, he does not have that literal function in the comedies with Hepburn. 'The dogs' in *Adam's Rib*, a surrogate son in Hucko in *Pat and Mike*, the Greek boy whom Hepburn wrongheadedly adopts in *Woman of the Year* are the only traces of the literal role. But everything else about him conflates father and lover into one. The straightness, moral and sexual; the cragginess unaffec-tedly displaying rather than effacing middle age; a certain rugged portliness; an authoritative bearing, relaxed but powerful, an undeviating maleness neither doubting itself nor finding the necessity to overdramatise itself, but which also conceals sentiment ('You're just a big sentimental slob', Pat tells him late in *Pat and Mike*). As is felt proper for the male, he seems to care nothing about his appearance; indeed in profile he sometimes looks a little simian, Neanderthal, squat, with his long-hanging arms, and certain habits of his acting underwrite (in a calculating art that suggests the character's uncalculatingness) everything else about him that contributes to this im-pression of the sincere. In gestures not sought by more glamorous stars, he puffs his cheeks, or, when he is in pensive mood, lolls his tongue in his cheek, and he has a way of letting his heavy head drop forward which fills his powerful, scrubbed face with folds, as well as rubbing and fingering it in a rough, unself-conscious way. As Hepburn, his wife Mary, puts it ironically in *State of the Union*, 'when he's cockeyed drunk with sincerity, people can't resist him'.

This last is important. Though the Tracy persona in these films is con-structed to please at many conscious and unconscious levels, part of the meaning of the Hepburn/Tracy films is their awareness of exactly that. After all, in *State of the Union* it is his image of paternal virtue that interests the manipulators, Adolphe Menjou and Agnes Moorhead, and makes him a possibility for father figure number one, the President. True, the film rescues his real sincerity at the end, but it hardly allows the image of Tracy to survive unexamined. 'I know he's a big man,' as Mary again remarks to Jim Conovan, 'you know he's a big man. My bad days are when he knows he's a big man. You don't suppose there's any way of getting Grant elected and keeping it a secret from him?'

Armed with his refined populist aura (if Cagney is Hollywood's demotic Dionysus, Tracy is the Apollo of the people), he is in *Adam's Rib* literally the defender and giver of the law, but it would be a dimly prejudiced reading of the film, or the other comedies, that granted him immunity from criticism. We are obviously meant to love him, but it is the films' logic that we recognise – and that Tracy himself eventually does too – the excesses of the father. Here not only, as he plays with and against Hepburn, does he have a lover/opponent who challenges the father's hierarchy, but it is no daughter he deals with. A widow in *Pat and Mike*, she is 45 to his 52 in real life, so there is no question of the kind of meaning, say, the younger *Audrey* Hepburn has in regard to her patriarchs, all to do with youth and regeneration, with the feeling of, not the conditions of, romance. Not only does the Katharine Hepburn character in the comedies (she is much more self-effacing in the non-comic *State of the Union*) have an approximate chronological equality with Tracy, she is also his professional equal, as lawyer in *Adam's Rib* and as journalist in *The Desk Set*. Or she is even superior, for good sports journalist as Sam Craig is in *Woman of the Year*, and symbolically important as sports may be in the film, her job, with its political, international, wartime connections is more important. If we see the combination of manager (him) and sports star (her) in *Pat and Mike* as symbiotic, there is still no doubt that the athlete falls into the category of the more extraordinary. Brilliant, even a prodigy (in *Woman of the Year* she seems to speak every European language, in *Pat and Mike* she doesn't stop at golf and tennis, but plays baseball, shoots and even boxes, though, as she quickly points out, with 16oz. gloves), she is the antithesis of Judy Holliday's Billie. Rather than yesterday, she seems born tomorrow. Typically in the comedies this seems at the beginning to hold no threat for the Tracy figure, too tolerant, too intelligent, too self-possessed to be threatened by a woman who equals or even, in certain ways, might surpass him. Yet, as we shall see, each of the films reaches a point where the Tracy character's conception of himself is tested to breaking point. Covert problems, hidden strains of sexual prejudice and aggressions cause crises that the films must attempt to resolve.

Pat and Mike, the third of the four comedies, has Tracy as Mike Conovan, a New York sports entrepreneur with various shady connections and a stable that includes an unsuccessful heavyweight fighter, 'Hucko' (Aldo Ray), and a racehorse ('Little Nell'). He sees Pat Pemberton (Hepburn), an unlikely Californian, competing in the women's golf matchplay Nationals and offers her an illicit deal to make certain money by coming second rather than trying to win. She refuses. Disturbed by the oppressive presence of her fiancé, she fails in the final. Then, insisting on an interim period of self-reliance, she seeks out Mike in New York. He becomes her 'manager' and she his 'property', her growing success – we see her in various professional tennis matches alongside Frank Parker, Alice Marble and others – only interrupted by bathetic failure when Collier is present. Slowly, without romantic or sexual involvement between them, the relationship grows, in the end threatened only on the one hand by Mike's criminal associates and on the other by Collier. Pat rather than Mike defeats the gangsters, something which in fact produces the main crisis of the film, and Collier walks out on Pat because he believes (wrongly) that she has been having an affair with Mike. Watched by Mike, she wins the matchplay Nationals.

Compared with *Woman of the Year* and *Adam's Rib*, *Pat and Mike* is distinctly relaxed, much less plot-orientated than its predecessors. Cavell talks of its being 'a gentle summery anthology of themes' from the other films, a statement with which one might agree if taken in the most positive sense – i.e. that anthologies rearrange known objects ('themes') and in that rearrangement create extra significances, and that an arrangement may be 'summery' (as distinct from summary) without being superficial. It is certainly easier to underestimate the comic seriousness of *Pat and Mike* than that of its predecessors. Britton, for example, regards it with contempt, though the empty generalities and mock-Leavisian ironies of the passage in which he does so suggest that the problem lies less in the film's art than with the critic's desire to denigrate and simplify the Tracy/Hepburn films. Thus:

> *Pat and Mike* in which the cycle's (feminist) thematic has been safely inoculated as an inert, cosy 'entertainment' formula by which we are to be disarmed, is merely embarrassingly arch, its grossly inflated reputation only being comprehensible, it seems to me, as evidence of the dazzling expertise with which it allows one to feel that the inequalities of patriarchal sexual relations, of which one has vaguely heard tell, can be convincingly rectified through the private mutual accommodation of loveable, exceptional people.

The formulaic rhetoric here is at such a distance from its object and its particularities that it would be equally meaningful to substitute *Holiday* or *Bringing up Baby* for *Pat and Mike*.

In spite of its deceptively relaxed ambience, *Pat and Mike* is the film of the cycle that most revealingly explores the image of Tracy as father. Two attributes, the criminal and the Godlike, infect this patriarch, and the film's progress, which is the union of Tracy and Hepburn as man and woman rather than trainer and athlete only, is also the investigation and shedding of them. Rather than self-reference being simply inert, Mike's surname of *Conovan* should remind us that it differs only by a single consonant from that of the cynical, manipulative Adolphe Menjou character in *Woman of the Year*, the political string-puller, Mike *Conova*. In other words, the name (despicable though Britton finds, for reasons which are never very clear, Cukor's screenwriters, Garson Kanin and Ruth Gordon) should signal the narrative's desire to criticise before acceptance, even where Tracy is concerned. Not only does he have gangster connections, but illictly entering Pat's apartment to make her his offer, he is dressed rather like an archetypal Godfather – dark shirt under his suit and stubby tie. The central metaphor of the film is an analogy between the trainer's contract with the athlete (in which the trainer is ceded powers of a kind by the athlete, to the advantage of both) and the contract of marriage in a patriarchal society ('It's a contract. It's the law', Adam says in *Adam's Rib*; 'It's a deal!' as Mike says in *Pat and Mike*). But for the analogy to work benignly, the criminality lingering about Mike – a more literal reworking of the moments noted by Cavell where Adam poses playfully as the melodramatic villain in *Adam's Rib* – which represents elements of potential abuse in the contract, must be shuffled off. The criminals, when we meet them, insist on exploiting Pat's talent by having her finish second 'for insurance' rather than first, the proposition which Mike makes at the beginning of the film but learns to reject. (Finishing second has obvious connotations in the domestic sphere of love relationships as well as in the world of sports.) The gangsters are also linked to an idea of ownership that Mike outgrows. As trainer–manager, Mike both owns his charges and has the power to dictate the conditions under which they live, something amusingly dramatised in the scene where he cancels Pat's dinner orders and imposes more spartan choices. The implications of his Jehovah-like power over Pat, Hucko and 'Little Nell' are drawn out in the film's running joke of the 'three questions' he asks of his charges. The horse of course cannot answer back, but when Hucko replies to Mike it is through words forced on him by his trainer.

> Who made you, Hucko?
>   You, Mike.
> Who owns the biggest piece of you?
>   You, Mike.
> What'll happen to you if I drop you?
>   I'll go right down the drain, Mike . . .
> And?
>   And . . . stay there.

This repeated question and answer sequence immediately recalls the beginning of the Catholic catechism which opens with the question 'Who made you?', followed by the answer 'God made me', and so on. (Tracy's own Catholicism, his inability to obtain a divorce from his wife and his relationship with Hepburn are, of course, all part of the film's subtext.)

The shadow of religion here, the invocation of divine models of behaviour, is not at all surprising if one agrees with Freud that patriarchal authority is linked with the rise of religion in the West. Fathers, abusing their power both in the family and in the public domain, can become as authoritarian as God himself in jealously decreeing that no other law must be obeyed. With Hucko, his surrogate son, Mike's divine rule is especially destructive for Hucko has been knocked out in his last four bouts. The problem, as Pat realises, is akin to hers with her fiancé, Collier. In either case paternalistic power has subjugated rather than encouraged. When, outside the training camp infirmary, Pat stands in the background watching Mike give Hucko a dressing-down for some minor infringement of training rules that culminates in the usual 'Who made you?', her face shows disapproval, and moments later she herself talks to Hucko, pointedly coming down from her superior station on the verandah to do so. Heretically she suggests to him that he is too old for the 'three big questions', i.e. that the father's power may be a good thing for the infant needing authoritative models, but continued too far it results in retarded growth and infantilism. ('Little Nell', we remember, dies in Dickens's novel without reaching maturity.) Hucko's defeat of himself in a contest in which the opponent is only incidental parallels Pat's own progress from being Collier's 'little woman' (a phrase that Amanda vented her anger on when she defined what marriage should be in *Adam's Rib*).

Collier Weld (William Ching) adds to his affirmation that Pat is his 'little woman' the addendum that he is her 'little man'. This accidentally Reichian allusion – he is clearly a prime target for the admonitions of *Listen, Little Man!* – is made jokingly, but the joke only part hides the truth. Far younger than Mike, whom he calls 'old man' when they meet, with considerable emphasis on 'old', he is much more the heavy father, the unrepairable *senex*.

Much recent film criticism has been concerned with the 'male gaze', both as the motivator of the camera in a patriarchal cinema and as regards the objectification of female characters by male characters on the screen. Collier, bland and handsome, never overtly offensive, embodies aspects of this proprietorial gaze. Indeed Pat remarks on it when she asks, after one of the moments when his presence causes her to fail, 'Why is it I always fall to pieces when you give me that look?' 'That look' is massively present in the social golf game with the Bemingers where he makes it clear that Pat's failure will let him down, and there is a significant moment where, as she crouches down to line up the putt, her eyes look up beseechingly at his which look down on her demandingly from an exalted position. To borrow Lacan's famous image of the 'mirror phase', Pat, facing Collier, is constantly translated back to a childhood image of herself as the 'little woman', reading her mind's misconstruction in Collier's patronising face.

The effects of that 'look' are played out in one of the film's most memorable scenes where Pat undergoes a series of hallucinations during her tennis match where the ball flying at her suddenly multiplies, where her own racquet turns into a pigmy toy, her opponent's into a giant's weapon and the net into an impassable barrier. The opponent is none other than 'Gorgeous Gussie' Moran, featured erotically in the press as an exposer of pretty panties: the sportswoman as erotic object first and skilful player second. In setting Pat against her, and making the contest the occasion of Pat's major breakdown, the film develops the consequences of its overall use of sports as a metaphor for female fulfilment, an arena not quite as 'ideologically innocent' as Britton claims, since not only is there the particular conflict pointed to above, but even with the growth of female sports in the 1930s alluded to in the chapter on *Bringing up Baby*, sports were still thought of as primarily a male field of endeavour. If, as Cavell half complains in passing, Cukor spends a disproportionate amount of time on Hepburn's 'physical accomplishments', making the film's first section extremely leisurely, the display perhaps has its Atalantan point alongside its longueurs.

Though the film replaces Collier with Mike as Hepburn's partner, a network of resemblances between the two insists that the switching is not automatic but a process in which, while she learns confidence from him, he learns from her as Collier never does. Like Collier, Mike is a sort of administrator (the one, assistant vice-principal at the college, the other, a trainer–entrepreneur). Both want to make a 'delicate deal' of a golf game. Both, as owner–protectors are rebuked together when they argue over Pat with much talk of 'owning' and 'property' (echoing the classic nineteenth-century exposures of the economic inequality of marriage), where her salutary reaction is 'Nobody owns anything or anybody except myself. Go away.' Finally, that first sign in the film of Collier's tyranny, where he objects to her wearing trousers for golf, has an echo late in the film where she and Mike dine together. Here his compliment on her dress ('the right silks') leads on to the suggestion that 'It does more for you than them pants you're always wearing.' The point she makes in reply is that she is 'not sure I'd be able to play in it', and the conversation ends. We might feel that the debate betrays Mike's confusion between sports and erotics, but at least he raises it only as a tentative suggestion to which he never returns, while with Collier it is much more like a command.

Moments of crisis

> Golf is what I call a nice game . . . I mean it's dignified and fresh air. Men and women both. Now you take those lady rasslers. Now that's something I can't stomach. That's something that shouldn't oughta be allowed.
>
> — Barney, the gangster, in *Pat and Mike*

Mike's definition of the 'man/woman thing' is that relationships have to be 'five oh, five oh', that the 'whole gismo' must be fully egalitarian. But here, as in *Woman of the Year* and *Adam's Rib*, a point of crisis is reached, leading to the possibility of divorce in the first two films and the possibility of non-marriage in the later. In each case Hepburn's drive for equality is felt by Tracy to have gone too far, to have transgressed at least his conception of the 'five oh, five oh' relationship. In *Woman of the Year* he is constantly placed in a position that is none other than a parody of the subsidiary wife's, the 'little woman's.' In *Adam's Rib* the explosion comes after he feels mocked in court. In *Pat and Mike* it occurs as he feels that his distinctive maleness has become redundant when Pat does his job of physically overpowering the threatening gangsters. In each case the male figure makes an angry speech in which he claims that equality has tipped over into non-differentiation. 'The woman of the year is not a woman', Sam tells Tess in *Woman of the Year*. In *Adam's Rib* Adam announces to Amanda that 'We've been close, but we've never been this close before', and in *Pat and Mike* he breaks away declaring that he likes 'a He to be He and a She to be a She'.

In *Pat and Mike* the moment that provokes this outburst is presented not once but twice, actually replayed with commentary by the principals demanded when, afterwards at the police station, explanations are required for the mayhem Pat has wrought among the gangsters. To Mike's intensely glowering embarrassment he is forced to watch Pat's re-enactment of her triumph and endure the admission of his own marginalised part in the proceedings. (*The Police Captain* (Chuck Connors): 'And just what were you doin' all this time?' *Mike:* 'Just watchin'.')

The original battle and the quarrel that follows as they leave the police station, the literal site of the masculine law, culminate in an allusion that for a moment invades the comedy with the world of the Gothic as Mike regresses to his old creator/creature analogies, as well as suddenly invoking the image of woman as monstrous in his claim that he has built her up into a 'Frankenstein monster'.

Pat and Mike is not, as we have already suggested, as overt in its statement of the 'feminist theme' as its predecessors (where, for instance, in *Woman of the Year* Tess's aunt is a noted feminist, the title 'Woman of the Year' that is awarded to Tess comes from a woman's organisation, and where, in a scene of notable comedy, Sam, arriving late, makes something of a fool of himself on the platform during a feminist meeting). Equally, it does not push its issues to the striking melodramatic extreme of inter-sexual aggression found in *Adam's Rib*, framed as that narrative is by Mrs Attinger's attempted shooting of her husband and by Adam's pretended shooting of Amanda and Kip. Nor does it have any parallel to the other films' assaults by Tracy on Kip and Gerald, characters who are coded as gay, or, at the very least, deficiently masculine. But if Pat's easy disarming of the gangsters is in no way an aggression aimed at Mike, the problem is that he feels it to be such, and for a moment in the night-lit scenes that follow with their anger and sudden invocation of the monster, *Pat and Mike* plays out its version of the same crisis.

The difficulty in discussing the way this trauma, and the ones it echoes, are acted out and resolved, is that since heterosexuality itself in the most influential recent criticism is identified with the regressive, the dictatorially Oedipal and the oppressive, any resolution or set of compromises that the heterosexual characters make in order to readjust their relationship will be seen simply as a surrender to dominant patriarchal ideology. Pat's only surrender is twofold: an admission, on the one hand, of a need for Mike's fatherliness in certain circumstances ('I need someone to look after me'), and on the other, of the attractions of certain external signs of femininity. We shall return to the former in a moment, but first let us take in the significance of the semiotics of Hepburn's hairstyle in the bedroom scene with Mike after their quarrel. Here is the only time that she wears it down instead of in the swept-up fashion or fuzzy bird's nest of the rest of the film, including the final golf scene. The style and the moment indicate – remembering also their previous discussion about dress and Mike's preference for dresses over pants – that outside the sports arena there is a place for pleasure in certain signs of sexual difference, provided they are not crippling. By this suggestion, and the sense that Mike has made many adjustments for her, the matter is settled, for when Mike comes back to her room to adjust the curtains and gently pull up her blanket (a parallel to an earlier scene where he settled her for an afternoon nap) he seems to have overcome the feelings that gave rise to his outburst.

One suspects that there are critics whose ideological absolutism will force them to be blind to the positive ways the scene places the partners in a multi-faceted relationship, acting out the roles for each other not only of lover and lover (husband and wife) but of father and mother, daughter and son. Of course if the father is simply typed as the source of all evil, then it follows that he can perform only negative acts, which means that we are likely to be asked to view the positives of such a scene only as the screen for more sinister meanings such as the reconstitution of the father's power, and as a strategy of infantilisation which turns the grown, equal woman back into dependent and nursling. However, to say this is not only to deny the complexity of the scene itself, but the complexity of human relationships; to be deliberately blind to the way the scene exhibits in Tracy qualities of tenderness and nurturing in which patriarchy has often been seen to be deficient. By this point in the film we have also seen Katharine Hepburn taking a kind of motherly care of him, insisting that he needs looking after in his relation with the gangsters, so that transactions involving protectiveness are by no means one-way. Again it is possible by a constricting effort of the imagination to read this negatively: i.e. the father, while infantilising the woman, still demands (yet at the same time resents) her maternal role. But it seems to us that if you can say only, or even primarily, this of *Pat and Mike*, then your reading of any male–female relationships has become entirely mechanical, simply the imposition of a predefined negative paradigm upon any possible instance. When Pat and Mike converse near the end of the film in her bedroom, their discussion centres round her statement that 'I need someone to look after me', his refusal to credit it and her insistence on it. Given the whole context, to see her statement as a climbdown, as the film's taking away from Pat what it has only pretended to give her, is to seek the doctrinaire at all costs. Mike knows it means nothing of the sort, for his response is not to dwell on it and build it up into the dominant meaning of their relationship, but to say 'Well, I don't know if I can lick you or you can lick me, but I do know one thing – together we can lick them all.' The question of such fatherliness and motherliness, of filial and daughterly roles within relationships can hardly be theorised, since the rightness or wrongness of a gesture – whether its meaning is finally liberatingly protective or unliberatingly over-protective – depends upon unique circumstance. While you can argue that specific social orders of a capitalist and patriarchal kind (as distinct, say, from socialist and matrilineal) are more likely to encourage the negative tendencies rather than positive ones, to declare that only the negative ones exist is absurd.

The fact that *Pat and Mike* is so much a film about a middle-aged couple – a middle-agedness which makes even the lissome Hepburn's athletic prowess look less a reality, at least in the tennis, than a metaphor for female striving – makes it easier for these qualities to be demonstrated as the erotic tends to be sublimated into the companionable, a tenderness not wholly unerotic, but never burningly so. In the whole film only a single kiss (Pat to Mike) is given, and Mike's reply to her agreement to marry him is a handshake and 'It's a deal!' Mike's apparent allergy to flowers (which we notice Collier is keen on sending as gifts) suggest itself as a sign of the film's wariness of the conventionally romantic, something it shares with many 30s comedies. The lovers' touches are, as it were, translated into the stethoscope Mike places on Pat's breast to check her heartbeat after exercise, the healing fingering of the massage table, and the not unsuggestive moment where Tracy leans over a supine Hepburn, working on her, bending her arm back and forth in a motion with obvious connotations. Here too the lovers' subjective views of each other are given comically as Pat fantasises Mike's head on a photograph of Collier, and Mike sees a sort of anamorphic image of Pat's face imposed on 'Little Nell's'.

A comparison with *Woman of the Year*, a much more riven and intense comedy, is instructive, for there, in the exceptionally emotionally-wrought wedding scene, the camera focuses on Tess listening to the minister's declaration of the demands on the marriage partners. 'As the bride gives herself to the bridegroom, let him be to her father and mother, sister and brother, and, most sacred, husband.' He continues, 'As he gives himself to her, let the bride inspire and sustain him, let her unite with him in all the experiences of life to which their paths shall lead . . .' The earlier film is able to redefine positively the role of the father/husband, but cannot quite bring itself to give the minister a speech which makes it 'five-oh / five oh' for the wife/mother, veering away from the missing symmetry of 'Let her be to him mother and father, sister and brother, and, most sacred, wife.' Clearly the less intense terms in which *Pat and Mike* sets up its dilemmas makes it easier to resolve them, but the same can be said of *Bringing up Baby* compared to, say, *His Girl Friday*.

Britton's negative reading of the whole Hepburn/Tracy cycle heavily depends on a view of the films as the negative, conservative term in a comparison with the anti-patriarchal, anti-capitalist *Baby* and *Holiday*. His reading, intermittently brilliant though it is, is faulty at both ends, exaggerating the conservatism of the late films and the radicalism of the earlier ones. The same scepticism aimed at the Tracy/Hepburn films could find equal evidence of ambivalence and backing-off in the Grant/Hepburn films, of which it could equally be said that they present 'the inequalities of patriarchal sexual relations . . . rectified through the private mutual accommodation of loveable, exceptional people'. Equally, the desire to find positive meanings – (a

desire that becomes too pressing, as in the castratory misquotation of *Baby* that turns 'your golfball' into 'your *ball*') – if turned on *Pat and Mike* would reveal a text far different from the one slightingly dismissed, with even its own version of the parody of phallic domination when Pat, having overcome the gangsters, holds the small, limp, exceedingly phallic cosh in her hand and asks Mike 'What is this?' Did you ever see anything like this at all?'

This is not to present *Pat and Mike* as a text without aesthetic flaws (its dilatory opening) or entrapments in conventional ideology (the fact that the crisis is caused by the least likely, and therefore the least worrying kind of equality between the sexes, that of physical strength, which evades more difficult questions, as, we might feel, does the proletarian–'upper-cruster' angle to the romance). But the combination of the Kanins and Cukor (perhaps interpretable as a happy balance of the female and male, heterosexual and homosexual sensibilities) and the by now intrinsic possibilities of meaning residing in Hepburn and Tracy together, manage to produce images of male and female companionability (always fewer than those of passion) rare in the cinema. The gains may be private and non-transferable; for instance, the police captain, a not wholly unregenerate character, judging by his interest in Pat as a golfer, still automatically misconstrues her explanation of winning the fight. When she says 'I've been around Physical Ed a long time', he assumes that Ed must be a strongman beau from whom her strength ultimately derives – 'Who's Physical Ed?' But the mixture of independence and interdependence as Mike turns the gaze associated with Collier into a conspiratorial wink at the final hole of the last playoff, or as the pair dismantle patriarchal, and even matriarchal, superiority in the final parody of the 'three questions', this time addressed to Mike by Pat, reassembling power as mutual, places *Pat and Mike* high among the most intelligently egalitarian products of the genre. The famous conceit/joke that closes *Adam's Rib* (Adam's 'Vive la différence', Amanda's 'What does that mean?' and Adam's reduction of the celebration to the 'little difference'), which plays intensely with the twin desires to assert sexual sameness and sexual difference, is subtle enough to benefit from an anachronistic reading out of Derrida – 'Vive la différ*ance*' – emphasises how much even of sexual meaning, outside the crucial 'little difference', is malleable, 'unfixed, in process, deferred'.

Pat and Mike

Five-0 – Five 0, the unholy trinity: the good father (Spencer Tracy) coaches his obedient 'son' (Aldo Ray) and no-punches pulled 'daughter' (Katharine Hepburn) in the arts of survival.

Grant, the narrative can be relied upon to save her from the danger. Having allowed her to demonstrate that she is a 'real woman' by desire, it rescues her from the contamination of actual premarital sex, a last gasp of the mythology that makes compatible female sexuality and purity. Spurned by the heroine, the promiscuous hero inverts the heroine's movement away from puritanism by accepting marriage and monogamy. Finally, as if compelled to underscore the reproductive function of the sexuality with which the narrative has been obsessed, a coda adds a pregnancy or birth. This super-plot does not cover all the films named, but it is a rough summary of three of the best of them, *Pillow Talk*, *Lover Come Back* and *That Touch of Mink*.

Though these films have as their heroine a determined career-girl (an interior decorator, an advertiser, a computer worker, in *Teacher's Pet* a professor of journalism), they are ambivalent about ultimately affirming her in that role. *Teacher's Pet*, where there is a real sense that both characters think and live journalism, is the least so. But in the remake of *My Favorite Wife*, *Move Over, Darling*, Ellen has declined from anthropologist – explorer and mother to mother alone, and at the end of *The Thrill of It All*, a film in which Hudson's/Grant's seducer's plot to sleep with the heroine without getting her pregnant is converted into the husband's plot to impregnate his wife to put an end to her television advertising career, Beverley Boyer is content to be 'a doctor's wife'. Does marriage automatically end the woman's role in the outside world? *Pillow Talk* and its successor *Lover Come Back* do not exactly say so, but the arrival in the coda of the earliest possible child is a broad hint in the affirmative.

If a female cannot have both career and marriage, characters like the alcoholic maid, Alma, in *Pillow Talk*, the alcoholic secretary, Maude, in Tashlin's *Susan Slept Here* (1959), or Millie in *That Touch of Mink* who carries round a wedding ring because she believes in 'always being prepared', point the moral of the incorrect choice. As Alma (Thelma Ritter) jaundicedly puts it: 'If there's anythin' worse than a woman livin' alone, it's a woman sayin' she likes it!' In *Pillow Talk* Brad (Rock Hudson) puts forward a temporary male resistance to the paradise of suburban marriage in a memorable scene where Jonathan (Tony Randall) argues in its favour. Brad confuses Jonathan by replying to his arguments for the 'adult' and 'maturity' (those loaded 50s words) with a reiterated 'why?' and then develops his comparison of the unmarried man to the 'tree in the forest . . . independent, an entity unto himself' which is then chopped down (a symbolic castration parallelled by the phone board's threat, after Jan's complaints, to 'disconnect him') and transformed into the impedimenta of the family home, 'a vanity table, the breakfast nook, the baby crib and the newspaper that lines the family garbage can'. It is a moment of witty subversion, made all the more so by Tony Randall's masochistically leering reply, 'With Jan you look forward to having your branches cut off', but a temporary resistance really only articulated by the male. Jan's parallel statement denying to Alma that she is missing anything in her single life is unconvincing, a mere gesturing at externals – a lovely apartment, a good job, charming dates, the best shows. Alma's scepticism – 'If you don't know what you're missin', then you're missin' it' – underlines the film's argument that while men may have to be trapped into domesticity, women naturally gravitate to it. In *Male and Female* (1949) Margaret Mead writes of the way 'Each known human society has tried to come to grips with these problems, with the incompatibility between man's spontanaiety and the monotony of the domestic hearth, with the over-compatibility between woman's docility and the perpetuation of some tight, outworn tradition.' Though its guarded mixture of the biological with the cultural will not find favour with critics who illogically reject any biological base from which the possibilities of culture are developed, and though we might feel that a later, more conservative climate makes for a less radical statement of the relation of biology to culture than is found in her work of the 1930s, Mead's terms usefully illustrate what *Pillow Talk* can and cannot openly come to terms with. On the one hand it gives a great deal of expression to male spontaniety, though in the end bringing Brad to heel. On the other, though in many ways responding to the excitements and reorientations that its career-girl heroine embodies, it is constantly tempted by the sirens of over-compatibility, especially where the female characters are concerned (1950s 'functionalism' and the repression within the myth of 'the happy housewife heroine' of what Betty Friedan was describing, almost as the film came out, as 'the problem that has no name').

All this is so, and yet to say only as much is to simplify the more various feelings *Pillow Talk* evokes. Three areas of the film contribute to these and demand attention: (i) the personae (individual and interlocking) of the two stars; (ii) the film's glossy *mise-en-scène* and (iii) the configuration of minor characters, sub-plots, parodies, pastiches and marginalised themes that lie beneath or border on the main areas of the narrative. In looking at these, one important distinction ought to be kept in mind. All films may be approached as possessing both a level of conscious intent and a level of unconscious meanings. It is clear that in some cases the conscious level is highly organised and self-aware, a self-awareness which may include a critique of ideology. *Pat and Mike* falls into this category, and can be seen as both within and without dominant ideology, being on the one hand a celebration of 'the ideology of the couple', yet on the other, clearly aware that it is dealing with a 'feminist theme' which interrogates the latter, and many – though not of course all – of the film's meanings are the product of this self-awareness. But a film such as *Pillow Talk*, inventively crafted though it is, is shaped more firmly by the demands of 'entertainment' and the laws of pleasing the greatest number of box-office patrons. (The film took $7.5 million on initial release.) As such it is certainly not devoid of self-consciousness, as the parodies and pastiches of *Giant* (1956) and the Rock Hudson Sirkean melodramas testify, but what rules the production of overt meaning is the mythic reconciliation of opposites which constitutes, as Robert Ray puts it, via Truffaut the 'certain tendency of the Hollywood cinema'. In a more conservative era this reconciliation is likely to take more conservative forms in films without the complicating possibilities set up by, say, the intervening presence of directors like Cukor and Wilder, writers like the Kanins and Axelrod, the licence of comical satire in *The Seven Year Itch* or the accumulated meanings of the Hepburn/Tracy partnership flowing into *Pat and Mike*. Viewed in the most reductive terms, *Pillow Talk* picks out of the air the theme of the career-girl and exploits its timeliness and appeal, without wanting to investigate too closely what these are, and then in the same or next, breath closes it off. Similarly it responds to the male critique of marriage given a new inflection (as Barbara Ehrenreich has interestingly argued) in the pages of *Playboy*, yet ends up by affirming the institution in its most traditional form, e.g. the sight of Brad as contemporary caveman lifting and carrying a protesting Jan, and the three-month immediacy of the arrival of the child. These manoeuvres have their own interest as renderings of felt ambivalences, but much of the fascination of the film resides in the way that, beneath these motions, at a level which often seems more unconscious than conscious, the regulation of meaning is much looser, resulting in the various complicating features which make the film much more than the sum of its most obvious mechanisms.

Star signs: he and she

He is a tree trunk.
                    — Fassbinder on Rock Hudson in *All That Heaven Allows*

With Jan you look forward to having your branches cut off.
                              — Tony Randall of Doris Day in *Pillow Talk*

As others have noted, Doris Day, though very much associated in the public mind with corn-fed, bouncy, girl-next-door roles (in sentimental musicals like *On Moonlight Bay*, 1951, or energetic ones like *Calamity Jane*, 1953), and later with the resisting, sexy but good girl of the sex comedy cycle, is a more multi-faceted figure than selective memory has made her out to be. 'The darker sides of Day' exhibited, say, in *Love Me or Leave Me* (1955), and *The Man Who Knew Too Much* (1956) are not aberrations but define important characteristics present but less immediately visible in later films like *Pillow Talk* where she tends to be flattened by memory into pure stereotype, 'the image' (Haskell) 'of a forty-year old virgin defending her maidenhood into a ripe old age'. This highly defensive sexual prudence, as exhibited by Ruth Etting in *Love Me or Leave Me*, the musical biopic in which Day as the famous singer accepts the support of, but later leaves, her gangster–sponsor–husband (James Cagney), can be seen as a melodramatic analogue to the comic situations. Those sexually ruthless qualities that Ruth Etting cultivates in order to achieve success and escape the degradations of the dime-a-dance hall in which she begins, that calculated investment of the resources which her attractiveness represents, are responses (not entirely dissimilar) to problems (again, given the transposition from melodrama to comedy, not wholly dissimilar) faced by the smalltown girl from Upper Sanduskie, Eureka or mid-Nebraska in the big cities of the comedies. Jan Morrow, no doubt, would be shocked by the comparison with Ruth Etting's calculated drive to achieve her professional and marital desires, but the con-straint on her own situation is that the uncalculating release of her libido is fraught with a double danger, however much parts of the film may define the problem as simply one of daring to 'let go'. Such a 'trip to the moon' may not only interfere with the struggle for professional success, but is also dangerous (apart from the pre-pill possibility of pregnancy) because it almost inevitably takes place only on the male's terms. The equation of marriage with respect and the possibilites of female assertiveness may be one that we want to question, but it is something that the film is being historically truthful about, and for Jan (whom we could hardly expect to be Emma Goldman or even Betty Friedan) the two tend to be synonymous, making her eventual decision to give herself to Rex more perilous than we might read it now. Brad's three mistresses might be freer than she is in their life of erotic indulgence, but they are really Brad's slaves and their sexual allure does not prevent them from being summarily despatched when Brad throws them over for marriage with Jan. Likewise the playgirl who drives Jerry to work at the opening of *Lover Come Back* and the ironically named 'Rebel' in the same film, in fact highly manipulated by Jerry, are similarly powerless, in the end little more than the 'rabbits . . . I mean girls' (an obvious reference to the Playboy Clubs) Jerry Webster supplies for his partying clients.

Jo McKenna's actions in Hitchcock's *The Man Who Knew Too Much* are less jarring then Etting's because they are free of the element of sexual manipulation. Here, in spite of her husband's (James Stewart's) pressure on her to abandon her singing career in favour of her duties as a doctor's wife, she is finally able to assert herself, initially by intelligently decoding a message, and subsequently through the power of the famous voice, used self-consciously in the film as a symbol of superiority over James Stewart's complacent drawl.

The pressures afflicting the character in the later comedies are perfectly illustrated by the early encounter of Gannon (Clark Gable) and Erica Stone in *Teacher's Pet*. After Gannon, the hard-boiled editor, discovers that the academic he has sneered at is a woman, his first instinct is to fill up the pages of his notepad not with his teacher's thoughts on the theory of journalism, but with a crude cartoon of her that emphasises what seems to him a comic disparity between her brains and her accentuated physique. When she asks him 'What would you like next?' mesmerised by her behind (lauded with memorable unrefinement by the producer, Ross Hunter, as 'one of the wildest asses in Hollywood!'), the only comment he can come up with is a puff of smoke at the retreating rump, the same that in the recognition scene at the nightclub in *Pillow Talk* draws a similar response from Brad: 'So that's the other end of your party line!' The problematic is further illustrated in the contrast with Day enacted by Gannon's girlfriend, the ersatz Monroe, Mamie van Doren, who sings a celebration of woman as dumb-blonde consumable goods:

> Now you've heard of instant coffee,
> You've heard of instant tea,
> See here, you guys,
> Just feast your eyes
> On li'l ol' instant me!

In *The Thrill of It All* a similar contrast is made between Beverley Boyer and the blonde starlet 'Spot' Checker, but there it largely focuses on the banal artifice of glamour versus the most obvious Day qualities Philip Shane catalogues in *That Touch of Mink* when he tells Cathy that she is 'direct, sincere, uncomplicated'. Remembering that the 50s are overridingly the age of almost instant everything, of innumerable domestic gadgets and devices to save time and labour and allow more human energy to be channelled into expanding leisure time, the contrast between Mamie's instant sex and Day's more typical recalcitrance becomes more than a simple moral one. It is not so much the male characters' appreciation of her sexuality that is the issue, for both Doris Day's healthy, physical look and the narratives make clear she is sexually vital, but rather the instantaneousness of that appreciation (unconsciously parodied by the lecherous Ivy-Leaguer, Tony, who, refusing to be rebuffed by Jan's reminder that he is Harvard man, replies by pointing out that he is on vacation – like the other men in the film apparently on a permanent sabbatical of the mind where women are concerned). *Pillow Talk* consistently surrounds Day with an inescapable ambience of sexual suggestion and fecundity, from Brad's erotic use of the phone disturbing the order of her business life, to the wood sculpture of the fertility goddess in M. Pirot's shop that so takes Mrs Walter's attention ('Savage little creature, isn't it!'), to accidental linguistic slips of desire such as Jan's embarrassing telephonic *double entendre* to Brad that they have got to live together. These are the mostly good-mannered but insistent urgings of an age preoccupied with unconscious sexuality, of which the demure yet infinitely suggestive famous advertisement of the day, 'I dreamed I stopped the traffic in my Maidenform Bra', was the memorable ultimate.

Pillow Talk's narrative, placing Jan in this world, is divided over how to deal with her, allowing her in places freedom and self-definition, in others, crucially at the very beginning and end, turning her into a highly conventional image of female sexuality. The film's opening shot after the title sequence concentrates on her in her slip as she pulls on a silk stocking and strokes her leg in a stereotypically narcissistic gesture that signifies the primary female interest as self-adornment, its primary place of definition the bedroom. The film's conservative drive is equally evident near its close when Day is dragged from her bed, literally swept off her feet, kicking and complaining but ultimately complaisant, by the now marriage-hunting Rock Hudson. Yet such moments are only partly definitive as the character continually draws in aspects built into the persona from previous films – the spunky, blue-collar commitment of Babe Williams in *The Pajama Game* (1957), the tomboyish, baseball-enthusing characteristics of many films, which suggest a determination not to be wholly defined by the external demands of the culture's design of femininity and not to be cut out of the world of male pursuits). Sometimes in tune with a more liberal working of the narrative, sometimes subverting a more repressive one, these positive, sometimes resistant qualities are often signalled in the names of the characters she plays in the comedies – Cathy *Timberlake:* pastoral values; *Beverley Boyer:* tomboyishness; Carol *Templeton:* a sunny inflection of the puritan sacramentality of sex, the body as temple of the soul; Erica *Stone:* the pastoral note again, but also connotations of a necessary hardness; and, in *Pillow Talk, Jan Morrow,* which, as you roll it round your tongue, becomes a clever and significant joke, an American reworking of *Jeanne Moreau,* the French actress already becoming world famous through films like Louis Malle's *L'Ascenseur pour L'Echafaud (Fran-tic*, 1958) and *Les Amants (The Lovers*, 1958), the latter especially an inter-national success. A homonymic joke which, as you think of the differences between the portrayal of women in the American and European cinemas, can have many significances, but one set of them is to assert, despite contrary drives in the narrative, a woman companionable rather than entirely 'other', and less bound up in the mystique of brooding femininity than her French namesake. The semiotic intuition behind the invention of the name 'Day' for Doris Kappelhoff, with its connotations of sun, light, and openness, ultimately stands behind all of these.

If Day in these films is a fascinating chrysalis, a cluster of living signs half expressing the orthodoxies of the times, half challenging them, what of her equally popular co-star, Rock Hudson, with whom commodity logic, based on the great popularity of both of them, dictated that she should star?

Hudson, like his female equivalent, Kim Novak, was a pure product of the old studio system (consider the vulgarly wonderful semiotics of the name thrust on him: Rock = strength, Hudson = America), picked along for beauty and the signs of manliness, and initially publicised shamelessly as bare-torsoed beefcake. Miss Dickenson, the telephone company's inspector in *Pillow Talk*, flaunts this in a female version of instant sexual appreciation when her unconscious replies 'you' when Brad asks her what she wants to inspect. In *Giant* George Stevens's camera cannot love even Elizabeth Taylor more than Hudson and, framing them side by side, is equally entranced by the raven hair and creamy skin of both. Later, in Frankenheimer's *Seconds* (1966), Hudson plays the retrospective part which comments most fully on the fantasy he embodies. The middle-aged Scarsdale executive who, given a second chance at life, lives it in the face and body of Rock Hudson, is a hyperbolised version of many a 50s film fan. Waking from the transfiguring operation, the patient, looking in the mirror at the image of his ego ideal, says, 'Well, I never, it's a masterpiece!' Jan, in the back of the taxi with Brad, is only a little more restrained in her soliloquised thoughts.

Like that of any star's, the initially simple Hudson persona was continually added to, with his more multi-levelled parts discovering and defining aspects in him that could in turn feed into later, and play back into earlier, roles. Predominant among these were the early films he made at Universal with Douglas Sirk, comedies such as *Has Anybody Seen My Gal?* (1952) and *Captain Lightfoot* (1955), which revealed the actor's talent for comedy, and more importantly the series of eminent Sirkean melodramas, *Magnificent Obsession* (1954), *Written On the Wind* (1957), *The Tarnished Angels* (1958), and above all, *All That Heaven Allows* (1956). In the last the 'Nature Boy' image (the little girl, Julia, in *Magnificent Obsession* calls him 'Tarzan' when she first sets eyes on him) is refined into the Thoreauvian character of Ron Kirby, keeping alive the virtues actual, or dreamed of, in a man free of the mock-civilisation of Stoningham's representative suburbia. The power of this image, no doubt enhanced by its success as a fabulous money earner for Universal, obviously stayed with the writers and director of *Pillow Talk* (Stanley Shapiro, Maurice Richlin and Michael Douglas), for they recall it in complex pastiche/parody (down to tree images, a cabin rendezvous, hushed tones, soft fireside shots in close-up, Brahmsian soundtrack when Jan and Brad almost go to bed in Connecticut), pastiche/parody that balances, with sophisticated urban ambivalence, between affirmation and cynicism.

It is tempting to bring later knowledge of Hudson's homosexuality, a Hollywood secret only publicly revealed when he was diagnosed as having *AIDS* in the 1980s, to bear on his films. Certainly from this perspective there is a particular irony about a great heterosexual icon of the cinema whose fabrication includes even the nature of his sexuality. In giving in to this temptation, it must be stressed that for the mass audience of 1959 there was no doubt about Hudson's sexuality at all. Nor does he even seem to have been a star appropriated by sexual minorities as their own. But – and it must be admitted that this is a very subjective point, impossible to prove and perhaps the imposition of our later knowledge on the texts – we may find it reflected in aspects of a facial configuration marginally at odds with the hypermasculinity averred (the softness of the set of the mouth, the somewhat retracted smile that lifts the upper lip off the front teeth, the luxuriant cocka-too's quiff of hair that he sports). It may also be perceived in discreetly noticeable reticences, a certain reserved distance about Hudson's acting in relation to the overwhelming heterosexuality which the narratives attribute to him, factors which, working with others in the film, add to the artifice of the comedies and perhaps even the ambiguity of their most obvious move-ments.

As befits the representations of a time of generally conservative male domin-ance, the comedies of the late 50s and early 60s often reverse the strategy of a number of major earlier comedies which allow the woman the place of the schemer and manipulator of plots within the plot, deceiving and mocking the male. There are exceptions (Lauren Bacall in *How To Marry A Millionaire*; or Maggie McNamara as Marie fooling Louis Jourdan as Prince Dino into thinking she is all he would like her to be in *Three Coins in the Fountain*), but now the males usually dominate, often attempting to trick and sexually possess without commitment the too trusting heroines. In *Lover Come Back*, as the pair talk in an aquarium, a big fish gobbles up a little fish behind

them, and in *Pillow Talk* Jan thinks of Brad's apartment as a spider's web.
In *Pillow Talk* and its mirror-image plot in *Lover Come Back* this deceit
actually involves the hero splitting himself into two in order to accomplish
his ends. Thus Brad becomes the second self of Jan's virtuous suitor, the
Texan, Rex Stetson (who engagingly parodies aspects of Hudson's role as
Jordan Benedict in *Giant*, 1956), and in *Lover Come Back* the good scientist,
Linus Tyler. From the point of view of the previous discussion of Hudson
this too is suggestive, for it is notable how often the actor, whom his greatest
director, Sirk, saw as definitively monolithic, is, to the contrary, cast in roles
that revolve around his pretence that he is someone he is not. For instance,
in *Magnificent Obsession* Hudson, as the playboy Bob Merrick, pretends to
be the virtuous Robbie Robinson in order to court the widow of the man he
has accidentally killed. In *Man's Favourite Sport* (1964) he is Roger
Willoughby, the writer of a textbook on fishing who has never actually fished.
In *One Desire* (1955), another 50s melodrama made at Universal, he is torn
between social status and marriage to Julie Adams and love, his relationship
with the woman of ill repute, Ann Baxter. Even in *Send Me No Flowers*
(1964), he is not what he seems, imagining that he is terminally ill when
he is not, and in *Seconds* (1966) his outer and inner selves are much more
deeply and irrevocably split.

Is this image of repeated duplicity an accident, or the writers' and directors'
coded play with that ironic secret, or a response to elements of distance and
non-commitment in his performances that may have the cause suggested?
Whatever the answer, and however we read the effects, what is undeniable
is that in *Pillow Talk* and *Lover Come Back* the conceit of the double is
significant in a number of ways. Most obviously it involves Doris Day in a
choice between two contrasting types of men, the playboy, attractive in his
sexual energy and refusal of the social norms but repulsive in his chauvinism,
and the feminised man, gentle, gentlemanly and uncorrupted, but naïve,
passive and less sexually exciting. As Molly Haskell has suggested, the deception allows both parties to experiment with roles and attitudes, so that in the
end Brad and Jerry both take on aspects of the virtuous pole without losing
the desirable energy and sexuality of the manipulative one, while Jan and
Carol, moving towards a less protective view of their own sexuality, realise
that it is a kind of half-way house between the two men that they want, i.e.
a 'sensitive' but not overfeminised man. But also, at a more unconscious
level, we might see this device, which allows the dynamic hero to assume
the passive role, as acting out the fantasy that Robert Warshow discovered
in *The Best Years of Our Lives* (1946), the dominant American male's secret
fantasy of passivity, with Doris Day in this comic version taking control of

everything, including sexuality. But, as if to counteract any such suggestion, the films are quick to fall back on corrective images of male strength and dominance such as the comedy made around the sheer masculine hulkiness of Brad as he fails to squeeze into Tony's sports car, his easy carrying of the drunken Tony off the dance floor, and his caveman hijacking of Jan.

At times, particularly in those scenes where Brad's and Jan's over voices are used as an equivalent to a thought bubble, *Pillow Talk* cultivates the feel and look of a comic strip. In a certain sense both Day and Hudson are stars who fit such flatness, personae of bland, pleasant surfaces, in no sense dangerous or difficult. Yet, within their clear outlines, within the safety of their seeming conformity, various subterranean currents stir, as representative of the transitional era that produced them as their more obvious ideological manipulability.

Mise-en-scène: the pastel shades of desire

A soft green – not as blue-green as a robin's egg, but not as yellow-green as daffodil buds.
    — Mrs Blandings (Myrna Loy) in *Mr Blandings Builds His Dream House*

Don't take your bedroom problems out on me!   — Brad to Jan in *Pillow Talk*

In the weakest glossy comedies of the time décor all but displaces narrative as the focus of interest. Thus in *Move Over, Darling* the wonders of the light, optimistic design of the Ardens' living room seduce the attention. Here yellow curtains echo carefully-placed chrysanthemums and the yellow cushion which highlights the subdued orange sofa. A sofa which stands on a greyish carpet that harmonises with creamy-slate walls, white drapes and woodwork and, as everything else does, with Doris Day's pastel green suit. Not at all, this, the vulgarity of the 'American Baroque' sardonically catalogued by the European observer, Nabokov, in *Lolita* (1959), but a kingdom of controlled taste, banishing the brash hues the Color Research Institute of Chicago reported appealed only to the lower classes, and thereby visually insinuating the pleasing myth of a wholly classless 1950s America. Post-war (1948) *Mr Blandings* had already begun the great suburban drift, but his 'dream house' was an old-fashioned fantasy, mock colonial with mod cons. The urban apartments and suburban homes of the later comedies have no such backward-looking historical commitments. Uncluttered, airy, spacious, clean, co-ordinated, their modified Bauhaus lines dismiss history for a present that is to be the fulfilment of history as an optimistic American text. No wonder in Tashlin's *Susan Slept Here* the prelapsarian lyrics of the theme

song *Hold My Hand* . . . 'So this is the Kingdom of Heaven . . . Let's never
leave again / Adam and Eve again' are addressed more to the lounge and the
kitchen than to the lovers.

While the décor plays synaesthesic rhapsodies on the colour organ of
desire, Doris Day's costumes elaborate such effects. Foregrounding her
clothes, these films expand the role of the fashion parade sections of films
like *How To Marry a Millionaire*. High profile opening credits emphasise
the interest in style, fashions and consumables, not as aristocratic exoticism
but as a hyperbolic version of what is available to all. 'Gowns for Miss Day
by Jean Louis . . . Miss Day's jewels by Laykin et Cie' we read at the
beginning of *Pillow Talk* (with 'Jewels by David Webb', 'Cameos by Carl
Reiner' and even a credit for the Rolls Royce in *The Thrill of It All*). But if
Day's costumes are very much part of a celebration of the unparalleled 1950s
middle-class luxury and what it, and the system that generates it, gives to
women in particular, they are also (something true too of the décor) involved
in meanings which float partly free of those others. Just as her hairstyles
represent a synthesis of traditional glamour and functional streamlining
(short but still feminine), so there is a distinct tendency for her outfits to
negotiate the same polarities, suggesting that one may not exclude the other
in a uniquely American blend that asserts Jan Morrow over Jeanne Moreau,
despite the French names of the designers and their associaton with Parisian
prestige. The older world, e.g. the Scarsdale Matron, Mrs Walters, still
clings to European influences as embodied by M. Pirot, Jan's boss, with his
decorative fourteenth-century crematory urn, but Pirot admits to Jan that
she is the real powerhouse in his design business (i.e. France has the name,
but America is the real force). Day's costumes signal themselves as glamorous, but at the same time throw out all elements of slinky, decadent allure
– no gauzes, plunging necklines, black stockings, or black negligees such as
are worn by Brad's French mistress – in favour of clean lines and colours.
Hats and gloves, and in two cases in *Pillow Talk*, huge muffs (one of them
leopard skin, a slightly decadent exception to the rule), often accompany
these as specifically feminine signs which also double as a kind of body
armour in the war of the sexes. Day's expansive posy of hats especially effects
a balance between allure and efficiency, feminine and frivolous to a point,
but somehow functional-looking as well, a badge of attractive efficiency rather
than an efflorescence of artifice. The most typical of her outer-world costumes, her suits, mimic the male businessman in his uniform of power, but
are softened into whites or yellows or pastel greens with matching high-heeled
shoes, or have placed over them a glamorous coat, e.g. the black fur she
wears in the first external scene of *Pillow Talk*. Her inner-world costumes,

the creations she wears for the romantic world of dates with Rex, are more conventionally glamorous, but significantly, while obviously outlining the female shape and, in doing so restricting its mobility, they avoid any sense of clutter, superfluity or decorative impediments. And moving, as the fashion compères say, from living room or office space to the bedroom, the pale blue that she often wears there rather than the usual female bedroom colours of pink, white or black (allegorically the flesh, purity, the devil), is the appropriation of a male colour ('blue for a boy/pink for a girl') though passed through a process of feminine softening.

In *Pillow Talk*, through a series of visual tropes, even the screen shape becomes an aspect of design, reviving timidly enough the more adventurous techniques of earlier cinema in split-screen compositions which not only place characters who are apart as they phone each other in the same composition, but also play visual jokes as they do so. Thus when Brad is on the phone to his mistress and Jan picks up her phone, the screen space becomes two upright triangles separated by an inverted one, each containing one of the speakers, with Jan placed as a disruptive force between the two hedonists. Likewise in the credit and closing sequences Jan and Brad lie tossing pillows in their separate beds separated only by the midscreen divide which is occasionally transgressed by the travelling pillows. This composition is varied in the sequence where by the luxury of modern technology they phone each other from their baths. These moments are presented as instances of technological wizardry by a cinema forgetful of its formalistically more radical past, but also, one feels, as a kind of unconscious analogue to the labour-saving devices of domestic life, the space and time-saving composition giving two, and even three, for one. Further, the very design of such images, bringing the characters together, yet separating them by bars, suggests collusion with a narrative matter of multiple deceits and misunderstandings, the essentially divided, distanced relationships – especially sexual relationships – typical of a society of abundant attractive surfaces but few depths. But at the same time other elements in the content of the frame (Brad placed as if lying on top of Jan as they communicate from separate beds, their feet touching along the screen divide as they take separate baths) identify a natural sexuality reaching out beyond the constraints of composition, prescribed roles and narrative ordering.

Any danger of overreading the significances of *mise-en-scène* in the film should be laid to rest by a reminder that Jan Morrow's profession is that of interior decorator, a fact which means that the narrative constantly draws attention to such meanings, in this very like Woody Allen's *Interiors*, dominated by another, though more negative, 'designing woman', Eve. The point where the designs of the film, the 'designs' Brad has on Jan and her 'designs' on him (both marital and environmental) most fully come together with *Pillow Talk*'s pervasive interest in interior space and colour is where Jan, having discovered Brad's deceit, takes her revenge on him by redecorating his apartment, not in the contemporary style he expects, but in a violent parody of the playboy's den, 'under the yum-yum tree', in the style of a harem-crazed sultan of old Constantinople.

This visual *tour de force*, a contradiction to the reign of taste elsewhere, suggests an extra significance in the way characters often choose figures of speech based on a contrast of colour and colourlessness to express themselves. So Alma says dreamily that Brad's phone calls have 'brightened up many a dreary afternoon for me', Jan snaps at Brad that 'I was waiting for you to make some off-colour remark', and Brad insults Jan by telling her that she listens into his conversations 'to brighten up your drab little life'. 'Brad', we may suddenly realise in this context, is an anagram of 'Drab', an effort of paronomasia, allied to a life of seduction, that is dedicated to fighting off conformity through the life style of the playboy. Brad's wealthy (many books and paintings) but visually unremarkable apartment (nonedescript colours, an unpainted brick wall) shows few signs of the style dominant in the rest of the film and Jan's apartment in particular, the significance of this being that his life is so replete with sexual release (Stanley Kowalski's 'coloured lights'?) that he not only feels no need to brighten his surroundings, but actively resists the ordering and cleanliness which contemporary taste connotes. Instead, the main feature of his apartment is the technological exuberance of his machinery of seduction, automatically dimming lights and locking doors, a sofa that transforms itself into a bed and a record player that issues seductive music at the right moment.

Jan's life as an interior decorator is, conversely, literally colourful, but Brad's accusation declares it to be essentially colourless because sexless. The implications cut both ways. His statements are conventionally and complacently chauvinistic, yet as far as Jan is concerned they are in some sense true since, lacking a satisfactory inner life (as she cannot but define it), she constantly exorcised the spirits of her sexuality through the refurbishing of her own and other peoples' houses and apartments.

This longing for 'colour', transferred into her costumes and the pastel lemons, oranges, greys, mauves and strawberries of her living space, is highly refined, as if her very unconscious is overruled by the ordered aesthetic in its expression. But her final piece of designing, towards which the narrative builds, is dictated not by the aesthetics of order but of rage, and, we might feel, of suppressed libido. Here decoration bursts from pastel into 'offcolour', from functionalism into libidinous allegory, from co-ordination into a riot of tumescent purples (remembered from the Copa del Rio nightclub?), demonic reds (the huge double bed in Brad's apartment has had throughout the film great red bolsters at its head and foot), and clashing greens and yellows. The redesigned den is also filled with the grotesque array of objects recapitulating her fevered vision of Brad's sexual life – the fertility goddess, the potbellied stove, a moose's head (for 'Moose' Taggart and for the 'big dame hunter', a joke from *An Affair to Remember*). Fleeing from such minor masculine terrors as Tony and Jonathan, whom she calls a 'pair of monsters', and apparently fleeing from the more really monstrous Brad, she ends, as it were, indirectly confessing her hidden longing for disorder and excess at the moment she completes Brad's domesticisation and her own.

The final unification of the pair – wish-fulfilment's reward for the watchers in a growingly youthfully married society – performs multiple functions. However unlikely the idea of a permanently monogamous Brad, it corrals the potentially disruptive in the playboy and the too outwardly orientated woman, while at the same time allowing certain of these traits to survive in both (how and where the film is not inclined to say). It enacts a tamed version of romantic love, an *amour fou* for the suburbs – 'Why does a man destroy himself?' Brad asks – and for a technologically oriented world with true love imaged as a rocketship 'trip to the moon', but crosses these with family responsibilities. It slightly eases Jan out of her puritanism and Brad towards his. Where the film seems to double back on itself questioningly is dealt with below, but one further moment from the central narrative repays consideration. As Brad and Jan speed towards consummation in Connecticut, the film modulates lyrically into the most romantic of the songs that are a convention of Doris Day's parts. Caressed by the breeze created by the moving car, caught in misty close-up, she sings the languid interior monologue of a song that celebrates her trusting decision to give herself to Rex:

> Hold me tight
> And kiss me right.
> I'm yours tonight
> My darling, possess me!

The clichéd lyrics of love (ironised anyway by her ignorance that she is with Brad) are given further resonances by their relation to the narrative's preoccupation with consumerism and the monstrous. It should hardly escape us that one way in which Rex definitely does not differ from Brad, even surpasses him, is in the scale of his wealth. In other words, the half-hidden condition of the drama of the dream of true romance is that it is the material possessor who may 'possess' (in all its senses, including the demonic) the woman, whom the woman is willing to be possessed by. Such implications – the sense of the woman as object and property – haunt even the delightful, delicately sensuous moment at the cabin when Jan, with Brad out of the room, wraps herself in his vast overcoat. For this very action, that calls up deliciously the most traditional feelings of male protection and female need for it, uncovers the evidence of Brad's fraud (doubly fraudulent in that the assignation takes place at Jonathan's house and with his champagne), the sheet music of the romantic song 'You are My Inspiration'.

At the edges: the hidden door

> Ya, ya, Roly!
> Ya, ya, Poly!
> Ya, ya, Roly Poly!

Away from the centre, at the peripheries, comic disorder threatens containment. Tony Randall as Jonathan Forbes in *Pillow Talk*, like his Peter Ramsay in *Lover Come Back*, and Gig Young in *That Touch of Mink*, plays the part of the hero's friend, confidant and either employer or employee. In each case he is a grotesque foil to, or whining parody of the confident hero, impotently caught between admiration for and envy of his superior maleness as manifested both in sex and a successful career. Tellingly, in the scene in *Pillow Talk* where we first see them together, Brad twice snaps the phallic cane Jonathan's psychiatrist has optimistically given him. Jonathan may be a millionaire, but as he ruefully complains to Brad, he suffers the disadvantage of being born rich, for it leaves him with nothing to attain, whereas Brad, beginning at the bottom, has acted out the mobile archetype of the American success story. Not surprisingly Jonathan and his confrères are long-term psychoanalysees, which in 50s comedy tends to signify weakness, here the failure to attain dominant masculinity. 'My analyst won't believe this', he mutters as Jan turns down his hopefully compromising gift of his car. His problem, as he sees it, is a mother fixation, while Peter Ramsey is oppressed by his late father whose portrait hangs in the office Peter is usually too neurotic to visit. In *That Touch of Mink* Roger's visits to his extremely materialistic analyst (Dr Gruber is only interested in probing him for stock-market information) are prompted by his liberal–conformist guilt at abandoning his job as professor of economics at Princeton for one with Shane at $50,000 a year. 'Every year you further humiliate me by raising my salary', this J. K. Galbraith *manqué* frets, but his unease at the seductions of the affluent society disappears when Shane asks, 'Would it help if I fired you?' 'No, no!', he quickly protests, 'Don't do that!'.

Trying to bribe Jan with his car, attempting to persuade her to marry him despite his three failed marriages, failing to 'hit the moon' when she grants him an experimental kiss, reduced from suitor to trying merely to protect Jan from Brad (more from envy than morality), Jonathan then suffers the indignity of becoming the scapegoat for punishments that are logically Brad's. As he takes her home from Connecticut they stop at a diner and his actions are misinterpreted by two protective hardhats as those of a callous seducer. The beating they give him parallels the similar assaults directed at Shane that Roger suffers in *That Touch of Mink*. Such punishments, the films seem to say, are deserved by the pusillanimous and ineffectual Jonathan for his failure to meet the standards of masculinity defined by Brad. But the distinction between parody and foil is a slender one and may encapsulate uncertainty as well as certainty. Rock Hudson may be the desirable *non plus ultra* of the time's masculinity, but Randall (like Young to Grant) is his alter ego, his doubtful self, an image of masculinity crushed by the very demands of masculinity, and also a character in whom the inevitable deviations from the master type are allowed to be voiced, albeit in a compromised and pathetic way which is then chastised. Harry, the elderly lift man, Alma's long-term admirer, who has been too cowed to approach her, is, however, infused with a sudden rush of masculine power as he watches Brad carry Jan off. His proposal, as we might expect, meets with success as Alma responds positively to the aggression every woman wants with the words 'Why, Harry, you're so strong!', which seem more a projection of her culture-bound fantasies than a reflection of reality. Indeed, the words of Harry's proposal tend to suggest otherwise – 'What you need is a man to take care of.'

The question of masculinity (the 'real' man complementing the 'real' feminine woman, that fetish of popular psychologising of the time) produces, as this shows, two sorts of dramatisations, one assured, dominant and conservative, the other much less certain. A heightened instance of the former occurs when Brad, in order to trick Jan into taking the sexual initiative with him, tells her that Rex's over-gentlemanly restraint can only mean one thing – that he is, as Brad euphemistically phrases it, one of those 'men who are very devoted to their mothers'. He then proceeds to list a number of infallible signs of homosexuality which, a little later as Rex, he gives out to Jan. These include collecting recipes, an interest in colours and fabrics (in *Lover Come Back* Carol Templeton remarks waspishly to a colleague who likes the colour lilac, 'Well, Leonard, everyone isn't as *artistic* as you are'), gossiping and devotion to mother. Alongside these Rex/Brad even allows himself a moment of crowning improvisation, lifting his little finger with emasculated elegance as he drinks.

But if here the mysteries of sexual orientation and the marks of manhood can be reduced to a few tyrannical externals (forbidding men to cook, for instance, something Spencer Tracy seems wholly at home with in *Adam's Rib*), in other parts of the film, as if unconsciously to deny these simplicities, there is the anarchy of the curious obstetrics plot which erupts again in variational form in *That Touch of Mink*. In *Pillow Talk*, as the scheming Brad ducks into a doctor's surgery to avoid an unwanted meeting with Jan, what he doesn't realise is that the doctor (Fred Clarke) is an obstetrician and that his innocent remarks to the nurse are being interpreted as announcing his pregnancy. Nurse Resznik rushes to Dr Maxwell to report the 'psychopath'. But in what develops into a running joke, a sort of antic sub-plot, Dr Maxwell's reaction is unexpected. Convinced that 'medical science still has many unknown regions to explore', he accepts Rock Hudson's pregnancy as possible, even probable, shanghaiing him with Nurse Resznik's help as he passes by at the film's end. In the parallel development in *That Touch of Mink*, because Dr Gruber leaves the room during Roger's analysis to phone his stockbroker, he misses vital parts of a monologue concerned with Philip and Cathy. Returning, the psychiatrist misinterprets what he hears as a confession of homosexual love between Roger and Shane. Gradually compounded, this finally results in the misreading of Roger wheeling a pram which belongs to the absent Philip and Cathy as a medical aberration of the same order of the one that obsesses Dr Maxwell. The arcane logic of this repeated plot would seem to be double-edged: either a grotesque warning of the dangers of ultrafeminisation facing the domesticated male, or (the possibilities are not mutually exclusive) an acting out in carnavalesque terms of a flouting of gender roles and even primary sexual attributes severely circumscribed in other parts of the film. Thus, in a comic return of the repressed, the most manly men are suddenly possessed of the most purely female possibility.

Another moment in the film obliquely questions other stereotypes dominant in it, in this case the very conventions of attractiveness embodied in Brad and Jan. The clever scene in 'The Hidden Door' where the black singer gives a musical commentary on the events of the plot, begins with a sort of community sing-song in which Jan, and eventually Brad, take part. The interesting thing about this apparently rather mindless novelty number called 'Roly Poly' with its naïve, handclapping action-game accompaniments, a primly orgiastic pre-Esalen experience for the nightclub patrons, is that in

a film committed to rather extreme sexual stereotypes and superhuman standards of attractiveness, its lyrics are about a love object who flagrantly escapes
such demands since 'He measures five feet up and down / And five foot front
to back.'

> When I first set eyes on him
> I laughed just like the rest.
> The more I saw the more of him,
> The more I liked him best.

As Jan takes over the lyrics in the later verses, what she sings flouts the
apparently immutable laws of desirability that impel her towards Rex/Brad's
'six foot six inches of opportunity'. It is interesting here to remember the
comedy based on Brad's ploy to get Jonathan out of the restaurant where
his presence threatens Brad's alias as Rex, a trick which scares him off by
threatening to land him with a girl who is a little 'different', known as 'Moose',
as his date, a date Brad further pretends is an enormous young woman across
the room tucking into her dinner. Whereas that scene shows a female 'Roly
Poly' with whom even the narrative's dismal non-hero could not declare
himself 'satisfied', the female voice of the song can celebrate a male version
of 'Moose' because, for all the force of Rock's physique in the film, there
are other ways than beauty in which a man can be attractive. The cry 'Ya,
ya, Roly Poly' which punctuates the verses must originally be a playground
taunt at the fat boy, but in the song it must mean something more like a
positive 'Yeah, yeah'. Though the lyrics finish with the female singer's confession that the singer is obese just like the man ('He's a Roly Poly Baby /
So am I'), neither the slim, attractive black singer nor Doris Day is like that
in the least, so that in the end the moment of release is reordered by more
conventional meanings – e.g. I'm Roly Poly's baby (i.e. beloved), or I'm a
baby who likes (comically euphemistic Roly Poly) sex. Brad, acting out the
part of the feminised Rex, for a moment released into over-the-top abandon,
can also suddenly echo the women with an address to the camera, 'Ah cawl
hah Rolah Polah', but, of course, that is even less believable.

FIFTIES SATIRE: *THE SEVEN YEAR ITCH*

> You have to imagine it sung by three chickens, Rufe.
> — Rock Hunter in *Will Success Spoil Rock Hunter?* (1957)

Despite its great box-office success, the passing of its title into a catch phrase

H

for the problems of long-term monogamy in contemporary marriage, and its invention of one of the most archetypal images of Marilyn Monroe, skirts rising as she stands astride the subway gratings, *The Seven Year Itch* (1955) does not enjoy a high reputation among Billy Wilder's films. Sinyard and Turner, for instance, even relegate it to a postscript on his 'failures' alongside an uncharacteristic film like *The Spirit of St Louis* (1957). Wilder himself has denigrated it in an interview more than twenty years after the event, seeing it as inescapably straitjacketed by early 50s sexual evasiveness: 'Unless the husband, left alone in New York while the wife and kids are away for the summer, has an affair with the girl, there's nothing. But you couldn't do that in those days . . . It didn't come off one bit and there's nothing I can say about it except I wish I hadn't made it. I wish I had the property now.'

While we can understand Wilder's attitude, and attempt below to explain why it is so negative, it is far from the last word on the subject. True, the film can be seen (and this, we maintain, is the view that lies behind Wilder's critique) as failing to attain either full satiric mordancy – i.e. the so-called 'bad taste' so offensive as to cause major exhibition problems for *Kiss Me Stupid* as late as 1964 – or to act out that fragile half-affirmation of conversion from cynicism to commitment characteristic of films like *The Apartment* (1960), *Irma la Douce* (1963) and *The Fortune Cookie* (1966), which Dr Dreyfuss encapsulates when he instructs C. C. Baxter to 'Be a Mensch. A Mensch. A human being!' Failing to fulfil conceptions of the most 'cynical' or 'romantic' Wilder, it can be seen as neither realistic enough in its gingerly treatment of problems of desire, nor complex enough in its 'one-dimensional man' of a central character, Richard Sherman (Tom Ewell). Nevertheless, while it is naturally interesting to speculate how Wilder might have developed the subject in the era of freedom attending, say, *Carnal Knowledge* (1971), such speculations draw attention away from the object itself which, in our definition, fascinates not in spite of but because of its massively ideologised hero's entrapment in the limited horizons and options of his marriage, work and life; an entrapment so remorseless that even in the movements of his unconscious, in his fitfully transgressive desires for release, he is still the creature of ideological conformity. If, as Wilder scathingly remarks, 'there's nothing', we would want to deny that (for the film, as distinct from its hero) nothing comes from nothing, asserting rather the film's critical interest in that nothing, that plenitude of inaction which fills it, that preoccupation with fantasies of transgression which would have been turned into something wholly different in Wilder's revised treatment. The rule of the Hays Code was in many ways something detrimental to the development of Hollywood film, yet here, as elsewhere, and at other times for other directors and writers, the necessities of censorship became a virtue for Wilder and Axelrod (author of the original stage play and co-writer with Wilder of the screenplay). Rather like a drama by Racine in which convention and decorum demand that all atrocities be committed off stage, *The Seven Year Itch* keeps the actual act of adultery off screen, absent yet at the same time obsessively present in the thoughts and fantasies of Sherman and those around him – Dr Brubaker's manuscript, *Man and the Unconscious*, with its sixth chapter called 'The Seven Year Itch', estimated to strike '84.6% of the married male population', being the presiding instance, an obvious analogue to the Kinsey Report, or at least the one on male sexuality of 1948. Thus Sherman's failure to sleep with the girl is essentially beside the point, at least as a criticism of the film, for its essence lies in dramatising the conditions and consequences of his dilemma. Writing of typical film stars of the 1950s, Molly Haskell has argued, 'they were all *about* sex, but *without* sex', and we might usefully transfer her statement, divested of its more negative implications, to *The Seven Year Itch*.

Conformity, consumerism and commodification are the pervasive subjects of the satiric cinema of the 50s and early 60s, the chief proponents of which are Billy Wilder and Frank Tashlin. The Kafkaesque open-plan workspace of 'Consolidated Life' in *The Apartment* (1960) expresses the numbness of the corporate ideal of 'other directedness'. The wit of *1,2,3* (1961) where the title draws together the military, the businesslike and the proto-fascist (his wife refers to the Coca-Cola director as 'mein Führer'), reinforces in its casting of James Cagney as businessman that sense of the gangster as the *doppelgänger* of the American capitalist that has often been remarked upon. The grotesque of Jerry Lewis's impersonation of the film audience as mindless consumers, ingesting junk food frantically along with the diet of screen images at the beginning of *Hollywood or Bust* (1956), recognises the cinema's involvement in the banalisation of American life. These three instances, two from Wilder, one from Tashlin, may stand as representative of the comic critique of materialist complacency which parallels, particularly in its versions of the business world, such melodrama of capitalism as the film version of *The Man in the Grey Flannel Suit* (1956) and *Patterns* (1956). Like theirs, the radicalism of the comedies is only partial since all, in their different ways, take the world they see as normative. However, in the 'serious' problem world of the melodramas the critique is less subtle and pervasive, concentrating on individual boardroom inhumanities (*Patterns*) or the cost exacted by corporation ambition on the individual (*Grey Flannel Suit*), problems solvable in the case of the latter by Rath's moderation – continuing to work in the system but not to a sacrificial degree – and in the former by the hero's decision to remain in the corporation in order to oppose the excesses of his boss. In the comic worlds of Tashlin and Wilder (so differentiated that it is a kind of *discordia concors* to bring them together) such solutions do not prevail: the fragile hope of romantic love in Wilder cannot promise an escape from constraining banality and corruption, while in Tashlin's films, implicated though they are in the consumerist fantasies which are their subject matter, the happy endings are transparent parodies, as when La Salle Junior retires to grow roses or the Tony Randall character to raise chickens and a family with Jayne Mansfield in *Will Success Spoil Rock Hunter?* Wilder's use in *Itch* of Tom Ewell, echoed by Tashlin's in *The Girl Can't Help It* (1957) two years later, adds, like other techniques of semi-alienation such as the commentator's over-voice at the beginning and the film's constant intertextual references to films, novels, Marilyn Monroe herself, a certain caricature or satiric flatness to the work. Ewell, like Tony Randall, is the perpetual comic second man, perfectly endowed to signify failure and incompetence, his failure to achieve the macho ideal not readable in any positive sense as protest, since we know all too well that the character he plays is wholly complicit with the most superficial values of his culture, just not expert in attaining them. Additionally, there are aspects of his physiognomy – not just his tired, regimented blandness, but more precisely that hangdog, harrassed look that is at once juvenile and senescent – which suggest that the lines of middle age have been engraved on an adolescent, with the whole period of growth and maturity omitted. In a different, more plastic, falsely confident version, Randall's characters play another variation on these films' interest in male incapacity, and recall in their range of interests the symbiotic pairing of Martin and Lewis, where the one parodies the lethargy of absolute patriarchal confidence (here doubly Italian and American), and the other embodies not only cretinous incompetence but a deep-seated fear of the female.

These films comically dramatise what is also towards the end of the 50s becoming the subject of sociological analysis, epitomised by Vance Packard's bestseller, *The Hidden Persuaders* (1957), the sense of a consuming society in which product and image are synonymous, where, above all, sexuality is manipulated as the key selling ingredient of almost any product, an age where Freud (of whom Richard Sherman has enough knowledge to give the Girl a popularised version of *The Psychopathology of Everyday Life*), has his ultimate recuperation in the psychoanalytical applications of Madison Avenue, as terms like 'motivational analysis' and 'sub-threshold effects' become part of the language of advertising. In connection with this we may notice how Dr Brubaker in *Itch* acts out this recuperation of psychoanalysis into the status quo in his replies to Sherman's hopes of an inexpensive analysis:

Tell me doctor, are you very expensive?
  Very.
I'm sure you occasionally make exceptions.
  Never!
Once in a while a case must come along that really interests you.
  At $50 an hour all my cases interest me.

The most extreme images of the commodification of sexuality are found in Tashlin's films, particularly his use of Jayne Mansfield in *The Girl Can't Help it* and *Will Success Spoil Rock Hunter?* Mansfield parodies the softer, more diffused, more natural-seeming Golden Girl charms of Marilyn Monroe, the quintessential sex goddess of the era, becoming a hyperbole of woman as the ultimate product of glamorising fantasy, her high-tech designed body contours, with zeppelin bosoms above a waspish abdomen, irresistibly calling up the slang of the time, 'chassis', with its comparison of the female body to an automobile. And indeed, like the Pontiacs, Oldsmobiles, Buicks and Cadillacs that marked hierarchical divisions within the corporations of the time, Mansfield (the name appropriately recalling the Koranic view of women as land tilled by the male) is the vulgarised fantasy and prize of commodity-stricken man. In Tashlin's famous jokes of heavy-handed excess, her singing voice reduced to a siren squeal, her girdle buttons popping as she kisses, milk bottles held up to her chest as doubles for her breasts, her sexual heat melting the iceman's ice and boiling the milkman's milk, she travesties that all-consuming interest in sex characteristic of 50s popular art culture, an interest which is at the same time unreal somehow, based as it is in repression and a regressive fantasy of the woman completely defined by sexuality, with the fashion for enormously-breasted women of the time (Sophia Loren, Mamie Van Doren, etc.), whatever else it may signify, marking the woman as utterly other than the male.

The plot of *Rock Hunter* hinges on the commercial use of the film star, Rita Marlowe (Mansfield) to advertise 'Staykist' lipstick. This clearly echoes the Girl's 'Dazzledent' 'kissing sweet' toothpaste ads in *Itch*, but the earlier film's interest in the intersection of sex and advertising does not stop there. Less overtly than in Tashlin, but with equal significance, the connection pervades the film, for it will be remembered that the Brady Publishing Co., alongside the Sherman's apartment the film's second setting, takes its profits from 25 cent reissues in 'pocket' editions with lurid covers of classical and serious works – 'pocket' editions suggesting trouser pockets and hence pocket billiards, or masturbation. *Little Women*, for instance, has been reissued with the subtitle *Secrets of a Girls' Dormitory*, redolent of voyeurism, male fantasies

of lesbianism, not to mention the comforting sound 'little women', or dependent, subservient girls, has for the immature male. It is highly ironic that
in the attempt to rid himself of the spectre of temptation in his wife's absence
Sherman frenziedly turns to his work, but his work only turns out to be a
further provocation, the encapsulation of his individual problems on a greater
scale – the manipulation of fantasies for a mass audience of Sherman-like
repressives driven by their frustration to images of sexuality rather than the
thing itself. Though Sherman's publications are somewhat more old-
fashioned and less sophisticated than Hugh Hefner's *Playboy*, already in the
third year of its sybaritically revolutionary life in 1955, *Playboy* is, as we
argue in the section below, very much in the film's mind, a symptom (as
Barbara Ehrenreich suggests) of a pre-feminist, wholly male-orientated reaction against the puritan conformities of monogamy, a bid for freedom
which is at the same time part of the sex-as-commodity nexus and, whatever
the rhetoric of equality, presenting women only as the playthings of the male.

The satire and preoccupations of these films are very much male-centred,
a focus on male problems through male characters. Remembering that the
Kinsey report on the female was published in 1953, we may very well ask
of the 84.6 per cent statistic given for husbands suffering from the 'Seven
Year Itch' where the relevant female statistic is? Brilliant but limited, *The
Seven Year Itch* is capable of anatomising the poverty of male categorisation
of women, while finding it difficult to escape some of the limitations it castigates in its characters. There are neither female nor male voices of maturity
in the film; without them the comedy of desire is denied the ballast of
exemplary ideals of living. On the other hand, with them, providing us with
more than the stereotypes of immature male, sexless wife and sexy playgirl,
the film might not have succeeded so well in creating its satire of a society
too consumerist to allow saner, healthier, more balanced voices and ideals
a hearing.

The underside of marriage

I'm married. Boy am I married!   — Richard Sherman

The Seven Year Itch, like a number of other Wilder comedies – in particular
The Apartment and *Avanti* (1972) – is structured around the tensions of
matrimony, monogamy, and their shadow, adultery. In *The Apartment* the
shabby, sordid adulteries of the 'Consolidated Life' executives and the slowly
growing romantic love between C. C. Baxter (Jack Lemmon) and Fran
Kubelick (Shirley Maclaine) seem to have nothing in common, nothing that

is, except their relation to marriage: the former seeking liberation from it, the latter driving towards it hopefully, the question being whether Jack Lemmon's or Shirley Maclaine's flight from the trap of cynicism is merely a journey back into the trap itself, a marriage bound to breed the habituation, cynicism and betrayal the characters flee from. Likewise, the ending of *Some Like It Hot* (1959): will Joe (Tony Curtis), the former exploiter of women, leave off his old ways in the married state? In both films do we believe that the female characters' masochism will be a thing of the past? The questions are not irrelevancies, but ones that the films deliberately raise in all their ambivalence; or if not deliberately, can hardly help raising in their dramatisations of the hopes and desires, pitfalls and illusions of relationships.

Structurally, *Itch* resembles a late Wilder film, *Avanti* which, however, moves in a different direction, granting its dull, married hero (Jack Lemmon) and heroine (Juliet Mills) a yearly release from the state of dutiful marriage, thus repeating the secret pattern of their fugitive parents. As in the later film, its premise is a longstanding marriage, but here, though tempted, the husband remains technically faithful, indeed in the end fleeing for the 8.47 out of New York as far away from the object of his desire as can be managed. Looked at with any sort of attention, though, this retreat from desire cannot be interpreted in any way as morality or loyalty, since Sherman's reasons are motivated more by fear and weakness, cowardice and conformity, than by nobler qualities.

Like the Hollywood cinema in general, of which they are so distinguished a part, Wilder's films are works of brilliant description, rather than theorising analysis. Over the course of his films, his attitude to marriage and adultery is profoundly ambivalent, replaying tensions most of his audiences feel between idealism, scepticism, cynicism and the middle ground. For instance, *Itch* does not place in an overtly argued sociological context the Shermans' marriage – a thing not seen on the screen but richly implied in many ways, and the source of the film's disruptions – but the descriptive detail tells us much about the particular pressures, over and above the more general ones on monogamy in modern societies, generated by highly conformist notions of marriage in the conservative atmosphere of the 50s. For certainly, as we follow the implications, the Shermans' marriage (which we are intended to see as representative, Sherman being described by the commentator at the film's beginning as a 'typical Manhattan husband'), seems stale and negative in the extreme, with the couple's drifting apart into over-separated worlds, the male as worker and money-earner in the outside world, the female as custodian of the domestic terrain which seems, apart from the record collection, to bear no trace of Sherman's imprint, to have been wholly taken over by Helen. This is in fact dramatised in the film's opening, for the occasion that makes possible his temptation is the summer separation, with wife and child on holiday, the father remaining in New York. (*Little Rickie*: 'Why can't Daddy come with us?' *Helen:* 'Poor Daddy has to stay in the city and make money.')

Returning alone to the apartment, Richard experiences a huge surge of relief which he expresses not only by breaking domestic rules (opening his bottle of fizz with the door handle rather than the bottle opener), but also by parodying the emptiness of a typical return-from-the office marital conversation: 'What happened at the office today darling? What happened? Well I shot Mr Brady in the head, made violent love to Miss Morris and set fire to 300,000 copies of *Little Women*.' Sherman's view of his wife seems to stem from his ineffectualness and childishness which both invites her role as the surrogate mother who organises him, especially as regards the various prohibitions (drinking, smoking, etc.) imposed on him in her absence, and at the same time is resentful of the marital Superego he has had his unacknowledged share in creating. Though he welcomes the immediate peace and solitude he finds in the empty apartment ('It's peaceful with everybody gone. No *Howdy Doody*, no *Captain Video*, no smell of cooking' – a series of statements suggesting disenchantment with his roles as husband and father), in reality he is totally, though terribly negatively, bound to his wife, as his panic at the self-created idea that she is seeking a divorce shows, an idea that frightens him not because it reveals a hidden store of affection, but because it is clear he would be hopelessly adrift without her. His fantasy of her knowing about his encounters with the Girl endows Helen with violent wishes for revenge against him (the daydream/nightmare in which she shoots him as punishment for his trespasses on behalf of the 'wives of America' who will give her a medal for it). This moment of fantasised violence no doubt expresses his own guilt and masochistic desire for punishment, as well as a displaced version of his own desires to do away with her (cf. those later films on the 'how to murder your wife' theme), and also introduces into the interstices of the narrative a premonition of the psychic violence of the feminist revolt that is brewing, as if the vengeance Helen seeks might be for more than her husband's lusts, for the whole unbalanced version of a marriage organisation whose rigid role separations are beginning to be found inadequate by both men and women in their different ways.

Another noticeable product of this marriage is its apparent solitude, for left alone in New York, Richard appears to have no friends at all to visit or be visited by, a detail placed as if to show precisely the debilitating effects of a concept of marriage that, in the interests of an ideal intimacy, separates

the couple off from all other social contacts into an exclusive enclave that
eventually becomes a prison. Until he begins to fantasise that Tom McKenzie
is seducing his wife on holiday, Sherman seems to have left no sexual
apprehension of Helen at all. It is little wonder that when he protests to
Brubaker, 'Look, Doctor, I love my wife', the doctor's unimpressed reply
is 'Don't we all? Your time is up.' His part helpless, part resentful confusion
of his wife with mother is underlined by his answering Helen's phone call
with the words 'Hello mother', an error whose immediate cause is his meditation, moments beforehand, on the 'simple biological fact' of women ageing
faster than men, which suddenly escalates, via a self-reference to the haggard
youthfulness we have noted in Ewell, to a horror of his wife ageing so fast
she will be mistaken for his mother. At the same time he appears to have no
more insight into his part in trapping Helen in essentially negative definitions
(Evelyn Keyes, a rather frumpy, wholly domesticated figure, thirty-two but
seemingly older to his thirty-eight, stripped of any of the glamour she had
in *The Jolson Story* (1946) than she has into her part in his discontent.

As Richard twists and turns on the rack of illicit desire, his dissatisfactions
pushing him towards thoughts of adultery, but his intense colonisation by
propriety filling him with guilt and fear, he takes on the form of a kind of
comic Hamlet unable to kill the monster of his anxieties, perpetually desiring
and retreating in a process to which his return to the family at the film's end
can only bring a temporary cessation since the conditions that cause it have
never been examined. In later Wilder films (*The Apartment, Buddy Buddy*,
1981, *Irma la Douce, The Fortune Cookie, The Front Page*, 1974), Jack Lemmon often plays the part of the 'little man', the eternal optimist, imposed
upon by the forces of dominant ideology and its restricted vision of the good
life. Tom Ewell and Tony Randall in *Rock Hunter* play that same part, but
more ludicrously; the difference being encapsulated in the pathos of the
sad-clown lineaments of Lemmon's face, a figuration that expresses a degree
of uncolonised mental space, the possibility of feeling leading to revolt, something quite different from the impotent satiric fixity of the other two. Often
in Wilder's films there are more cynical characters whose role is to join and
benefit from the system rather than mutely to suffer under it, and to remind
the virtuous sap that his devotion to the most hypocritical of its values is
absurd. The most self-seeking and scathing of these *eirons* is Walter Matthau
in his various roles, cynically, wittily, with all the history of disillusioned
experience streaming from his lugubrious eyes and dropsical cheeks, telling
the truth that there is no ideal nobler than the self, 'Numero uno', in a system
built to create and screw the sucker.

There is no Walter Matthau, or Matthau surrogate – like Tony Curtis, for most of *Some Like It Hot* – letting the devil take the hindmost in *Itch*, but this absence draws attention to the fact that all the other men in the film are if not Walter Matthau lookalikes, then his actalikes in their cynical attitudes towards marriage. For while Richard havers and hallucinates at the behest of his Superego, everyone else seems to be enjoying their summer liberty. At the lower end of the social scale, Krahulic the janitor, though he has a wife and four children, suffers no middle-class sexual inhibitions, stripped to his singlet, smoking a phallic cigar and constantly talking about big fat poodles (women's behinds). And Mr Brady, Sherman's grandfatherly publishing boss, echoes Krahulic's stripping to his singlet as he shaves, his search for pleasure (announcing to Sherman that he hasn't been to bed since sending the family off to Nantucket), and the lewd laugh of an aspiring Id, a laugh that Sherman soon finds himself unconsciously imitating, all indicators of a libido running wild. Though never seen in the film, an acquaintance of Sherman's called Charlie is much in his mind, for Charlie went off the rails when left alone the previous summer and ended up with tattoos of butterflies on his shoulders and of a green dragon on his chest. (No fear of flying there!).

It is apt that a film so caustically concerned with the claustrophobia of married life should largely take place in an apartment. Literally a place in a building partitioned off from others, the site of the misguided attempt to exclude the world for the sake of intimacy, but at the same time a place that cannot exclude the close proximity of others. In this case the vertical map of the apartment building reveals a kind of polymorphous world that Sherman cannot escape: in the basement the lustful janitor, the household's own 'Creature from the Black Lagoon'; on the top floor two interior decorators (the usual code for homosexuals); and, renting the Kaufmann's place above him, the overwhelmingly sensuous Girl. In *Itch* the apartment has the meaning of the married couple's habitat. In the later film of 1960 it has the opposite meaning as the trysting place for the rather sleazy rebels of love among the executives. In fact we may meditate that the opposition between the meanings is equally a close relationship, since marriage and adultery are inextricably linked together, each the implication of the other. What is interesting about the return of the repressed in this film is that the occasion of adultery presents itself not in some exotic place like Acapulco or Palm Beach or a rural motel, but in the very heart of the home, as if to express most insistently its presence in the outwardly well-adjusted marriage of the time. Though, of course, Richard's wishes are never consummated, the Girl, the phantom of his desires in the white dress with the large polka dots that mirrors the wife's similarly patterned but more restrained dress, actually occupies her bed, each round stain on her dress a visual sign of a more acknowledged sexuality all but obliterated in the domesticated wife. As if looking down in sardonic commentary on all that is taking place, from its perch on top of the air conditioner, a large ornamental wooden duck, prominent in the frame, surveys Sherman's attempted seduction of his visitor. This duck, which in a minor way may say something about the conformity of the Shermans via the banality of their aesthetic taste is, more importantly, the dead duck of their conventional marriage, an image which returns us to the momentary backward movement in the film's prologue from contemporary to Indian Manhattan, where the adulteries of the contemporary husbands are paralleled by the Indian husbands sending their wives up-river in the summer while they occupy themselves 'setting traps, fishing and hunting' (i.e. having sex with younger squaws). In the marriages of the Shermans and the business clones we see at the beginning of the film, semi-identical in their lightweight suits, ties and hats, excitement has vanished and the instinctual has been buried under the impedimenta of consumerism, the claustrophobia of domesticity and middle-class rituals. The attempt that Sherman makes to revive the sexual wilderness is extremely half-hearted, for when his patter to the Girl invokes, as an invitation to intercourse, the idea of civilised man as savage under the surface, and the Girl then tells him she wants to stay the night to take advantage of the air-conditioning, he hurriedly temporises, ' . . . When I said that we were savages, well, there are savages and savages . . .' Clearly, also, there are playboys and playboys, for Sherman in his guilt-ridden introduction into the marital apartment of the female who is sex but not responsibility is trying (as Barbara Ehrenreich ingeniously argues of the significance of Hefner's *Playboy* in *The Hearts of Men*) to make the apartment his own, to reclaim the indoors for men, to escape into an erotic rather than a husbandly identity with all its monetary and familial cares, the latter trenchantly suggested in the brief non-communication between Sherman and his space-helmeted son at the film's beginning, and the connotations of the business of the paddle (clearly big Rickie's renounced penis) that he is trying to post to his son throughout the narrative, and finally does so wrapped up in a bandage. This last is the culmination or nadir of the riotously phallic entourage of symbols (the champagne corks, fingers in champagne bottles, toes in tap and so on) that pervade the film's knowing progress.

The Girl

Sherman: (referring to the presence of the Girl in the apartment) This may
               seem unnatural to you. But actually it's the most natural thing in the
               world.
Krahulic: I'll say!

In Nicholas Roeg's ingenious film *Insignificance* (1985), which brings
together in mythic relations Marilyn Monroe, Albert Einstein and Joseph
McCarthy during the filming of none other than *The Seven Year Itch*, Monroe
(Teresa Russell), questioned by her taxi driver about the part she is playing
replies: 'I play this girl. She's a "what", not a "who". It's just a figment of
this guy's imagination. He imagines me hangin' around the place, y'know.
I spend the entire movie in the kitchen, or in the bathtub, or havin' my skirt
blown up – round my fuckin' ears.' It is a complex moment, this sophisticated
piece of intertextuality, asking for a response from an audience in the 1980s
that is aware of Monroe herself as a contradictory text dwelt upon by cultural
analysis: the universal blonde sex symbol, the child–woman, the vehicle for
the tenor of a male dream of spontaneous sexual sweetness (Mailer in *Marilyn*
and *An American Dream*), or of abused womanhood and lost sisterhood
(Steinem), and so forth, palimpsest upon palimpsest. Particularly, in commenting on the role Marilyn Monroe played in *The Seven Year Itch*, as the
'Girl' who haunts Tom Ewell's waking dreams, it is informed by a sharpened
post-50s, post-feminist critique of her significance not just as sexual symbol
but as victim of aspects of that sexual mythology which she embodied. Her
speech (referring us implicitly to the side of her that expressed intellectual
ambitions connected with Lee Strasberg and Arthur Miller) becomes the
possibility of what a radicalised Monroe – freed of her various real-life com-
plicities – might have articulated if 1955 had been 1985, a protest at the
literally nameless role (like the 'girl' or 'blonde' of some of her earliest films)
she plays.

The screen image of Monroe, particularly in *Itch* where there is little or
nothing of the more ethereal qualities associated with her in films like *Bus
Stop* (1956) and *The Misfits* (1961), is heavy with objectification. Indeed in
Billy Wilder's later use of her in *Some Like It Hot*, where there is (whatever
else may also unconsciously be there) a conscious heightening as well as
dissolving of sexual stereotypes, the overflowing female excess of her is almost

---

The Seven Year Itch
Festooned with jokey symbols of consumerist sex-appeal the fantasised girl (Marilyn Monroe)
speaks through female 'fan' and phallic loaves of her own struggling authenticity.

embarrassing in scenes like the yachtboard encounter with Tony Curtis, and the singing of 'I Wanna Be Loved By You'. Embarrassing, that is, to habits of mind accustomed to a different ideal of slimmer, athletic female body shape – e.g. Jane Fonda – and to images denying rather than confirming the destiny of anatomy that seems written in her softness of flesh, the large beautiful breasts offered in that characteristic forward tilting pose full on to the audience as the absolute otherness to the biological and cultural hardness of the male. And in the slight seeming flaw of her nascent pot belly, less streamlined than those of her many imitators, affecting the watcher, could there be a subliminal image of the maternity which, ironically, in real life, with her surgical history of miscarriage and abortion, she could never attain?

Yet the 'what' played by Monroe in the repertoire of memorable but narrow roles given her by Hollywood – those variations on the dumb blonde incarnate in the bar girl, the secretary, and the entertainer – is also a more complex 'who', the tension of the two providing much of the fascination of those roles. True, these were conceived within an exceedingly closed range (with only *The Misfits* as a partial exception), yet to read her presence in many of her major films (e.g. *The Seven Year Itch, Some Like It Hot, Bus Stop, Gentlemen Prefer Blondes, The River of No Return* (1954), *The Misfits*) as something always struggling, consciously or unconsciously, against a mono-lithic objectification forced on her by the script and director is to simplify the issue, for in many of her films, at least in the ones named above, she is used by directors and scriptwriters in a far from simple way as a register of feelings about the female and, beyond this, to register the feelings of the female. In other words, in however rudimentary or fleeting a way, however much limited by the conventions of typecasting and the restrictions of the dumb-blonde role, these films enact the emergence of a 'who' over a 'what', though of course the autonomy of the 'who' that emerges is very severely structured by dominant 50s preconceptions of hierarchical relations between the sexes and the dependence of the woman on the man, however much she may educate him in the marriages the endings of most of the films imply.

The part Monroe plays in *Itch* is at the same time a contradiction and a confirmation of these remarks. In many ways the film is an exception, with the investigation of stereotypes and fantasies central to rather than peripheral to its satiric intent. *Gentlemen Prefer Blondes* (Hawks, 1953) is also satirical and concerned with analysing stereotype, but the character of Lorelei is more touching, more rooted in relationships with other characters, not just a wraith. Compared with *The River of No Return* which precedes it, and *Bus Stop* which follows it, *Itch* is deliberately regressive, moving back to the totally nameless character of the earliest films whose sex is her identity. But the regression is calculated, the double constraint productive, returning the character more explicitly than any other of her films to its roots in a male fantasy of an idealised female sexual otherness – open, giving, spontaneous, innocent, exciting but unthreatening, all those images of Sugar Kane sweetness created for her by celebrants like Wilder and Mailer. But whereas in other films the combination of a three-dimensional character (e.g. Cherie in *Bus Stop*) and the star's charisma tend to make all those characteristics cohere, the satiric method of *The Seven Year Itch* tends to make them fall apart, to reveal their basis in fantasy by placing them as the product of an inadequate and immature consciousness, Richard Sherman's. Though the combination of the star's charisma and the film's obvious wish to display her as a sexual spectacle at the same time as it criticises the operation produce strands that pull in a contrary direction, many moments are firmly placed as the fetishisation of Sherman's comically inadequate consciousness: for instance, the Girl's first appearance, clutching the emblematic fan and the shopping bag with its rampant stick of French bread, and her ascent of the stairs while Sherman voyeuristically cricks his neck (a repetition of a motif which, throughout the film, underlines his look). Though the narrative does not signal conventionally that she is 'just a figment of this guy's imagination' by, for instance, revealing it all as a dream (as is the case with another star, Joan Bennett, and in another context, Lang's *The Woman in the Window*, 1944), or by conventionally blurring the screen when she appears, the structure of the film with its multiple daydream episodes (e.g. where Sherman demonstrates to his absent/present wife his erotic potential with other women) suggests it strongly. In line with this, the Girl's first appearance in the film is given in a shot as Sherman goes to answer the doorbell which, unmistakably from his point of view, shows her merely as a shape visible behind opaque curtain and glass door, suggesting the arrival of some sort of wraith from the unconscious. Later, her re-entry down the blocked-off staircase into the apartment after he has expelled her from it carries the suggestion of an immaterial force gliding through the walls, accompanied by ethereal music, only later explained as the result of her unnailing the floorboards. The extreme implausibility of her remaining nameless throughout the whole narrative, breaking a major rule of realistic narration, adds to these effects, which are, of course, placed not to establish the action as an undeniable dream but to assign it to that realm somewhere between the real and the imagined that is the space of the comic 'return of the repressed'.

It is easy, all too easy, to write about the film in a simplified way which labels the display of Marilyn Monroe's beauty as in itself an objectionable objectification, a corrupt fetishisation. Such a position seems to us impossibly

and undesirably puritanical, reasonable only from a viewpoint hostile to
heterosexual desire itself. What, though, is different is the perception that
the terms in which this beauty is formulated, the series of oxymoronic opposi-
itions (sexuality and childishness, purity and availability, etc.) that are held
together in it, are in the end limiting and oppressive ways of seeing. Because
it is not committed like her other major films to creating pathos around her,
The Seven Year Itch is actually able to anticipate the deconstructionist critics
of the star image by breaking down momentarily the subtle balances holding
the desirable image together. For instance, in the scene where Sherman
imagines her on TV delivering the 'kissing sweet' 'Dazzledent' ad, the most
famous and characteristic of Monroe's facial expressions, the vulnerable,
open-lipped invitation, is seen as integrated in the service of a product.
Equally, the childish side of the childish/mature paradox is so stressed (e.g.
when she asks for a gin and soda), as is the ordinariness against the glamour
(e.g. when she is too distracted by thinking about the price of repairing her
fan to listen to Sherman), that the image drifts into its constituent parts and
invites a more critical reading; i.e. her inattentive monologue as Sherman's
punishment for wanting an ignorant woman.

  Sometimes, though, the movement is more deliberately ambivalent,
involving first deconstruction and then attention to a positive residue left
after it; that set of positive connotations that the image of Monroe has for
both women and men, and of which the vast amount of writing about her
is the proof. The appeal to women (Gloria Steinem, for instance) rests on a
complicated set of determinants simultaneously drawing sympathy for her
from the processes of her exploitation, while arousing envy on account of
an effervescent inner radiance, excitement and playfulness, all qualities
achieving their visual revelation in the exaggerated gestures and milky abundance of a body brimming over with the voluptuous undulations of a Rubens
nude. But the effects of the lustrous figure, tremulous voice and caressing
look of combined injury and tenderness in the eye, coupled with the ana-
chronistically superimposed images of elegiac feeling created by her tragic
suicide, have all too easily prompted a narrow feminist redefinition of Marilyn
Monroe wholly in terms of women's cultural victimisation under patriarchy,
a redefinition that has sometimes too simplistically side-tracked analysis of
the affirmative qualities that she also inescapably projected. In *Itch* the Girl's
childishness, vulnerability and innocence, those definitions of her essence
now so indelibly branded on the Marilyn myth, are not simply inevitable
routes to victimisation, but, more positively, and paradoxically, her most
reliable exits from conformity. Her transgressions of social norms in this
film range from the debunking of pretentiousness (while he plays

Rachmaninov she talks of Eddie Fisher), to candour (while he furtively hides
US Camera, she takes pleasure in displaying her photo), to playfulness (her
full of gusto piano rendition of 'Chopsticks'), to gender-crossing DIY initia-
tives (she unnails the boards), to creative wilfulness (she refuses to stay away
even after her expulsion from the apartment), this last trait of character
something to which even Sherman himself is sensitive, though it leads him
mean-spiritedly to think of her only as a gold-digger poised to ruin him by
blackmail.

The equivocal rhetoric of the Monroe presence even stretches in this film
to the most banal remarks, as when she replies that she has no 'imagination
at all' to Sherman's boastful references to his own. Understood with the
subtlety that the text deserves, the reply has three levels of meaning: first,
she has no imagination because she is stupid; second, she has no imagination
– though he has – because the female is conventionally seen as wholly the
imagined, the male as the imaginer; third, much more positively, she has
no imagination because she is so innocently unrepressed (imagination in
Sherman's terms meaning guilt-shadowed thoughts of the forbidden). This
is also true of those moments playing with another opposition that is resolved
in the star persona of Monroe, the conjunction of heat and cold, the demand
for the ultimate in sexuality and chastity simultaneously, expressed by the
Girl's constant search for breezes (the subway vent, Sherman's air-conditioning) to relieve her body heat, even to the point, as she disarmingly informs
Sherman, where she keeps her panties in the ice-box (as Mailer crudely but
memorably puts it, the art of the film resides in how close 'one can come to
the concept of hot pussy while still living in the cool of the innocent'). Mailer's
rhetoric here is totally male-centred; how much the film's satire criticises,
how much it collaborates with the point of view is open to argument, but
again there are moments where the Girl's innocence seems to pass beyond
the limitations of the ideologically-loaded trope it carries, to assert something
more basic, an uncorrupted, unrepressed delight in sensation: 'It's delicious',
as opposed to her sillier, more pretentious 'Just elegant'.

Thus, though the Girl is apparently wholly without autonomy, wholly the
product of Sherman's wish-fulfilment, there are times when she becomes
something more, not as in some other films where the sensitivity and pathos
of a character is deeper than the stereotype, but through a kind of residue
whereby her words and actions reach a meaning beyond the one that Sherman
gives them. So, for instance, she says of marriage, 'Getting married. That'd
be worse than living at the Club [a sort of YWCA from which she has been
expelled]. I'd have to start getting in by 1 o'clock again.' Here her antipathy
to marriage can be seen on a primary level as fitting in exactly with Sherman's

playboy dreams, for his attempted flight from domesticity requires a girl
who will make no demands on him, who will not look on him as a potential
breadwinner and support. At a second level, her words become a statement
of his own dissatisfaction with the married state which his actions and words
may often obliquely imply, but which he can never bring himself to utter
openly. But the Girl's words are also, more threateningly, a female voice of
dissatisfaction, expressing opinions which only the male is expected to have.

The meaning again circles round the significance that Barbara Ehrenreich
has drawn out in *The Hearts of Men*, the *Playboy* philosophy (if not an original
subscriber, Sherman will obviously soon be eagerly buying it rather than
US Camera for secret reading), as a masculine protest against the demands
of 'manhood', solidity, self-sacrifice and 'maturity' (a protest that finds its
history more delicately and ambivalently fixed in Philip Roth's novels,
Portnoy's Complaint, *When She Was Good* and *My Life As A Man*); the nexus
of meanings having as its key reference the fact that Monroe herself was
exhibited as the first *Playboy* centrefold two years before Sherman ogled her
in *The Seven Year Itch*.

At one place, towards its end, the film seems to drop its primarily satiric
intent. Here Sherman finally confesses the truth of his low self-esteem and
mocks the idea that his wife might be jealous of him: 'How can anybody be
jealous of somebody with a briefcase who's getting a little pot? Who gets so
sleepy by 9.30 he can't keep his eyes open? Let's face it . . . No pretty girl
in her right mind wants me. She want Gregory Peck.' The Girl replies solicit-
ously, and at length:

> Is that so? . . . How do you know what a pretty girl wants? You think every girl's
> a dope? You think a girl goes to a party and there's some guy in a fancy striped
> vest strutting around like a tiger, giving you that I'm-so-handsome-you-can't resist
> me look and for this she's supposed to fall flat on her face. But there's another
> guy in the room. Way over in the corner. Maybe he's kind of nervous and shy
> and perspiring a little. First you look past him, but then you sort of sense he's
> gentle and kind and worried and he'll be tender with you. Nice and sweet. That's
> what's really exciting. (Touches him.) I'd be very jealous of you. (Kisses him.) I
> think you're just elegant.

If we look through the flattery of the male part of the audience, the Girl's
words may be seen as having the function of reassuring her male progenitor
(and his prototypes in the film audience) of their potency and desirability:
just as the doll-like paralysis of the *US Camera* pin-up (lying down on her
front, in a still polka-dotted bikini, looking at the viewer, beckoning him to
feast off sanctioned pleasures) do the same for the voyeur. And when Sherman
mentions Gregory Peck he is probably thinking of him in such heroic roles

as *Duel in the Sun* (1946) and *Captain Horatio Hornblower* (1951). There is a predictive irony in this choice since it is Peck who will play a year later the serious version, in *The Man in the Grey Flannel Suit*, of the little man as executive parodied by Ewell and Randall.

Yet inextricably mixed up with this there is another and more positive text than the massaging of the pusillanimous ego of the 'little man' (again, the fierce Reichian invocation seems appropriate). The Girl's words recall moment after moment in films previous and yet to come in which the Monroe character articulates her desire for 'respect' and 'regard' and her longing for a man of tenderness and sensitivity. This, the text of the 'who' as against the 'what', is pervasive in the films (e.g. her statement in *Bus Stop* that 'I just got to feel that whoever I marry has some real regard for *me*, aside from all that lovin' stuff'). The tone of the utterance in *The Seven Year Itch* is different to the norm in that it comes both from a character who is less 'real' than the others and less vulnerable, but to read it merely as a sop to Sherman is too crude. Against all the odds, through the visual and verbal language of a culture programmed to exploit her, she is also speaking for herself, coming through to express her authenticity and difference, not content, like those women of whom Virginia Woolf speaks in a discussion of women writers struggling to free themselves from the presuppositions of patriarchy, to be bullied by 'that voice which cannot let women alone'. If conformist, male-orientated eroticism demands the fetishisation of hips and breasts, Marilyn Monroe succeeds (where Mansfield and others fail) in being, as even a feminist erotica would allow, truly polymorphously perverse, drawing attention away from these twin focuses to every other atom of her sexual presence. If conformist, male-orientated expression of dumb-blonde speech is at best crassness, and at worst, silence. Marilyn Monroe succeeds (where Mamie Van Doren and others fail) in breathing life into her scripted clichés, turning the platitudes of love and identity in her morale-boosting monologue (where at one point only her voice and not, for once, her body speaks, as the camera focuses instead on Sherman), into the light but impassioned, resilient but also self-consciously theatrical and spirited homily of a girl–woman not yet brow-beaten by a system sometimes unexpectedly subverted by its own comic child-monsters of desire.

THE OTHER SIDE OF MIDNIGHT:
SIRK'S FAMILY COMEDIES

The sub-genre – from romance to ritual

The matrimonial attachment between the two partners has to be regarded biologically as an intermediate stage leading up to paternal attachment.
— Malinowski, *Sex and Repression in Savage Society*

Romantic comedy centres on the couple, celebrating the passionate but hopefully companionate love that brings them together, and typically ending at
the moment of passage into the responsibilities of marriage. Family comedy,
holding up its mirror of pleasurably idealising reflection to that later stage,
must be defined in very different terms. The deep structurings that underlie
its lyrical charms can be summarised thus: (i) It foregrounds the reproductive function of love and sexuality demoted in romantic comedy. (ii) It is
group centred, leaving the couple's world of passionate sexual love for the
more diffused ties of family love. (iii) It acts out the family's crucial educative
function of being (in Talcott Parsons's terms) 'factories' which produce
human personalities. (iv) It is marked by a celebratory tone, for in a society
where almost everyone comes from a family and where it is normative to
found one, family comedy's most basic function is to generate feelings of
pleasure (conscious and unconscious, nostalgic, present and anticipatory)
about the family. Equally it is characterised by (v) deflectionary strategies
which diminish (or sometimes just deny) anything that threatens the family
or makes it a site of displeasure. And where common wisdom sees a conflict
between positive and negative feelings about the family, the sub-genre is
marked by (vi) reconciliatory mechanisms which ease conflict by appeal to
concepts like the naturalness of family life and the inevitability of repression
and tension in any social formation. Lastly, these films may contain – by
conscious design or unconscious expression – (vii) sub-texts which exist in
critical opposition to aspects of the dominant ideology of the film, its repressed, so to speak. In these latter aspects family comedy is similar to the family
melodrama, but such expression will be more secondary and more contained
within optimism than in melodrama, which is licensed to greater excess and
greater disruptiveness in its use of the weak 'happy ending', the closure that
satisfies the requirements of optimism and morality, but in such a way as
potentially to challenge them. Hollywood family comedy follows the pattern
of its classic American archetypes in the drama and the novel (O'Neill's *Ah,
Wilderness!* and Alcott's *Little Women*, both twice filmed in major versions)

in their idyllic, fuller closures, yet even here irony may be a powerful presence
– and, we will argue, with Sirk's comedies often is – questioning the reconciliations of the comic finale.

   A shortlist of some significant films of the sub-genre, alongside the six
Sirk texts we will examine, includes *Ah, Wilderness!* (1935), *Little Women*
(1933 and 1949), *Life With Father* (1948), *The Easy Way* (1952), *Cheaper by
the Dozen* (1950), *Father of the Bride* (1950), *The Courtship of Eddie's Father*
(1963), Milos Forman's *Taking Off* (1971), and the musicals – for this lyrical
genre often seeks its embodiment in music – *Meet Me in St Louis* (1944),
Summer Holiday (1948), *On Moonlight Bay* (1951), *By the Light of the Silvery
Moon* (1953) and *Mary Poppins* (1964). Such films resolve in some form or
other such problems as the power of the father in the patrilineal family, the
problems encountered in the process by which the young males and females
of the family are socialised into their cultural manly and womanly roles, and
sometimes the erotic difficulties of both generations, the children in adapting
desire to the approved pattern, and the parents (or, rather, almost always
the father, since the mother in these films is usually presented in a state of
exaggerated stasis) in leaving the primarily erotic world of the couple for the
affectionate, ethical, other-oriented world dominated by the needs of the
children.

   The ideal of the family in 1940s and 50s comedy necessarily appears archaic
from a later perspective acutely aware of trends unknown or less visible then
– e.g. increasing divorce, increased premarital sex, the tendency towards a
restricted form of serial monogamy, the lessening of sanctions against unmarried parenthood, efficient contraception and a high population level leading
to a lessening of the absolute importance of reproduction, with a related
growing tolerance of non-heterosexual practices and extra-familial life styles.
If we treat reports of the imminent death of the family as exaggerated, then
we will see the family comedies of that period not as absolute evidence of
the view (Cooperian, Laingian, some gay and lesbian criticism) of the family
as the *fons et origo* of all repression, gender injustice and unhappiness, but
as representations of a growing disymmetry between a highly conservative
ideology of the family and changing social circumstances rendering that
ideology increasingly obsolete, a disymmetry that the sub-genre finds itself
reluctant to admit, though impelled to represent, however obliquely. Comparison of the two versions of *Little Women* provides a useful measure of the
conservatism of the period, for the later film not only omits the Civil War
realities glimpsed briefly at the start of Cukor's film, but through June Allyson's much cosier version of Jo defuses much of the force of the gender
conflicts acted out by Katharine Hepburn. Here too there is no hint, except

for the bare repetition of the occurrence, of the extraordinary moment where the March patriarch returns, but so old, weak and white-haired that the viewer is invited to consider how much the power of the father is an idea that functions without reference to the actual holder of the power. Instead, in Le Roy's film a hale and hearty Leon Ames returns briskly to the fold. This later version of *Little Women* also underlines the sub-genre's tendency, most pronounced in the 40s and 50s, to emigrate from its modern suburban settings to an idyllic past – the late nineteenth century, the pre-First World War years, the 1920s, and pastoral and smalltown settings – in which family and gender roles were perceived as more stable than in the difficult present. In melodrama we are within sight of *Rebel Without a Cause* (1955) which centres so much on the traumatic reactions of the younger generation, not to the power of the father but to a confused situation in which the fathers are incapable of living out the roles demanded of them, their failure condemning the young males to swing violently between extreme poles of cultural masculinity and femininity. In the well-lit, idyllically middle-class loci of family comedy such problems are contained, modulated into optimistic shapes, Oedipal crises resolved into patterns of inheritance.

Whether more or less conditioned to over-idealisation and evasion rather than recognition of conflict, the fundamental point characterising the sub-genre is that, beneath its lyricisms, family comedy takes the longer – what we might call the Malinowskian – view, after the argument put forward in works such as *The Sexual Life of Savages in North West Melanesia* and *Sex and Repression in Savage Society*, that structurally marriage universally exists for the reproduction and nurturing of children. Indeed, in a number of films, including four of the Sirk comedies (*The Lady Pays Off* (1951), *Weekend with Father* (1951), *Meet Me at the Fair* and *Take Me to Town* (1952), as well as Minnelli's much better known *The Courtship of Eddie's Father*), this view is embedded in a remarkable conceit by which the impossible idea that a child could choose its own most perfect parents is expressed in a plot in which the child (single-parented or orphaned) either deliberately causes or accidentally precipitates the formation of a new marriage and family. As Jimmy John, the foster-child, puts it in the slightly differently plotted *The Easy Way* (1952), 'I had the chance to choose my own parents'.

The underlying ethos of such films is further clarified by that curious tragic-comic work, George Stevens's *Penny Serenade* (1941), where 'The Story of a Happy Marriage' is the fact that Roger's and Julie's (Cary Grant's and Irene Dunne's) marriage cannot survive the multiple tragedy of her miscarriage, subsequent sterility, and the death of the step-child. Sinking into extremes of despair and on the point of parting forever, they are only rescued for each other by the social worker Miss Oliver's last-minute offer of another stepchild. Other more dominantly comic films such as *Cheaper by the Dozen* (1950) and *The Easy Way* hyberbolise the primary function of the family over subjective desire by sheer weight of numbers, literally twelve children in the former, a mere five in the latter, though enough to drive Cary Grant to repeated jokes about the children's interference with his sexual life. In *The Remarkable Mr Pennypacker* (1959) Clifton Webb is so enamoured of the family that he bigamously has two of them, moments before the invention of the contraceptive pill producing no less than seventeen children. Similarly/differently *Every Girl Should Be Married* (1948) is a romantic comedy in which the values of romance are rather grotesquely and ambivalently put into perspective by Betsy Drake's obsessionally baby and home-orientated desire for marriage.

Spare though these few notations are (an example of a more complicated, psychoanalytically based thematic is found in *Father of the Bride* where Spencer Tracy has to trace a difficult route away from his daughter and back to his wife), they provide at least a basic generic context in which to examine the six comedies made at Universal by Douglas Sirk during 1951-52: *The Lady Pays Off, Weekend With Father, Has Anybody Seen My Gal?* (1951), and *No Room for the Groom, Meet Me at the Fair* and *Take Me to Town*.

Comedy and melodrama

> I wish I could find something to laugh about. This used to be such a happy home.
> — Vincent in *There's Always Tomorrow* (1955)

Douglas Sirk's 1950s melodrama became in the 60s and 70s a paradigm for analysis of the ways in which Hollywood films sometimes managed, consciously or unconsciously, to transgress, as well as celebrate or abide by, the norms and conventions of an industry rooted in the capitalist traditions of post-industrialised American society. The distinctiveness of Sirk's case was that the radical readings given to his films could appeal both to a major body of work in the highly art-conscious tradition of European cinematic melodrama (such UFA films as *Schlüssakkord*, 1936, and *Zu Neuen Ufern*, 1937) and later to Sirk's detailed statements of his intentions and models in writers as different as Euripides, Thoreau and Calderón. Cogent attacks on 'intentionalism' and unreconstructed *auteurism*, centring round the provocative slogan of 'the death of the author', disallow a naïve conception of Sirk as absolute source of all meaning in his work, but his statements should not be ignored, since they constitute the most articulate record of a struggle by a

highly self-conscious film-maker to produce works sufficiently within Hollywood norms to be commercially successful, yet able to use the potentialities
of those norms – e.g. the different kinds of excess allowed by melodrama
and comedy – critically against the reactionary conformism of many elements
of Cold War America. Inevitably there are sharp disputes as to the success,
and even the degree of radicalism, that Sirk achieved through his many
different strategies, but especially through distancing techniques and the
subversion through style of the usual processes of audience identification
with the narrative. What cannot be doubted, though, is that Sirk seized upon
the formal possibilities and the typical content of the Hollywood melodrama,
its interest in class, race and, above all, the family (especially, though not
exclusively, woman's place in the family), the socialisation of children, the
psychopathology of family relations, and very self-consciously manipulated
them.

Curiously, in view of the reputation of Sirk's American melodramas, his
comedies have been all but ignored (only a few pages in Michael Stern's
Douglas Sirk (1971) breaking the pattern of neglect, making useful preliminary points, especially about the films' relation to melodrama and their satiric
edge). An important reason for this has been that until recently melodrama
has been critically privileged over comedy as the more disruptive genre. It
is also probable that the conditions under which the American comedies
were made (with the exception of *Captain Lightfoot*, 1954, all before *Magnificent Obsession*, 1954, established Sirk as a major commercial director at
Universal and allowed him greater freedoms) were perceived as unpropitious
– low-budget B films, shot quickly in black and white when not musicals,
employing only minor stars (e.g. Sterling Hayden, Dan Dailey, Linda Darnell, Ann Sheridan at the end of her career, Tony Curtis and Rock Hudson
at the start of theirs) – and in a genre seen perhaps as the most conservative
of all the popular forms.

Yet referring back to our brief outline of the characteristics of family
comedy, centred as they are on family life and the home as both refuge from
the turbulence of public life and a microcosm of the norms, hierarchies and
tyrannies of the outside world, it is surely clear that family comedy and
family melodrama are mirror-images of each other – with the family in the
one case idealised, in the other seen claustrophobically, as oppressed by
external (but internalised) social forces. Both genres address basically middle-
class values, offering the bourgeoisie images of itself in usually modern settings. That conviction of some feminist critics that melodrama is the only
genre to highlight female problematics must be obviously untrue when we
turn to romantic comedies like *Bringing up Baby* and *His Girl Friday*, and

though Family Comedy in the first instance wants to resolve rather than display contradictions attending the female as mother, wife, and independent person, object and subject of desire, nevertheless it highlights (or can highlight) these problematics. Indeed, though 40s and 50s family comedy tends to make of the mother a wholly static figure, as if her immobility can provide a fixed point of security amidst the tensions explored in fathers, sons and daughters, this is an area in which Sirk's comedies stand apart from the norm, since *The Lady Pays Off*, *Take Me to Town* and *Meet Me at the Fair* all contain mothers (or fairly mature mothers-to-be who are no longer inexperienced girls) very different from the almost post-sexual mother figures of many of the films. Of all the melodramatic topics and conventions, only adultery – too traumatic a form of comic release for 50s audiences, though Lubitsch in the 30s treated it relatively freely – is significantly absent from the comedies. In *All I Desire* (1953) Sirk's most powerful melodrama of adultery, the issue is part of the melodramatic ambience of shock and failure, female desire, questioning of marriage as an institution, and the illusion of romantic love. Even so, in a comedy like *No Room For the Groom*, we are entitled to wonder whether after the honeymoon period a pair as ill-matched as Alva and Lee will not succumb to the pressures of their already noticeable incompatibility.

While family comedy is likely to be more conservative aesthetically than melodrama, with all the excesses and hysteria of transference and displacement noted by its analysts, comedy too has its areas of excess that violate normality. Melodramatists like Sirk and Minnelli, turning to comedy, are adept at importing values from the mirror-genre (the moment, for instance, in *The Courtship of Eddie's Father* of Eddie's discovery of the death of the goldfish, or Spencer Tracy's Gothic, semi-incestuous nightmare in *Father of the Bride*). But beyond that there is the set of categories laid out by Bakhtin in his work on the comic in *Rabelais and His World*: comedy as carnival, as festive madness, as a degradation of the high and elevation of the low, as a celebration of the ludic and the bodily, of masks, play-acting and creative pretence. In 40s and 50s family comedy such release is carefully limited in the sub-genre's search for order and harmony, but we cannot but be aware of its presence (sometimes open, sometimes fugitive) in Sirk's comedies, arguing that the social formation that demands more than the necessary repressions of culture endangers itself and creates unnecessary unhappiness. For instance, consider the different aspects of celebration of the body as sexuality in 'Vermilion O'Toole' in *Take Me to Town* and in Clara in *Meet Me at the Fair*, and, more complicatedly, in the Tarzan figure of *Weekend With Father*, or of the body as indulgence in Charles Coburn's 'Mr John

Smith' in *Has Anybody Seen My Gal?* Or the celebration of trickery and creative pretence in the shapes of 'Doc' Tilbee in *Meet Me at the Fair*, May alias 'Vermilion O'Toole' in *Take Me to Town* and Samuel G. Fulton alias 'Mr John Smith' in *Has Anybody Seen My Gal?*

One constant point of reference that runs through both the melodramas and the comedies is Henry Thoreau's great refusal of the veneer of civilisation and its life-denying impulses, *Walden*. Sirk, very well-read in classic American literature, remarked that he was given *Walden* by his father when he was thirteen or fourteen, and either explicitly (as when Alida and Cary discuss the book in *All That Heaven Allows*) or implicitly, its echoes resonate through the films. The pastoral as theme is common in the 1940s and early 50s (something we have discussed in detail with reference to *Summer Holiday* in *Blue Skies and Silver Linings*) and coincides with the mass emigration of the time by the middle classes from the cities to the suburbs which, as Richard Polenberg in *One Nation Divisible* notes, were often christened with sub-Thoreauvian names like 'Woodbury Knoll' or 'Park Forest'. Sirk's films constantly invoke Thoreau and this context in complex ways, sometimes as a positive ideal almost wholly disguised in the pleasant but ersatz pastoral individualism of the suburbs, criticising the 'resignation' that is 'confirmed desperation' lived by 'the mass of men (who) lead lives of quiet desperation'; sometimes embodied in characters like Ron Kirby who move to 'a different drum'; at other times, equally positively, embodied in the pastoral settings of Oregon and North-West America that Sirk loved; and on other occasions present perhaps as nothing more than a frustrated memory of a vanished, or almost vanished, ideal – the river in *Written on the Wind*(1956), the beach house in *The Lady Pays Off*, Alva's vineyard in *No Room for the Groom*, the 'jungle' hothouse of Claudette Colbert's mansion in *Sleep My Love* (1948), or Camps Hiashwaka and Mineshwaka in *Weekend with Father*.

While the melodramas usually end with instincts to freedom withered and imprisoned, the comedies allow space for greater hope – one index of which is the more positive role played by the children in the marriage and remarriage situations. Sirk made some well-known remarks on the negative meanings children often have in his films, and in the self-centred, wholly ideologised siblings of *There's Always Tomorrow* and *All That Heaven Allows* the future generation is certainly the antithesis of comic growth.

In the comedies, however, they are generally a more positive force, bringing the adult lovers together and sometimes, especially in the case of the three little sons in *Take Me to Town*, who recognise in Vermilion a fellow free spirit, genii of release. Yet ambiguities still tend to attach themselves to the younger characters. For instance, the two sets of children in *Weekend*

With Father for a long time desire more conventional partners for their parents, and it is hard not to feel that the optimism of Ann Stubbs's conversion to desiring her father's happiness is clouded by the glimpses given of the tyranny of the regime of pre-pubescent dating, set in motion during the child's latency period, which threatens to negate any individual development outside the most petrifying social norms. Similar doubts may touch the adult characters in their happy endings, for instance the shadows of the window bars behind Vermilion as she sits on the veranda of Will Hall's house suggest not just the prison she has happily escaped, but the possible prison of domesticity towards which she is heading.

The six Sirk family comedies made at Universal in 1951 and 1952 also benefit from being seen not just in relation to Sirk's output in melodrama, but in relation to the less discussed interest in comedy that runs through his career. Both before and after his film work he directed major stage comedies, some of which he translated and adapted, by Shakespeare, Wilde, Shaw and Molière among others, and in his cinema (both European and American) there is a continuing commitment to comedy, secondary but parallel to his work in melodrama – *April, April* (1935), *Accord Final* (1939), the use of Lucille Ball in *Personal Column* (1946) and Don Ameche and Dorothy Lamour in *Slightly French* (1948), as well as the 1954 adventure comedy *Captain Lightfoot*. Finally, to note that Sirk worked on the six Universal comedies under consideration for something like twenty months during 1951 and 1952 without other projects intervening is to point to a period of sustained preoccupation with comic versions of the family theme, which argues also that, however lightly he regarded some of these films many years later, they will bear a more detailed examination than has up till now been given to them.

The Lady Pays Off (1951)

Plot synopsis

Evelyn Warren (Linda Darnell) has won a Teacher of the Year award, but languishes in frustrated melancholy because teaching has failed to bring her romance. Her schoolmarm's aura has only succeeded in attracting men with mother-fixations.

So, determined to live a little, she finds herself on vacation in a casino where, not realising she is playing roulette with $100 instead of $1 chips, she ends up $7,000 in debt. When Matt Braddock (Stephen McNally), the owner, is informed, he is attracted to her and offers to cut cards: if she wins, the debt is cancelled; if she loses, he will tear up the bill provided she agrees to tutor his motherless nine-year-old daughter (Gigi Perreau).

Evelyn loses because Matt cheats. Reluctantly she agrees to be Diane's tutor. Scornful of Matt and his life-style, Evelyn plots to revenge herself on him by making him fall in love with her. Doing so, she sees off a super-sophisticated rival, Kay Stoddart (Virginia Field). Matt declares his love and sells his casino, ready now to lead a more respectable life with Evelyn. She then tells him she has tricked him and leaves.

Marie, the housekeeper, and Diane come to the rescue by pretending that Diane has run away from home as a result of Evelyn's going. Evelyn returns to search for the 'lost' Diane, who suddenly reappears to pronounce Matt and Evelyn 'Mummy and Daddy'.

How to Handle a Woman

> Women are suited to being the nurses and teachers of our earliest childhood precisely because they themselves are childish, silly and short-sighted, in a word big children their whole lives long.
>
> — Schopenhauer, 'On Women'

The first of Sirk's comedies at Universal announces themes and structures which will dominate the whole set. Thus Evelyn and Matt's romance is between parties at least one of whom is already a parent, making the romantic plot a family narrative as well (three out of the six films). The adults around whom the new family will be formed are (with the exception of *Has Anybody Seen My Gal?*) relatively young and sexually-motivated which means that even when the narratives are most family-directed they have a large romantic component. This characteristic emphasis away fom the autumnal, largely unproblematic adult sexuality of films like *Summer Holiday* and *Meet Me in St Louis* is important because it potentially places in the foreground tensions between the monogamous family and sexual drives, as well as rescuing the mother (or here the mother-to-be) from her totally inward-looking role as angel of stasis. The first and last (*Take Me to Town*) of the sextet of films indeed place the mother-to-be in the position of protagonist, so that though there are still elements of the conventional 'Perseus and Andromeda' situation being played out – in the simplest movement of the films the heroines are rescued from discontent or seeming degradation by their males – the viewer in invited to read the heroine, her problems and her rescue more critically, despite Sirk's comment many years after the event on *The Lady Pays Off* that 'I have no feeling for this picture at all'. '*Was wünscht das Weib?*' The question is raised in comic form by Linda Darnell's Evelyn, sultry discontent written in every part of her hispanically aggrieved features, her heavily

sensuous figure exaggerated by dresses that flagrantly find ways of accentuat-
ing her hips and breasts. As she frankly explains to her headmistresss, she
wants a man, but the only ones she attracts are Oedipally-stricken suitors of
the sort her memory conjures up during the presentation banquet speech
that casts her as 'Universal Mother', men she amusingly fantasises as trapped
in pygmified form in the womb-like concavities of a wine glass or ashtray or
in the wobbling breast-like mounds of a jelly. Seeking appreciation as a
woman, not as a mother, she reacts with hostility and a desire for revenge
when she is forced by Matt's trick to be Diane's surrogate mother (a situation
that parallels her fears of marriage – economic submission to a man whose
main use for her, she fears, is child-bearer, childminder and child-educator).

   In the film's optimistic surface movement Evelyn's problems are solved.
Growing attachment to Diane proves she is a true mother. And Matt, 'all
man', as the headmistress describes him, free from Oedipal fixations, strong
enough to knock out a gangster but sensitive enough to have Impressionist
prints in his private room at the casino, finally breaks down her defences,
healing the split that troubles her. Any man, he says, who loves a woman
would also want her to be the mother of his children. Evelyn is released
from her frustrations, the cure presumably *'dosim repetatur!'* and motherhood
in equal parts, her release triggered by the deep-sea fishing episode where
she enters a crazy, positively grotesque realm of degradation, release and
wish-fulfilment on the boat that rescues them, run by the perpetually drunken
captain – a sequence that ends with her drunkenly raiding the trawler's new
catch, a wealth of fish-phalluses which she claims and then tries to return
to the sea.

   But also, in ways that have their reflection in the other films, optimistic
comic completion only half-covers ambiguities and uncertainties that run
through the narrative. It is hard to forget that twice in the earlier part of the
film Matt calculatedly deceives Evelyn, initially with a stacked pack of cards,
trumping the King of her gender discontent with his spurious Ace, then
pretending to destroy the IOU by which he controls her. Such discords, and
Evelyn's revengeful response to them in her plan to make a fool of Matt
when she makes him fall in love with her, shadow the rhetoric of romantic
strolls on the beach where surf crashes and the strains of 'I'll Take You
Home Again, Kathleen' float in the night. Here too in minor form the
Thoreau motif is sounded, but in a way that hardly promises untramelled
release: the retreat to nature in Carmel being to a luxurious bourgeoisified
beach mansion complete with patio, barbecue and drinks trolley, not to
mention French housekeeper – items certainly of the good, but hardly of
the renovated life. The house invites comparison with the mock primitivism

of Matt's casino with its decor of paintings of demurely provocative Victorian pin-ups, animal horns and tribal masks. The combined effect provokes ambivalence; a sense of limited characters reaching for a concept of the natural life they can no longer grasp, but also a sense of powerful natural forces in the background even though they manifest themselves in diminished forms (e.g. the horsehead lampstands associated with Matt, and Diane's toy dog, Pluto).

Diane's melancholy (paralleling Evelyn's, so that the film centres on two unhappy females) stems fom the nine-year-old's need for a motherly and female role-model, that need for both male and female parents at the centre of four of the six comedies. The need is in no way doubted, but the relation/opposition of Diane's two favourite toys (anticipating the use of the toy 'Rex', the 'walkie-talkie robot man' in *All I Desire*), the Disney dog, Pluto, and her ultra-feminine doll, suggests some area of doubt about this mother–daughter relationship. One strand of the text shows Evelyn's effect as a role-model on the child leading to Diane's claim in her farewell letter that she is running away to be a teacher. However, this is the only moment where Evelyn's profession is viewed positively, and the overall implication is that, in finding love, her other-world orientation will wholly give way to an inner, domestic one. Pluto, Disneyfied but still an animal force, and if a god of the underworld, then the underworld of the little girl's unconscious, is associated largely with Diane's life without Evelyn, while the doll (an ego ideal of feminine conventionality) increasingly displaces him during the film, so that it is the doll whom Diane ecstatically embraces as her parents-to-be finally kiss. A related moment earlier finds Evelyn (presumably as an aid to a lesson in mythology) having drawn on the blackboard a pair of pretty centauresses copied straight out of the notoriously sentimental Pastoral Symphony section of *Fantasia*. The suggestion acted out is that as Evelyn surrenders her teacherly self rather than finding a way of balancing it with her roles of lover and mother, so she may hand on to Diane only the most conventionalised version of womanhood.

Evelyn's defeated rival, Kay (Virginia Field), is clearly meant to be disapproved of for her combination of masculinised aggression, absurd ultra-femininity (wearing high-heels and gloves on a hike), and brittle affected camp mannerisms. But seen in structural relation to, rather than just in competition with Evelyn, her role in the film is more complicated, particularly when the two women are viewed in relation to Marie, the French housekeeper whose old-world femininity openly admires Matt for his tough surface and 'veree, veree kind' interior. These words provoke a notably fierce reaction from Evelyn who repeats them in angry mockery. The anger and the mockery are those of the strong American woman, brought up to be the rival and equal of the male, who then finds she is required to adopt an inferior and more limited role (something Margaret Mead analysed as a major structural contradiction in American life in *Male and Female*, 1949), and which may be seen as a major factor behind second-stage feminism, a trauma that Marie, the traditional European woman, more content with her time-honoured role, does not suffer. Evelyn's discontent which so dominates the film may unconsciously relate as much to the conditions under which the strong woman can have the strong man, as to being without one.

Weekend With Father (1951)

Plot synopsis

Brad Stubbs (Van Heflin) and Jean Bowen (Patricia Neal), widow and widower, he with two young girls, she with two young boys, meet at the station as they send their children away on a Summer Camp holiday. They meet again by accident, and through discussing their children and the problems of single parenthood, get to know each other. Romance and the desire for marriage follow, and the pair decide to break the news to the children at Camps Hiashwaka (Hiawatha) and Minneshwaka (Minnehaha) over Independence Day weekend.

Brad has been involved with a glamorous TV singer Phyllis Reynolds (Virginia Field again) whom he has decided to drop both because of her deficiencies (her career and her lack of interest in children) and meeting Jean. Phyllis, unaware of what Brad has been trying to tell her, arrives at the camp, where the supervisor, Don Adams (Richard Denning), a Tarzanesque athlete, is trying to move in on Jean. These problems are compounded by both sets of children identifying with the wrong role-models, the boys with the exuberant he-man, the girls with the TV star. Attempting to win the boys over, Don fails miserably in various father–son athletic contests against other pairs. The two sets of children also begin to fight amongst themselves. The marriage seems to be impossible. However the situation is rescued by Brad's older daughter, Ann (Gigi Perreau) who stage-manages a reconciliation that institutes the new family.

Fathers and sons and daughters

Trouble with you Phyllis, is you don't know what it means to be a mother. I do!
— Brad Stubbs in *Weekend with Father*

The second of the black and white comedies of contemporary life, *Weekend with Father* almost wholly inhabits the everyday, giving its audience mirror-images less of their fantasies than of their most socialised selves – or at least the selves they mundanely aspire to – the rewards and worries, duties, concerns and pleasures of middle-class parenthood. Brad's and Jean's vicissitudes are those of characters without the literal topographic freedom and psychic space for manoeuvre of the characters in the musicals set in the more spacious west, like 'Doc' Tilbee and Vermilion O'Toole. Even in *The Lady Pays Off*, Marie, the housekeeper, with her magic tricks and previous career in a circus, represents a diminished element of carnival as lacking in the film that follows it as is the negative grotesque of *No Room for the Groom*. The world of *Weekend with Father* is one of PTAs and Summer Camps, the problems of ten-year-old daughters who want to paint their nails and have boyfriends, and adjustments to a status quo of roles that the characters largely accept rather than evade as 'Doc', Vermilion and Clara do in *Meet Me at the Fair*, and *Take Me to Town*. When, for instance, Jean's black maid considers her mistress's marital prospects she invokes within a hoped-for love a set of highly conservative suppositions when she asks for 'Just one good solid citizen with enough money to take care of you and the boys for the rest of your natural lives'.

These 'good solid citizens', Brad and Jean, inhabit a seemingly stable world only destabilised by the deaths of their partners a few years back, leaving each of them a single parent; though at the time of the film fewer marriages were dissolved after children were born than was to become the case (the majority of divorces still happening in the early, childless years of marriage). Death might well be seen here as decorously playing a role beyond metaphysics, providing a screen image for marital breakdown in a period where comedy is too decorous to dramatise the growing divorce rate problems of second marriages with step-parents and step-children.

As in *The Lady Pays Off* the reconstruction of the family is seen as a primary good. Indeed the lovers actually meet through their children as they see them off on their holidays, their first conversation is about them, and their growing attraction to each other is underpinned by a belief they refine in conversation that a parent of each sex is indispensable. He, lacking a mother for his girls, sees mother's 'care' as more important. She, lacking a father for her boys to be disciplined by (the categories exhibit very conventional ideas of motherly and fatherly roles), sees the father as more important. The debate is ended by Jean's 'Maybe they're equally important' and Brad's agreeing with her, 'It's like sort of trying to decide whether you can get on without the left foot or the right foot.'

If Brad, as played by Van Heflin, is not unlike a latter-day Charles Bovary of the advertising world (Bovary was the role he took in Minnelli's film of 1948), Jean (Patricia Neal) is no Emma to find him dull, though his surname *Stubbs* with its connotations of stubby, stubbed out, stub-end – suggests a critical overview of him. (The name recurs in variations in two more scripts Joseph Hoffman wrote for Sirk, Will Stubbins in *No Room for the Groom* and Dan Stebbins in *Has Anybody Seen My Gal?* in each case suggesting in these films with contemporary settings something less expansive and promising – regardless of the positive roles of the individual characters – than is possible in the world of the period Western musicals.) Brad and Jean are perfectly suited in their plain, honest decency in a world where the only hint of the adulterous or any sort of unregulated passion is in the episode where the hotel clerk at the Valhalla Lodge, obviously accustomed only to the simplest categories of the licit and illicit, cannot cope with the complicated request that the unmarried Brad and Jean make for separate rooms for themselves and the children they have even though they say they aren't married, and clearly feels that something infinitely salacious if not quite definable is afoot, a view confirmed when Phyllis arrives as Brad's second 'fiancée'.

The couple's hopes of marriage have to survive two related obstacles – first the intense conservatism of the children in resisting the marriage-to-be and integration into the planned new family unit, and second their preference for the other more stereotypical potential mothers and fathers, Brad's girls for Phyllis, the TV singing star, and Jean's boys for Don Adams, the super-athletic camp commander. Each of the three more quotidian black and white comedies has a place rather than a character vestigially associated with nature and release (though Alva in *No Room for the Groom* is a character who to some degree embodies these lost qualities, seen only in a parodied, simplified form in Don). In *The Lady Pays Off* there is the deep-sea fishing expedition, in *No Room for the Groom* the more limited locus of Will's apartment, and here Camps Hiashwaka and Minneshwaka, where a kind of highly regulated memorial of more nature-oriented days is re-enacted. It is in this setting that Brad gives in to the pressures which emanate from Jean as well as her boys to present himself to her sons as a surrogate for their dead 'marine pilot' father, and involves himself in a series of humiliating attempts to win their esteem, despite the fact that he knows he is 'not exactly the athletic type'. In this diminished Walden where oneness with nature is reduced to ultra-competitive sporting contests where winning is all and the fathers vie with each other as much as the sons (Transcendentalism decayed to Social Darwinism in the American ideology of nature), Don, who 'would make Tarzan look anaemic', shines much more than Brad. The conventionality of children is a favourite Sirkean theme that runs through melodramas like *All That*

Heaven Allows and *There's Always Tomorrow*. Here the children eventually see the light and a more optimistic conclusion is generated, but what is dramatised before the end suggests a general infection by ideologised stereotypes that qualifies optimism. Brad too surrenders to pressure in his eagerness not to fail the boys' demands of him, finally getting himself knocked down by an irate diminutive father when, for all his liberal disclaimers, he can't quite bring himself to say that he couldn't lick the other father. And clearly Jean finds it difficult not to think he is failing the boys.

If Don Adams, despite the connotations of his surname, represents only a false primitive, a mock frontierism outdated as a male role-model, 'Auntie Phyllis', the girls' first choice, seems to represent woman's mistaken progression in the other direction of an escalation of culture over nature. Played by the same actress as Kay in *The Lady Pays Off*, she adds to the qualities on display there not only an ill-disguised lack of interest in children, but an all-absorbing interest in her own career as a television star. 'Darling, you wouldn't ask me to give up my career, would you?', she asks Brad, but plainly he would and the audience is expected to sympathise, given Phyllis's bossy narcissism and attachment to trivialising television (though logically some of the odium attached to the latter should adhere to Brad, whose job as a television advertising executive is inescapably bound up with what Phyllis represents). The restrictiveness of the world of social possibilities in *Weekend with Father* is very much dramatised in the person of Phyllis, whereas in the freer milieu of *Take Me to Town* and *Meet Me at the Fair* the familiar antithesis of career and marriage and the pejorative connotations of the female as actress are broken down.

The ending finds Brad's older daugher, Anne (Gigi Perreau again) engineering a plot rather similar to the one in *The Lady Pays Off* to bring everyone together. Overhearing her father saying on the phone that the marriage can't go on because of the children's opposition, she has a 'heart-to-heart' with him, in which she collapses the seeming antithesis between the adults' and the childrens' desires – 'How could Patty and I be happy if you're not?' This ideal solution is made possible by the cessation of the hostilities that have grown up between the two sets of children (foreshadowed by the moment earlier in the film where one of Jean's boys seems destined to be punished by the forest ranger and is protected in the crisis both by Brad and his daughters). Yet beneath the concluding symmetries certain doubts prevail, relating particularly to the characters' (both adults' and childrens') entrapment in stereotype which makes the resolution more hopeful than indubitable. Notably, the banishing of Don from serious consideration by Jean and the children does not come about from any sort of revised estimation of the over-simple ideas of manhood he embodies, but is precipitated by the he-man's single area of deviance from the norm, the passionate vegetarianism with its 'potassium cocktails' and 'Swiss gluten steaks' which he tries to force on the boys. So in the end the family could be said to be united (with surely sardonic implications) by a hamburger.

Has Anybody Seen My Gal? (1951)

Plot synopsis
When Samuel Fulton (Charles Coburn), one of 1920s America's richest men, makes his will, he decides to leave a great deal of money to the descendants of a fondly-remembered girl friend of his youth. She, in fact, preferred another man and her choice released Fulton to pursue undistractedly his business career.

Before endowing the smalltown family with the fortune, he visits them, pretending to be a Mr John Smith, to see whether they are the sort of family who will benefit from his philanthropy. He inveigles his way into their home by forcing himself upon them as a lodger.

The family, comfortable but not wealthy lower middle-class, consists of an amiable father who owns the local drugstore where Fulton/Smith finds employment as ice-cream apprentice to Rock Hudson, soda-jerking his way out of provincial life; an ultimately benign mother whose social pretensions do, for a spell, get the better of her and cause the temporary financial downfall of the family and the temporary disruption of the engagement between her older daughter and Rock Hudson's soda-jerk; and three charming children, two of whom are teenagers (Piper Laurie as Millicent, and William Reynolds, who plays two much more unpleasant sons in *All That Heaven Allows* and *There's Always Tomorrow*) and a young tomboy (Gigi Perreau).

Millicent's engagement is broken off by the mother when news of the $100,000 legacy from a nameless source reaches the family. Pushed by the mother's social ambition, they move to the top of the hill to live beside the snobs of the high bourgeoisie. Millicent is about to marry one of the rich kids from the neighbourhood until, with the news that the $100,000 is all spent, the family's world crashes. Their new-found friends abandon them and they return to their old house, Millicent to Dan, and Smith (also known as 'Gramps') takes his leave, in the knowledge that families do not need wealth to find happiness.

Deus ex machina

You don't know how important success is till you've had it.
— Naomi in *All I Desire*

Has Anybody Seen My Gal? hinges on a cliché of conservative ideology –
virtue (i.e. not wealth or social status) is the true nobility. Pull the other
one, the film seems to say. Telling good Americans that wealth is a respectable
enough ideal to strive after, but that it does not necessarily bring true happiness, is as good a way as any of convincing those who do not have it that
they should be content with their lot. In a society where, despite the pieties,
wealth is everything, the moral – whatever its general truth – can only have
a conservative force.

As Samuel G. Fulton, Charles Coburn, the instigator of the plot, is a split
figure (literally split, when he takes on his other name of John Smith to visit
the Blaisdells). Part Falstaff, disobeying the doctor's ban on cigars and soon
abandoning his diet for Mrs Blaisdell's stews, his rotundity another reminder
of those Bakhtinian categories lurking within the comic world, his fleshliness
(a 'full ton') is equally the emblem of his past entrepreneurial greed,
materialistic self-interest and rampant *laissez-faire* of 'a nation', as *Walden*
puts it, of debauched nations in general, 'without fancy or imagination,
whose vast abdomens betray them'. Yet beneath the second, the first still
lives in his disenchantment with his economic success and in distant
memories of love, and he turns himself back into a symbol of abundance as
he prepares to celebrate a (limited) collectivity in the release of at least a part
of his fortune to others. Typical of his two-tiered function as spirit of abundance and representative of capital, he prepares to hand his gifts to others,
yet only to the single set of others to whom he feels related, who represent
to him his former, less corrupted self. The name he takes on to do this, 'John
Smith', not only essentially symbolises the virtuous commonality, but is also
a name that calls up the story of Captain John Smith and Pocahontas (alluded
to in *The Lady Pays Off* where Evelyn crossly tells Diane that it is just a
legend). Again the implications point several ways. As Smith he is representative of advancing capitalism coming amongst the Blaisdells, civilisation's
Indians, the contented 'noble savages' of bourgeois myth. Bearing precious
gifts, obliquely seeking the Pocahontas of his past who symbolised the different directions his libido might have taken (that libido still vestigially alive
in its displaced passion for cigars), he is at once a principle of future life and
a bearer of corrupting presents.

As Samuel G. Fulton (the Samuel like Enoch's name in *Meet Me at the*

Fair, with biblical reverberations, here of authority and judgement) descends into the world of ordinary smalltown life like some *deus ex machina* from Greek drama, or like the duke in *Measure for Measure*, leaving the higher world to learn the perhaps more vital truths of the lower one, so, in a kind of criss-cross pattern, Mrs Blaisdell climbs from the lower to the higher and reaches her partial self-discovery when the family's new wealth disappears. For Fulton, dedication to big business has been a metaphorical death of Alcestis-like proportions (the Alcestis plot being a structure Sirk draws attention to in his remarks about *Magnificent Obsession*). His 'death' has meant life for his rival who went on to marry his sweetheart (Mrs Blaisdell's dead mother). The result of Fulton's defeat has been the flourishing of the all-American family with its smalltown contentments and stasis, which his ambition would have broken up, a myth which the industrial capitalism into which he advanced cultivates as sentimental vision of its true self even as it rushes to escape from it. This, of course, is an irony that the film cultivates, for while Fulton yearns to return to the small town, its citizens, with the ineffective exception of the Father (who is the unambitious mirror of the relative economic failure his wife's mother married), dream of climbing, or at least are willing to be pushed, in the opposite direction. Thus even the virtuous Dan Stebbins (Rock Hudson) is not content to work his way up from soda-jerk to store owner in the sticks, but seeks the opportunities of the metropolis where he may become the mirror-image of his rival Carl Pennier, whom the son of the family, Howard Blaisdell, already mimics.

The 1920s setting of the film and its quasi-musical form (fragmentary versions of songs like 'Five Foot Two', 'When the Red, Red Robin' and 'Gimmee a Little Kiss, Will Ya, Huh?') creates a pleasant aura of nostalgia, but its fairy-tale nature is pointed out by the film's epigraph: 'This is a story about money . . . Remember it?' Underneath, the hypocrisies of prohibition, class snobbery and sexual prurience are rampant, resulting in the comic victimisation of the innocent Smith who finds himself in jail accused of gambling, drinking and then petting with a young girl in a public place.

The psychic imprisonment of the Blaisdells in their new mansion is given further expression through effects of décor reminiscent of the melodramas, e.g. as Rodin-like statues of naked lovers embracing in the lifeless house are framed beside the characters, saying all that needs to be said about the petrification of desire, friendship, love and feeling that their new life in the better suburbs embodies.

As Mrs Blaisdell takes tango lessons (forgetting the dance's origins in the brothels of Buenos Aires), buys fashionable gowns and cultivates the socially desirable Pennicks in the hope of an advantageous marriage for her daughter, it is she and women's vanity that in the bourgeois comedy of manners (like Mrs Eyre in the prototype of comic celebrations of the virtues of the bourgeoisie, Dekker's *The Shoemaker's Holiday*), bears the most blame. Again we may feel merely mysogynistic conventions at work, but if we think of her in comparison with Mrs Kingshead in *No Room for the Groom*, the film that immediately follows this, we may be struck by the logic she enacts, the frustrated, wholly housebound woman's desire for power and prestige in the distorted forms of fashion and keeping up with the Joneses, providing a kind of preliminary working for the monster of the later film.

Yet even so the film is complex enough to realise that, just as the mythology exaggerates the purity of the small town, so it exaggerates the defects of the city; that *objets d'art* (part of Smith's disguise is that he is an artist who has worked in Paris), social graces, elegance, are not simply to be despised. If even Thoreau craved for tinned food after months of home-grown beans, we can see why 'John Smith' leaves the backwaters of provincial America for the civilised corruptions of his former life.

His intervention in the lives of the Blaisdell family has, ultimately, been pointless. Dan and Millie would have got married without him; Charles and Harriet Blaisdell end as they began, resigned to the modest contentment that the ideology of constant achievement and progression will render impossible. Being 'John Smith', then, has been a holiday for Samuel G. Fulton, a festive release as in the brief moment of extra-familial community he enjoys in the jail leading the singing of 'It Ain't Gonna Rain No More', but, as he returns, we know that Fulton, not Smith, still rules the world.

No Room for the Groom (1951)

Plot synopsis
In Las Vegas Alva Morrell (Tony Curtis), a young GI on furlough from the Korean War, marries Lee Kingshead (Piper Laurie) after eloping. When he comes down with chickenpox the marriage cannot be consummated and, after hospital, he has to leave immediately for the front. Lee and her mother (Spring Byington) are living in Alva's house in Suttersville, California, despite the mother's disapproval of Alva as a prospective husband.

Posing as an invalid, though secretly indulging her vices, Mrs Kingshead tyrannises Lee to the extent that her daughter has not been able to confess to the marriage. When Alva arrives back on another leave, he finds that Mrs Kingshead has brought into the house a vast collection of her cousins, invited to California to provide labour for the town's cement works, booming in the war economy, owned by Herman Strupel, the suitor she has favoured.

In the home that belonged to his paternal grandfather and where as a viniculturist he grows the vines that produce 'Delicioso' champagne, Alva is forced to queue for his own bathroom, get served last, if at all, at his table, suffer the persecutions of an abominable child, and even after the news of the marriage has been broken, be repeatedly frustrated in his attempts to sleep with his wife.

Mrs Kingshead plots to have the marriage annulled, Herman Strupel to get possession of Lee (who works as his secretary) and to drive a railway line for business reasons through Alva's home. Eventually Lee discovers that her mother's illness is faked and a seemingly final breach between husband and wife is healed, the film closing on the expectation of consummation and the promise of a relative-free future.

Eldorado

Gaily bedight,
A gallant knight,
In sunshine and in shadow,
Had journeyed long,
Singing a song
In search of Eldorado.

— Edgar Allan Poe

Though the most obvious structure of the film is one of long-delayed release ending with the young couple about to consummate their marriage and escape from the tyranny of the family's occupation of Alva's home, *No Room for the Groom* is the bleakest of the Sirk comedies, the one closest to the melodramas in its depiction of family relationships as tyranny and emotional frustration. The film's second shot has an ornate complexity that seems intent on announcing more than the obvious, Alva's and Lee's arrival in Las Vegas. In it we first see the couple through the bus window in which a neon sign reading 'Eldorado' is reflected. Las Vegas (literally, 'The Meadows'), as its name signifies, is a once pastoral locale that has become the purely material treasure place of a New World that has betrayed its ideals to materialism, a place where the riches of capitalism and the American dream of overnight success are offered in their most arbitrary form, the wheel of fortune. Seeking their own new world of romantic love and pastoral self-sufficiency (Alva's viniculture and 'Delicioso' champagne), the couple are all but oblivious to the meanings of the place they have come to and hardly register the conveyor-belt cynicism of the city's marriage industry. ('McCain's the cheapest, but McCoy's the fastest, and I oughta know, I tried them both', a passer-by, referring to rival marriage factories, advises them). But, as if unconsciously infected by the surroundings, Alva's desire immediately turns to illness as the fever of love turns out to be the fever of chickenpox.

Though Las Vegas, the place of tawdry glamour to which the innocent lovers have been drawn (a pessimistic thought in itself) for their elopement, disappears from the narrative, its replacement, smalltown Suttersville, seems to be repeating the pattern on a more intimate scale – changing socially and ethically as the large-scale capitalism of the cement works spreads its influence under the war economy. Even the site of eventual erotic release, Will Stubbins's apartment, speaks half of the pastoral, half of its antithesis, the print on the wall Bingham's 'Fur Traders Descending the Mississippi', signifying the pre-industrial, but the neon sign of the Strupel cement company visible through the window commenting on the translation of those traders into the fullness of industrial capitalism. (The name 'Suttersville' may also be Sirk's ironic echoing of Eisenstein's aborted American project, *Sutter's Gold* – also with a setting in pastoral California – whose critique of the capitalist ethos proved too radical for its sponsors, an attitude if anything more alive in 1951 than in the 30s).

The simplest trajectory of the narrative has the lovers escape the influence of the presiding deities of War, Chance and Capitalism that rule over its opening, but much is enacted to temper such optimism.

Alva (Tony Curtis in an early leading role) is a kind of minor foreshadowing of Ron Kirby (Rock Hudson) in *All That Heaven Allows,* a man in whom Thoreauvian virtues still marginally exist, though 'Delicioso' champagne suggests a diminution of their power almost to the point of parody. Rooted to the earth, he treasures his house as an inheritance from his grandfather to be handed on to his '*bambinos*'. As such he is far from the world of the grey flannel suit or even the television executive (Van Heflin) in *Weekend with Father* or slick urbanite (Stephen McNally) of *The Lady Pays Off.*

Alva's entrapment in a grotesque variant of the family, consisting of Mrs Kingshead's motley relatives, points to the central paradox of a film that both excoriates and idealises the family, presenting it on the one hand as rapacious, uncaring, manipulative, repressive (with only the unmarried Aunt Elsa an exception), while on the other looking forward optimistically (an optimism tempered by some doubt) to the new version of the unit that Alva and Lee struggle to initiate. This of course replays a familiar ambivalence in attitudes towards the family, pessimism about life in the intimate group versus the hope that this time things will be better. But in the film the opposition takes additionally a more particular form since the organisation in which Alva is trapped is not so much the 'isolated' or 'nuclear' family

defined by the sociologists of the 40s and 50s, but a huge parodic version of
the extended kinship family, doubly distanced from him because it is wholly
from his wife's side not his own. Even Lee has no feeling for them (*Mrs
Kingshead*: 'You ought to be proud of your heritage. Our family came out
to California in a covered wagon.' *Lee*: 'Now that I've seen them I know
why the wagon was covered'). In this grouping the exact status of relationships may even evade aficionados of kinship systems – 'She's your mother's
brother's brother-in-law's daughter, or is it your mother's brother's sister-in-
law's son . . . ?' Many family films of the period appear to be compensating
a felt lack in the growingly isolated parent–children family group by building
a more than nuclear structure, but this one, if it celebrates anything, endorses
an ultra-isolated family (*Alva*: 'You know, Lee, this is what I used to dream
about. You and me alone'). It is as if the attack on the vanishing extended
form of the family allows an intense idealisation of the 'isolated' or 'nuclear'
variant.

The vast oppressive family that takes over Alva's house is ruled by Mrs
Kingshead. The casting of Spring Byington in the role reverberates with
subversive possibility since that actress is none other than the idealised 'Mar-
mee', the wife–mother of Cukor's *Little Women*, turned into a Tartuffe-like
monster of comic hypocrisy, ruthlessly maintaining her power over her
daughter by the fiction of her illness. At the most conventional level she is
a grotesque version of masculine fears of matriarchal rule (stemming from
the female domination of the household and the American woman's mirroring
of male aggesssion in a culture prizing aggression). At another she is
extremely interesting in the way her name (Mrs Kingshead, i.e. the head of
the king, the ruler of the male) points not just to her assumption of authority
(preventing Lee from sleeping with Alva, trying to get the marriage annulled),
but also to her appropriation of envied but forbidden male activity. In the
licence of her seclusion she eats, drinks, smokes, gambles and reads stories
like 'Blondes are Dynamite' in *Love Confessions*, like Tartuffe cloaking sex
with piety as she hides her bedside reading, *Love Confessions*, in a copy of
the *Church News*. This phallic mother (a status symbolically underlined by
her association with the huge trophy fish in Will Stubbins's apartment) can
be read as a comically monstrous explosion of the cultural repression of the
daughter – visited back on her own daughter, Lee – that grasps for fulfilment
not only at patriarchal authoritarianism but also at forbidden patriarchal
excesses. Significantly Mrs Kingshead closely identifies herself with Herman
Strupel, Lee's industrialist suitor, who in turn identifies himself with her,
his own sexuality repressed almost as effectively, save when on occasions he
is betrayed by a slip of the tongue such as when he persistently confuses the

words 'neurotic' and 'erotic'.

Alva and Lee eventually escape from outmoded kinship relations to an idyll of nuclear bliss, but the ending is marked by various pessimistic ambiguities. Although Lee, dousing herself in the 'Fille d'Eve' perfume that signifies the triumph of the 'erotic' over the 'neurotic', sheds some of her extreme passiveness to become a more dominant character as she seduces Alva, it is hard to see her ignorance of what viniculture actually is, something stressed in the film's last moments, as pointing to a positive future, particularly since the huge phallic stuffed fish, clearly associated with the banished mother and all she represents, is so prominent in the final frames. Nor do the terms of Alva's reprimand to Lee when Strupel offers her a fur coat breed excessive optimism, for his experience with Mrs Kingshead seems simply to have confirmed him in the very patriarchalism which may be seen as the root cause of Mrs Kingshead's aberrant queenship. 'You didn't have a husband round to teach you any better.'

Meet me at the Fair (1952)

Plot synopsis

Tad Bailiss, a young orphan, escapes from the grim Springville Detention Centre. 'Doc' Tilbee, an itinerant showman and seller of fake medicines (Dan Dailey) and his partner Enoch Jones ('Scat Man' Crothers) pick him up. Tad is being sought by an earnest young woman, Zeralda Wing (Diana Lynn), who, shocked by the conditions of the centre, intends to get it reformed when she returns Tad to it. Zerelda is the fiancée of the District Attorney of Capital City who (though of course she doesn't know it) is in the pay of corrupt politicians, themselves seeking the boy in order to prevent anyone using him as a witness in the scandal that threatens them over funds misappropriated from the Boys' Home.

Zerelda tracks Tad down, but 'Doc' evades her, though not before possibilities of love are raised. In order to keep Tad with them and away from his pursuers, 'Doc' and Enoch head for the Fair at Capital City (on the principle that Tad will be least visible in the most obvious place). Here 'Doc' meets up with an old lover and professional partner, Clara Brink (Carole Matthews), who is still hoping to marry him, and persuades her to look after Tad for a while. Meanwhile Zerelda is approached by an elderly couple who claim to be relatives of Tad and wish to adopt him. When she tells 'Doc' of this, he meets the couple and reluctantly agrees to give Tad up to them, convinced that the boy needs education and a settled way of life. Shockingly it is revealed that (unknown to Zerelda) the couple are a pair of actors hired by the corrupt politicians, who then short-circuit their more involved plans by arresting the boy and putting him back in custody. 'Doc' and Enoch attempt to rescue Tad from the Detention Centre, but succeed only in freeing eleven other boys whom 'Doc' persuades Clara to harbour temporarily. In fact Zerelda, now alienated from her fiancé, has rescued Tad herself. Finally 'Doc' and his friends expose the politicians at a concert and 'Doc' decides to marry Zerelda. Accompanied by Tad and Enoch, they drive off and Clara reappears to close the film with a reprise of her festive song 'Meet Me at the Fair'.

Families and counterfamilies

And each heart is whispering, home, home, at last.
— Thomas Hood, quoted by 'Doc' to Zerelda

A starting point for the discussion of Sirk's injection of radical positive and/or critical elements into his comedies might well be – at a narrative, characterological and socially critical level more obvious to his majority audience than more formalist manoeuvres likely to be picked up only by a minority – the use of the black actor 'Scat Man' Crothers to play 'Doc' Tilbee's partner, Enoch Jones. Nothing in the role itself suggest that it has to be played by a black and, indeed, that constitutes part of the positive point, for Enoch's partnership with 'Doc' is never commented on favourably or unfavourably by anyone in the whole course of the film, but simply (remarkably) is an unremarkable narrative fact. If the three musicals (*Meet Me at the Fair, Take Me to Town* and *Has Anybody Seen My Gal?*) are, as Sirk felt, imbued with a nostalgia that makes each of them 'a little lyrical poem to the American past' (said of *Take Me to Town*, but true of all three), the nostalgia is complicated here, consisting of a gesture through an idealised past to a utopian future (rather than America's racist past and present, the latter given terrifying embodiment in the scene in *Imitation of Life* where the black girl is beaten up by her white boyfriend), made concrete in the happy scene where 'Scat Man' sings 'The Shiniest Mouth in Town' to a relaxedly happy crowd of white spectators. Enoch might, at first glance, seem to be conventionally encumbered with the good-natured naïve religiosity that is such an ambivalent stereotypical virtue in Hollywood's good blacks, but here his dignified biblical name is meaningful as he rescues Christianity from mere formalism (e.g. the Springville Detention Centre) by first of all insisting on rescuing Tad (he talks 'Doc' into it) and then freeing all the other boys from the home. Just as 'Doc', fraudulent though his title is in the strictly medical sense, is,

like Doctor Dan in *All That Heaven Allows*, a voice of life and health, for even if his elixir is fake, he himself is a force to defeat 'that tired, run-down feeling', so Enoch, recalling the enigmatic figure of the Old Testament who 'was not, for God took him', represents a vital religious feeling that overflows into charity, a feeling preserved perhaps from bourgeois taint in the subordinate world of black life and here oriented towards the present, unlike Annie's ornate black funeral in *Imitation of Life*.

Though Enoch must, through the inescapable basic proprieties that underlie the narrative, give way to 'Doc' and assume both a sexless and secondary role while 'Doc' is involved with both Clara and Zerelda, at the peripheries of the film the text – consciously or unconsciously – comments on itself, acting out the miscegenation which the ideological framework of the film cannot tolerate, for when Clara sings her version of 'Bill Bailey, Won't You Please Come Home' the male dancer who accompanies her in a dandified, erotic way is, though light-skinned, clearly negroid.

Enoch's blackness, and his playful but, we might feel in the context, meaningful assumption as barker of the role of Apache medicine man, also plays into the debate about the family which informs the action. Orphaned Tad (even if mature Bill Bailey doesn't) needs a home, which ultimately means a parent of each sex, but with whom will he share it? Springville Detention Centre, as 'Doc' tells Zerelda, doesn't sound right. On the other hand the ideally homely pair, the grandfatherly and grandmotherly couple from Wisconsin (*Racine*, Wisconsin to underline the discovery made later), 'nice people' redolent of healthy living and the more benign protestant virtues, to whom Zerelda and 'Doc' cede Tad for adoption, prove to be a couple of actors. The ironies of the narrative here not only find these two characters deceived, but also the audience who have shared their trusting perspective, only to have it betrayed. The reversal of expectation is more than a minor plot-shock, for it invites a scrutiny of the untrustworthiness of signs, asking us to consider how much our stereotypes of the family rest on a gallery of sentimental cameos that may deceive.

Tad's adopted on-the-road 'family', from which both the virtuous Zerelda and her corrupt fiancé, Chilton Corr, try to separate him becomes a kind of alternative fantasy image of the family detached as far as possible from the most static norms – peripatetic, imaginative (all 'Doc's' tall stories), joyfully religious in deed as well as word, protective but open rather than closed, its

---

Meet Me at the Fair

Comedy as carnival. In flight from the corruptions and entrapments of conventional society, Doc (Dan Dailey), Enoch ('Scat Man' Crothers), Tad (Chet Allen) and 'Spook' pursue alternative values.

double father figure 'Doc'/Enoch, both medicine man and preacher, good man and picaresque rogue, a beneficent version for a latter-day Huck of the actor–rogues 'The King' and 'The Duke' in *Huckleberry Finn*. Like Jim on the raft with Huck, a black man, who here is also a red man, makes up a psychic totality lost to white middle-class imagination.

The problem here (apart from the attempts of the authorities) is the lack of a mother figure, that vacuum caused by the missing parent of the other sex which runs through so many of the comedies and which provides an opportunity to debate here, as in *Take Me to Town*, the constitution of an ideal (as distinct from idealised) mother. Whereas in the other films the opposition provided by third parties is purely formal (for instance in *Take Me to Town* only the closest acolyte of Cotton Mather could prefer Mrs Stoffer to Vermilion), here 'Doc' is involved with two potential wives/ mothers, both such positive figures that when he chooses Zerelda it in no way involves a diminution or degradation of Clara.

Like Phyllis Reynolds in *Weekend with Father* and Vermilion in *Take Me to Town*, Clara Brink (the name Brink, like Zerelda's surname 'Wing' suggesting female mobility, change, a flight-to-be) is both a career woman and an actress, but very much associated with the positive world of the latter rather than with Phyllis's world of narcissism and fake glamour (cf. Lana Turner in *Imitation of Life*). Like Vermilion she combines the oppositions of unrepressed sexuality (she has been 'Doc's' unmarried lover) and mater- nity, marriage and career, release and tradition (in her dressing room Tad sings 'Ave Maria' to a backstage audience). It is the requirement of joining the puritan and the unconstrained, rather than any deficiency in her, that pushes Clara, who, played by Carole Mathews, has the further favour of a marked resemblance to Barbara Stanwyck, Sirk's favourite actress, to one side to make way for Zerelda (Diana Lynn) who bears a facial resemblance, though she is much younger and prettier, to Mrs Stoffer (Phyllis Stanley), Will's grim wife-to-be in *Take Me to Town*. The basic affinity between Zerelda and Clara is given a characteristically Sirkian touch as through colour (Zerelda's vivid yellow costume, Clara's bright greens) these women are seen to triumph over the moral drabness of their society.

The project of the love plot of *Meet Me at the Fair* – again a plot that pronounces man and wife simultaneously with 'Mummy and Daddy' – is not to marry 'Doc' to Clara, which would be to marry liberty to liberty, but to wed 'Doc's' freedom, imagination and eroticism to Zerelda's rectitude, moveable constraint and social concern. No doubt aspects of this coincide with conservative ideological patterns, remnants of the younger, purer woman being preferred to the sexually mature one, as well as the granting of greater freedom to the man, but, as if to resist any such simple placing, Clara has the last word in the film as she reappears in the post-narrative coda/epilogue as the presiding genius of the Fair (another Bakhtinian locale) with its release of oral and genital pleasures highlighted in the lyrics of her song. 'Doc's' obvious interest in the polygamous (he twice talks about Brigham Young to Zerelda) yields to monogamous choice, the rule of the family world as distinct from the erotic, but a choice which in some sense embraces both women rather than the one, since near the end of the narrative various of Clara's attributes pass to Zerelda. This is what is dramatised when Zerelda finds a copy of *As You Like It* in 'Doc's' wagon and begins to act out Pheobe's speech (III. v) to the mirror. This acting motif (Zerelda in some limited sense becoming Clara) is present again in her movement into 'Doc's' *Romeo and Juliet* fantasy late in the film.

Thus when an ideal family for Tad is finally made up, it consists of Father ('Doc') and stepfather (Enoch), mother (Zerelda), and a sort of fecund presiding godmother (Clara). It represent at once a commitment to stability and education (what Enoch warns Tad he will need :'Cowboys and rollin' stones don't get anywhere'), yet also preserves something of the cowboy and rolling stone, and a world wider than the wholly white vision of all those middle-class Hollywood comedies whose sole black presences are maids with names like Delilah. It is of course a fantasy, as the film's concern with fantasy in 'Doc's' dramatised tall stories tells us clearly. Sirk's preference is for implication rather than the tradition of overt didacticism of Godard via Brecht. There is nothing so didactic as the 'There must be happy endings: must, must, must' of *The Good Person of Sechzuan*, but the implication is similar, if subtler – the fantasy ending as an image of what ought to be over what is.

Take Me to Town (1952)

Plot synopsis

A woman (Ann Sheridan) has been arrested, though she is innocent, along with her corrupt lover, for fixing games in a casino. The time is nineteenth-century America, the place is the West.

She escapes from the Marshal to the Town of Timberland where, under the name of Vermilion O'Toole, she sings and dances at the Elite Opera House 'Palace of Chance' and hides out from the law. When her ex-lover, Newt Cole, and the Marshal show up, she seeks refuge in a house in rural Pine Top, the home of Will Hall (Sterling Hayden), a widowed and rugged lumberjack, with three young sons, who is also the local preacher. His boys have discovered Vermilion on a visit to Timberline looking for an alternative wife and mother to their father's probable choice, the prudish widow, Edna Stoffer.

Returning from the woods, Will is surprised to find Vermilion acting as the boys' housekeeper, but after he tastes her home cooking and is informed of how she has rescued the youngest son from a bear, he allows her to stay on.

Will encourages the outraged townspeople to take 'the Christian way' and welcome Vermilion into the community. When she helps to raise money for the new church building fund, she thinks up the idea of putting on a play.

When Newt and the Marshal again turn up, she is recognised, but the Marshal realises Vermilion must be innocent when she tries to help him arrest Newt. Newt escapes again, but is chased by Will, and the climax of their fight on the mountain coincides with that of the melodrama now being staged for the church fund. Will defeats Newt, marries Vermilion, who becomes a mother to the boys – a transformation she has ironically been observing throughout the narrative – and Sunday-School teacher at the new church.

There is Nothing Like a Dame

I'm a flaming redhead. If you play with fire you'll get burned.
> — Vermilion O'Toole in *Take Me to Town*

Take Me to Town dramatises the tensions in the national psyche between the Puritan ethic, the clean God-fearing life of Middle America, and the glossy razzmatazz life of the wicked city. While holiness and hard work are epitomised by Will Hall, the lumberjack preacher, the corruptions of the urban world are characterised by 'Vermilion O'Toole', the town floozy of the title song, astray in the wilderness and accused by a local zealot of being there on the Devil's business.

The film's primary focus is on the culture's desire to reconcile notions of clean family living with values not too drastically anti-life and anti-sex. In this it takes up some of the interests of its predecessor, *Meet Me at the Fair*, but in one way is more interesting, for it drops the Zerelda Wing figure and leaves the field and hero to Clara as reconstituted in Vermilion. By the end of the film Vermilion – a mellower Ann Sheridan in the twilight of her career, but still with something of the 'oomph-girl' aura – will have progressed from familial and sexual outcast to almost fully socialised and respected member of the community, in the process achieving the seemingly impossible combination of what had seemed like polar opposites. The transition is neatly encapsuled in the rhyming ballad about the heroine with which the film begins and ends, with crucially altered lyrics at the end signalling her recuperation by the community. The lyrics at the beginning are:

> This is the tale of Vermilion O'Toole
> Who started a crime wave
> When she was in school.
> At first she stole kisses,
> And then she stole hearts.
> The Warden says this is
> The way it all starts.

The alliance between sex and criminality, almost axiomatic to the Puritan mentality, a conviction that at its crudest only tolerates sexuality as reproduction, is expressed through Old-Testament-inspired clichés in which Vermilion, a daughter of Eve, has stolen the virtues of the innocent male. Her disruptive sexuality is only ultimately controllable either through public acknowledgement of her evil, marked if not by a scarlet letter then by her profession as burlesque entertainer at Palaces of Chance, or, eventually by marriage. Before the transformation and containment are complete the film takes a comic look at the repressive mechanisms of culture.

Rose, the Elite's brassy doyenne, points to them when she travels into the heart of Middle America, and with innuendo worthy of Mae West, tugs at the repressed sexuality of Timberline's pent-up males, luring them with the gaudy attractions of her anti-Walden empire of the senses – 'Us city girls is partial to you country [matters?] men. They don't grow so big in the city.' Sidling up to a rugged blacksmith, she cries 'Timber!' as he crashes down some manly tool on an anvil. The phallic joke, too, in all the pines and timbers, is picked up again after Vermilion's decision to follow the three boys into the wilderness: the camera cuts away from the characters and in a montage sequence concentrates on a series of low-angle shots of the sky-high pine trees, at first tall and sturdy emblems of phallic power, but then cut down and collapsing. Sex has been so repressed that the only snap it has left, as Vermilion complains to Edna Stoffer, is in her garter; so efficiently displaced that when even Will Hall, who initially has such a stifling conception of motherhood he is ready to marry Mrs Stoffer, is attracted to Vermilion it has to be made out it is in no way related to her voluptuousness (epitomised by an ample bosom constantly on the verge of spilling out of her dress), but for her meat pies. As one of the little sons explains: *Boy:* 'Miss O'Toole, I think he likes you.' *Vermilion:* 'What makes you think that?' *Boy:* 'The way he looked at your meat pies!' From the child's point of view meat pies may well be a priority, but though as audience we are invited to approve of 'Bucket' and his brothers' search for a woman who will be both mother/nurse and satisfactory erotic prototype for their later life, the film also suggests the problems of a culture so given to displacement that it finds great difficulty in reconciling the maternal and sexual functions of women. The film suggests in many ways that what the boys find easy to do, accept Vermilion both as someone who makes pies and smells nice (perfume or more natural female odours?) the men find it harder. Displaced into the shadier corners of burlesque, the repressed nevertheless rages on, not least in Vermilion's red hair and the extraordinary connotations of her name, conjuring up no less than a post-virginal blood covered member.

That a preacher should pave the way towards the rehabilitation of a woman in the clutches of the Devil is something that seems to chime in with Sirk's conviction that Christianity has often been a radical force for good as well as evil. 'The Christian Way', as Will puts it, is charity, mercy and love, a plea for self-improvement and the raising of expectations. Before her conversion Vermilion has expected nothing of her men (Newt is clearly an exploiter), and now, with Will, she has more. On the other hand, as Thoreau argues, Christianity tends to teach reverence rather than self-awareness. From St Paul ('Wives submit yourselves to your own husbands . . . Children obey your parents in all things', *Colossians* 3,18-21) down to Cardinal Spellman and the conservative papacy of Pius XII in the 1940s and 1950s, not to mention the patriachalism of the American low churches, 'decent' women have been badgered into accepting that their only true place is in the home.

> This was the story of Vermilion O'Toole
> Who now is a teacher
> In the new Sunday School.
> She has a cute family
> As you ever saw,
> The former O'Toole
> Who is now known as 'Maw'.

As the anonymous balladeer sings about Vermilion's transformation, our last image of this provincial Mary Magdalen, following the shot of her teaching children at Sunday School, is as she troops with the family (the three children and Will) into the river for a family swim, all ready for the purgation of their unruly desires in a Pine Top River Jordan, all signalling their conformity to the dullest Middle American values in their wearing identical bathing costumes, which in their stripes even hint at prison uniforms. Yet

Take Me to Town
Küche, Kirche und Kinder? An essay in Sirkian ironies. Will Hall (Sterling Hayden), the preacherman, confronts the baroquely named Vermilion O'Toole (Ann Sheridan). His little sons more freely admire their Mom-to-be's combination of allure and domesticity.

172

we might take heart from the colour symbolism of the stripes, red and white, the colours of desire and purity, suggesting that Vermilion as the film's main force for life will be allowed to spread a little red into Will's exaggerated purity, just as she will take some of his lily-white virtue to moderate her carnality in the new family life to which she will henceforth belong.

As ever, in the comedies we have been discussing, the film's mode is to mix realism and fantasy, comedy with melodrama. The 'showgirl and the preacher' narrative has all the makings of high melodrama, but Vermilion's humour, the antics of the preacher's sons and various other elements ensure that comedy triumphs. This is reinforced by the anti-illusionistic, typically Sirkian device of distancing the audience from the narrative through *mise-en-abyme* structures which reach their climax at the end of the film. As the incidents of the outer comic frame reach a crescendo, so those of the inner melodrama frame (the play performed for the church building fund, significantly entitled *The Lady's Good Name, A Melodrama in Three Acts*) reach theirs, reminding us again of the symbolic relation of the two modes and their view of the family. Equally, as Will and Vermilion prepare to share their lives, we might remember the formulaic closing line of the boys' bedtime stories, 'What happened ever after?' As in the other comedies, as in the melodramas, there is no real closure – the apparent certainties of happiness are offered through a perspective of ambiguity.

5

'Starting over'

Romantic comedy today

NOTES TOWARDS A DEFINITION OF CONTEMPORARY ROMANTIC COMEDY

Divorced husbands' and wives' seminars

In *Starting Over* (Alan Pakula, 1979) the recently divorced hero, Phil (Burt Reynolds), attends a therapy group for divorced husbands which is regularly interrupted by the arrival of a similar group of divorced wives demanding possession of their room. Apprehension and hostility are expressed on both sides (a male 'Fuck off!', an antiphonal female 'Eat shit!'). Whenever the group meets, religious music is heard faintly in the background. Later it is revealed that the meeting place is next door to a church. This neat piece of symbolism reminds us of the once sacramental status of marriage (cf. the power of the scene in *Woman of the Year* where Katharine Hepburn attends her aunt's wedding) – in which, except for widow and widower, the idea of 'starting over' did not apply. It also reminds us of the quasi-religious burden of expectation that marriage bears in a contemporary society where sexual love is felt as the highest good, not merely a universal urge or the ground of social life. However much the actual forms of the marriage service are assaulted in recent films (*The Graduate*, 1967, *Semi-Tough*, 1977, and *Private Benjamin*, 1980, all end with broken wedding ceremonies rather than the transformed ceremony – i.e. from wrong partner to right partner – of a film like *The Philadelphia Story*), the general presupposition, or, at least, hope is that somewhere along the path of relationship and serial monogamy things will be, as Jessie (Candice Bergen), Phil's wife, sings, 'Better than Ever'. At the end of *Starting Over*, just before the hero goes to be reconciled with his girlfriend, there is a brief scene in which a Christmas *rapprochement* takes place between the ex-husbands' and wives' groups, halting and nervous, like hostile troops from the Great War trenches for a moment forgetting their differences. Such a moment could not be imagined taking place in, say, *Midnight* or *Bringing Up Baby*, so far are the earlier films from feeling that they are obliged to place their 'pursuits of happiness' (Stanley Cavell's felicitous phrase) within a general statement about the difficulties of relationships between men and women. Romantic comedy, as distinct from the non-romantic comedy of the sexes, by definition ends with the hopeful triumph of romantic love, but in the modern variant not only are its costs calculated along with its rewards, but also its almost infinite difficulties. Perhaps today only in a film whose voice justifies itself by novelty and a sense of cultural suppression (e.g. Donna Dietch's lesbian 'woman's picture', *Desert Hearts*, 1985) can a sophisticated film-maker simply present old-fashioned romantic affirmations.

Semi-tough or impossible?

Brian Henderson has provided the only attempt to map the theoretical terrain of present-day romantic comedy. In 'Romantic comedy today: semi-tough or impossible?' he reaches the conclusion that romantic comedy may indeed now be impossible, or, more temporisingly, be 'vaguely problematic, extinct or transformed'. Though Henderson is a highly sophisticated writer with a considerable range of reference to the theory of comedy, his argument is almost wholly pinned to an analysis of a single film, *Semi-Tough* (Michael Ritchie, 1977). Though very intelligent, extrapolations from such a narrow sample must run the risk of contradiction. His major conclusions may be summarised thus: (a) The film *Semi-Tough* demonstrates by its interest in satire at the expense of romantic material, 'a loss of faith in the interest of romance as a subject'. (b) The present may be forming a future that will bring changes that presage 'the death of romantic comedy'. 'Romantic comedy posited men and women willing to meet on a common ground and to engage all their faculties and capacities in sexual dialectic . . . it seems that when the new self pulls itself together, it is away from the ground of full sexual dialectic.' (c) 'Social and political changes have transformed the making and reception of romantic comedy.' These changes include growing divorce, single parenting, feminism, gay rights and, above all, 'the rise of the working woman'. Henderson varies between diagnosing growing pains and terminal illess. The bravura (or silliness) of theorising from a single not wholly representative instance possibly leads him to a too generalising and simplifying negative. Nevertheless he is right that major tensions, problematics and transformations are to be perceived.

Our love is here to stay?

The comedy of the sexes, non-romantic comedy, comedy of the events arising from the sexual impulses as they intersect with the demands of cultural life, priapic comedy which may be as crude as *Porky's* (1982) or as sophisticted – indeed quasi-tragic – as *Shampoo* (1975), is hardly in danger of disappearing. Though radical Freudian-influenced critics often forget how much the meaning of psychoanalysis is grounded in the necessity of repression (the amount demanded is open to debate, but the principle stands), such comedy is universal. Which is to say that sexuality is of its nature incapable of being organised without frustrations, disappointments and forbearings (to say the least!), though certain modes of organisation in certain conditions may to some degree lessen those elements that can be lessened. If such a definition stresses the negative, the comedy of repression, it is clear that there also exists a comedy of the celebration of the pleasures and meanings of sexuality, and that most sexual comedy combines the two. If criticism puzzles more over the fate of romantic than of non-romantic comedy, it is because the former involves specifics that are in a state of flux in advanced Western cultures. For instance, how much does the nexus of attitudes at the centre of romantic comedy depend upon an extreme cultural differentiation of the sexes based upon the passivity and subordination of women? Or is mutual delight in differences that are not necessarily hierarchical possible? Is it too naïvely optimistic to read the Hollywood romantic comedy as a profound unconscious meditation on these two questions?

Audience/audiences

In *Jokes and their Relation to the Unconscious* Freud is very much aware of the problems of audience reception of jokes, comedy and humour. For instance, in the chapter 'Jokes as a Social Process' he quotes *Love's Labour's Lost:*

> A jest's prosperity lies in the ear
> Of him that hears it, never in the tongue
> Of him that made it.

In a later chapter he writes:

> The comic is greatly interfered with if the situation from which it ought to develop gives rise at the same time to a release of strong affect . . . The affects, disposition and attitude of the individual in each particular case makes it under-

standable that the comic emerges and vanishes according to the standpoint of each particular person, and that an absolute comic exists in only exceptional circumstances.

The subjects of male and female sexuality and their relation with each other today unmistakably constitute an area that, touched on, tends to generate 'a release of strong affect', especially among sections that see themselves in some sense as marginalised and oppressed. While it has often been said (usually belittlingly) that women think differently from men, it is only recently that the implications of such a view have been seriously formulated into attempts to theorise audience by gender (e.g. Laura Mulvey and others). Primitive though such attempts may be, and with them a parallel interest in male homosexual and lesbian responses, they very much complicate the idea of audience and further undermine the sense of 'an absolute comic'. Further, the sense of part of the audience disapproving may create displeasure where there was originally pleasure. For instance, Doris's (Barbra Streisand's) 'fag'-centred tirades in *The Owl and the Pussycat* (Herbert Ross, 1970), or Vicky Alessio's (Glenda Jackson's) quip about wanting to be raped in *A Touch of Class* (Melvin Frank, 1973) may now produce embarrassment in 'liberal' audiences who would have laughed unembarrassedly when the films were first released. A sense of probable fragmentation of audience response undoubtedly makes much contemporary comedy edgily nervous. Who will laugh at what? How can particular potentially hostile sectors be placated? Such questions did not force themselves upon the makers of, say, *The Awful Truth*.

Loving by the book

How often the heroes and heroines of contemporary romantic comedies are pictured reading, and how little those of earlier films – an emblem of their happy unself-consciousness. (*The Shop Around the Corner* is a notable exception, but there the characters read novels rather than polemics.) Examples are Vicky Alessio with *The Female Eunuch* in *A Touch of Class*; Susan showing Gary his wife, Roberta's, secret bedroom word-hoard in *Desperately Seeking Susan – How to Be Your Own Best Friend*, *I'm OK, You're OK* and *Dr Ruth's Guide to Good Sex*; Eli's obsessive researching of the psychology and physiology of sex in popular scientific books and journals in *Can She Bake a Cherry Pie?*; Charlie Partanna's readings in the popularised psychology of love in the magazines in *Prizzi's Honor*; the example from *Tootsie* discussed below.

Endings

The large question of the intricate relation, the mass of discontinuities within continuities, or vice versa, of contemporary to 'classical' Hollywood comedy, can at least be approached in a shorthand way by a consideration of the comic ending. To say that the endings of earlier romantic comedies are optimistic and full is not to say that their optimism is simply naïve. Ambivalence and doubt have their subordinate place within those narratives, but they do give us myths of lasting love, an energy devoted to ideals of happiness which overrides doubt even where it is spoken. Their art is ultimately an art of the ideal. Contemporary romantic comedy still grasps at the ideal, but in a way that stresses difficulty and scepticism, with the drift into nihilism of films like *Carnal Knowledge* and *Shampoo* always possible; likewise the movement towards uncoupled self-assertion in the post-feminist comedy of independence (e.g. *Private Benjamin*, Howard Zieff, 1980, in which the Goldie Hawn character refuses at the altar her third marriage and ends assertively alone). Some key examples: *Blume in Love* (Paul Mazursky, 1973) threads its way between versions of this Scylla and Charybdis with a hero (Blume – George Segal) whose obsessive, angst-ridden love for his ex-wife threatens to break the bounds of the comic, and a heroine, his wife, Nina (Susan Anspach), threatening to move beyond the couple. The end of the film sees the pair reunited, with the birth of their child imminent, though the child has been conceived during Blume's rape of Nina. However, Nina, in reaccepting Blume, refuses to marry him, so that although the film is a report from a male perspective, the female largely dictates the terms of reunion, denying that she is his wife, so that he laboriously refers to her as 'the mother of my daughter'. Further, with its closing scene in Venice, Italy, rather than the Venice, California, that is its everyday world, the wish-fulfilment aspects of the closure are admitted and even heightened, with the band in the square playing the *Liebestod* from *Tristan und Isolde*. (A comparable but less highly-wrought instance is *10* (Blake Edwards, 1979), where Sam (Julie Andrews) accepts back George (Dudley Moore) after his adventure, but also refuses to marry him, though much less decisively than is the case with Nina.) In *Starting Over* the happy closure which reunites Phil with Marilyn (Jill Clayburgh) is not only set within a perspective of common divorce and marital breakdown, but is emotionally complicated by the film's refusal to make the third party, here Jessie, Phil's ex-wife (Candice Bergen), in any way like the easily dispensable third party of earlier romantic comedy (e.g. Ralph Bellamy in *The Awful Truth* and *His Girl Friday*, Miss Swallow in

Bringing Up Baby). Though the narrative hurriedly skates over the failure
of the attempt Jessie and Phil make to reorganise a comedy of remarriage
after their divorce, in various places her feelings are given prominence,
particularly in the extraordinary and ludicrous scene, both touching and
highly embarrassing, where she courts him with her song 'Better than Ever'.
And though the narrative finally abandons her to follow Phil and Marilyn,
it is Jessie's voice that sings over the final images, reasserting her presence
over her absence, and her pain and loss, as well as the loss any choice by
Phil involves. An exemplary instance of the strain attending closure in contemporary versions of the sub-genre is the ending of *Bob and Carol and Ted
and Alice* (Mazursky, 1969) where after the couples have felt unable to have
group sex, the film pushes into a final movement which, calling on the
European precedent of Fellini's *8½*, goes outside linear narrative realism by
introducing a kind of circus of couples (including a Red Indian and a
homosexual pair), who first of all seem to fall apart to mingle promiscuously,
but then drift back into the pairings, their actions accompanied by a curious
song, the burden of which is a defence of the couple, not so much in terms
of morality as of expediency – i.e. one relationship is difficult enough! The
ending of *Can She Bake a Cherry Pie?* (Henry Jaglom, 1983) may be taken
as an exemplar of a certain thickening of subjective reality which draws
contemporary films away from the ideal forms of earlier ones. As Henderson
remarks, the past of the the characters in 'classical' comedies is unspoken.
Here, though, Eli's photos and home movies speak disruptively of a
remembered past not obliterated by the present. We confess ourselves not
sure whether the couple dancing on the film are a younger Eli with his
wife/girlfriend, or his parents, but in either case the film closes on a dream
of the past to which Astaire's singing of 'The Way You Look Tonight' adds
the further dimension of a nostalgic lament for simpler, fuller, impossible
versions of romance.

Elmo and others

Committed though they are to the couple, recent romantic comedies often
dramatise, through one of the characters, an attitude casually inimical to
romantic love, which suggests that somehow it belongs to an archaic phase
of perception and behaviour. Elmo (Kris Kristofferson), Nina's peripatetic
lover in *Blume in Love* who is puzzled when asked by Blume if he loves her
and later just decides it is 'time to split', is one of these, as are three female
characters who come immediately to mind – Susan (Madonna) in *Desperately
Seeking Susan* (1985), the Kelly Le Brock character in *The Woman in Red*,

and Jenny (Bo Derek) in *10*, the last two married, yet finding time for sex with the heroes that the idealising males find too uncommitted. The films usually seem to want the watcher to feel that these characters' attitudes miss out on certain valuable feelings, are in some way lightweight, devoid of gravity, but nevertheless their laid-backness troubles and questions the romantic premises of the narratives.

Difference/sameness: sameness/difference

The perennial structuring principle of romantic comedy, but raised to a new height of self-consciousness in the contemporary cinema. What we would call conservative comedy ('progressive' and 'regressive' are terms of judgement widely and variably used in contemporary criticism, often to denote simply a universalisation of the writer's minority sexual orientation) is ordered by the priority encoded in the first pairing, while what we would call more radical comedy is ordered by that in the second, the search for definitions of difference not caught up in subordination and hierarchy. In certain ways these motions are more clearly traced in films of a less inventive or even banal kind where the desire to give a two-way pleasure (affirmation of the pleasures of sexual difference/pleasure in the destruction of outmoded signs of difference) is highly transparent, less a complex renegotiation of categories in the post-feminist era than a contradictory play of opposites, having it both ways. *A Touch of Class*, in its time (1970) very popular, is a good example, a film that now looks in many ways merely a product of faded chic and trendy implausibility (the heroine being kept in a flat in Macclesfield Street, of all places!). Yet its great success rested on its play with difference and sameness which, even in this rather low-grade instance, is not wholly covered by the concepts of 'inoculation' and 'recuperation' (the former the view that bourgeois ideology – the film industry – allows a little radicalism but only in order to defuse it). On the one hand, Glenda Jackson, her beauty rather mundane and minatory, is an image of female independence – attractive rather than glamorous, unawed, professional, ready with the putdown for male arrogance, throwing around slightly shocking terms like 'having it off'. But, on the other hand, there is an exceedingly banal plot movement which, with extreme implausibility given her character, turns her into a mistress passively kept in a flat waiting for the odd visit from her married lover (George Segal), and in doing so blatantly reaffirms male power (it is only he who can end the affair). Rather than being worked into any convincing pattern, the contradiction exists in unmediated blatancy, though it should be said that a purely narrative-based interpretation, emphasising the film's old-fashioned closure, would underestimate the pervasive force of the Jackson persona and what it signifies. In *The Main Event* (Howard Zieff, 1979) the handling of the dichotomy is more ingenious, a sort of low-level paradigm of the sub-genre's workings. The film begins as Hilary (Streisand), a brilliant businesswoman, invents a unisex perfume, thus strongly stating sameness (dissolution in unisex of traditional sexual difference, already undermined by her work success). Immediately, in reply to this, debt forces her to become a manager in the ultra-masculine world of boxing, a world of male otherness where ritualised aggression insists on biological difference. The narrative then proceeds with its series of oppositions/relations – male/ female; boxing/fashion; O'Neal/Streisand – but with the meanings merged and modified as well as opposed. Thus: her power over him as manager, reversing the roles of *Pat and Mike;* her dynamic persona contrasted with his passivity; his 'pretty boy' looks contrasted with her kooky ones (though in order to apply the brakes, to prevent too great a dissolution of roles, the great 'fight that never was' is a grudge match that has as its source an opponent's taunt of effeteness).

The words, the act

The last section of Henderson's argument revolves around the question the heroine of *Semi-Tough* addresses to the hero – 'How come we never fucked?' – as signalling the death of romantic comedy. The blatancy of this query, both shocking and, by now, almost unremarkable, can be paralleled in film after film. Henderson is clearly right in seeing displacement and sublimation into metaphor as the grounds of the art of the romantic comedy of the past, producing the delicate 'libidinal glow' of comedies like *Bringing Up Baby,* and in seeing the difficulties for contemporary romantic (as distinct from non-romantic) comedy consequent upon this lowered threshold of the forbidden. From the vantage point of the present and the forseeable future, where not only does it seem that almost 'anything goes' in the realm of sexual representation but also a heavy weight of material that is directly unpleasurable is allowed display, our attachment to the earlier comedies is to something close yet very distant, a nostalgia for an art of graceful allusiveness and lightness. The problem of the sexual explicitness of contemporary romantic comedy is that it is suited to display the erotic base, but not the superstructure of feelings deriving from it, which precisely reverses the powers and limitations of earlier comedy. In the latter, the absence of the directly sexual makes for one form of unreality; in the former, its accentuated presence makes for another. Yet when these heroes and heroines talk of 'fucking', in almost all cases we are meant to know that they use a shorthand term, whether in self-assertion, self-protectiveness, mere trendiness, or a desire to ballast flights of romance with their origins in the sexual act; that 'fucking' (even when an obsessive like Eli in *Can She Bake a Cherry Pie?* tries to prove his love by physiological tests during intercourse) is somehow more with the right partner, not quite coterminous with the basic physiology of the act. For better or worse (and the films see the worse as well as the better) romantic monogamy survives, even in a character like Charlie Partanna in *Prizzi's Honor* (1985) with his heartfelt distinctions between 'love' and merely 'in love'.

Girls on top

An often reiterated moment in the literal depiction of sexual relations meditated above: the woman is seen above the man, sometimes followed by a return to the man-on-top position. The significance of this is openly stated in *The Owl and the Pussycat* (1970) where Felix Sherman resists Doris's usurpation and insists on 'a simple respect for tradition'. Banal and simple though the symbolism is (and liable to deceive, since Larry's victimised girlfriend in *Can She Bake a Cherry Pie?* wears a T-shirt that proclaims 'A Century of Women on Top'), it functions as a sign of change and of desired or actual shifts in power.

'I like myself'

Brian Henderson notes *Semi-Tough's* cultivation of satire of 'psychotherapies, body therapies, and human potential movements' at the expense of the matter of romance. Clearly this thematic, most defined perhaps in Mazursky's films, but observable across the sub-genre (e.g. the therapy group in *Starting Over;* Roberta's reading in *Desperately Seeking Susan*) is not random but, rather, intimately related to what it tends to displace – whether we define it as a salutary return to older philosophical traditions of transcendence through the self rather than the couple, or whether we see it as another manifestation of 'the culture of narcissism' (possibly as both). Perhaps, too, Henderson's term 'lampooning' is not quite the most accurate for what is going on. In the historically defining instance, *Bob and Carol and Ted and Alice* (1969), the opening sequence concentrates on a range of body and soul therapies while the soundtrack plays the Hallelujah Chorus and 'I Know that My Redeemer Liveth' from Handel's *Messiah*. Here the effects seem to us complex, relying in part on our criticism of such narcissism, but at the same time appealing to growing scepticism about romantic love as the source of transcendence, and to changing ideas of self-definition and self-fulfilment.

Masculine-feminine: the marginalisation of romance

In the late 1980s self-definition is often seen in terms of one's sexuality – the meaning of one's maleness or, more especially, femaleness. Such concerns, appearing in the Hollywood romantic comedy, do not wholly disrupt the traditional dynamic of the heterosexual couple moving towards union, but they do in certain key instances push it away from the centre and towards the margins of the narrative. Two such films, antithetical in almost every other aspect, are the Clint Eastwood comedy *Any Which Way You Can* (Van Horn, 1980) and *Desperately Seeking Susan* (Susan Seidelman, 1985), the one concerned with protecting a bedrock of 'masculine' activities and concerns for an audience that in a very untheorised, gut-reaction way feels itself under threat, the other, very much feminist-influenced, appealing to an audience receptive to sexual–political changes. Both are in some sense structured around heterosexual romances, in the first case that of Philo Beddoes (Clint Eastwood) with Lynne (Sondra Locke), in the second Roberta's (Rosanna Arquette's) with Des, and Susan's (Madonna's) with Jim. But in both cases it is the process of definition of 'masculinity' or 'femininity' which is the main interest of the film, Roberta's search for/identification with Susan, Philo's relations with Wilson, the Hell's Angels, and Clyde, the orangutan, the last a sort of masculinised, literally redneck version of Baby in the classic film. *Any Which Way* begins with an extra-narrative duet in which Eastwood and Ray Charles sing, *amigo* to *compadre*, about male companionship and 'all the women we've been through', while *Desperately Seeking Susan* has in fact two endings, the first minor, celebrating the couples, the second major, the newsreel clip of Susan raising Roberta's hand in gynopsychic triumph.

Prizzi's Honor (John Huston, 1985)

A fascinating cross-generic film, the serious revisionist gangster film as romantic comedy, paralleling the tendency of contemporary romantic comedy to invade melodramatic modes (e.g. *Blume in Love* with its tormented narrative overvoice, contradicting Henderson's blanket assertion, as, less interestingly, does *The Woman in Red*, that romantic comedy is all *histoire* and no *énonciation*). A 'family romance', the Mafia providing an extreme image of the pressures of a brutally competitive society. Hero and heroine meet, as they ideally should, as equals, but in this society as *mafioso* / hit-man and tax-consultant / hit-woman. Maerose makes the generalising point to Charlie: 'You and she is in the same line of business . . . You are lucky you found each other . . . She's an American. She had a chance to make a buck and grabbed it.' In the film's penultimate scene the lovers prepare for bed with no option but to kill each other. The film opens up in at least one major strand of its meaning to a reading that is a dance of intelligence around the survivals and corruptions of love (in which Charlie Partanna is so philosophically interested) in a ruthlessly predatory society.

Carnal Knowledge: masculine guilt and dystopia

In certain key comedies of the 70s and 80s masculine guilt becomes a basic, if not the basic thematic of the contemporary sub-genre – guilt at male objectification of women, at patriarchal dominance, at the unequal rewards and divisions of labour. This issues at the extremes in either nervously self-conscious *utopian* comedies or flagellantly *dystopian* ones where romance turns to satire or something close to it. The utopian is the norm since comedy tends to reconciliation, and such films as *Tootsie* and *Victor Victoria*, discussed in detail below, dramatise reconciliation following (mostly male) reorienta-tion. Dystopic comedy (much rarer in the popular Hollywood cinema, though more common in the European, e.g. the films of Marco Ferreri and Fellini's *Casanova* and *City of Women*) plays out the nightmare that relations between the sexes may now indeed be impossible. Both kinds are in their own ways fuelled by male guilt, with utopian comedy overtly displaying its good, reparative intentions. *Carnal Knowledge* (Mike Nichols, 1971), perhaps the closest to a purely dystopic comedy of the sexes that a cinema committed to optimism has produced (*Who's Afraid of Virginia Woolf?* also by Nichols, 1966, is a second instance, but with its genesis in the art theatre) embraces that guilt to a massive degree. The oddity of its low reputation among feminist critics presumably comes from a dismay that the film's women (historically and ideologically trapped like its men) are unable to formulate alternatives to the disastrous misperceptions of the males, and perhaps from the critics' misperception that a film about misogyny is bound itself to be misogynistic. *Carnal Knowledge* dramatises – as is signalled in the opening conversation between Nicholson and Garfunkel – what is analysed in the essay 'On the universal tendency to debasement in the sphere of love', the common failure in men to bind together the two currents of 'the affectionate' and 'the sensual' which together constitute 'a completely normal attitude in love'. The poles of predatory masculine aggression and idealising sensitivity are represented by Jonathan (Nicholson) and Sandy (Garfunkel) in a series of tableaux that progress from college days to the present. While Sandy moves from calf love to sanitised liberal marriage to ludicrous idealisation of a flower-child ('She's

my love-teacher . . . in a lot of ways she's older than I am'), Jonathan takes
the road of excessive objectification of female sexuality ('I would have settled
for the legs if she'd had just two more inches here and three more here!').
Jonathan's actual fear of women, activated by any resistance of independence
on their part ('The women today are better hung than the men!'), though
he is in fact driven almost to madness by Bobby's (Ann Margret's) exaggerated passivity, leads eventually to his psychic impotence and the two terrible
scenes where, first, he compères his slide show of the women in his life,
'Ballbusters on Parade!', and, second, where he is visited by the call-girl
played by Rita Moreno. This second is a sexual rite built around his economic
power, his self-sufficiency and a grotesque celebration of his male strength.
'A man', she croons, 'who inspires worship because he has no need for any
woman because he has himself.' Here the reciprocity of romantic comedy is
reduced to the mocking female's observation of a male sexuality completely
turned in on itself, the phallus wholly, disastrously, perceived by its owner
as the instrument of power and self-assertion. The hopelessness of the film
– but a critical rather than a luxurious hopelessness – is increased by its
women, the poles of masochistic passivity in Bobby, the mirror-image of
male aggression in Cindy, with Susan reduced early in the film to the off-
screen nullity of the taken-for-granted wife. If Jack Nicholson (who finally
gets to play the devil in *The Witches of Eastwick*) preserves a kind of Miltonic
Satanic status and pathos for Jonathan it is because his character, unlike
Garfunkel's, is capable of perceiving the depths of his own degradation,
pushing the satiric comedy *à thèse* into regions of mourning for the perverted
powers of masculinity.

The death of masculinity?
Jack Nicholson, the hero and comedy

In some notes on *Raging Bull*, the feminist critic Pam Cook raises central
questions pushed to the margins in much sexual-political criticism when she
writes of the spectacle of the decline of the boxer Jake LaMotta (Robert DeNiro).

> In the tragic resolution of the film we're asked to look with pity on the shell of a
> man who has lost all the attributes necessary to masculinity. Some might want to
> celebrate that loss (*Schadenfreude*, pleasure in another's misfortune is built into
> tragedy), and there is, I think, a sadistic pleasure in the spectator's pitying look

Carnal Knowledge
Jonathan's (Jack Nicholson's) picture-show, 'ballbusters on parade'. The apotheosis of the
humour of male guilt and castration.

at Jake at the end of *Raging Bull,* partly explained by the space opened up for
female desire when the powerful male is brought low. But, as the sister of tragedy,
melodrama, tells us, there is no desire without the phallus . . . and though we
may take it up we can do so only at the expense of male castration. So what does
it leave us? Our desire is folded in with the man's desire for himself, and like him,
we mourn the loss of masculinity.

Raging Bull, of course, is far from comic, but its concern with masculinity
forms a link with contemporary romantic comedy where it might be said
that the enigma of masculinity rather than the traditional enigma of femininity
has become the central issue of many films. Nowhere is this more fascinatingly so than in the films of Jack Nicholson, one of the central male stars of
the Hollywood cinema over the last twenty five years, a star whose career
has not on the surface been dominated by comedy, but in whose complex
persona certain comic elements are constantly emphasised (e.g. in films as
various as *The Little Shop of Horrors* (1962), *The Shining* (1980), *Chinatown*
(1974), *The Last Detail* (1974), *Terms of Endearment* (1983), and *One Flew
Over the Cuckoo's Nest* (1976), and whose later career has made interesting
turns towards romantic comedy (e.g. *Goin' South,* 1978, which he directed,
Prizzi's Honor, and *The Witches of Eastwick,* 1987). Nicholson's enormous
power as a star actor is based on a combination of extreme intelligence (a
febrile sensitivity allied to a mocking knowingness) and sexual charisma
which has been nicely explained by Teresa Grimes in 'The Chameleon Smile',
some notes for a season of Nicholson films.

> Nicholson links the charisma of the forceful, active, masculine, 'complete' hero
> . . . with the appeal of the contemporary, fragmented anti-hero . . . It can therefore
> be suggested that Jack Nicholson as star persona . . . has metaphorically 'held
> together' that sense of cultural crisis endemic to America of the seventies, and held
> it together precisely because he embodies the potential for subversion, while at
> the same time reinforcing the power and dominance of the male hero and all it
> represents.

Indeed, apropos of this definition, we may note that in one of his major
roles, in *Five Easy Pieces,* the character he plays literally divides into separate
versions of the two roles mentioned, the sensitive, tormented East-Coast
classical pianist, and the macho hardhat.

The emphasis in both serious and popular journalism on Nicholson's famous
smile ('the chameleon smile' of Grimes's piece; 'The Star With the Killer
Smile', *Time* cover story, 12 August 1974), points to an element of danger
about him which we find extremely interesting. Nicholson, in the extremes
of positive and negative response he arouses in women, might be posited as
the most provocative male star of the feminist/post-feminist era, grating

against the desire to place the male under female control or to assert the insignificance of differences between the sexes. The antithesis of the feminised man as represented by, say, Dustin Hoffman in *Kramer versus Kramer* (1980), yet he is in no way conflatable, in his irony and self-awareness and willingness to choose roles which portray the male in crisis, with simpler versions of rearguard masculinity as embodied, say, by Charles Bronson. Nicholson not only gives offence by his complex, insolent male resistance, but in various of his roles – perhaps most startlingly in *The Shining* – acts out culminating images/parodies of patriarchal wickedness, ferocious in their energy of self-mortification, yet played with an edge of irony that mocks too simple a response to the various punishments his fictive presumptions earn him. *Goin' South* gives us a studied comic extension of this when Nicholson, as Henry Moon, is to be hanged for horse-thieving. Unaware of the town's law that he can be saved from death by any woman who will marry him, he sneeringly insults the ladies who inspect him in his death cell. Later, informed of the law, he reverses his tone as he begs them not to judge a book by its cover. The scene, with its interior audience of outraged females watching over the renegade male's threatened execution and penance, might be given the status of a self-conscious allegory of the star's relation to the time's sexual-political changes. Rescued by Mary Steenburgen, he finds himself in a parody of the traditional wife's role of merely legalised labour, and it is only after this further penance that the film moves, through the pair's interdependence in a working partnership, to renegotiations that honour the woman's autonomy and the *male*'s difference.

REPARATIVE FICTIONS

Tootsie (1982)

Toot-Toot-Tootsie goodbye!

Next week our programme will be 'Transvestism: aberration or altered life-style?'
— TV presenter in *House Calls* (1978)

When in *Tootsie* Sandy Lester (Terri Garr) suspects her boyfriend Michael Dorsey (Dustin Hoffman) of having an affair with another woman, she tries to control her anger by proclaiming she has read *The Second Sex* and *The Cinderella Complex*. By this stage it has become perfectly clear that the film is acutely aware of the sexual revolutions sparked off by feminism. Among its many achievements, one stream of feminism has succeeded in giving greater credibility to philosophical traditions rejecting essentialist notions of selfhood in favour of those recognising social determinants and presuppositions in the constitution of the self. And even though the most unswerving radical feminists have consistently rejected any kind of alliance with men ready to restructure traditional notions of sexual relations and identity, *Tootsie*, pleading its case with women prepared to acknowledge sympathetic male overtures, attempts to deal with the 'woman question' boldly, even if in paying due regard to the legacy of victimisations suffered by women in the past, its mission to provide an optimistic outlook for the future history of the relations between the sexes remains surrounded by edginess and unease. The film's formal method of approaching these labyrinths of sexual politics is created primarily through the provision of two major and well-worn devices of comic tradition: cross-dressing and *mise-en-abyme*.

Cross-dressing, an inflection of the looser, more all-embracing device of comic deceit, of mistaken identity, has an ancient ancestry: in literature it reaches at least as far back as the Greek myths (with, for example, stories about Achilles in drag in the pursuit of sexual gratification), though its most prolific periods are in the Elizabethan and Spanish Golden Age dramas. In the cinema, cross-dressing has characterised films as diverse as *Queen Christina*, *Sylvia Scarlett*, *I Was a Male War Bride* (1949), *Some Like It Hot*, *Psycho* (1969), and *The Crimson Pirate* (1952), where in each case, of course, the device has its own set of specific historical and aesthetic determinants. On the whole, strikingly different effects are created by male and female transvestism, for as Mary Ann Doane puts it, 'male transvestism is an occasion for laughter; female transvestism only another occasion for desire'. So while Burt Lancaster dressed as a folksy Nereid in the closing stages of *The Crimson Pirate* is a spectacle designed to make us laugh both at his mimicry of ridiculed female gestures and mannerisms, and at the presumed feeble daintiness of the female form, here in no way the equal of Lancaster's trapeze-artist build, Garbo as the incognito Swedish count in *Queen Christina* is the source of a whole variety of forbidden pleasures, at once exciting thoughts of lesbianism for the male (a constant motif of much male-orientated porn), softening and making more overtly sensual traditional images of masculinity, and in her transgression of gender limits creating a *frisson* of delightful shock at the sight of her release from the ususal trappings of her sex.

By the time of *Tootsie*'s making, and in the aftermath of the post-60s reformulations of sexuality, the device can dispense with some of the unnecessary ambiguities and camouflage about sexual preference and identity characteristic of films like *Queen Christina*. One of the more colourful minor knock-on effects of the sexual revolution has been a concerted assault, especially among the young, on the previously hide-bound limits of gender-specific fashions. Furthermore, with a climate seemingly more propititious for the flourishing of all kinds of sexual life styles once classified as deviant, the 70s and 80s were suddenly ready to allow gayness, lesbianism and trans-sexualism if not exactly to prosper then at least more uninhibitedly to speak their names. Yet, to confuse sexual liberation, a flower-power left-over from the days of letting it all hang out, with that project of defining the role and place of women through analysis of the cultural and economic modes of their exploitation, is an error *Tootsie* seems content enough both to acknowledge and to avoid.

The liberation of sexual–libidinal as distinct from political tastes and tendencies reached its peak perhaps in notions of free love and public admissions of difference from the norm, something that was given its most dramatic form in the phenomenon of more widely publicised incidents of trans-sexualism and gender clinics both in the USA and in foreign countries where the more notorious gender-bending surgeons practised their genital theodicies.

Tootsie is plainly not a comedy about actual trans-sexualism. At all times in his cross-dressing Michael Dorsey only ever pretends to be a woman, never in his most self-indulgent moments considering mutilating himself as a man in order to be physically reborn, like his more grotesque comic and ironised antecedent Myra Breckenridge, a woman. Nevertheless, since it takes great pains to show in various scenes the minutiae of his cosmetic application, depilation, strapping, and so on, as a man becomes if only in appearance an apparently convincing woman, it is useful to place *Tootsie*'s interest in cross-dressing against the background of recent feminist readings of trans-sexualism, some of the underlying premises of which seem sometimes to coincide with the film's grasp of the difference between femaleness and femininity. If *Tootsie*'s heart is in the right place, its head, like its sex, is ultimately too confused by more traditional perceptions of femaleness. Admittedly, the film does not reach the nightmarish depths of Angela Carter's partisan view of sexual relations in *The Passion of New Eve* (also dating from 1982), in which the ex-public schoolboy Evelyn is mutilated and refashioned as the voluptuous centre-fold lookalike Eve, becoming through this act of psycho as well as body surgery the object of the uncouth desires and masturbatory fantasies of the average *Playboy* reader. But, on the other hand, Tootsie's transvestism is readable in part as an atonement for the sins of the patriarchs, even if in becoming a 'woman', he/she is doomed to be, like the

novel's Tristessa, the male transvestite who becomes Hollywood's most
famous actress, '. . . the perfect man's woman . . . the shrine of his own
desires . . . the only woman he could have loved', an outrageous male fiction
of femininity, a complicated part-bad, part-good mother-figure, 'Dorothy
Michaels', redeeming her own ideology-fleeing son, Michael Dorsey.

What ultimately becomes a process of self-discovery and a partial critique
of the socialisation of sexual identity begins as the twin narcissistic desires
of exhibitionism and domination of others, in this case through deception.
Michael Dorsey, an aggressive, argumentative actor, is out of work and
decides to audition, disguised as a woman, for the soap opera part of a female
hospital administrator. As he tries for the role, one that his girlfriend Sandy
has failed to land (on her own admission she has a problem with anger,
something that has feminist implication beyond the matter of her range of
dramatic expertise), he responds with an aggression and unladylike language
worthy of Myra Breckenridge to the patronising attitudes of the male director.
The unusual mixture of twin-set and pearls, genteel looks and barrack-room
repartee becomes irresistible to the show's producer, a woman, and despite
the misgivings of the director, Dorothy/Michael gets the part. Once placed
under contract, Michael Dorsey as Dorothy Michaels begins to see the truth
of a remark made by Julie (Jessica Lange), playing a nurse in the series, a
woman to whom, off screen, he is very soon drawn: 'Don't you find being
a woman in the 80s complicated?' The answer from both audience and
Dorothy is too obvious to need enunciation.

'You'll have to deal with my mind and not with my lips', Dorothy tell the
ageing Lothario who plays the show's Dr Brewster, an actor also known as
the 'Tongue' by all the women on the set. The comedy of desire finds its
roughest edges in the portrayal of Brewster's designs on the studio-floor
women, something motivated by the twin urges of appetite and undiscriminating conquest. Though equally deceived by appearances, and in this
case exclusively attracted to strong matriarchs rather than youthful nymphs,
Julie's father, Les (Charles Durning), plays out in his pursuit of Dorothy
Michaels the comedy not only of homosexual threat but also of what Freud,
paraphrased by Denis de Rougemont, has called '. . . a mother fixation
haunting the recesses of his memory'. These relationships, like those in the
sub-plots of Shakespeare's comedies, while anchoring the principal pair of
lovers in a baser reality, make them seem simultaneously more lustrous than
the less fancy-free characters who surround them. But, as in the Shakes

---

Tootsie
Finding out how the other half lives, Dorothy's (Dustin Hoffman's) journey through sexual
difference to knowledge of socialised attitudes to gender.

pearean comedies, the central characters must suffer ordeals of awareness and reorientations of ideals and desire before they can truly merit one another's love. So here, Michael will reach self-awareness by first of all learning something about the social victimisation of women, a process of which no male can ultimately claim total innocence.

She/he is compelled at all tines to deal with a whole range of intolerably patronising attitudes, epitomised by the director's normally demeaning use on set of terms like 'Toots', 'Baby' and 'Honey'. 'Stop thinking of me as a woman and start thinking of me as a person' is a line from the series script, but one of equal relevance to her off-screen life as a woman, and as he bludgeons his colleagues into submission, Dorothy/Michael discovers unexpected truths not only about himself but also about relationships between men and women in general, in particular, that in identifying himself as much with women as with men, the emphasis on sexual difference dwindles to a degree that makes more tolerable both his own sexual identity and his relations with others, especially, of course, women. The film does not set out to abolish sexual difference, since Michael is restored to his maleness at the end of the film; the point is rather that in a society which has produced flux and in some ways broken down difference, absolute polarities of gender-based difference can no longer be sustained.

Although the film ends with a reimposition of visual conformities (Michael has lost all visual trace of Dorothy as he and Julie walk down the street together towards their enjoyment of a heterosexual relationship), Michael's last speech reflects the extent of his *education sentimentale:* '. . . I was a better man with you as a woman than I ever was with a woman as a man. You know what I mean? I just gotta learn to do without the dress. At this point in the relationship there might be an advantage to my wearing pants. Hard part's over, you know? We were already good friends.' The speech is edgy, but at the very least, as Michael recognises the Dorothy in himself, the film manages at this point to give male audiences only lukewarmly interested in the social humiliations and victimisations suffered by women a vicarious experience of that history. Through Michael Dorsey's ordeals as Dorothy Michaels, male audiences may begin to know something of what women have historically endured, though the public humiliations he heaps on the traditional male both in the audience and as represented by the chauvinistic TV director are as nothing by comparison with Myra Breckenridges's vengeance in the name of 'the eternal feminine made flesh . . . dealing with man as incidental toy, whose blood as well as semen' is needed to make her whole.

Neither the 'eternal feminine', nor a synthesis of femininity, nor a dehistoricised emblem of her sex, 'Tootsie' is a specific 80s image of a common stereotype. Michael Dorsey's desire to be a woman is, firstly, linked to the whole acting metaphor in which the need to be admired is recognised as something culturally identified with femaleness; but, secondly, it can also be viewed as a wish at once to possess and to take revenge against the phallic mother. Given his slight but somewhat unmaidenly, unsylphlike looks Hoffman is restricted, as more androgynous and youthful male stars like Alain Delon or James Dean would not have been, to a limited range of feminine stereotypes. The maternal image created by Dorothy/Michael is commented on twice: First, when his room-mate cries 'Mum?' when as he wakes up he first sees Michael as Dorothy; second, when framed in the foreground at the studio with an all but naked Julie doing stretching exercises before going on the studio floor, Dorothy herself remarks, '. . . what kind of mother would I be if I didn't give you tits . . . tips'.

The positive side to Dorothy's mother image (the Freudian slip is a double gesture to glamour and motherhood), means that a man begins to see something of the humiliations suffered by women, in this instance the specifically middle-aged woman, no longer of primarily sexual interest; but, on the negative side, the woman Michael Dorsey becomes is an incarnation of a discredited stereotype. The force of this stereotype is in its insidiousness even more powerful that the overt prejudice of the kind the Jack Lemmon character displays in the early stages of *The War Between Men and Women* (1972), a misogyny so comprehensive as to be applied even to animals, so that when a pregnant dog comes into view, he comments unhesitatingly, 'It couldn't have been love. She must have been raped'. All this remains quite separate from a further area of ideological subservience, in that for an age in which women have largely dispensed with male chivalry and taken it upon themselves to fight their own sexual/social battles it seems almost insulting that in this film a man should not only be following tradition in deceiving other women (Sandy and Julie) – though admittedly with growing guilt – for his own gratification, but also doing battle on their behalf. (Crudity of this type must, however, be set against more radical elements, and it is surely not insignificant that the person enjoying the highest position of authority in the film is a woman, the producer of the series.) But in his parthenogenesis, like some Athena emerging from the womb of his own creative imagination ('Dorothy' means 'gift of the gods'), he seems in looks a caricature of a maternal, middle-class, demure lady stereotype, all perms, softness, sweetness, hushed tones, short quick-stepping walk and genteel gestures. 'Dorothy' becomes, in part, a fetishisation of femaleness, every detail of her lovingly, painstakingly constructed anatomy a reminder of the social construction of her sex. As Michael tugs at his hair, torturing it into acceptable matronly Middle-American contours, plucks his eyebrows, shaves his legs, and straps his waist, transforming each sectionalised area of the body into a symbol of femininity, in the process distancing them and establishing their convention-bound arbitrariness for the audience, the images further recall Freud's remarks on the Chinese custom of mutilating and then revering the bound feet of women: 'It seems as though the Chinese male wants to thank the woman for having submitted to being castrated.'

Though it has to be said in the film's defence that Dorothy actually says she is not attracted to men who find over-made-up women desirable (i.e. the film knows that too much make-up sometimes reduces women to sex objects), the negative implications of the Dorothy character are to some extent echoed by the portrayal of Jessica Lange's Julie. Conventionally placed, if we exclude Dorothy herself, as the film's leading lady, and the eventual object of Michael's desire – once he has dispensed with Sandy – Julie is also to a certain extent a victim of stereotype: there is a redeemable intelligence, and she reveals a capacity for self-awareness, but there is also a part of her that projects an image of the nice but basically limited California beach-girl type, the kind of woman, moreover, who falls for strong, cheating, macho men.

'When I find the one who can give me the worst possible time, that's when I make my move', Julie is made to say as she tries to explain a temperament attracted to cheats like the egocentric director. Is this the film's knowing echo of Freud's recognition that excessive masochism in women originates in social customs (though Freud also maintains everyone is to a certain extent masochistic), 'which similarly force women into passive situations', or is it another example of the film's unconscious acceptance of stereotype? The answer is unavoidably equivocal, but even so, in a film so sensitive to the whole complex area of women's victimisation by culture, it would be difficult to feel that serious issues were not also deliberately being raised through its focus on Julie's problems.

Less equivocally treated, though, is the film's *mise-en-abyme* of the fictionalisation of experience through soap opera. In part a satire of what by the 80s has become the immensely popular phenomenon of soaps like *Dynasty* and *Dallas*, a genre whose origins date from the 30s radio serials sponsored by soap companies, *Tootsie* also specifically concerns itself firstly with the divergences between fact and fantasy (Julie at one point says she wants directness and openness in sexual relations, but when she is given them by Michael replies by throwing water all over him), and, secondly, with the specific relevance and meaning of medical soaps in the culture.

Medical soaps, like all other types, are, as Dorothy Hobson notes in a remark about the genre as a whole, basically 'escapist or fantasy programmes through which women could realise the romance missing from their own everyday lives'. What makes this one so different from, say, *Dr Kildare* or *Ben Casey* is that a 'woman' thrusts herself here into the centre of the narrative. Moreover, as the beneficiary of male privilege and manipulation, Michael/Dorothy can see through the false pieties, the ersatz religiosity, the blatant hypocrisy of male-orientated attitudes in which hysterical women patients are cured by strong male doctor figures, a pattern already treated with some sophistication in great film melodramas like *Now Voyager* (1942) and *All That Heaven Allows* (1954). Michael is consequently better placed than most to explode the conventions of a genre all too frequently serving only the interests of the male. Not only subverting the language and conventions of the series through outrageous ad-libbing, he also invents a totally ludicrous ending for himself as the hospitals's administrator, an exit from the part that simultaneously sends up the inbuilt absurdities of the genre's twists and turns of narrative (how many more long-lost brothers, daughters, half-sisters and brothers will Blake Carrington turn out to have in *Dynasty?*) and, through settling an old score against her fictive father's original tyranny against his family, takes on the Lacanian significance of revolt against the Law of the Father, the authority constantly delimiting the mother-child relationship which in his role as Dorothy, the good/bad mother redeeming the son, Michael has so triumphantly defied. As someone for whom his womanhood has been the 'best part of his manhood', Dorothy/Michael questions the predominantly patriarchal ideology which has consistently placed prohibitions both on the loosening up of relations between the sexes, and, more generally, on the whole question of the redefinitions of role, gender and sexual identity.

Victor Victoria (1982)

How do you solve a problem like Julie?

I am not what I am.   — Viola in *Twelfth Night*

The TV announcer's definition of Sally Miles in *S.O.B.* (1981) as the 'Silver Screen's symbol of sweetness, sinlessness and sobriety' is nothing less than a world-wide audience's perception of the meaning and status of the actress who portrays her, Julie Andrews. In a quasi-autobiographical film, Blake Edwards embarks on an interrogation of this complex audience response, a

process he pursues perhaps even more dramatically in *Victor Victoria*. While everyone recognises that Julie Andrews's star persona suggests, superficially at least, a soufflé of clean-living, nursery-room hygiene and wholesomeness, Edwards further knows that beneath the veneer lie much more complicated elements solidifying the image. *The Americanization of Emily* (1964) and *Torn Curtain* (1966) had already delighted in placing her respectability and demureness under various kinds of threat, but in Blake Edwards's work what *S.O.B.* initiates *Victor Victoria* develops, drawing further attention to the complexities of sexual allure underlying the unmistakable aura of purity and virtue.

Julie Andrews may well be a nursery madonna, but the phenomenon of her box-office popularity cannot simply be explained in terms of the U-certificate audience, and a way of unravelling the complexities of her screen representation can be found through preliminary concentration on her well-publicised failure to land the highly prized role of Eliza Doolittle in the lavish film version of *My Fair Lady* (1964). That failure had fed into the dynamics of the whole Andrews persona, exposing it as being in some senses vulnerable to rejection as much on the grounds of glamour as of pedigree. Whatever the reasons for her rejection as the screen Eliza it seems clear, if one judges by the final choice of Audrey Hepburn for the part, that what Andrews lacked – besides mileage as a major star – were the kind of *petite*, fragile, pretty-pretty, gawky, Swiss Finishing School qualities so much in abundance in Hepburn.

Though Julie Andrews is often associated with children, and is herself, especially in her early career, frequently presented as a spirited embodiment of youth and energy, this is something not restricted to the aristocratic or high bourgeois drawing-room world in which Hepburn sometimes moves (*Roman Holiday, Charade*, etc.); her youthful zest, on the contrary, is more usually identified with pastoral (*The Sound of Music*) or suburban (*Mary Poppins*) nurseries. The nuns in *The Sound of Music* say Maria is as unpredictable as the weather, fond of the outdoors, animals, and childish pranks. *S.O.B.* plays on these Mary Poppins attributes by giving us our first glimpse of her in a number set in a playroom where large-as-life toy soldiers and monstrous toy bricks surround her as she sings 'Polly Wolly Doodle All the Day'. Like Katharine Hepburn in *Holiday*, Julie Andrews seems wholly at ease in this infant world, an unthreatening space for uninhibited indulgence

---

Victor Victoria
Julie Andrews, a woman impersonating a man impersonating a woman, and Robert Preston (Toddy), the homosexual as 80s father-figure, looks as if they have their doubts about the reactions of a minatory world.

of her good sport's breezy, clean-thinking tomboyishness and good humour, qualities condensed, moreover, into an image projecting both chumminess and materialism.

Julie Andrews personifies the good sport and the good mother, these twoseparate strands in the persona forming part of the complex inner texture of her sexual allure. If Mae West or Dorothy Michaels in some ways represent comic hyperboles of the phallic mother, Julie Andrews, for all her tomboyish-ness, personifies in one facet of her dual nature, the vaginal, suckling matri-arch. While Mae West and Dorothy Michaels thrive in public places, the early Julie Andrews usually makes of domesticity a virtue, listing crisp apple strudels and girls in white dresses with blue satin sashes as being among her favourite things. She perfectly fits the job description in the ad sent out by the Banks children, Jane and Michael, in *Mary Poppins*, in which any appli-cant to the post of nanny must be 'of cheerful disposition, rosy-cheeked, free of warts, game-loving, witty, very sweet and faintly pretty'. With a face that seems to be a cross between Joyce Grenfell and Ursula Andress, Julie Andrews combines the scrubbed, blooming look of the outdoor, good sport type – her upturned nose an emblem of optimism, cheerfulness and, though it does not stretch so far as his, Pinnochioesque childishness – with the taut, clear skin of an oval face showing off beautiful, sympathetic eyes to create the aura associated with motherhood. Shot through all this an element of authority provides an additional reminder of the medicine she conceals in the spoonful of sugar. In as late a film as *10*, she continues to play a sort of erotic mother figure to Dudley Moore's strange and naughty child.

It is as though the partly Oedipal basis of her sexuality is being acknow-ledged in *S.O.B.* when her breasts are so dramatically exposed to the public view. (In the narrative, the film she has been starring in has bombed, and an attempt to salvage something from the wreckage is made when the director decides to re-shoot it as a soft-porn shocker.) The breasts alone are laid bare, virtually all the rest of the body remaining under wraps. On this level, what at first might have seemed like an act of cinematic sacrilege – the eroticisation of a star whose image personified demureness, whose sexual exposure seemed motivated exclusively by prurience and voyeurism – might be interpreted as the visual recognition and celebration of her Oedipal meaning for the mass audience.

This Oedipal side of the duality of Julie Andrews, in which the good sportiness provides the more homely basis for her fertility goddess sexuality, is partly what first draws James Garner's King Marchand to her in *Victor Victoria*. But even her relationship with her homosexual partner Toddy (Robert Preston), who normally behaves towards her like a protective mother (at one point calling her 'poor baby' when she rests her weeping face on his shoulder), reveals a maternal streak occasionally finding expression, as when she defends Toddy against the jibes of his ex-lover, with a firm right to the jaw. The discipline of the sugar and medicine-dispensing mother receives here its most violent expression in the film. Victoria also takes responsibility, despite all the necessary compromises the film ultimately demands of her (restored feminity, career compromises, life at King's side), for developing King's more mature understanding of sexual identity and the relations between the sexes, just as Maria had once turned an immature, severely patriarchal Captain Von Trapp into a loving father for children he had only previously known how to treat like a military troop. But the good mother qualities of the Andrews persona are in *Victor Victoria* perhaps ultimately eclipsed by the film's interest in the more androgynous implications of her good sportiness. These elements are signalled in *Star!*, among other ways, through another display of boxing skills, on that occasion against her drunken first husband, but in *Victor Victoria*, within the contradications of the persona as a whole, they are stressed through the narrative's demands on her becoming a transvestite, here, like Jessie Matthews in the British musical, *First a Girl* (1935), before her, a woman claiming to be a man impersonating a woman. Both films are based on Reinhold Schunzel's *Viktor und Viktoria*, made in 1933.

Victoria's cross-dressing questions in various ways presuppositions legitimising social norms. Julie Andrews as Victoria Grant, as unsettlingly beautiful here as Greta Garbo's transvestite nobleman in *Queen Christina*, invokes a tradition of female sex-transcendence through cross-dressing as fitting now in the 80s as in the 30s setting of the film, decades in which a woman might well echo Victoria Grant's complaint that 'there are things available to me as a man that I can never have as a woman'. In the image of Toddy's cropping of her hair all kinds of taboos are lifted (cf. St Paul's less indulgent views on hairstyles for men and women in *Corinthians* 1, 11:14-15), while in her effortless wearing of her Hungarian count's Dandy suits she becomes an androgyne suppressing her femininity not to unsex herself but, on the contrary, as a means of ultimately being more truly a woman, to place in confusion masculine/feminine polarities, and to become someone whose ambiguous sexuality, in an age in some ways no longer bound by rigid conventions, can be more easily tolerated than in earlier less flexible ones. In her pretence to be a Hungarian count, moreover, she becomes, as a Hungarian, a stranger set on making the strange more familiar, and, as an aristocrat, the sexually marginal more respectable. In reverse process, Victor becomes Victoria, a victor or Amazon of sexual identity, not like her mythical forebears paring off her right breast to remove impediments to her skills in archery, but flattening them, denying her womanhood in the public, male-privileged domain until, as she herself notices, they look like empty wallets. If a woman's social and sexual exchange value are not infrequently invested in her breasts, to be deprived of them entails social devaluation. Significantly, when at the end of the film Victor returns as Victoria, she wears a dress of generous décolletage, revealing a great expanse of what in *Some Like It Hot* Jack Lemmon called his chests, covered only by the peekaboo device of a veil that rather more proclaims than conceals the primacy of their sexual-social value. As Victor, she replaces the power invested socially in her breasts with that endowed naturally in her voice, here the modern Amazon's equivalent of the traditional arrow or spear. Julie Andrews's powerful soprano, the instrument that first thrust her into public awareness, is here pressed into the service of the female's struggle with the male: sometimes using it overtly like a weapon, as when she deliberatly pitches it high enough to fracture the night club owner's apéritif glass after his rejection of her at the audition (memories of *My Fair Lady*), at other times using it to outwit her audiences, especially men, but always ultimately in a sweet and unthreatening way, by making them accept her travesty of the truth.

The most sceptical of her male admirers is King Marchand, James Garner teaming up again with Julie Andrews for the first time since *The Americanization of Emily*. King's attraction to Victor seems confused, ambiguous, even incomprehensible at first. But if this is so, it seems less a fault of the narrative than a development of Blake Edwards's acknowledged interest in the antics of voyeurism, a motif reaching its most complicated comic form both in the detective figure of Jacques Clouseau in the Pink Panther films (in this film a private eye tries to prove Victor is a woman) and in *10*, where Dudley Moore's playboy spends much of the first part of the film spying through a telescope on the nubile young ladies living in a neighbouring suburban house, who in turn spy back on him, both sides fuelled by a desire to establish sexual difference.

In *Victor Victoria* King's relationship with Victor/Victoria is at first very probably governed by voyeurism (his fascination with her stage act, and his spying on her when she takes a bath). Beyond that, though, detailed exchanges of dialogue, romantic comedy's standard barometer of the relations between the sexes, are to a large extent relegated in importance in a film where it is enough simply to know that the principal male character feels strongly attracted to her. In some ways, then, the film pales by comparison with what we have come to expect from films like *Bringing Up Baby*, *His Girl Friday*, and even *Tootsie* and their witty articulation of desire. This film relies more heavily on conceit: the spectacle of Julie Andrews in the Victor/Victoria role as a person of apparently uncertain gender, combined with the whole aura of the self-consciously dramatised history of the Andrews persona, that combination of Oedipality and good sportiness we have been defining, works its spell here on a 30s Parisian audience. The ambience is so exaggeratedly theatricalised as to make the whole setting of the film's night club sequences an elaborate objective correlative for the real audience, the cinema-going public responding voyeuristically and compulsively to the complex surface and hidden meanings of the Star!, Julie Andrews.

Of the dramatised spectators, two are privileged. One, Leslie Ann Warren's Norma, King's mistress, caricatures the straight woman, taking to a *reductio ad absurdum* the conformist society's stereotyped notions of femininity: peroxide platinum blonde, figure emphasising hips and breasts, the jello-on-springs effect defined by Jack Lemmon in *Some Like It Hot*, and dumbness (though in fact her spirit has not been totally annihilated, periodically struggling for release and sometimes returning in monstrous form as she hurls pieces of furniture at her lover when her temper becomes too sorely tested). In her anxieties over King's attraction to Victor/Victoria the narrow issue of a woman's fears of being overtaken by a rival is offset by the narrative's interest in exposing the straight, feminine woman's vulnerability in the 80s consciousness of men perhaps satiated by more traditional standards and definitions of feminity. The matter is complex, though, for Norma's aggression sometimes triumphs over her passive femininity, so that she becomes, ironically, a woman who mutates from femininity without realising it.

The second privileged spectator is King himself, once again a character of specific relevance to the fictive world of the narrative itself, and, additionally, imaged as a comic hyperbole of the average straight male devotee of the Andrews persona. There are affirmative (handsomeness, humour, strength, *savoir-faire*, flexibility) as well as negative (voyeurism, deceit, gangsterism) features in his characterisation. The film confronts him – and, through him, male audiences in general – with his own prejudices. As Victor/Victoria puts it to him herself at one point, 'Your problem, Mr Marchand, is that you're preoccupied with stereotypes . . . I think it's as simple as you're one kind of man, I'm another.' Once King (with all the resonances of that patriarchal, law-giving name) has been faced with his sexual and moral myopia, he can perhaps begin to find release from trivialising, dehumanising modes of sexual behaviour and, far from veering away from an admission of attraction to Oedipal/Peter Pan objects of desire, can actually begin all the better to appreciate his attraction to them once he has been made to notice their force in his life. As someone on the fringes of gangsterism, he is an outlaw of culture too in his pre-Victor/Victoria identity; as a boxing aficionado (it seems fitting that Victoria, the upper-cut-happy fair-play matriarch should be attracted to him) he is all too easily, in the negative implications of the metaphor, drawn to violence. In this context one recalls Queen Christina's point about using her womanliness to undermine male aggression built into the fabric of seventeenth-century Swedish society.

But the film is not King's. In terms of character interest he even takes second place to Toddy. Victor/Victoria, not King, despite the name, is at the centre of this narrative. As Rosalind overshadows Orlando in *As You Like It*, so Victor/Victoria eclipses King in this film where the comedy of love is projected through the eyes of a woman, through whose stratagems of disguise and confusion we begin to question ideals of sexuality and identity, and to wonder whether women must be idolised, fantasised or idealised before they can truly be loved. By having Julie Andrews, epitome of normality, star as Victor/Victoria, the outrageousness of the film is both more surprising and more acceptable. Significantly, she is herself released from conformism by the homosexual Toddy as a prelude to her own rescue of King. Through Victor/Victoria King can begin to speak the unspeakable, name the unnameable, tolerate the intolerable. She plays the unpredictable catalyst challenging the certainties of sexual norms, in whose company and through whose influence deviancy need no longer be classed as deviant, eccentricity no longer thought of as eccentric. Even ring fans turned heavyweight bodyguards like Mr Bernstein, King's minder, can now come out of their gyms, unashamedly owning up to their gayness. However dull the number, the lyrics sung by Toddy and Victor testify to the pre-Aids sexual revolution of the early 80s:

> You and me
> we're the kind of people
> other people would like to be,
> wandering free.

As Toddy and Mr Bernstein cuddle up in bed, and as first Victor/Victoria, and then Toddy, do a camp Latin American number that in its exaggeration, irony and theatricalisation dramatises the homosexual's historical social marginalisation, the film is able to lay claim, if only transiently, before the realism of its closure somewhat shakily restores the characters to their social and sexual places (Victoria at King's side in the audience at the night club, a spectator now, and no longer a participant), to a freer climate both for the relations between the sexes and for sexual identity itself. Toddy takes over Victoria's role on stage at the end, an action simultaneously re-emphasising the stereotype of the camp, comic drag queen, while removing the heterosexual female from the setting – here the stage-setting, film equivalent of Arden, Illyria, the wood near Athens – of psycho-sexual experiment, reversals and metamorphoses of sex and identity.

Romantic comedy may now well be in the 80s, as Brian Henderson argues, something semi-tough, but it is surely not impossible, even if the post-feminist, gay revolutions mean that the old certainties are henceforward incessantly subjected to interrogation. If, however, radical attitudes to sex have taken to impossible extremes the theory of the desirability of hetero-sexuality's extinction – on the grounds that it leads *per se* to tyranny and oppression – at least in drawing attention to the limitations of this view most people can simultaneously take the point that equality between the sexes is the only conceivable basis for the kind of love likely to be here to stay.

Sources

PREFACE

The texts to which specific mention is made are as follows: Sigmund Freud, *Jokes and their Relation to the Unconscious*, vol. VI, Pelican Freud Library, (Harmondsworth, 1976); and on the Schreber case, 'Psychoanalytical notes on an autobiographical account of a case of paranoia', *Case Histories ii*, Pelican Freud Library (Harmondsworth, 1979); E. Ann Kaplan, *Women and Film: Both Sides of the Camera* (London, 1983); *The Cinema Book*, ed. Pam Cook (London, 1985); Robin Wood, *Hollywood from Vietnam to Reagan* (New York, 1986); Andrew Britton, *Katharine Hepburn: The Thirties and After* (Newcastle upon Tyne, 1984) and *Cary Grant: Comedy and Male Desire* (Newcastle upon Tyne, 1983); Richard Dyer, *Heavenly Bodies: Film Stars and Society* (London, 1987); Stanley Cavell, *Pursuits of Happiness: The Hollywood Comedy of Remarriage* (Cambridge, Mass. 1981); Raymond Durgnat, *The Crazy Mirror: Hollywood Comedy and the American Image* (New York, 1974). *Screen* has spasmodically given attention to comedy (e.g. in vol. 22, no. 2 (1981), and vol. 25, nos. 4-5 (1984)).

The point about bisexuality (or, as they call it, 'ambisexuality') comes from William H. Masters and Virginia E. Johnson, *Homosexuality in Perspective* (Boston, 1979). References are also made to Andrea Dworkin, *Intercourse* (London, 1987), Adrienne Rich, *Of Woman Born: Motherhood as Experience and Institution* (London, 1977), Margaret Mead, *Sex and Temperament in Three Primitive Societies* (London, 1952) and *Male and Female* (London, 1950) and Bronislaw Malinowski, *The Sexual Life of Savages in North Western Melanesia* (London, 1957), *Sex and Repression in Savage Society* (London, 1927) and *Sex, Culture and Myth* (London, 1963). The quotation that ends the preface comes from the Penguin edition of Virginia Woolf, *A Room of One's Own* (Harmondsworth, 1972), p. 6.

1 — BRINGING UP BABY

For the adverse criticism of Katharine Hepburn in *Bringing up Baby*, see *The New York Times* review of 1938 by Frank S. Nugent. Our definition of Screwball comedy draws on Wes D. Gehring, *Screwball Comedy: Defining a Film Genre* (Muncie, Indiana, 1983), but see also Thomas Schatz, *Hollywood Genres: Formulas, Film-Making and the Studio System* (Philadelphia, 1981). For us, as for many others, Robin Wood's *Howard Hawks* (London, 1968) was the first serious piece on *Bringing Up Baby* that we ever read.

Instances of the limited 'sociological' approach to 30s comedy that we criticise are (though they are not negligible books) Andrew Bergman, *We're in the Money: Depression America and Its Films* (New York, 1972) and Robert Sklar, *Movie-Made America* (London, 1978).

For comedy in general, see Northrop Frye, *Anatomy of Criticism* (New York, 1969) and, pervasively, Sigmund Freud, *Jokes and their Relation to the Unconscious*. Mention should also be made of Gerald Mast, *The Comic Mind* (Indianapolis, 1973) and Raymond Durgnat, *The Crazy Mirror: Hollywood Comedy and the American Image*. Meredith's notion of 'comic pain' comes from 'An essay on comedy', in *Comedy*, ed. Wylie Sypher (New York, 1956). Stanley Cavell's thought-provoking and witty writing on *Bringing Up Baby* (even if he stretches definitions to the point of meaningless in order to type it as a comedy of remarriage) and other 30s comedies is found in *Pursuits of Happiness: the Hollywood Comedy of Remarriage* (Harvard University Press, 1981). Andrew Britton's mostly highly perceptive comments on Hepburn, Grant and *Bringing Up Baby* come from *Cary Grant: Comedy and Male Desire* (Newcastle upon Tyne, 1983) and *Katharine Hepburn: The Thirties and After* (Newcastle upon Tyne, 1984).

Freud on Jensen's novel, *Gradiva* (1903), is found in 'Delusions and dreams in Jensen's *Gradiva*' (1907), Vol. xiv, Pelican Freud Library (Harmondsworth, 1985). On the subject of parapraxes, verbal and physical, see Freud, *The Psychopathology of Everyday Life* (London, 1948). We are far from unaware of the major critique of Freud's methods by Sebastiano Timpanaro in *The Freudian Slip: Psychoanalysis and Textual Criticism* (London, 1976), but make the point that, whatever the debate about Freud's interpretations, the comedies and melodramas of the period accept the idea of 'the Freudian slip'.

Since we refer approvingly to Herbert Marcuse's arguments about the re-eroticising of reality (which, arguably, is part of the meaning of *Bringing Up Baby*), it is important to note, lest our position seem contradictory, that we are aware of his apparent endorsement of the bisexual release argument which we look upon somewhat sceptically. While gay theorists (e.g. the Argentinian novelist Manuel Puig in *Kiss of the Spider Woman* London, 1984), call on Marcuse's authority in *Eros and Civilisation* (London, 1969), we are impressed rather by the way he uses the argument less as a substantive than as a formal means to move to the ideal of 'the conceptual transformation of sexuality into Eros' and 'libidinal work-relations'. Marcuse certainly invokes the release of homosexuality, but only to argue quickly for a 'non-repressive sublimation' that 'would not simply reactivate precivilised and infantile stages, but would also transform the perverted content of those stages'. What is most noticeable is the hurry with which he leaves for 'non-repressive sublimation' any concrete manifestation of homosexuality. This leads us to find him unconvincing as a prophet of bisexuality.

On questions of the artistic representation of 'historicity' see Vladimir Propp, *Theory and History of Folklore* (Manchester, 1984), and also, on magic animals, *Morphology of the Folktale* (Austin, Texas, 1968). For Engels on the economics of marriage, see *The Origin of the Family, Private Property and the State* (Harmondsworth, 1985). Margaret Mead is quoted from *Sex and Temperament in Three Primitive Societies* (London, 1952): Anaïs Nin claims that women have a closer identification with nature in *In Favour of the Sensitive Man* (London, 1976); Pauline Kael celebrates Cary Grant in 'The man from dream city' in *When the Lights Go Down* (London, 1980); Northrop Frye considers the function of 'blocking' characters in *Anatomy of Criticism;* Bergson's notion of the mechanical as the cause of laughter is stated in 'Laughter' in *Comedy*, ed. Wylie Sypher. The 'loon' references are from Henry David Thoreau's *Walden* (New York, 1982). Ortega y Gasset's remarks on hunting are in *Sobre la Caza* (Madrid, 1975). William E. Leuchtenburg in *The Perils of Prosperity* (Chicago, 1958) mentions the influence of John B. Watson on pre-Spockian child-rearing.

2—LUBITSCH

The books and articles that we have found most useful are the following: *Ernst Lubitsch: A Guide to Reference and Resources*, ed. Robert L. Carringer and Barry Sabath (Boston, 1978); Enno Patalas, 'Ernst Lubitsch: German Period' and Andrew Sarris, 'Ernst Lubitsch: American Period' in *Cinema: A Critical Dictionary*, vol. ii, ed. Richard Roud (London, 1980); William A. Paul, *Ernst Lubitsch's American Comedy* (New York, 1983), though the latter is unconvincing in its dogmatism about what is significant Lubitsch (i.e. not *Bluebeard* and none of the musicals except *The Merry Widow*). See also Molly Haskell, *From Reverence to Rape* (Baltimore, 1974) and, on the experimental elements of Lubitsch's early films, Barry Salt, *Film Style and Technology: History and Analysis* (London, 1968). For other information on early Lubitsch, though in the context of unhelpful comparisons of Lubitsch's comedy with other expatriate directors' non-comic work, see Graham Petrie, *Hollywood Destinies: European Directors in America, 1922-31* (London, 1985). Our own *Blue Skies and Silver Linings: Aspects of the Hollywood Musical* (Manchester, 1985) contains material on Lubitsch's European and American themes.

On Lubitsch and actors see, for instance, David Niven, *Bring on the Empty Horses* (London, 1975). On Hecht and Raphaelson as screenwriters for Lubitsch see, though with sceptism about his crude judgements of *Angel* and *Design for Living*, Richard Corliss, *Talking Pictures: Screenwriters in the American Cinema, 1927-73* (New York, 1974). Further opinions of *Bluebeard* are quoted from Graham Greene, *The Pleasure Dome: the Collected Film Criticism 1935-40* (London, 1972) and *The Daily Express*, 22 May 1938. For instances of the 'confectioner' image in contemporary critical reactions to Lubitsch, see the piece on *That Uncertain Feeling* in *The New York Times Film Review 1932-38* (New York, 1970), p. 1785, and, more complicatedly, James Agee on *Heaven Can Wait* in *Agee on Film* (London, 1963), pp. 49 and 50, where the 'kidded clichés' are also noted. Bosley Crowther's review of *Heaven Can Wait* comes from *The New York Times Film Reviews 1939-48* (New York, 1970), p. 1952. Pauline Kael's remarks about Lubitsch and Raphaelson are found in *Three Screen Comedies by Samson Raphaelson*, introduced by Pauline Kael (Madison, 1983), which also contains Raphaelson's memoir, *'Freundschaft: How It Was with Lubitsch and Me'*. The statements by Lubitsch himself on *Heaven Can Wait* are from Herman G. Weinberg, *The Lubitsch Touch: A Critical Study* (New York, 1977), the source also of Raphaelson's anecdote about a rare act of censorship.

Thorstein Veblen on 'conspicuous consumption' is from *The Theory of the Leisure Class* (London, 1970); the figures on divorce in America in the 20s come from William E. Leuchtenburg, *The Perils of Prosperity* (Chicago, 1958); Bergson, 'Laughter' in *Comedy*, ed. Wylie Sypher (New York, 1956) is alluded to with regard to *Bluebeard's Eighth Wife*. Other texts mentioned in the discussion of the same film are: Anaïs Nin, *In Favour of the Sensitive Man* (London, 1976); Angela Carter, *The Sadean Woman* (London, 1979); Simone de Beauvoir, *The Second Sex* (London, 1969); Anthony Storr, *Human Aggression* (London, 1982); Kate Millett, *Sexual Politics* (London, 1977), and Adrienne Rich, *Of Woman Born: Motherhood as Experience and Institution* (London, 1977).

Arguments from Lacan and Freud on the nature of desire are found respectively in *Ecrits, I and II* (Paris, 1966, 1967) and 'On the universal tendency to debasement in the sphere of love' in *On Sexuality*, p. 258.

3—THREE COMEDIANS
Bob Hope

Information about the popularity of Hope (and Crosby) is taken from David Pirie, *Anatomy of the Movies* (London, 1987), pp. 108-9. Briefly summarising, in the period 1941-45, Hope was the number one male box-office star, from 1946-50 number 2, from 1951-55 number 6: while in the period 1946-50 Crosby was number 1 (4 in 1941-5, 5 in 1951-5).

Bob Hope, agreeing with Brooks Riley about his image, is quoted from *Film Comment* (May/June 1979, vol. XV, No. 3) – (B.R.: 'Full of lust, but never getting the girl.' B.H.: 'A coward with phoney bravado and all that stuff'). On Tashlin, see *Tashlin*, ed. Claire Johnston and Paul Willemen (London, 1973). Richard West on Hope is quoted from *New Statesman*, 31 December 1972; for Thai feet see *The Times*, 28 December 1972.

Freud's remarks on the infantile in comedy are found in *Jokes*, pp. 286-92, an interest which, as he notes, is prefigured by Bergson in his 'Laughter', p. 104. On the significance of 'Painless' Potter's toothpulling, see *The Interpretation of Dreams*, vol. iv, Pelican Freud

Library, (Harmondsworth, 1976), pp. 507-16. For Freud's distinction between 'innocent' and 'tendentious' jokes, see *Jokes*, pp. 132-5. For his speculations about narcissism and homosexuality, see 'On narcissism: an introduction' in *On Metapsychology*, vol. xi (Pelican Freud Library, Harmondsworth, 1984), especially pp. 81-4. For his ideas about 'masculine' sexuality in the pre-feminised girl (appropos Jane Russell) see 'Female sexuality' in *On Sexuality*, p. 338, and 'The transformations of puberty' in 'Three essays on sexuality' *(ibid.)* p. 141.

Parker Tyler very briefly remarks on the 'sissy', quasi-homosexual element in the Hope persona in *Screening the Sexes: Homosexuality in the Movies* (1972). Angela Carter writes about dandyism in *Nothing Sacred* (London, 1982). William A. Paul on Jack Benny as both *alazon* and *eiron* comes from *Ernst Lubitsch's American Comedy* (New York, 1983). On the heroic status which Hope fails to achieve, see C. M. Bowra, *Heroic Poetry* (London, 1952), Joseph Campbell, *The Masks of God* (Harmondsworth, 1983), and C. G. Jung, *Man and His Symbols* (London, 1978). The passages from Herbert Marcuse are from *Eros and Civilisation* (London, 1969) and the closing Narcissus quotation comes from Ovid, *Metamorphoses*, Book 3. Steve Seidman, *Comedian Comedy: A Tradition in Hollywood Film* (Massachusetts, 1981) has usefully distinguished 'comedian comedy' from other forms. Frank Krutnik, 'The clown-prints of comedy', *Screen*, vol. 25, no. 4-5 (1984) does little more than summarise the latter.

Mae West

Freud's phallocentric emphasis in discussing jokes, especially obscene ones, see *Jokes*, pp. 140-1 and 142-5. His remarks on female narcissism are found in 'On narcissism: an introducion', in *On Metapsychology*, vol. xi (Pelican Freud Library, Harmondsworth 1977), pp. 351-7. Cinema as a form of fetishism is discussed in chapter 5 ('Disavowal, fetishism') of Christian Metz's *Psychoanalysis and Cinema* (London, 1982). The idea of Mae West as a fetish against male castration fears is found in Claire Johnston's 'Woman's cinema and counter-cinema', reprinted in *Movies and Methods*, ed. Bill Nichols (Berkeley, 1976).

Various views of Mae West may be found as follows: Parker Tyler briefly in *Screening the Sexes: Homosexuality in the Movies* (New York, 1972); Susan Sontag in 'On camp' in *Against Interpretation* (New York, 1969); Angela Carter in *The Sadean Woman* (London, 1979), Graham Greene in *The Pleasure Dome: The Collected Film Criticism 1939-40* (London, 1972).

Following various trails, Gershon Legman is quoted from *The Rationale of the Dirty Joke* (London, 1969); Charles Baudelaire on comedy from 'L'Essence du rire' in *Oeuvres Complètes*, vol. ii, ed. Claude Pichois (Paris, 1976); Alison Lurie from *The Language of Clothes* (London, 1983); Thorstein Veblen from *Theory of the Leisure Class* (London, 1970); while the quotation from John D. Rockefeller about the American Beauty Rose is taken from J. K. Galbraith, *The Affluent Society* (Harmondsworth, 1984).

Mae West's statements about herself come from her 'autobiography', *Goodness Had Nothing To Do With It* (London, 1960). The phrase 'monumental maiden' is, of course, borrowed from Marina Warner; Steve Seidman, *op. cit.*, is again quoted on the conventions of 'comedian comedy'. The passage from Zola's *Nana* (Nana, like Mae West is a song and dance lady) is found on p. 11 of the Penguin edition (Harmondsworth, 1972), and the passage from Virginia Woolf's *Orlando* is quoted from the Triad Grafton edition (1977), p. 24.

Woody Allen

Allen's confessions of 'female' pastimes are made in an interview with *The New York Times*, reprinted in *El País*, 2 February 1986. Much has been written in general terms on Allen, but three of the more analytical studies are Douglas Brode, *Woody Allen: His Films and Career* (London, 1986), Robert Benayoun, *Woody Allen: Beyond Words* (London, 1986) and Maurice Yacowar, *Loser Take All: The Comic Art of Woody Allen* (New York, 1979).

For Freud's definition of 'Humour', see *Jokes*, pp. 293-302. For comparisons with Lenny Bruce, see *The Essential Lenny Bruce: His Original Unexpurgated Satirical Routines*, ed. John Cohen (London, 1973). Questions of sincerity, authenticity and identity are discussed by Lionel Trilling in *Sincerity and Authenticity* (London, 1974).

On the intricacies of love and sexuality, see the two Kinsey Reports, Alfred C. Kinsey, Wardell B. Pomeroy and Clyde E. Martin, *Sexual Behaviour in the Human Male* (Philadelphia and London, 1948), and Alfred C. Kinsey, Wardell B. Pomeroy, Clyde E. Martin and Paul H. Gebhard, *Sexual Behaviour in the Human Female* (Philadelphia and London, 1953). Also William H. Masters and Virginia E. Johnson, *Human Sexual Response* (Boston, 1966). See especially Michel Foucault, *The History of Sexuality*, vol. i (Harmondsworth, 1981). For Freud on the precariousness of sexual functioning, see 'Inhibitions, symptoms and anxiety' in vol. xx, *The Standard Edition of the Complete Works of Sigmund Freud* (London, 1959). See also Stephen Heath, *The Sexual Fix* (London, 1982) and Erich Fromm, *The Art of Loving* (New York, 1974). The Schreber case is documented in Freud, 'Psychoanalytical notes on an autobiographical account of a case of paranoia', *Case Histories II*, vol. ix, Pelican Freud Library (Harmondsworth, 1979). The short story, 'The Kugelmass episode' is in Woody Allen, *Side Effects* (London, 1980). Alison Lurie's comments on the Annie Hall look are in *The Language of Clothes* (London, 1983). On the comparison between Philip Roth and Woody Allen, see *Portnoy's Complaint* (London, 1969), *The Breast* (London, 1973), *My Life as a Man* (London, 1974) and *The Anatomy Lesson* (London, 1984).

4—THE FIFTIES
A brief overview

On the period generally we have found Godfrey Hodgson, *America in Our Time* (New York, 1976) unfailingly useful. The two specifically filmic works we refer to as in some measure asserting the complexity of films of the period are Brandon French, *On the Verge of Revolt* (New York, 1978) and Peter Biskind, *Seeing is Believing: How We Learned to Stop Worrying and Love the 50s* (London, 1984).

Pat and Mike

Other notable instances of patriarchal December/May romances are Clark Gable with Sophia Loren in *It Started in Naples;* a very elderly Dick Powell with teenage delinquent Debbie Reynolds in *Susan Slept Here*, and Audrey Hepburn's septuagenarian Parisian father-figure (lover?) in *Sabrina Fair*, the latter perhaps parodying the whole tendency. Andrew Britton's arguments against the Tracy/Hepburn cycle appear in *Katharine Hepburn: The Thirties and After*, pp. 81-93; for his low opinion of *Pat and Mike* see pp. 83-4. Stanley Cavell's point about Tracy being figured momentarily as melodramatic villain comes from *Pursuits of Happiness*. We allude to *Listen, Little Man!* by Wilhelm Reich (Harmondsworth, 1975, first published 1948). For the 'mirror phase' see Jacques Lacan, *Ecrits I and II* (Paris, 1966 and 1967). The closing quotation is from Jacques Derrida, *L'Ecriture et la Différence* (Paris, 1967).

Rock and Doris

On the 'liberal consensus' and 'the end of ideology', etc. see Godfrey Hodgson, *America in Our Time*, pp. 48-98 in particular.

For Betty Friedan on 'Functionalism', 'The happy housewife heroine' and 'The problem that has no name', see *The Feminine Mystique* (Harmondsworth, 1983; first published 1963). For ideas on the 1950s male revolt against domesticity ambiguously embodied by Brad, see Barbara Ehrenreich, *The Hearts of Men: American Dreams and the Flight from Commitment* (London, 1983).

Our writing on 50s styles owes a large debt to two books by Vance Packard, *The Hidden Persuaders* (Harmondsworth, 1986, first published 1957) and *The Status Seekers* (Harmondsworth, 1961, first published 1959).

A much publicised, though rather superficial dossier of articles on Doris Day was published under the title *Move Over Misconceptions* by the British Film Institute, Jane Clarke, Mandy Merck and Diana Simmonds (London, 1981). Molly Haskell's remarks on the doubling of the male in *Lover, Come Back* are found in *From Reverence to Rape*. Fassbinder's likening of Rock Hudson to a tree comes from the essay 'Six films by Douglas Sirk' in *Sirk*, ed. Laura Mulvey and Jon Halliday (London, 1972), while Sirk's words about him are on p. 98 of *Sirk on Sirk* (London, 1971).

The Seven Year Itch

Neil Sinyard and Adrian Turner refer to *The Seven Year Itch* as one of Wilder's failures in *Journey Down Sunset Boulevard: The Films of Billy Wilder* (Ryder, Isle of Wight, 1979). Wilder on the film is quoted from their book; on Tashlin, see *Tashlin*, ed. Claire Johnston and Paul Willemen (London, 1975). On 50s styles, psychological selling by sex, and the world of the executive, see again Vance Packard, *The Hidden Persuaders* and *The Status Seekers*. For an influential fable of the time, see Sloan Wilson, *The Man in the Grey Flannel Suit* (New York, 1955). See also Herbert Marcuse's *One-Dimensional Man* (London, 1968) and Barbara Ehrenreich's *The Hearts of Men* for the significance of *Playboy*, Marilyn Monroe and the male rebellion half-embodied by Richard Sherman.

On Marilyn Monroe, see Norman Mailer, *Marilyn* (London, 1973); Gloria Steinem, *Marilyn* (London, 1987) and Richard Dyer, *Heavenly Bodies: Film Stars and Society* (London, 1987).

Sirk's: Family Comedies

For Talcott Parsons on the nuclear family, see 'The isolated conjugal family' (1955) in *Sociology of the Family*, ed. Michael Anderson (Harmondsworth, 1982). For Bronislaw Malinowski's views on the family in both primitive and modern cultures, see *The Sexual Life of Savages in North Western Melanesia* (London, 1957), *Sex and Repression in Savage Society* (London, 1927) and *Sex, Culture and Myth* (London, 1963).

Jon Halliday's *Sirk on Sirk* (London, 1971) is copiously referred to in quoting the director's views – e.g. Walden and America (pp. 40-1, 63-4), children (pp. 107-8), irony and American audiences (p. 73), and *Alcestis* and the *deus ex machina* (pp. 95-6). Comments on the comedies are found on pp. 87-9, 158-60, while the Sirk Edition of *Bright Lights* (Winter, 1977), contains an interview in which Sirk says more positive things about the non-musical comedies than are contained in Halliday. On the comedies see also Michael Stern, *Douglas Sirk* (Boston, 1979). Details of Sirk's earlier films are taken from Halliday, *Sirk on Sirk*.

The main source of M. H. Bakhtin's comic theory is *Rabelais and His World* (Cambridge, Mass. 1968). We generally acknowledge a long tradition of writing in *Screen*, *Movie* and elsewhere on Sirk's melodramas, in particular Thomas Elsaesser, 'Tales of sound and fury' reprinted in *Home is Where the Heart is: Studies in Melodrama and the Woman's Film*, ed. Christine Gledhill (London, 1988). Laura Mulvey uses the Perseus/Andromeda model in 'Afterthoughts on "Visual pleasure and narrative cinema" inspired by *Duel in the Sun*', *Framework*, no. 15-17 (Summer, 1981).

For information (relevant to the discussion of *No Room for the Groom*) on Eisenstein's *Sutter's Gold* project, see Yon Barna, *Eisenstein* (London, 1975). In the section on *The Lady Pays Off*, Margaret Mead's views are quoted on the conflict between the American girl's upbringing and her later role. These are found in *Male and Female* (London, 1950). In the introductory material on Sirk and Walden, reference is made to Richard Polenberg on the post-war suburban pastoral in *One Nation Divisible: Class, Race and Ethnicity in the United States since 1938* (New York, 1980).

5—STARTING OVER: ROMANTIC COMEDY TODAY

Brian Henderson's essay 'Romantic comedy today: semi-tough or impossible?' first appeared in *Film Quarterly*, 31, no. 4 (Summer, 1978). Freud writes on the relativity of comedy and the instability of perceptions of it in *Jokes*, pp. 196-7, 203-4, 280-5. Laura Mulvey's arguments on sex differentiation in audience response are found in 'Visual pleasure and narrative cinema', *Screen*, vol. 16, no. 3 (Autumn, 1975), and 'Afterthoughts on "Visual pleasure and narrative cinema",' *Framework*, no. 15-17 (Summer, 1981). Freud's essay on 'The universal tendency to debasement in the sphere of love', alluded to in the discussion of *Carnal Knowledge*, was consulted in *On Sexuality*. Pam Cook's piece on masculinity in *Raging Bull*, 'Masculinity in crisis: tragedy and identification in *Raging Bull*' was published in *Screen*, vol. 23, no. 3-4 (September, October, 1982), while the programme note on Jack Nicholson by Teresa Grimes, 'The Chameleon Smile' was consulted in the British Film Institute Library.

Tootsie and *Victor Victoria*

On cross-dressing see Mary Ann Doane, 'Film and masquerade: theorising the female spectator', *Screen*, vol. 23, no. 2-4 (1982); Gore Vidal, *Myra Breckenridge* (London, 1985), and Angela Carter, *The Passion of New Eve* (London, 1977). Mother-fixation is discussed by Denis de Rougemont in *Passion and Society* (London, 1962); Freud's references to footbinding are in 'Fetishism' in *On Sexuality;* masochism is discussed among other places in 'The sexual aberrations' in *On Sexuality* and in 'Anxiety and instinctual life', in *New Introductory Lectures in Psychoanalysis*, vol. ii (Pelican Freud Library, Harmondsworth, 1981). On TV soap operas, see Dorothy Hobson, *Crossroads: the Drama of a Soap Opera* (London, 1982). On the 'Law of the father' see Jacques Lacan, *Ecrits I and II* (Paris, 1966, 1967).

On Blake Edwards's career, see Peter Lehman and William Luhr, *Blake Edwards* (London, 1980). For further writing on cross-dressing, see Janice G. Raymond, *The Trans-sexual Empire* (London, 1980), Annette Kuhn, *The Power of the Image: Essays on Representation and Sexuality* (London, 1985), and E. Ann Kaplan, *Women and Film: Both Sides of the Camera* (London, 1983) and Rebecca Bell-Mettereau, *Hollywood Androgyny* (New York, 1985).

On *Victor Victoria* specifically, see Robin Wood, *Hollywood From Vietnam to Reagan* (New York, 1986).

Index of names and titles

Accord Final, 241
Adam's Rib, 179, 183, 184, 185, 186, 187, 188, 190, 191, 195, 214
Affair to Remember, An (1954), 180, 181, 211
Affairs of Anatol, The, 14, 32, 45
Agee, James, *Agee on Film*, 88, 301
Akins, Zoe, 14
Alice Adams, 14, 17, 19
Alice in Wonderland (1933), 76
All I Desire, 239, 244, 250
All That Heaven Allows, 200, 204, 240, 247-8, 249, 259, 289
Allen, Woody, vii, x, 95, 99, 134, 152-78, 209, 302, 303, 'The Kugelmass episode', 162
Ameche, Don, 10, 22, 85, 86, 241
American Werewolf in London, An, 33
Americanization of Emily, The, 290, 294
Ames, Leon, 182, 236
Andrews, Julie, 271, 289-97
Angel, 51, 57, 59, 61, 62-7, 70, 71, 72, 301
Animal Crackers, 32
Anne of the Indies, 129
Annie Hall, 155, 157, 159, 163, 165, 166, 167, 168, 169, 171, 172-8
Ann-Margret, 279
Any Which Way You Can, 276
Apartment, The, |216, 217, 220, 223, 224
Apocalypse Now, 96
April, April, 241
Arise, My Love, 11
Arquette, Rosanna, 276
Arthur, Jean, 10, 12, 24
Arzner, Dorothy, xi, 125
Avanti!, 220, 221
Awful, Truth, The, 5, 11, 12, 22, 28, 29, 30, 32, 270, 271
Axelrod, George, 200, 217

Bachelor Knight, 23
Bachelor Mother, 11, 12, 26, 32, 37
Bakhtin, M. H., *Rabelais and His World*, 239, 250, 261, 304
Ball, Lucille, 118, 241
Ball of Fire, 6, 30, 35, 37, 76, 180
Bananas, 157, 165, 168
Bara, Theda, 119
Barna, Yon, *Eisenstein*, 254, 304
Barrault, Marie-Christine, 167
Barth, John, 'Night sea journey', 162
Baudelaire, Charles, 'L'essence du rire', 125, 302

Baum, Vickie, 14
Beau James, 101
Becky Sharp, 67
Bellamy, Ralph, 25, 28, 101, 271
Belle of the 90s, 120, 123, 125, 129, 137, 138, 139, 140, 141, 142, 143-6, 147, 148, 149, 150, 151
Benayoun, Robert, *Woody Allen: Beyond Words*, 302
Benedict, Ruth, 12
Benny, Jack, 20, 102, 110, 111, 149, 302
Bergen, Candice, 267, 271
Bergkatze, Die, 82
Bergman, Andrew, *We're in the Money: Depression America and its Films*, 10, 298
Bergman, Ingmar, 156, 167, 169
Bergman, Ingrid, 181
Bergson, Henri, 'Laughter', 26, 39, 41, 72, 79, 299, 300
Big Broadcast of 1938, The, 101, 114
Bill of Divorcement, 17, 20
Bluebeard's Eighth Wife, vii, 47 49, 51, 72-83, 300
Blume in Love, 271, 272, 276
Bob and Carol and Ted and Alice, 272, 275
Bogart, Humphrey, 162, 165, 182
Bogdanovich, Peter, 41
Bonaparte, Marie, *Edgar Allan Poe: His Life and Works*, 34
Born Yesterday, 182
Borzage, Frank, 76
Bow, Clara, 119, 149
Bowra, C. M., *Heroic Poetry*, 104, 105, 302
Brecht, Bertholt, 124, 148, 261
Bringing Up Baby, vii, x, 1-44, 186, 189, 193, 195, 238, 268, 272, 274, 294, 299
Britton, Andrew, vii, viii, ix, x, 11, 12, 16, 23, 24, 186, 187, 189, 193, 195, 298, 299, 303
  Cary Grant: Comedy and Male Desire, x, 11, 16, 17, 23, 24, 298, 299
  Katherine Hepburn: The Thirties and After, x, 12, 16, 186, 187, 193, 195, 298, 299, 303
Broadway Danny Rose, 170
Brode, Douglas, *Woody Allen: His Films and Career*, 302
Broken Lullaby, 49, 56, 82
Brooks, Mel, 151
Bruce, Lenny, 153, 159, 302
Buber, Martin, 163

Buchanan, Jack, 21, 23, 50
Buddy, Buddy, 223
Bus Stop, 226, 228, 229, 233
By the Light of the Silvery Moon, 235
Byington, Spring, 252, 255

Cagney, James, 185, 201, 217
Caine, Michael, 171
Calamity Jane, 200
Call Me Bwana, 113
Camille, 14, 150
Campbell, Joseph, *The Hero with a Thousand Faces*, 104, 301
Can She Bake a Cherry Pie?, 270, 272, 275
Cancel My Reservation, 101
Capra, Frank, 48, 76
Captain Horatio Hornblower, 233
Captain Lightfoot, 204, 238, 241
Carnal Knowledge, 216, 271, 277-9
Carringer, Robert & Sabath, Barry, *Ernst Lubitsch: A Guide to Reference and Resources*, 61, 62, 300
Carroll, Madeleine, 14
Carter, Angela,
  Nothing Sacred, 116, 302
  The Passion of New Eve, 283, 305
  The Sadean Woman, 79, 127, 301, 302
Casanova (Fellini), 277
Casanova's Big Night, 100, 104
Cat and the Canary, The, 101, 104
Cat People (Tourneur), 32, 34
Catlett, Walter, 26
Cavell, Stanley,
  Pursuits of Happiness: the Hollywood Comedy of Remarriage, vii, x, 8, 30, 37, 60, 187, 189, 268, 299, 303
Chaplin, Charles, 45, 115, 153
Charade, 290
Cheaper By the Dozen, 235, 237
Chevalier, Maurice, 61, 76
Chinatown, 280
Ching, William, 168
Christopher Strong, 14
City of Women, 277
Clarke, Fred, 214
Clayburgh, Jill, 71, 271
Cleopatra (1934), 75
Clift, Montgomery, 117, 126
Cluny Brown, 45, 46, 49, 50, 60, 66
Coburn, Charles, 25, 85, 92, 249, 250
Colbert, Claudette, viii, xi, 13, 49, 73, 75, 76, 79, 82
Cook, Pam, vii, 279, 298, 305
  (ed.) *The Cinema Book*, vii, 299

'Masculinity in crisis: tragedy and identification in *Raging Bull*', 279, 305
Cooper, Gary, 13, 22, 35, 51,, 67, 68, 69, 73, 75, 76, 82
Cooper, J. Fenimore, *The Deerslayer*, 106, *The Leatherstocking Tales*, 105
Coppola, Francis, 96, 268
Corliss, Richard, *Talking Pictures: Screenwriters in the American Cinema, 1927-1973*, 69, 301
Cosby, Bill, 151
Courtship of Eddie's Father, The, 235, 236, 239
Coward, Noel, 21, 23, 51, 55, 58, 69, 70, 71, 84
Design for Living, 51, 69, 70, 71, 84
Crawford, Broderick, 183
Crawford, Joan, 5, 17
Creature from the Black Lagoon, The, 224
Cregar, Laird, 85, 86
Cries and Whispers, 167
Crimson Pirate, The, 282
Crosby, Bing, 97, 99, 101, 103, 111, 112, 117, 118, 301
Crothers, 'Scat Man', 256, 258, 259
Crowther, Bosley, 85, 301
Cukor, George, 46, 49, 187, 189, 195, 200, 255
Curtis, Tony, 22, 221, 223, 228, 238, 252, 254

Dailey, Dan, 238, 256, 258
Dance, Girl, Dance, 125
Darnell, Linda, 238, 241, 242
Davis, Bette, 58
Day, Doris, 37, 182, 197-215, 303, 304
Dean, James, 116, 126, 287
De Beauvoir, Simone, *The Second Sex*, 83, 301
Delmar, Vina, 14
Delon, Alain, 129, 287
Demarest, William, 25
De Mille, Cecil B., 14, 45, 60
De Niro, Robert, 179
Derek, Bo, 273
De Rougemont, Denis, *Passion and Society*, 285, 305
Derrida, Jacques, *L'Ecriture et la Différence*, 195, 303
Desert Hearts, 268
Desert Song, The, 97
Design for Living (Lubitsch), 48, 50, 51, 52, 60, 61, 62, 63, 67-72, 76, 78, 79, 84, 301
Desire, 76
Desk Set, The, 183, 185
Desperately Seeking Susan, 270, 272, 275, 276
Dietch, Donna, 268
Dieterle, William, 39
Dietrich, Marlene, 58, 62, 63, 65, 145, 182
Disney, Walt, 32, 172, 244
Doane, Mary Ann, 'Film and masquerade: theorizing the female spectator', 282, 305

Douglas, Melvyn, 62, 64
Drake, Betsy, 237
Duel in the Sun, 233
Dunne, Irene, viii, 12, 29, 182, 236
Durgnat, Raymond, *The Crazy Mirror: Hollywood Comedy and the American Image*, x, 4, 299
Dworkin, Andrea, *Intercourse*, ix, 299
Dyer, Richard, *Heavenly Bodies: Films Stars and Society*, x, 298, 304

Easter Parade, 134
Eastwood, Clint, 276
Easy Living, 6, 10, 12, 24
Easy Way, The, 235, 236, 237
Edwards, Blake, 271, 289, 290, 294, 305
Ehrenreich, Barbara, *The Hearts of Men: American Dreams and the Flight from Commitment*, 200, 220, 225, 232, 303, 304
8½, 154, 172
Elsaesser, Thomas, 'Tales of sound and fury', 304
Engels, Friedrich, 11, 13, 55, 83, 96, 299
The Origins of the Family, Private Property and the State, 11, 55, 83, 299
Erotikon, 45
Every Day's a Holiday, 120, 121, 123, 141, 142, 143, 146, 150, 151
Every Girl Should Be Married, 237
Everything You Always Wanted to Know about Sex but were afraid to Ask, 160, 161, 162
Ewell, Tom, 216, 218, 223, 226, 233

Fairbanks, Douglas, Sr., 21
Fantasia, 177, 244
Farrow, Mia, 152, 153, 169, 170
Fassbinder, Rainer Werner, 'Six films by Douglas Sirk', 200, 304
Father Goose, 37
Father of the Bride, 182, 184, 237, 239
Feld, Fritz, 26
Fellini, Federico, 154, 272, 277
Femme Mariée, Une, 82
Ferreri, Marco, 277
Field, Virginia, 242, 244, 245
Fields, Dorothy, 14
Fields, W. C., 123, 140, 145, 148, 149, 151
Fifth Avenue Girl, 12, 40
First a Girl, 293
Fitzgerald, Barry, 27
Fleming, Rhonda, 106, 118
Fonda, Henry, 4, 22, 23
Fonda, Jane, 228
Forsaking All Others, 15
Fortune Cookie, The, 216, 223
Foucault, Michel, x, 157, 160, 303
The History of Sexuality, (vol.i), 157, 160, 303
Framework, 304, 305
Frantic, 204
French, Brandon, *On the Verge of Revolt: Women in American Film in the 1950s*, 179, 303

Freud, Sigmund, vii, viii, ix, x, 3, 8, 28, 39, 40, 53, 55, 60, 89, 95, 97, 104, 111, 112, 116, 117, 118, 119, 127, 128, 131, 153, 154, 162, 174, 188, 218, 249, 278, 285, 287, 288, 299, 301, 302, 303, 305
'Anxiety and instinctual life', 288, 305
'Being in love and hypnosis', 174
'Delusions and dreams in Jensen's *Gradiva*', 8, 299
'Female sexuality', 118, 302
'Fetishism', 127, 128, 305
'Inhibitions, symptoms and anxiety', 303
The interpretation of dreams, 104, 301
Jokes and their relation to the unconscious, x, 3, 4, 95, 97, 112, 119, 154, 156, 269, 299, 301, 305
'On narcissism: an introduction', 89, 111, 116, 117, 131, 302
'On the universal tendency to debasement in the sphere of love', 55, 60, 278, 301, 305
'Psychoanalytical notes on an autobiographical account of a case of paranoia [Schreber], ix, 165, 299, 302, 303
'sexual aberrations, The', 288, 305
'transformations of puberty, The', 302
Friedan, Betty, 199, 201, 303
The Feminine Mystique, 199, 303
Fromm, Erich, *The Art of Loving*, 162, 303
Front Page, The (Wilder), 101, 223
Frye, Northrop, *Anatomy of Criticism*, 3, 25, 299

Gable, Clark, 1, 5, 16, 182, 197, 202, 303
Galbraith, J. K., 213, 302
The Affluent Society, 302
Garbo, Greta, 126, 129, 282, 293
Garfunkel, Art, 277, 279
Garner, James, 197, 292, 294
Gehring, Wes D., *Screwball Comedy: Defining a Film Genre*, 299
Gentlemen Prefer Blondes, 108, 228
Giant, 200, 204, 206
Girl Can't Help It, The, 218, 219
Glyn, Elinor, 14
Godard, Jean-Luc, 82, 124, 148, 261
Goin' South, 280, 281
Gordon, Ruth, 187, 195, 200
Grable, Betty, 128
Graduate, The, 267
Grant, Cary, x, 1, 2, 6, 7, 13, 15, 16, 18, 21-5, 26, 37, 38, 41, 56, 101, 137, 147, 148, 150, 151, 152, 182, 197, 198, 213, 236, 237, 299
Great Lover, The, 103, 106
Greene, Graham, *The Pleasure Dome: The Collected Film Criticism, 1939-40*, 48, 76, 120, 301, 302

Grimes, Teresa, 'The Chameleon Smile', 280, 305

Halliday, Jon, *Sirk on Sirk*, 304
Hands Across the Table, 12, 14
Hannah and Her Sisters, 157, 170, 171, 173
Harlow, Jean, 119, 149
Has Anybody Seen My Gal?, 204, 237, 240, 242, 247, 249, 252, 257
Haskell, Molly, *From Reverence to Rape*, 62, 179, 201, 206, 217, 300, 304
Hawks, Howard, vii, 2, 13, 22, 23, 30, 34, 46, 49, 108
Hayden, Sterling, 238, 261, 265
Heath, Stephen, *The Sexual Fix*, 160, 303
Heaven Can Wait (Lubitsch), 48, 51, 60, 62, 65, 77, 78, 83-94
Hecht, Ben, 46, 47, 51, 69, 301
Heflin, Van, 245, 246, 254
Hefner, Hugh, 103, 220, 225
Hemingway, Ernest, *The Green Hills of Africa*, 34
Hemingway, Meriel, 168
Henderson, Brian, 'Romantic comedy today: semi-tough or impossible?', 70, 268, 274, 275, 276, 297, 305
Hepburn, Audrey, 182, 185, 290, 303
Hepburn, Katharine, viii, x, 1, 2, 6, 12, 13, 16-21, 22, 38, 41, 126, 181-96, 200, 290, 299, 303
Hershey, Barbara, 170
His Girl Friday, 11, 22, 26, 30, 31, 40, 41 .
His Woman, 75
Hite, Shere, 160
Hodgson, Godfrey, *America in Our Time*, 179, 303
Hoffman, Dustin, 281, 284, 287
Holden, William, 181, 182, 183
Holiday, 5, 11, 19, 20, 21, 22, 26, 30, 31, 36, 37, 186, 193, 290
Holliday, Judy, 119, 182, 183, 185
Hollywood or Bust, 217
Hope, Bob, x, 9, 20, 95-118, 124, 134, 148, 149, 153, 155, 159, 166, 177, 301
Hopkins, Miriam, viii, 50, 54, 58, 63, 67, 68, 69, 76
Horse Feathers, 32
Horton, Edward Everett, 67, 69, 77, 82, 102
House Calls, 281
How to Marry a Millionaire, 14, 182, 205, 208
Hudson, Rock, 37, 197-215, 238, 249, 251, 254, 303, 304

I Was a Male War Bride, 23, 282
I'm No Angel, 65, 121, 122, 123, 124, 129-36, 137, 139, 141, 142, 143, 144, 149, 150, 151
Imitation of Life (Sirk), 257, 259
Indiscreet, 22, 180, 181
Insignificance, 226
Interiors, 167, 170, 209

Irma la Douce, 216, 223
Irreconcilable Differences, 46
Irving, George, 26
It Happened in Naples, 37, 182, 303
It Happened One Night, 1, 16, 43, 75
It's a Wonderful World, 12

Jackson, Glenda, 270, 273, 274
Jaglom, Henry, 272
Jensen, Wilhelm, *Gradiva*, 8, 299
Johnston, Claire, 'Woman's cinema and counter-cinema', 126, 302
Johnston, Claire & Willemen, Paul, *Tashlin*, 96, 301, 304
Jolson Story, The, 223
Jung, C. G., *Man and His Symbols*, 104, 302

Kael, Pauline, 24, 48, 299, 300
   'The man from dream city', 24, 299
   Three Screen Comedies by Samson Raphaelson (introduction by Pauline Kael), 48, 301
Kafka, Franz, 162, 217; 'Investigations of a dog', 162
Kane, Carol, 167
Kanin, Garson, 187, 195, 200
Kaplan, E. Ann, *Women and Film: Both Sides of the Camera*, vii, 298, 305
Keaton, Buster, 115
Keaton, Diane, 152, 161, 169, 172, 175
Keyes, Evelyn, 223
King of Kings (De Mille), 14
Kinsey, Alfred C., *et al.*, 6, 160, 161, 164, 217, 220, 303
Kiss Me, Stupid, 216, 316
Kramer Versus Kramer, 281
Kristofferson, Kris, 70, 272

Lacan, Jacques, x, 53, 55, 189, 289, 301, 303, 305
   Ecrits I & II, 301, 303, 305
Lady Eve, The, 4, 5, 12, 19, 23, 30, 32, 180
Lady Pays Off, The, 236, 237, 239, 240, 241-5, 247, 248, 250, 254, 304
Lady Windermere's Fan, 49
Laing, R. D., 2, 35, 36
Lamour, Dorothy, 112, 116, 117, 118, 241
Lange, Jessica, 285, 288
Lasser, Louise, 169
Last Detail, The, 280
Laurie, Piper, 249, 252
Le Brock, Kelly, 113, 272
Legman, Gershon, *Rationale of the Dirty Joke*, 138, 302
Lehman, Peter, and Luhr, William, *Blake Edwards*, 305
Leiris, Michel, *Manhood*, 157
Leisen, Mitchell, 13
Lemmon, Jack, 22, 220, 221, 223, 287, 294, 295
Lemon Drop Kid, The, 103, 104, 113, 116
Le Roy, Mervyn, 236

Leuchtenburg, William E., *The Perils of Prosperity*, 36, 299, 300
Lewis, Jerry, 149, 217, 218
Life With Father, 235
Little Shop of Horrors, The (Corman), 280
Little Women (Louisa May Alcott), 219, 222, 234
Little Women (Cukor), 20, 234, 235, 236, 255
Little Women (Le Roy), 234, 235, 236
Lombard, Carole, 12
Loos, Anita, 14
Love and Death, 99, 156, 161, 162, 164, 165
Love Me or Leave Me, 201
Love Parade, The, 49
Lover Come Back, 180, 197, 198, 201, 205, 206, 212, 213, 304
Lovers, The, 204
Loy, Myrna, 207
Lubitsch, Ernst, vii, x, 11, 12, 26, 31, 45-94, 110, 125
Lukács, Georg, 96
Lurie, Alison, 120, 173, 302, 303
Lynn, Diana, 256, 260

McCarey, Leo, x
MacDonald, Jeanette, 50, 61
MacLaine, Shirley, 220, 221
McLuhan, Marshall, 155
MacMurray, Fred, 14
McNally, Stephen, 241, 254
McPherson, Jeannie, 14
Madame Bovary (Minnelli), 247
Madame du Barry, 49
Madonna, 272, 276
Magnificent Obsession (Sirk), 204, 205, 206, 238, 251
Mailer, Norman, 159, 226, 229, 231, 304
   Advertisements for Myself, 159
   An American Dream, 229
   Marilyn, 226, 231, 304
Main Event, The, 274
Male and Female (De Mille), 14
Malinowski, Bronislaw, x, 234, 236, 299, 304
Mamoulian, Rouben, 67
Man From Wyoming, The, 76
Man in the Grey Flannel Suit, The (1956), 217, 133
Man Who Knew Too Much, The, (1956), 201
Man's Favorite Sport, 206
Manhattan, 157, 159, 163, 168, 169, 170
Mansfield, Jane, 218, 219, 233
March, Fredric, 13, 51, 67, 68, 69
Marcuse, Herbert, 28, 110, 299, 302, 304
Marion, Frances, 14
Marriage Circle, The, 47, 49
Marshall, Herbert, 13, 51, 53, 58, 62, 64
Martin, Dean, 6, 111, 218
Marx Brothers, 32, 125
Marx, Groucho, 153, 161
Mary Poppins (Robert Stevenson), 235, 290